DICKENS AND THE BROKEN SCRIPTURE

DICKENS

AND THE

BROKEN SCRIPTURE

JANET L. LARSON

THE UNIVERSITY OF GEORGIA PRESS   ATHENS

© 1985 by the University of Georgia Press
Athens, Georgia 30602

Designed by Kathi L. Dailey
Set in Linotron 202 Bodoni Book
with Bodoni Open display

The paper in this book meets the guidelines for
permanence and durability of the Committee on
Production Guidelines for Book Longevity of the
Council on Library Resources.

Printed in the United States of America

89   88   87   86   85   5   4   3   2   1

Library of Congress Cataloging in Publication Data

Larson, Janet L.
Dickens and the broken Scripture.
Includes bibliographical references and index.
1. Dickens, Charles, 1812–1870—Religion and ethics.
2. Dickens, Charles, 1812–1870—Sources.
3. Bible in literature.   I. Title.
PR4592.B5L3   1985   823'.8   84-24001
ISBN 0-8203-0769-6 (alk. paper)

The illustration on the title page is an etching by Hablot
K. Browne for the title page of *Little Dorrit*.

A portion of this book first appeared in slightly different
form in *Nineteenth-Century Fiction* (vol. 38, no. 2
[September 1983]: 131–60) as "The Battle of Biblical
Books in Esther's Narrative." © 1983 by The Regents of
the University of California.

TO

VIRGINIA AHLBRAND KARSTEN
WALTER JOHN KARSTEN

No one can paint more picturesquely by an apposite epithet, or
illustrate more happily by a choice allusion. . . . [Dickens]
freshens with new life the oldest facts and breathes into thoughts
the most familiar an emotion not felt before.

John Forster, *The Life of Charles Dickens*

. . . they who should have oped the door
Of charity and light, for all men's finding,
Squabbled for words upon the altar-floor,
And rent The Book. . . .

Dickens, poem written for Lady
Blessington's Keepsake Book (1843)

Contents

Preface

"OF MAKING MANY BOOKS there is no end." So Ecclesiastes, anticipating the modern publishing trade in literary criticism, cautions the reader near the close of his text. Like Ecclesiastes' final inscriptions, the writing of this Preface marks only an apparent closure, as industrious Dickensians, undaunted by biblical warnings against "the vapours," go on remaking the novels of so conflicted and protean a writer as the Inimitable was and is.

Let it be said at once that this book is not an attempt to reclaim Dickens for Christianity; to my mind, the Christian tradition has clearer and stronger spokesmen and women than the multivoiced Charles Dickens. The historical starting point of this study has mooted such a reconstruction: if the Bible became a fractured Code for so many in the nineteenth century, and if Dickens was a writer peculiarly attuned to his times, the Scripture to which he alludes more frequently than to any other text is likely to be less stable than he probably believed it was whenever he invoked it most explicitly in his fiction. Reading the biblical Dickens then becomes not an act of conflict resolution, of settling this Victorian Proteus down into one interpretable shape, but of attending to the multiple meanings generated by the irresolutions, discords, and even ruptures that Dickens' Scripture can bring into his work.

Although some readers may scent deconstructionist influences in this hypothesis, in fact the intention throughout to assess the fictive strategies of the text owes much to my graduate training in more traditional kinds of criticism. Even if one could bracket out what one knows about the historical and biographical contexts for Dickens' novels, attention to their verbal textures and structures discloses moments when his Scripture comes up against its own self-engendered paradoxes. None of what follows needs a Derrida to point out Dickens' aporias in matters of faith; Walter E. Houghton's account of nineteenth-century perplexities in *The Victorian Frame of Mind* (which I first read under the benignly stimulating tutelage of the late Frederick E. Faverty at Northwestern) has made its lasting impression on the readings of Dickens in this study. My introductory chapter more fully explains what I am about; its last section attempts to reconstruct the theoretical scaffolding from which the argument has been built. The rest of the book gets down to business.

The aim of this study is to weigh Dickens' biblical allusions in their fictional and historical contexts. This aim has required me to take up major representative novels one by one, allowing each text to establish its own multilanguaged world in which Dickens' scriptural words sound. *Oliver Twist* (1837–38) conveys a sense of his beginnings and sharply defines some of the problems religious words have in establishing their own weight and cogency in the Dickens world. *Dombey and Son* (1846–48) proves transitional in its handling of biblical allusion as in much else. Here, against a background of multiplying social languages, Dickens tries to articulate more firmly than before a religious perception of his world's malaise and what might prove an antidote to it; but he does this through heterogeneous religious voices, not necessarily consonant with each other or efficacious in their contexts. Here, too, the ideas and biblical prose style of Thomas Carlyle as Dickens' mentor most audibly enter into the dialogic imagination of the fiction, in Mikhail Bakhtin's phrase. With the indecisive double narration of *Bleak House* (1852–53), the biblical and liturgical voices begin to quarrel among themselves and with others; and against the New Testament quotations through which Esther Summerson reads herself and her world, the Book of Job establishes its importance as a means of interpretation, even obsession. Dominant subtexts like Job in this novel manifest the Dickens who was, as John Forster said, "very much a man of one idea, each having its turn of absolute predominance" (*Life* 1:195)—although nothing is "absolute" in *Bleak House*, not even the Joban ironies darkening its vision of the whole world as a desolate habitation.

Little Dorrit (1855–57) seems to me constructed to confess, suppress, and cope with a religious and vocational crisis of the mid-1850s. It also introduces Dickens' most successful "religious" heroine, set within a context skeptically envisioned through the lenses of a subsequent influential subtext, the Book of Ecclesiastes. In this central and longest chapter, the net is cast wider than elsewhere to catch nearly all the biblical allusions. This is Dickens' most shadowy, indecisive novel, calling for the reader's "Patience" (as Dickens exhorts his reader) in sorting out and weighing its moral and religious words. My reader, too, will require patience while moving through the labyrinth of intertextual connections traced in chapter 5 between Dickens, Carlyle, and the Bible: for *Little Dorrit* seems to me the work in which Dickens' transactions with his mentor's texts—themselves a reconstructed Bible for the nineteenth century—become fraught with aporias suggesting Dickens' own reservations about the scriptural tradition as translated in part through Carlyle's style and thought. With *Our*

Mutual Friend (1864–65), Dickens cycles back to some of the biblical themes and archetypes he had employed earlier, especially in *Dombey and Son*, gesturing toward religious values he maintained publicly and in his letters to the end of his life. But in this late novel we also find ourselves in the graveyard of "dead quotations" to which Bakhtin would banish religious rhetoric in the novel. Whatever it came to mean to Dickens personally in his last decade, Scripture in the context of this highly self-conscious, multiperspectival work proves almost wholly depleted of its literary resonance for the mature novelist.

BOOKS' BEGINNINGS are as elusive as their ends. Nonetheless, in making the journey backward to trace them, one can salute at least some of the living presences who helped to generate, abetted, constructively thwarted, or redirected the course of this book. First introduced to me by my dissertation directors Lawrence G. Evans and Christopher Herbert in the early 1970s, the scholars and critics who have over the years influenced my sense of what Dickens was about are Legion, as he might say; but I would be remiss not to acknowledge here my debts to George H. Ford and Sylvère Monod, Julian Moynahan, Barry V. Qualls, Andrew Sanders, Susan Shatto, Dennis Walder, and Alexander Welsh for their work on Dickens and the Bible. More broadly, the writings of M. H. Abrams, Mikhail Bakhtin, John Dominic Crossan, Northrop Frye, Frank Kermode, George Levine, and J. Hillis Miller—a mixed but goodly company—have served as stimuli to my own efforts.

To the editors of the *Dickens Studies Annual*, the *Dickens Quarterly* (formerly the *Dickens Studies Newsletter*), and *Nineteenth-Century Fiction*, I owe thanks for permission to republish material verbatim or revised. David Parker, curator of the Dickens House Museum; Nicholas H. MacMichael, keeper of muniments at Westminster Abbey (along with Canon Trevor Beeson); and librarians at the British Museum, Harvard University, and Cambridge University have all been generous in giving access to their collections. To Margaret Reynolds, in 1981 a research assistant at the Dickens House, I am grateful for numerous excavations of things Dickensian and for the special brightness of her friendship. David Burke, Kenneth Diable, John David Larson, Merle Longwood, and William Shafer have given indispensable help in biblical studies. George H. Ford, Rosemary Jann, Fred Kaplan, John McClure, Julian Moynahan, David Paroissien, Branwen Bailey Pratt, Barry V. Qualls, and John Richetti have read versions of the manuscript and, in their gracious gifts of time and critical attention, have proved to me that collegiality is no chimera, even in academic Vanity Fair.

One's personal debts to guiding daemons and Good Samaritans grow as one thinks backward to the beginnings. Jacqueline Berke first said to me, in effect,

"Janet, you must write a book"—and later helped to make it possible not only by her example as a fine writer, but also by her willingness to release me from an important project in order to finish this study. Virginia Cremen-Rudd, chair of the University College English Department (Rutgers at Newark) and one of the last romantics, made gracious allowance for the inroads upon my time demanded by this project and always encouraged, often inspired. Dean Charles Nanry, a former seminarian with special relish for the "Jesuitism" quotations from Carlyle that pepper this book, played several supporting roles. Thanks are also due to Martin E. Marty and James M. Wall for our continuing dialogue on writers and religion, and for the grace of letting me off the hook awhile from my editor-at-large duties with the *Christian Century*. And without the more than generous support of the Rutgers Research Council, the Faculty Academic Study Program, and the Graduate School at Newark, the work of the past four years would not have been possible; I thank especially Charles F. Main and Francis Baran.

Others of the daemonic company who offered words in season that provoked thought or kept me from the depths I name with special gratitude: Patricia Gartenberg, Victoria Harrison, David Hoddeson, Mary Howard, Dick Lee, Jewel Seehaus, Maryann Siebert, Mary Scott Simpson, and Thomas Werge. A relay team of proofreaders—Donna Gustafson, James Hale, Mary Howard, Scott McGrath, and Jewel Seehaus—held out for late hours in my kitchen reading my words back to me and sometimes new words that I have gratefully adopted. Susan Tiller, a typist of the first order, not only did her work professionally but (as Dickens once said of an audience) sympathized with me and divined my purpose. Larry Qualls gave his expert and generous attention to the illustrations. From the beginning of our association Karen Orchard and Debbie Winter at the University of Georgia Press have given abundantly of their wise and gentle counsel.

Reaching farther back, I dedicate this book with love and gratitude to Virginia and Walter Karsten, who brought me up in the spirit of Martin Luther to read the Scriptures and bequeathed to me their love of the King James language.

Nurturing and clarifying that love over the years, since our first Victorian seminar at Northwestern, has been the special gift of the Rutgers colleague to whom I owe most, Barry Vinson Qualls—most judicious and indefatigable of manuscript readers, font of allusion sacred and otherwise, and more Bunyan pilgrim than knows.

A Note on Texts
and Abbreviations

THE FOLLOWING ABBREVIATIONS are used for works cited in the text. Nonfiction prose citations indicate volume and page numbers; novel citations include volume or book, chapter, and page. Scriptural quotations are from the King James Version.

B   John Bunyan. *The Pilgrim's Progress*. Ed. Roger Sharrock. Harmondsworth: Penguin, 1965.

BCP   The Book of Common Prayer. Oxford: Oxford University Press; and London: Henry Frowde, n.d.

BH   Charles Dickens. *Bleak House*. Ed. George Ford and Sylvère Monod. Norton Critical Edition. New York: W. W. Norton, 1977.

CB   Charles Dickens. *Christmas Books*. Vol. 4 of the Nonesuch Dickens, ed. Arthur Waugh, Hugh Walpole, Walter Dexter, and Thomas Hatton. Bloomsbury: Nonesuch Press, 1937.

CME   Thomas Carlyle. *Critical and Miscellaneous Essays*. Centenary Edition. Vols. 26–30 of *The Works of Thomas Carlyle*, ed. H. D. Traill. New York: Charles Scribner's Sons, 1896–1901.

D   *The Letters of Charles Dickens*. Ed. Walter Dexter. Vols. 10–12 of the Nonesuch Dickens, ed. Arthur Waugh, Hugh Walpole, Walter Dexter, and Thomas Hatton. Bloomsbury: Nonesuch Press, 1938.

DS   Charles Dickens. *Dombey and Son*. Ed. Alan Horsman. World's Classics Edition. New York: Oxford University Press, 1982.

ED   Charles Dickens. *The Mystery of Edwin Drood*. Ed. Margaret Cardwell. Oxford: Clarendon Press, 1972.

FR   Thomas Carlyle. *The French Revolution*. Vols. 2–4 of *Works*.

H   Thomas Carlyle. *On Heroes, Hero-Worship and the Heroic in History*. Vol. 5 of *Works*.

Life   John Forster. *The Life of Charles Dickens*. Ed. A. J. Hoppé. Everyman's Library Edition. 2 vols. New York: Dutton, 1966.

LD   Charles Dickens. *Little Dorrit*. Ed. Harvey Peter Sucksmith. Oxford: Clarendon Press, 1979.

LDP   Thomas Carlyle. *Latter-Day Pamphlets*. Vol. 20 of *Works*.

LOL   Charles Dickens. *The Life of Our Lord*. London: Associated Newspapers, 1934.

MC   Charles Dickens. *Martin Chuzzlewit*. Ed. P. N. Furbank. Harmondsworth: Penguin, 1968.

MP   Charles Dickens. *Miscellaneous Papers, Plays, and Poems*. Ed. B. W. Matz. Vol. 18 of *The Works of Charles Dickens*. National Library Edition. New York: Bigelow, Brown, and Company, n.d.

OCS   Charles Dickens. *The Old Curiosity Shop*. Ed. Angus Easson. Harmondsworth: Penguin, 1972.

OMF   Charles Dickens. *Our Mutual Friend*. Ed. Stephen Gill. Harmondsworth: Penguin, 1971.

OT   Charles Dickens. *Oliver Twist*. Ed. Kathleen Tillotson. World's Classics Edition. New York: Oxford University Press, 1982.

P   *The Letters of Charles Dickens*. Pilgrim Edition. 5 vols. Oxford: Clarendon Press. Vol. 1 (1820–39), ed. Madeline House and Graham Storey, 1965. Vol. 2 (1840–41), ed. Madeline House and Graham Storey, 1969. Vol. 3 (1842–43), ed. Madeline House, Graham Storey, and Kathleen Tillotson, 1974. Vol. 4 (1844–46), ed. Kathleen Tillotson, 1977. Vol. 5 (1847–49), ed. Graham Storey and K. J. Fielding, 1981.

PP   Charles Dickens. *The Pickwick Papers*. Ed. Robert L. Patten. Harmondsworth: Penguin, 1972.

P&P   Thomas Carlyle. *Past and Present*. Vol. 10 of *Works*.

SB   Charles Dickens. *Sketches by Boz*. Vol. 1 of *The Complete Works of Charles Dickens*, ed. Richard Garnett. London: Chapman and Hall, 1900.

SR   Thomas Carlyle. *Sartor Resartus*. Vol. 1 of *Works*.

UT   Charles Dickens. *The Uncommercial Traveller*. Vol. 29 of *The Works of Charles Dickens*. New York: Charles Scribner's Sons, 1911.

1

The Fractured Code
in Dickens' Fiction

TOM-ALL-ALONE'S
(Hablot K. Browne)

And with many such parables spake he the word unto them, as they were
able to hear it.

Mark 4:33

NORTHROP FRYE finds his generating text for *The Great Code: The
Bible and Literature* in Blake's aphorism: "The Old and New Testaments are the Great Code of Art." Biblical imagery and narrative, in
Frye's words, constitute "an imaginative framework—a mythological universe,
as I call it—within which Western literature had operated down to the eigh-
teenth century and is to a large extent still operating."[1] From the sentiments
about the Bible conventionally if sincerely expressed in Dickens' letters, we
would not guess that the Great Code was an imaginative resource for his fiction.
When we turn to the major novels, we encounter a far more imaginatively engaged response to the Old and New Testaments—the Pentateuch (especially
Genesis), the historical books, major and minor prophets, Psalms, Wisdom literature, the Book of Esther, the Gospels, Acts, the Epistles (especially Romans
and Corinthians), Revelation, and some of the Apocrypha (bound into the
Dickens family Bible). Dickens alludes to the Bible and the Book of Common
Prayer more often than to any other texts. But in his hands the Authorized
Version is no longer the simple readable book of his professed belief, nor even
the coherent "mythological universe" of Frye's literary creed. Especially in
Dickens' mature novels, the Bible becomes a paradoxical code that provides
him with contradictory interpretations of experience; it is drawn upon as though
it were still a source of stable values, resonant familiar images, and reassuring
conventions of order, but it is also becoming a locus of hermeneutical instability
reflecting the changed status of the Bible in his time. This book is about that
paradox; its aim is not merely the tracing of allusions, even less the discovery of
a mythological system implying a Christian philosophy in Dickens' work, but
the rather more delicate task of examining the status of the Bible texts he replays and revises in five novels from the beginnings to the end of his career.

1

WE CAN GLIMPSE the bearings of this paradox on his work by considering at the
outset two kinds of parable Dickens tells.

In Westminster Abbey the Sunday following Dickens' funeral there, Dean

Stanley preached a sermon on Dickens as parabler. Taking his text from Luke 16, the story of the rich man and Lazarus, Stanley argued for "the sacredness of fictitious narrative" and urged his hearers to "see how the Bible itself sanctions a mode of instruction which has been, in a special sense, God's gift to our own age. . . . the gift of 'speaking in parables'; the gift of addressing mankind through romance and novel and tale and fable."[2] In his long series of novels, Dickens was "the special teacher" of the day's text: through his "modern human Parables . . . [Dickens was] the advoca[te] of the absent poor. . . . By him that veil was rent asunder which parts the various classes of society. Through his genius the rich man, faring sumptuously every day, was made to see and feel the presence of the Lazarus at his gate."[3] Dean Stanley's sermon is typical, for as George Ford notes, Dickens' "social criticism had acquired a New Testament aura of considerable importance to its status" by the time of his death.[4] More generally, the writer who came "Next to the Bible and Shakespeare" in sales (as *The Book Monthly* reported in 1906) achieved in his own time the stature of a religious figure whose works (like those of other great Victorians) were compared with Holy Scripture.[5] Such a characterization helps to define one unquestionably influential way Dickens used the Bible in his fiction: to clarify the moral outlines of his "parables" and, by invoking the Book appealed to by all parties, to strengthen his relation with a wide Victorian audience.

But there are also in Dickens' fiction, as in the Bible, "some things hard to be understood," which the "unstable," Peter says, "wrest . . . unto their own destruction" (2 Pet. 3:16). Preaching on Ezekiel 20:49 (where the prophet entrusted with a dreadful oracle exclaims, "Ah Lord God! they say of me, Doth he not speak parables?"), Dean Stanley's mentor, Dr. Arnold, wrestled with the fact that "Scripture has its parables . . . which cannot now be understood"—"not only . . . the obscurities of God's word, but . . . its perpetual and invincible obscurities. . . ."[6] The Greek *parabolē* and the Hebrew *mashal* encompass a wide range of meanings, from the simple metaphor and the exemplary tale to the riddle and the dark saying. When the Psalmist says, "I will open my mouth in a parable: I will utter dark sayings of old" (Ps. 78:2), he promises the kind of total disclosure that Dean Stanley praised in Dickens' rending of the veil between the classes "by the dramatic power of making things which are not seen be as even though they were seen."[7] But speaking in parables means the opposite of open proclamation when Jesus tells his disciples in Mark 4:11–12: "Unto you it is given to know the mystery of the kingdom of God: but unto them that are without, all these things are done in parables: That seeing they may see, and not perceive; and hearing they may hear, and not understand; lest at any time they should be converted, and their sins should be forgiven them." In his prolonged meditation on this text in *The Genesis of Secrecy,* Frank Kermode takes parable as paradigmatic of unstable and enigmatic stories, "narratives that mean more and other than they seem to say, and mean different things to different people." The reader of such riddling texts remains on the outside; and Kermode insists that there are only outsiders' interpretations, for one is never completely "inside" a story text, in full possession of its latent meaning although it may yet be glimpsed as a momentary "radiance."[8]

In his later novels, Dickens creates enigmatic, disturbing fictional worlds that resist any easy, concordant interpretation. They anticipate the modern narratives Kermode describes as "intermittent, forgetful, at times blind or deaf": their "varying focus, fractured surfaces, overdeterminations, displacements, have constituted a perpetual invitation to all inquirers after latent sense,"[9] yet the text eludes us even as we are interpreting it; and the accumulation of such unstable meanings in a Dickens novel affects the way we can take in even the clear moral parables he continues to tell. Searching for the key to the meaning of the whole, some readers have looked to Dickens' biblical patterns; and indeed he reaches for such patterns himself as a mode of containment and assurance against his darker parables of social and metaphysical evil. But in the protean works of his maturity, the biblical patterns are fractured, counterpointed, contradictory, "forgetful" of other, rival patterns or "deaf" to the undertones of his own subtexts from the more notoriously obscure or troubling biblical books. Early Bible commentators, Kermode reminds us, "would have attributed the darkness of the tale to the intention of a divine author,"[10] as Ezekiel does. But when Dickens is working as parabler in this second sense, he must relinquish his cherished role as the providential novelist proposing and disposing of his story in a "finished" design, as he presents himself in the 1857 preface to *Little Dorrit* (p. lix), and can only attend faithfully upon the mysterious outlines of his story, like Kermode's St. Mark and Kafka's doorkeeper in his parable, "Before the Law." As a parabler in this darker sense, Dickens writes in figures of which even he does not "know" the meaning although he generates them; he remains on the outside of the very riddles he would rede. Entering into the play of his text to reconstruct the unstated meanings, the reader discovers that "being an insider is only a more elaborate way of being kept outside," although not without occasional glimpses of the radiance that Kafka's petitioner also sees through the barred door of the Law.[11]

This riddling Dickens only began in the occasional indignation G. B. Shaw hailed that "spread and deepened into a passionate revolt against the whole industrial order of the modern world."[12] This outrage often enough found vent in parabolic utterances of the most transparent kind, although they become more enigmatic as the angry voices accumulate in the later fiction. The steady increase in ironic biblical allusions exposing this modern order as disorder testifies to Dickens' deepening sense that his culture had outgrown the Bible's scheme, perhaps any scheme—a historical fact that exposed even the biblical ideals the prophetic Dickens invoked as impossible fictions of belief. It was, therefore, a deeper malaise than indignation that put the Bible itself through this crux and compelled Dickens to tell the darker parable. Of his contemporaries who responded to this unease,[13] Thomas Carlyle was perhaps the most congenial to the darker Dickens, even though Carlyle celebrated the novelist in his lifetime (when not damning the novels) for his cheer and manly heart. I am thinking especially of Carlyle's letter to Forster upon the publication of the *Life*, in which Dickens' mentor saw his "bright and joyful sympathy" but also, "deeper than all, if one has the eye to see deep enough, dark, fateful, silent elements, tragical to look upon, and hiding, amid dazzling radiances as of the sun, the elements of death itself."[14] While, as will soon become clear, I tend to read Dickens' novels as Carlyle does the *Life* in this letter, there are still the not wholly "uninterpretable radiance[s]"; and any reading of Dickens' fiction that aims to take as much of the biblical allusion as possible into account must remain poised on the paradox of a Dickens who both discloses and withholds his meanings, who "may proclaim truth as a herald does" with his allusions but also uses them in ways that "conceal truth like an oracle."[15]

2

ALTHOUGH SEVERAL BOOKS treat Dickens' uses of the Bible in his novels, this essential aspect of his art has not been much studied in comparison with his plots, characters, imagery, or symbolism. One suspects that the main cause of this relative neglect is the stumbling block presented by one kind of biblical usage in Dickens—those sentiments of "the New Testament in its broad spirit" (*Life* 2:422), as he put it in his will, that are sometimes implicated in the worst stylistic excesses of his work. There are several problems of audience and artistic coherence with this language, which will first be taken up with *Dombey and Son*. In this unimaginative phase of Dickens' style, the Bible and the Prayer Book become repositories of clichés from which to draw to evoke automatic reactions for certain kinds of novelistic occasions, such as the child's deathbed or the exaltation of the heroine's virtues. Such bids for Victorian solidarity, when Dickens bribed his readers' uncritical assent with the small change of conventional religious language, have become prime exhibits of the least attractive side to us of "that particular relation (personally affectionate and like no other man's)" which he savored with his public (letter to John Forster, March 1858, D 3:15). Allusions that call upon the reader to do no creative work, merely to respond to an abstract stimulus, can foster the worst sort of complacency; while passively consuming "truths" thought to be ennobling, the consumer is invited comfortably to withdraw from experience. Shaw recognized the dissonance that then disturbs Dickens' art when he charged that the novelist's "sentimental assumptions are violently contradicted by his observations."[16] Although the Bible is not in itself a complacently optimistic book, it gave Dickens language of idealistic simplification and premature closure he was not loath to use when the psychological or social facts could bear no, or no more, examination. His religious allusions can then take on what a *Blackwood's* reviewer called "the strangest counterfeit air": in such defensive transactions, Dickens self-consciously calls upon the Bible to lend its authority to the putative sincerity of his own "higher sentiments . . . calling upon heaven and earth to witness how genuine they are"[17]—while his own facts belie it all.

That the biblical Dickens can be embarrassing, caught out at his least inventive and most pandering, must be admitted. But as Alexander Welsh observes about David Copperfield's parting apotheosis ("O Agnes, O my soul . . . pointing upward!"), "the more [such words] have been regretted, the less they have been examined"; and his book, *The City of Dickens*, itself makes an impressive case for examining such Victorian conventions as the salvific female attending the dying on their journey to another world.[18] Dickens' use of similar conventions will also be treated here, but in relation to larger fictional contexts that allow familiar religious formulas to be placed in question. Beyond this, the Inimitable Boz puts his Bible to many more imaginative, and some more disturbing, uses than the imposture of religious sentimentalism. A brief survey of this range will help us anticipate some of the problems with reading the Dickens who does not speak in only one biblical voice.

For one thing, his Scripture does not "repudiat[e] all familiarities" like Mr. Dombey's "glazed and locked" bookcase (5.44); Dickens freely plays with the Bible and the Prayer Book, his imagination ever stimulated to improve upon the convention and the set phrase. This inventiveness ranges from the fanciful—as in his description of the Dutch tiles paving Scrooge's fireplace, where there were "angelic messengers descending through the air on clouds like feather-beds," and "Apostles putting off to sea in butter-boats" (*CB* 14)—to the potentially blasphemous, as in *Edwin Drood*'s jocular reference to "the highly-popular lamb who has so long and unresistingly been led to the slaughter" (10.80).[19] In *Bleak House* Peepy replays the drunkenness of Noah by dipping this toy figure from his ark "head first into the wine-glasses, and then put[ting] him in his mouth" (30.376); at the other end of the scale are Reverend Chadband's pastiches of pious proof texts, which might be less brutally funny if they were not addressed to Jo. These variously playful kinds of allusion, in a context also fostering pious ones, add a flavor of inconsistency to the novels that is Dickens' way, as though (to borrow the words of the *North British Review* from another context) "the strong spices of Punch were to be mixed up with the savory morsels of the Churchman's Monthly Magazine."[20]

Besides these sentimental, fanciful, jocular, and parodic biblical Bozes, there are also the satiric, ironic, skeptical, and elegiac voices that draw some of their power from scriptural allusion and precedent. Here again, too often this heterogeneity has been missed while only the more obvious and pious features have been noted. Humphry House observes, for example, that when Dickens requires "a special burst of eloquence, he returns again and again to the scenes and forms and language of the Church."[21] But House does not distinguish here between the early and the later Dickens and misses altogether the subversive potential of his heavily ironic uses of liturgical language. It is also notably absent in some scenes where a rite is being enacted, either because Dickens is satirizing empty forms or—quite a different reason—because he is unconcerned himself with the full traditional meaning of the ritual. Such silences and inattentions, paradoxically occurring within contexts that attend carefully otherwise to biblical tradition, must also be accounted for, as must lapses like the botched allusion in *Great Expectations* that Julian Moynahan has made famous: Pip's inadvertent "pharisaic rewording of the publican's speech" while he is attending the dying Magwitch ("I thought I knew there were no better words I could say beside his bed, than 'O Lord, be merciful to him, a sinner!' ").[22]

The desideratum for an assessment of the biblical Dickens is some reasonably precise method of accounting for such contradictory attitudes and strategies. We risk blunting the sharpness of the text if we abstract from it only the continuities that shape our artificially coherent picture of the religious Dickens— the biblical archetypes, a "Christian philosophy," even the "social gospel" that does unify parts of *Bleak House*.[23] Yet the assumption that scriptural reference lends coherence to the fiction underlies most studies of this subject.[24] Dickens' biblical allusions are generally seen as obvious performances in his Victorian "repertoire of [the] familiar" (to borrow Wolfgang Iser's phrase)[25]—pious gestures toward his culture's most cherished treasury of sacred stories, archetypal images, stable moral values, and privileged inspirational language that nineteenth-century readers required. What has not been carefully examined by some is the assumption that, whatever else might be fractured in his world, the Bible according to Boz is an unbroken book, like Carlyle's Scripture "before all things, *true*, as no other Book ever was or will be" (*LDP* 323). Even without this premise, the Word in Dickens is read as a univocal presence providing interpretive stability within the welter of human voices that strain the limits of orderly discourse in the major novels. Thus are his uses of the Bible thought to clarify the "religious centre" of fictional works that are "about ends," in Alexander Welsh's words: "whatever sense of direction or purpose can be salvaged from experience."[26]

Certainly Dickens does use the Bible in these ways. His Esther Summerson, for example, reaches for consolation in the resurrection miracle of Luke 7:12–16 ("that young man carried out to be buried, who was the only son of his mother and she was a widow," 31.389), assuming her reader will immediately recognize this story of the widow of Nain. But as I will suggest, darker "resurrection miracles" in *Bleak House* jar the reader's acceptance of Esther's Gospel pieties. The repeated appearance of such antithetical allusions in single novels, wherein an even wider range of biblical voices can be heard, suggests that not the unifying Logos but a broken Scripture lies behind Dickens' mature work. As Carlyle very well knew, and taught Dickens to observe, in their times of religious uncertainty and babble of doctrines, the Bible like nineteenth-century religion had been "smote-at . . . needfully and needlessly" until it was "quite rent into shreds" (*SR* 184). Certainly Dickens deplored the acrimonious religious debates of his day—what he called "Gorham controversies, and Pusey controversies, and Newman controversies, and twenty other edifying controversies" which were driving "a certain large class of minds in the community . . . out of all religion."[27] Yet even as he deplored these "unseemly squabbles about the letter which drive the spirit out of hundreds of thousands" (to Rev. R. H. Davies, 24 December 1856, D 2:818), Dickens' whole procedure with Scripture presupposed developments in biblical interpretation that had "rent The Book" and jeopardized its claim to absolute authority. Although Higher Critics debated the Bible's authenticity in intellectual circles from which Dickens was excluded by temperament and education, echoes of that larger battle had reached his ears, as his letters show.[28] More generally, all around him far-reaching cultural dislocations were shaping a world that seemed no longer to fit the Bible's concordant design of history. In his transactions with the Authorized Version, Dickens is very much a widely experienced man who "underst[ood] the temper and tendency of the time," as he wrote to W. F. de Cerjat on the *Essays and Reviews* controversy (21 May 1863, D 3:352)—a time when the Bible was "the subject of accommodation, adaptation, varying interpretation without end" (25 October 1864, D 3:402).

Dickens' most avowedly religious Victorian creation is *The Life of Our Lord*, a document suppressed in his lifetime (he even forbade Georgina to remove it from the house) and not published by the family until 1934.[29] This "history" he constructed for his children because, as he wrote his son Edward, the New Testament "is the best book that ever was or will be known in the world, and because it teaches you the best lessons by which any human creature who tries to be truthful and faithful to duty can possibly be guided" (26 September 1868, D 3:668). Despite such avowed intentions, this manuscript of eleven chapters, moving from the birth of Jesus to the persecution of the early Christians, is not only a pious work translating the New Testament's language for children's hearing and turning it into more readable continuous narrative.[30] Nor is it merely a simplified religious testament to replace what Dickens called "the church catechism and other mere formularies," which unnecessarily "perplex" children's minds "with religious Mysteries that [they] . . . can but imperfectly understand."[31] Rather, *The Life of Our Lord* is symptomatic of an age in which the Bible was the "subject of accommodation, adaptation, varying interpretation without end." Deliberately constructed according to Dickens' one conscious principle of interpretation—which was that there need be none, for as he wrote Edward, "the interpretations and inventions of Man" cannot improve upon the New Testament's simple story and must be "pu[t] aside"[32]—*The Life of Our Lord* represents Dickens' effort to recapture the essence of Christianity.

First he follows the line of defense advocated by his friend, Rev. Chauncy Hare Townshend, to "throw overboard" the Old Testament and Judaism "in order (to use Paley's words) 'to lighten the sinking ship of Christianity.' "[33] *The Life of Our Lord* is the prime example of Dickens' often-expressed belief that one can take "the New Testament as a sufficient guide in itself" rather than "forc-[ing] the Old Testament into alliance with it—whereof comes all manner of camel-swallowing and of gnat-straining," as he wrote Frank Stone in 1858 (13 December, D 3:79). Then like many other Victorians, Dickens tries to harmonize divergent Gospel accounts, basing his on Luke but with additions from John and Matthew and ending with selected stories from Acts. Like the Gospel writers themselves, Dickens freely compresses and moves around material to suit his thematic purposes: for example, Jesus' words from the cross ("Father! Forgive them! They know not what they do!") become his response to Pilate's cruel soldiers (*LOL* 102). Instead of Luke's Sermon on the Plain we have Matthew's Sermon on the Mount, which is reduced to the Lord's Prayer in the narrative but so infuses the spirit of the whole account that the themes Dickens recapitulates in his own concluding homily are all from Matthew's Sermon. Luke's themes of the great pardon for all men and the gospel of the poor were undoubtedly attractive to Dickens, the "Great Physician" persona he would have admired, and Luke's softening of the violent and strong emotional reactions were congenial to Dickens' purposes,[34] but certain of the Lukan themes and stories did not fit his "essential" gospel: notably, the fulfillment of Jewish prophecy in Christ's messiahship as well as the temptation of Christ, the sacramental significance of the Last Supper, and the story of Pentecost. With his narrative of the Passion and Resurrection, Dickens seems to shift into John's Gospel, from which he also borrows other stories such as the Cana miracle and the raising of Lazarus. There is some irony in the choice of John because this account more than any other insists that Jesus is the Son of God, whereas *The Life of Our Lord* articulates no clear doctrine of the incarnation. The Christmas angels announce Dickens' Jesus as "a child . . . who will grow up to be so good that God will love him as his own son" (and they add, "people will put that name [Jesus Christ] in their prayers" not because Jesus is God but "because they know God loves it," 14). Such a rationale makes Dickensian sense, then, of the voice of God offstage at Jesus' baptism, announcing, "This is my beloved Son, in whom I am well pleased!" (23–24), as well as the unavoidable divine titles Dickens is careful to put only in the mouths of characters who "said" or "believed" them (see 60, 83, 102–3, 109–10). Dickens makes no such claims himself, carefully explaining, "because he did such Good, and taught people how to love God and how to hope to go to Heaven after death, he was called *Our Saviour*" (34).

Thirty years in advance of *God and the Bible*, Dickens' *Life of Our Lord* was illustrating the dilemma Matthew Arnold bluntly summarized in 1875: "two things about the Christian religion must surely be clear to anybody with eyes in his head. One is, that men cannot do without it; the other, that they cannot do with it as it is."[35] Dickens believed that the Church should "considerately yiel[d]" to "the more thoughtful and logical of human minds . . . [so] as to retain them, and, through them, hundreds of thousands" (letter to de Cerjat, 21 May 1863, D 3:352), and *The Life of Our Lord* is an example of what that yielding might mean. Nonetheless, had this manuscript been published in the author's lifetime, it would have brought down on his head the very controversy that his revised New Testament tries to settle. If his refusal to confess Jesus as "Very God of very God" would have offended conservative Anglicans and evangelicals, the fourteen miracles he includes, climaxing with Christ's resurrection, would have amused the rationalists among his readers,[36] although they might have been content enough with the moral parables Dickens retells in stressing Jesus' teaching ministry. Like William Ellery Channing abandoning some points of faith disproved by reason but not others, Dickens inadvertently courts the ironies of a Mr. Facing-Both-Ways. He does not allow that Jesus is really divine (he only "look[s] so divine and grand," 60),[37] yet he credulously reports the miracles, the most powerful signs that Jesus is God; the forgiveness stories are particularly important,[38] yet Dickens insists that heaven is the reward of Duty Done. The duty theme is paramount: John baptizes people who "promise to be better" (23); the early Christians "knew that if they did their duty, they would go to Heaven" (124); and Jesus is the exemplary human being who teaches us "TO DO GOOD always" so that we may be forgiven and "live and die in Peace" (124, 127). If one might expect this emphasis from a father to his children, one also hears in this reconstruction the voice of the Victorian who cannot believe in Bible promises of Christ's full atonement for sin, a religious mystery even adults "can but imperfectly understand," and Unitarian sympathizers like Dickens not at all.[39] Although he uses much from the biblical accounts down to the red-letter words he cites verbatim as though they were *ipsissima verba*, the Gospel according to Dickens attempts to stabilize "varying interpretation" of the New Testament by substituting one of his own that raises more questions than it resolves, while it implicitly makes his private "accommodation" to the attenuated authority of the New Testament as God's self-revelation in Christ. As for other "essentialists" of the nineteenth century, there can be no impeccable naiveté for Dickens, although this "simple New Testament Christian" (as Angus Wilson and dozens of others have called him)[40] has tried to recover it.

In House's influential chapter on Dickens and religion, he concludes that no one could gather from the novels that "during the years in which they were written the English Church was revolutionized."[41] True, it would be folly to look there for Tractarian figures (although one recalls Mrs. Pardiggle, with her High Church notions of liturgy "very prettily done"). But the revolution in attitudes toward the Bible does find practical expression in certain telling strategies of Dickens' fiction, as well as broadly implicative thematic expression in the darker novels to be discussed. Some of the practical effects can be summarized here: While eminent theologians inconclusively debated their views on future punishment, Dickens refers to the Devil and hell "ambiguously," as House writes; "they might be either literal or metaphorical, so that details of belief are left open."[42] While rationalist critics were treating Scripture as a book of myths, Dickens was drawing upon some of its stories as divine fairytales—the Book of Esther on the level of Cinderella. While orthodox typological interpretation was being discredited, with its elaborate readings of Old Testament characters as types or prefiguring shadows of Christ, Dickens' David, Esther, Job, and Christ figures are wholly humanized; they represent only religious and moral ideals severed from the fuller implications of the typologist's sacred text.[43] Like other nineteenth-century writers Dickens secularized sacred plots; Victorian Adam and Eve figures leave their latter-day Gardens of Eden at the ends of *Little Dorrit* and *Great Expectations*, just as Tom and Maggie pass the Golden Gates at the close of book 2 in *The Mill on the Floss*. Such juxtapositions can ennoble characters, but they can also produce the incongruous effect of Dorothea Brooke's appearance in provincial Middlemarch, "the impressiveness of a fine quotation from the Bible,—or from one of our elder poets,—in a paragraph of to-day's newspaper."[44] Further, such dislocations of biblical references can produce irony at the Bible's as well as a character's expense. On occasion in the novels Dickens even shifts from implicit to direct statement about the inadequacies of Scripture to modern life,[45] although he also expressed his belief in progressive revelation (see letter to de Cerjat, 21 May 1863, D 3:352), of which he may have believed himself a human instrument; his frequent assumption of the prophetic mantle suggests as much. Most important for the argument developed in the following chapters, the Bible's contradictions, given such alarming attention in nineteenth-century intellectual circles, turn up in the popular novelist's work, as he invites rival allusions from quite different parts of the sacred book to coexist uneasily in the same fictional world.

Such free uses as Dickens made of the Bible could not have emerged but in a climate where, for example, with the breakdown of the figurative interpretation of Scripture, there is growing unconcern about the unity of the canon, so that specific texts can be read (and adapted for fictional purposes) as self-contained units.[46] In a climate where the historical facticity of God's Word in all its parts is no longer assured, nor even deemed necessary (as for Dean Stanley preaching on "the sacredness of fictitious narrative"), biblical character types or paradigmatic plots do not have to be thought historical to have emotional resonance; for Dickens as for Matthew Arnold, such things are part of the "poetry of religion" that is still available to the writer although the fact may be failing it. In an intellectual milieu where, as Erich Auerbach writes, "the doctrine which [the biblical stories] had contained, now dissevered from them, becomes a disembodied image,"[47] the novelist who wants the design of a vicarious atonement for a Sydney Carton can borrow it from the New Testament without having to believe the doctrine as rooted in fact or as necessary to salvation.

In the multivocal works of Dickens' maturity, their miscellany of biblical allusions is hardly concordant; capable of being harmonized only selectively, they more often arrange themselves in patterns of contradiction and dissonance. Studying these configurations will not bring us to that condition of literary grace, interpretive certitude, but it will help us understand more about how Dickens read his Bible and take us to the heart of his novels' formative tensions. Like other Victorian novelists George Levine has described, Dickens could not totally "acquiesce in the conventions of order" he had inherited, not even the Authorized Version; yet he struggled as they did "to reconstruct a world out of a world deconstructing, like modernist texts, all around" him.[48] Although Levine excludes Dickens from his survey of Victorian realists, these conflicting aims, I would argue, produce the form of Dickens' mature fictions and direct his manipulations of biblical texts in "a time to break down, and a time to build up" on the ruins. In Dickens' mature fictional reconstructions, which never achieve the "new Mythus" Carlyle had called for, the Bible becomes a paradoxical book: it is at once a source of stability, with its familiar conventions of order, and a locus of hermeneutic instability reflecting the times of religious anxiety in which Dickens wrote.

3

LITERARY ALLUSIONS are only one element among the heterogeneity of things brought into that expansive, polyglot phenomenon, a nineteenth-century novel—itself a fabricated context for the allusion and one embedded in other contexts (literary, biographical, historical, and more). Dickens' big novels are such phenomena par excellence, or *ad nauseam* according to one's taste, that to read even a modestly complex allusion is to venture into a network of interpretive possibilities, if one tries to keep these dynamic contexts in mind as one reads. The folly of then writing a book about those provisional interpretations comes home in the problem of definition—of terms and of focus. In the absence of a received definition of allusion, I would like to begin by offering an expansive one that, reaching from the direct quotation to the merest reference, allows for the multiplicity of "plays" Dickens makes on and with biblical words.

In two common literary handbooks, allusion is defined as a brief "reference," tacit or explicit,[49] but our common use of the word also includes the sense of quotation, as Michael Wheeler is right to insist in *The Art of Allusion in Victorian Fiction*. The reference points to an adopted text without stylistically mimicking it, as when a mother in *Bleak House* declares of some rowdy children, "you cannot expect them specially if of playful dispositions to be Methoozellers which you was not yourself" (11.134). The direct quotation need not necessarily be flagged typographically; characteristically, the Inimitable prefers the unmarked quotation.[50]

Dickens' playfulness with received religious formulas requires other broad categories between the reference and the direct quotation that include the echo and the adapted text. A truncated form of quotation, the echo may use a key

ATTORNEY AND CLIENT: FORTITUDE AND IMPATIENCE
(Hablot K. Browne)

Ashes to ashes, dust to dust. (Order for the Burial of the Dead)

word or phrase from a particular Bible passage, but frequently it calls up a host
of associations from assorted texts that may, or may not, converge in meaning.
When Mr. Vholes, legal advisor to Richard Carstone, raps on his hollow desk
("your rock, sir!") "with a sound as if ashes were falling on ashes, and dust on
dust" (39.485–86), the conjoining of several echoes produces a complex effect
because of the discordant sets of passages they bring to mind.[51] The first set
confirms the novel's satiric reading of Richard's Chancery foolishness, possibly
by recalling ironically Jesus' words to Peter ("upon this rock I will build my
church," Matt. 16:18) but more obviously by drawing without irony upon his
parable about builders of houses on "rock" and on "sand" (see Matt. 7:24–27).
As counterpoint, the second set of echoes from the Anglican Burial Service
("ashes to ashes, dust to dust") and the numerous Bible passages on which it is
based (especially from Genesis, Job, and Ecclesiastes) accumulates an elegiac
reading for Richard's sad course leading to his death. Beyond this, the biblical
allusions produce a generalizing effect that sets Richard's downfall into a larger
cosmic scheme in which even the brightest and best can be deluded, fail, die—
a Joban theme in *Bleak House* that tends to undermine the novel's satiric certainties. Other allusions in this chapter uphold them, however; Vholes' pledge,
"The suit does not sleep; we wake it up, we air it, we walk it about" (486),
exposes the soullessness of English law by mocking the resurrection promises in
the Burial Service while making ghoulish parody of Esther's favorite miracle (the
ruler's daughter who "is not dead but sleepeth," Matt. 9:24).

In this last instance, we have the adapted quotation. In a sense, this term
could be used for all allusions to adopted texts, for adoption becomes adaptation
as soon as the original bit of discourse is placed into a new verbal context. More
specifically, in what I call the adapted quotation, besides recontextualizing the
original, Dickens has made lexical and/or syntactic changes in his source, as
when he ironizes the spirit and application of Isaiah 40:6 ("All flesh is grass";
cf. 1 Peter 1:24) with Vholes "making hay of the grass which is flesh" (482). The
range of Dickens' adapted quotations is very broad, from facetious plays on
Bible words to revisions of its theological ideas, as in the narrator's apostrophe
to Jo, "thou art not quite in outer darkness" (*BH* 11.138; cf. Matt. 22:13).

Finally, Dickens employs subtextual allusion, in which a biblical passage,
chapter, or whole book (or other popular religious text) signaled by local direct
reference, quotation, or echo also forms an underpattern for longer stretches of
Dickens' text. Two types of subtexts in his novels offer different kinds of structuring. One is the narrative that parallels events in Dickens' plot while providing a
running commentary, *sub voce*, on his characters who are analogous to its own;
such are the structural allusions to *The Pilgrim's Progress* in *Oliver Twist*, *The*

Old Curiosity Shop, and Esther's narrative in *Bleak House*. The second type of subtext is the nonnarrative but pervasively influential parallel text, which can serve in two ways: for parts of a novel it may provide a medium of interpreting episodes or characters (the Sermon on the Mount for Amy Dorrit); or a biblical book or passage to which sets of allusions in the fiction point can act as an analogical matrix for part of a novel[52] or for wider reaches of its imaginative vision. To further complicate matters, a novel can have rival subtexts, which may persist in a state of unresolved tension, as the allusions to Ecclesiastes and Revelation do in *Little Dorrit;* or they may have a hierarchical relationship, with one subtext mediating the other, as in the opening of *Bleak House,* where a Genesis subtext is present but reinterpreted skeptically through Joban lenses. Dickens' uses of subtextual allusion create some of his richest, most complex effects because a subtext can comment ironically as well as supportively on Dickens' story, or to reverse the relation, his story can place the biblical material in perspective.

More important for this study than the classifying of instances into these general categories are the multiple functions of allusions as they work to stabilize meaning or to make it more indeterminate. Allusion is a poetic device with potential for introducing some dissonance into literary work because the original text is never completely assimilated into its new environment. There will always be difference between the two texts simultaneously activated— Dickens' alluding text and the text he quotes or evokes—for the writer's act of alluding and the reader's act of decoding are both performed in new linguistic settings. Beyond this irreducible difference, the relationship between the two texts is likely to move in one of two general directions in the mind of the reader. Either they will be brought closer together through the reader's perception of multiplying correspondences between them, or else "the more elements are recalled and the more patterns are formed, the farther apart the [two texts] grow." Imagining these intertextual patterns, as Ziva Ben-Porat has put it, we "reconstruct a fuller text."[53] In simpler terms, we have enhancing allusions and ironic ones that operate through discrepancy. This distinction will prove important for the chapters that follow if we understand further two kinds of undercutting that can take place. Wayne Booth's discussion of stable and unstable irony is useful here: in the first kind, the author gives us "an unequivocal invitation to reconstruct [to recognize and interpret unstated meanings], and the reconstructions have not themselves been later undermined"; in contrast, unstable irony does "not yield to clear and final classification . . . our interpretations will slip away from us even as they are made."[54] Stable allusions, then, may enhance or undercut but their immediate significance will be clear, whereas unstable allusions will invoke complexities that increase indeterminacy, teasing us into thought as we try to interpret the fuller text.

As I have suggested, Dickens critics have emphasized the role of scriptural allusions to stabilize meaning. Michael Wheeler, who reads the allusions to the Four Last Things in *Hard Times* this way, generally associates such authorial strategies in Victorian fiction with the omniscient narrator-persona.[55] On such a reading, allusions are a form of highly self-conscious controlling rhetoric, one of the writer's means, in Booth's phrase, of "impos[ing] his fictional world upon the reader"; he controls the reader's response by making him both aware of the value system that gives meaning to events and willing to accept those values.[56] Booth's rhetorician of fiction is Dean Stanley's parabler who makes us see.

The pragmatic functions of such stable scriptural reference points for reader and author should be sufficiently obvious. Grounding Dickens' fictional world in an eternal order of value, they help us to judge characters and read plots as moral designs. Enhancing allusions serve the purpose of thematic magnification: they may ennoble a character by associating him with a hero of faith, such as Arthur Clennam with the Good Samaritan, or they may raise a social practice to the level of a spiritual issue, as in the *Hard Times* chapter on schooling entitled "Murdering the Innocents" (book 1, chapter 2). The biblical identification of a Dickens character early on—such as George Rouncewell with the Prodigal Son—can also adumbrate plot developments, building into the book in this instance the anticipatory structure of absence and joyous return. Stable allusions can also help the reader to chart a moral path through the morass of plot. Titling the three books of *Hard Times* "Sowing," "Reaping," and "Garnering," for example, provides a parabolic structure that counteracts the potential chaos of the novel's title by suggesting that the temporal flow of events, however hard the times are, unfolds as a natural and moral action.

One subcategory of stable allusion is the implicit valuation of a character in terms of how he misuses, misinterprets, or misses the point of religious texts. Pecksniff's speech abounds in this sort of comic deflation; Sairy Gamp's misquotations and mispronunciations of Scripture and Bunyan ("this Piljian's Projiss of a mortal wale," *MC* 25.471) make for wonderful Dickensian parody of the sober moralist. Other parodies expose misquotation with humor that shades into black. Smallweed cursing Hawden turns the Litany inside out: "Plague pestilence and famine, battle murder and sudden death upon him" (*BH* 26.334; cf. *BCP* 35). The most elaborate of such ironic placing in *Bleak House* is Reverend Chadband's misappropriations of Scripture texts. When he addresses Jo, "My young friend, it is because you know nothing that you are to us a gem and jewel" (19.242), he reverses Proverbs 20:15 ("the lips of knowledge are a precious jewel") in order to make Jo a likely prospect for his own lessons of wisdom. When he blesses the Snagsby dwelling, "May this house live upon the fatness of the land; may corn and wine be plentiful therein; may it grow, may it thrive, may it prosper, may it advance, may it proceed, may it press forward!" (242), Dickens' allusion to Isaac's blessing meant for Esau but given to the dissembling Jacob (Gen. 27:28) revises the roles in this classic case of deception: Chadband is the false patriarch blessing other impostors as well as himself, their well-fed guest who wants another invitation. In such instances of ironic allusion, the reader readily reconstructs the unstated meanings which the controlling author has built into the text.

To the reader of a novel seasoned with biblical language, obviously the serious stable allusions serve as a form of psychological reassurance as well as pragmatic aids to reading. In a quasi-religious way, they function like the rescuing texts in *Pilgrim's Progress* that fix Christian's mind on heavenly things and stabilize his drift toward the heresies his tempters put forward. But in nineteenth-century fiction the sacred *language* takes on a peculiar urgency, like the "songs in the night" of Job 35:10. In 1837 Henry Melvill, Queen Victoria's chaplain, preached a sermon on this rescuing text, in which he declared his complete confidence that "there cannot be imagined, much less found, the darkness, in passing through which there is no promise of Scripture by which you may be cheered."[57] Of course, Dickens' words in season are not always biblical, but Esther Summerson's are; and in her narrative, salvation by quotation is a strategy as urgently useful to the "writer," to calm her own troubled heart, as stable biblical allusions of any sort are to the reader of the chaotic *Bleak House* world. Further, for the novelist recording the impact of rapid historical change, all the more important is the Bible as "the familiar model of history," as Kermode has called it. This book "begins at the beginning ('In the beginning . . .') and ends with a vision of the end ('Even so, come, Lord Jesus'); the first book is Genesis, the last Apocalypse. Ideally, it is a wholly concordant structure, the end is in harmony with the beginning, the middle with beginning and end."[58] In secular novels even the brief biblical allusion can invoke this concordant scheme, in which past reality and future hope give meaning to the present, faintly or vividly reminding the reader that such a reassuring model of history exists or at least had existed. Finally, for the adult reader whose memories of childhood training, earlier reading, and past authorities might be reawakened through encountering a familiar Bible text, a scriptural framework for his present acts of interpreting the novel at hand as a "book of life"[59] might help him to imagine that he can unify the different stages of his experience. Then, at least during his reading, might a Victorian see his life steadily and whole.

If stable allusions give readers hermeneutic aid and psychological assurance, the Victorian writer employing such strategies gains several advantages for himself. Those modes of literary criticism that reduce novels to meanings which are already common knowledge offer a special temptation to the investigator of Dickens' biblical allusions precisely because their most evident function was to connect what the novels portrayed with what was commonly known. In an *Uncommercial Traveller* piece in which Dickens goes to see a Sunday night religious service on a London stage, he reflects on his own problem: " 'A very difficult thing,' I thought, when the discourse began, 'to speak appropriately to so large an audience, and to speak with tact. Without it, better not speak at all. Infinitely better, to read the New Testament well, and to let *that* speak. In this congregation there is indubitably one pulse; but I doubt if any power short of genius can touch it as one, and make it answer as one' " (40). In Dickens' novelistic discourse, he takes his own advice, touching that single pulse and building a powerful ethos into his works by making charismatic appeals to Everyman's Book. In the very act of handing on this cherished cultural possession, the writer secures at once authority over and solidarity with his reading public.

To stop here, however, to treat Dickens' biblical allusions only as a form of controlling rhetoric, is to leave them, his readers' responses, and the Bible itself at the level of the unproblematic, whereas my argument is that in Dickens we see signs of the Great Code's fracturing. It seems to me significant that in literary handbooks, nineteenth-century examples of allusion are rarely used; typically, Milton, Nashe, or Pope illustrates the enhancing type of allusion, while *The Waste Land* or *Ulysses* exemplifies the undermining kind. One might well expect that major Victorian texts provide, line for line, fewer pure instances of either kind of literary allusion in a period when the authoritative testimony of the past is both desired and suspect. Under such conditions of uncertainty, it is not necessarily always clear how an allusion should be read; one person's correspondence may be another's ironic discrepancy. Thus, to the pious reader, Esther Summerson's rescuing texts are in-breakings of the mercy of God; to the skeptical, as to Victorian readers who found her unconvincing, her piety undermines itself, sounding suspiciously self-ingratiating toward the dear reader she wants to win. Dickens unleashes the subversive capacities of unstable biblical allusion in many different ways; here two types might be illustrated with a range of examples from *Bleak House* for the sake of contextual continuity, although as we shall see, biblical allusion becomes problematic from *Oliver Twist* onward.

In the first kind of instability, an allusion that can be read in divergent ways creates ambiguity in characterization—not to dissolve the Victorian notion of "character" altogether, but to lead us into the perception of more complexity than the model outlines at first suggest. In chapter 18, Esther Summerson, with her simplistic religious language, undergoes a crux of the sort that the Bible itself, or at least its more idealizing elements, suffers in its exposure to the *Bleak House* world. Meditating complacently on the beautiful woods near Chesney Wold in terms Romantic poetry had made familiar, with grace notes from popular religious language, Esther looks "through a green vista . . . upon a distant prospect made so radiant by its contrast with the shade in which we sat, and made so precious by the arched perspective through which we saw it, that it was like a glimpse of the better land" (228). When a storm breaks "so suddenly," Esther, "while thinking with awe of the tremendous powers by which our little lives are encompassed," emphasizes "how beneficent they are, and how upon the smallest flower and leaf there was already a freshness poured from all this seeming rage, which seemed to make creation new again." Although the repetition of "seem" provides a clue, the irony of this allusion to Revelation 21:1 and 5 cannot be constructed until the reader knows Esther's secret, although the tables will ultimately be turned on that irony, too, by Esther's renewal after much more than "seeming rage" by her story's end. But long before that, we must come to see the limits of her religious perspective uninstructed by later experience. In her ordered world, Esther, like a good typologist, sees sermons in stones and God's voice in everything. The illegitimate child rescued by the Hand of Providence who habitually speaks of being renewed projects the new heaven and new earth too readily on her own scene, as though the kingdom has already arrived. In this moment of peace it is natural but ironic that she should turn to a text which also promises, "And God shall wipe away all tears from their eyes; and there shall be no more death, neither sorrow, nor crying, neither shall there by any more pain" (v. 4).

With her romantically detailed descriptions, Esther involves us in this apocalyptic hypothesis of desire until its insubstantiality is verbally "exposed" by a voice breaking from the gloom: "Is it not dangerous to sit in so exposed a place?" (228). Suddenly the storm comes up again from Esther's own gloomy interior, when "there arose before my mind innumerable pictures of myself" like those she saw the Sunday before when "something quickened within" her upon beholding her unknown mother's face. Esther's religious piety has not prepared her for the complexities of identity her relation with this woman will bring to life. Although her conventional phrases can give her a structure of meaning for the "rage" without, she will find she cannot frame the rage within in any beneficent prospect until she has been exposed to all her outlook excludes—tears, sorrow, pain, death—and undergoes a rather more difficult transformation than the earth made new by the rain.

The allusions here foster the heuristic process through which Dickens takes us and his heroine: we form a configuration of meaning she invites us to form, but that illusion of "meaning" is disrupted and we must reconstruct it to fit the new facts. As the biblical allusions become destabilized, we are invited to reconsider their truth, along with their function for the speaker, and by extension the import and utility of all such common religious language. In the *Bleak House* passage, the model Esther as well as the biblical model she cites are put in question, not to be discarded but to be transcended by a more complex mode of consciousness. Usually, there is a limit to this kind of instability, and its muted didactic purpose gives to the reading process a dialectical form. When at this chapter's close Esther reasserts her old optimistic vision as she looks at Chesney Wold, peaceful and rain-refreshed, with "the little carriage shining at the doorway like a fairy carriage made of silver" (231), the jarring cruxes we have undergone help us now to see through this hypothesis of reality as a fiction of belief. So does its contrast with the final thing Esther "still" is forced to see: "Still, very steadfastly and quietly walking towards [the carriage] . . . went Mademoiselle Hortense, shoeless, through the wet grass." The Bible as fairytale must be corrected by a vision that more nearly sees the world as it is: Hortense represents an "earth . . . filled with violence" (Gen. 6:11) like the world before the Flood evoked on the novel's opening pages. As I will argue, Dickens' corrective vision in *Bleak House* comes not only from secular sources, but also from those parts of the Bible that speak to sorrow, pain, death. If ironic deflation of idealizing biblical language is implicit in passages like these of chapter 18, other texts come, in effect, to the rescue—not to arrest the destabilizing of meaning but to remind us that the Bible also has a word in season for the indeterminacies of life.

It should be added here that unstable allusions do not always signal genuine complexities of character; they may also indicate Dickens' ineptness or indecision. Such a muddle occurs in an apparent eleventh-hour attempt to provide Lady Dedlock with a Passion story subtext. Chapter 48 climaxes in the mysterious murder of her enemy Tulkinghorn, who plays an unambiguous antichrist to her ambiguous Christ. Leading up to this, when Lady Dedlock tells Rosa, "what I do, I do for your sake, not for my own," her words may recall Christ's "not my will, but thine, be done" in the Garden of Gethsemane (Luke 22:42); she adds cryptically, "It is done" (574; cf. John 19:30). In the next scene with Tulkinghorn—her Judas, "Always at hand" (575; cf. "he is at hand that doth betray me," Matt. 26:46)—Lady Dedlock has "a steady hand," with which she drinks the cup (of water, 581) as steadily she tells Tulkinghorn she is "quite prepared" for the course he will take (presumably, to bring her downfall, 582).

Later, "Her soul . . . turbulent within her" and "sick at heart," she goes to "walk alone in a neighboring garden" (583) to wrestle with her fate. Meanwhile, Tulkinghorn returns to his quarters; a shot rings out and all "is soon over" (584; cf. "It is done"). But not until "a little after the coming of the day" (585)—a phrase echoing the Easter morning passages in the Gospels—is the body found by witnesses who shriek and flee like the disciples who "trembled and were amazed" at Jesus' empty tomb (585; Mark 16:8). No angel but the "paralysed dumb witness" on the ceiling announces this demonic Easter parody, complete when Tulkinghorn is later "resurrected" as an evil force: "Her enemy he is, even in his grave" (55.666).

What do these sketchy allusions accomplish? Tulkinghorn's associations with the Antichrist ally him with Krook and the Lord Chancellor—anti-Shepherds all in the "valley of the shadow of the law" (32.391)—and firmly place him in a critical light. Lady Dedlock, however, remains a muddled figure. Her echo of "It is finished" becomes an unstable allusion merely mystifying her intentions: it suggests some decision taken, but what?—a murderer's vow to do the deed? a brave woman's resolution to spare others her shame? a victim's resignation to her pitiable fate? a fatalistic heroine's heedless self-sacrifice for a past deed done that cannot be undone? no decision at all, but mere bravado to cover her terror and irresolution? With these shadowy Christ-associations Dickens may have wanted to ennoble Lady Dedlock as heroine in the central passion story of *Bleak House*, as well as create some sympathy for her at the hour of her betrayal into the hands of sinners; yet the allusions neither settle nor enrich our view of a woman who remains (as Tulkinghorn says) "a study" (48.581).

Biblical allusion becomes indeterminate in a second way when what begins as a critical or satiric reading of events turns into something else. In the apparently ironic but ultimately beneficent allusion to Jacob's dream in chapter 12, we also have an instance of a biblical text that becomes predictive in more than one sense. Lady Dedlock, "in the . . . clutch of Giant Despair," cannot "go too fast from Paris" in her carriage: "And, when next beheld, let it be some leagues away, with the Gate of the Star a white speck glittering in the sun, and the city a mere mound in a plain: two dark square towers rising out of it, and light and shadow descending on it aslant, like the angels in Jacob's dream!" (139). At first this may seem merely a picturesque Sunday school leaflet effect, perhaps one Dickens had recalled on his own restless flights between Paris and London. But the more one meditates on the allusion, the more stable ironic discrepancies appear between Jacob's dream and Lady Dedlock's illusions that help the reader to judge her and anticipate her doom. Unlike the spiritually sleeping beau monde, Jacob awakens from his dream to declare, "Surely the Lord is in this

place; and I knew it not" (see Gen. 28:10–22). Jacob's vision of angelic messengers becomes a theophany in which the Lord promises, "in thee and in thy
seed shall all the families of the earth be blessed." But the Dedlock set denies
Jacob's divine world; they have replaced its God with an "exhausted deity . . .
terribly liable to be bored to death, even when presiding at her own shrine"
(150). Instead of Jacob's Bethel ("House of God"), where he built his shrine,
Lady Dedlock sees "a mere mound in a plain"; the "gate" of her heavenly city,
Paris, has been reduced to "a white speck" in what might be seen as a descrip-
tively desacralized landscape, with the towers of Notre Dame also reduced to
"dark square" shapes. Unlike Jacob on his journey, my Lady is fleeing from the
House of God and, unwittingly, toward her own judgment. The iconographic
representation of "light and shadow descending on it aslant" in this passage
merges visually with the allegorical "bend-sinister of light that strikes down
crookedly into the [Dedlock] hearth, and seems to rend it" (two paragraphs
earlier, 138). Together these pictures "seem" to suggest that unlike Jacob's
seed, Lady Dedlock's has not been blessed to her; in the Philistine categories
operating here, illegitimacy in the Dedlock line will rend the family hearth, and
she has no further legitimate issue with Sir Leicester. Her nightmarish revelation will shortly appear through a dark messenger, Tulkinghorn, whose threat to
her blasphemous position will drive her to only a graveyard "gate." When one
meditates skeptically on it, Dickens' biblical similitude moves from the pretty
and pious to the ominous.

Yet, ironically, the ironic vision is not the only one in *Bleak House*, for Lady
Dedlock's seed has already been blessed through the daughter who moves from
one end of the novel to the other dispensing benedictions. Through the natural
love (for Hawdon and her child) that "saves" Lady Dedlock morally, she has
been a vessel of God's promise after all, the promise in which Esther believes
and on which she acts. On this reading, then, the descending slant of light
replaces and redeems the "bend-sinister." The initial impression of a pious
allusion to Jacob's dream will be justified, if deepened in human significance,
and the reader of the *Bleak House* world will be surprised to learn that the Lord
is even in this place, though he knew it not.

In this novel, the interpretation invited by the more disturbing variety of the
second type of unstable allusion takes a self-reflexive rather than a progressive
form. Such a reading occurs when a seemingly containable irony breaks the
bonds of moral closure to turn back on the standard of valuation initially employed. This is the built-in liability of satire that exploits religious language: as
William Hone discovered in the heresy trials of 1817 for his political parodies of
the Prayer Book, because the satiric reduction of the religious standard exposes

the standard as well as the current heresies to ridicule, the satire can be charged with blasphemy.[60] A less extreme instance of self-reflexive destabilization occurs in Dickens' use of the Prayer Book to judge the aristocracy in *Bleak House*.[61]

With "it's to be hoped they line out of their Prayer-Books a certain passage for the common people about pride and vainglory" (12.142), Watt Rouncewell begins the satire lightly enough ("Forgive me, grandmother! Only a joke!") but with the awareness that the joke may be perceived as a trifling with holy things (cf. *BCP* 35). Although pious where Watt was impious, Esther, another social outsider, picks up the satire again in chapter 17 at the Chesney Wold chapel, where one of the coachmen "looked as if he were the official representative of all the pomps and vanities that had ever been put into his coach," forgetting his baptismal vows (224 and n. 6; cf. *BCP* 321).

By chapter 28 a shift in ironic implication occurs in the course of a political argument between Watt and Sir Leicester—new class meeting old class. A slur of the ironmaster's on the village school prompts the landowner to meditate upon "the whole framework of society . . . receiving tremendous cracks in consequence of people . . . not minding their catechism, and getting out of the station unto which they are called—*necessarily and for ever, according to Sir Leicester's rapid logic, the first station in which they happen to find themselves;* and from that, to their educating other people out of *their* stations, and so obliterating the landmarks, and opening the floodgates, and all the rest of it; this is the swift progress of the Dedlock mind" (354; first emphasis added). The catechism passage he has stumbled upon is the prescribed answer to the question, "What is thy duty towards thy Neighbour?" Sir Leicester has forgotten the spirit of the question and remembers only part of the response: "My duty towards my Neighbour is, to love him as myself, and to do to all men, as I would they should do unto me: . . . To submit myself to all my governors, teachers, spiritual pastors and masters: To order myself lowly and reverently to all my betters: To hurt no body by word nor deed: . . . and to do my duty in that state of life, unto which it shall please God to call me" (325). Even as he shows satirically that Sir Leicester has reduced this part of the catechism—perhaps all of it—to a class oath, however, Dickens also turns his critique back upon the Book of Common Prayer itself in the reforming spirit of the times that Sir Leicester, circa 1832, fears. *Bleak House* was written in a decade when controversy over changing the Prayer Book was becoming noisier and the parties for reform better organized, and when the Religious Census of 30 March 1841 had revealed that in an officially Christian nation less than half the populace were attending Sunday services.[62] In the latitudinarian spirit of Dr. Arnold's *Principles of Church Re-*

form (1833), but with his own later humanist urgency, Dickens is demonstrating that the interpretation of these Prayer Book words must be revised if it is to command the respect of the newly rising classes; the ironic clause beginning "necessarily and for ever" implies that people might change their stations, do their duty there, and still faithfully repeat the catechism response. Notably, however, Dickens' revisionary impulse does not arise in the *name* of the Book of Common Prayer or the Church so much as for the sake of social responsibility on the part of all classes, in a newly fluid society putting ever greater pressure on his chief stabilizing principle of "love thy neighbour as thyself."

Right after this catechism response on "My duty towards my Neighbour" is the recitation of the Lord's Prayer, by which the child is to call for God's grace in order to do his duty. Dickens' most bitter reflections on the Church's language emerge when he draws attention to its neglect of the poor, graphically emphasized in the distant churchtower of Browne's dark plate etching, "Tom-all-Alone's." In a novel where a primal catechetical scene is often replayed—such as Mrs. Pardiggle's grilling the brickmakers out of a religious book—the most disturbing is the final catechizing of Tom-all-Alone's prime prospect for Church charity, who is "a moving on right forards with his duty" towards "that there berryin ground" (47.567, 571). As Alan Woodcourt fails to teach Jo the Lord's Prayer—for his "immortal nature" has been sunk by ignorance "lower than the beasts that perish" (564; cf. Ps. 49:20)—we have a darker instance of the ironic, self-reflexive destabilizing of liturgical allusion.

The prayer comes into Dickens' text in a series of truncated quotations, whose poignant revisions by Jo might have stabilized the scene as pure pathos. Woodcourt starts the train of antiphonal responses between living and dying voices:

> "Jo, can you say what I say?"
> "I'll say anythink as you say, sir, for I knows it's good."
> "OUR FATHER."
> "Our Father!—yes, that's wery good, sir."
> "WHICH ART IN HEAVEN."
> "Art in Heaven—is the light a comin, sir?"
> "It is close at hand. HALLOWED BE THY NAME!"
> "Hallowed be—thy—"
> The light is come upon the dark benighted way. Dead! (571-72)

But the passage does not end in pathos and piety. This dialogue's defamiliarization of the old, old words releases the narrator's most bitter ire toward the nominal Christians in his audience who have not done their duty: "Dead, your Majesty. . . . Dead, Right Reverends and Wrong Reverends of every order. . . .

And dying thus around us every day." Taking his readers through a more violent crux than he had with Esther Summerson's religious language, Dickens so sets up the scene that he invokes readers' sentimental responses to Christian death-beds, as Dennis Walder has noted,[63] in order to betray them. Although the pious reader may hope the kingdom comes for Jo in "the light a comin," Jo never gets to that petition and dies, like Gridley, without accepting the "blessing" (see 25.315); pinioned on the hard words, "Hallowed be—thy—," Jo can scarcely know what a blessing is, or a name.

The violence that breaks out then in the narrator's rhetoric not only turns on Dickens' audience, but also implicitly puts in question the providential scheme the "Our Father" expresses, a scheme that fails when "Heavenly compassion" (572) dies out in the human heart. Moving through a series of destabilizations, this passage may ironically clarify where duty lies, but like so many of Dickens' darkest reflections on human nature, it holds out little hope that duty will be done in any rank of society on any significant scale. Despite the real presence of a few compassionate souls "close at hand," the fact remains that lives like Jo's and Gridley's were accursed—and no amount of private Good Samaritanism, or the "magic balsam" of half-crowns duly administered (569), seems likely to change the larger condition of indifference which permits such "dying thus around us every day." Despite the passage's tantalizing "radiances" in kind words and allusions to heavenly light, the only "light" that "is come" for Jo is that thrown by the narrator on the social causes of this creature's "dark be-nighted way." The rest is darkness indeed. Rather than being charged with stable irony indirectly affirming belief in the afterlife (as some readers interpret it), the language of Jo's deathbed scene—defamiliarized, truncated, unable to affirm any belief—submits more evidence for the power of "KING DEATH!" (33.413) in *Bleak House*, where more than Chancery suits or Bad Samaritanism is on trial before the "great eternal bar."

Read this way, Jo's deathbed does not effectively counteract the earlier pauper burial service it recalls, like beneficent slants of light reinterpreting sinister ones, but tends rather to confirm (and personalize) the dark parable of "Our Dear Brother." This "dread scene" (11.137) will offer a final extended example of how apparently stable ironic allusions become indeterminate at the expense of the religious values they invoke, especially for the orthodox Christian reader. Spending some time here on the concluding paragraphs of chapter 11 will antic-ipate a recurrent hermeneutic crux in these readings of the biblical Dickens, for in this passage we discover that how far the indeterminate meanings extend is a matter of interpretation—and not one definitively closed by the satiric, proph-etic, and allegorizing impulses here. Nonetheless, I shall argue, what makes the biblical ironies most disturbing, as so often in the later Dickens, is their amplification within the novelistic context.

In the passage describing Nemo's burial near the close of "Our Dear Brother," it seems at first that Dickens borrows the priest's lines from the funeral service simply to contrast, in Stephen C. Gill's words, "the horror of what is going on . . . with the meaning of genuine Christianity":[64] "Into a beastly scrap of ground which a Turk would reject as a savage abomination . . . they bring our dear brother here departed, to receive Christian burial" (137). In *Oliver Twist*'s precursor scene, where a clergyman on the run reads over the pauper coffin "as much of the burial service as could be compressed into four minutes" before Sowerberry tells the grave-digger, "fill up" (5.33), Dickens' refusal to quote any Prayer Book words signals the utter failure of this perfunctory rite to console the two wretched mourners. By the time of *Bleak House*, Dickens has refined his technique. Now, through a persona who does not narrate or re-present the scene so much as turn it into an occasion for prophetic discourse, he uses just enough of the Burial Service to remind readers of the meaning lost, playing upon the phrase "our dear brother" until they feel the hollow form of words it has become. Whether such an echo does its work depends upon some vestigial belief in Dickens' readers that the burial liturgy should mean something, as a powerful reminder of the brotherhood of all under the Fatherhood of God. On a stable first reading, it seems that the writer manipulating this narrative voice seeks to reactivate this belief in the hearts of his brothers and sisters.

Yet, as one meditates on this bitterly disillusioned passage, its controlled ironies dissolve into ambiguities that tend to undermine the "genuine Christianity" on which Dickens calls. For it is specifically the Christian world view that the whole passage fails to endorse and even puts in question. First, by so emphasizing the phrase "our dear brother," Dickens collapses the fuller implications of the traditional rite upon its one, not necessarily Christian, idea of brotherhood. If those who say the rites over the poor without feeling and allow such churchyards to exist deny the ritual's witness of Christian hope, Dickens seems uninterested in reinstating it at least through this narrator, who implies only that the conduct of the ceremony should show proper respect for the dead (and the participants more respect for life). More disturbing is the way the other religious allusion here is handled—an adapted Bible quotation picked up from the background mumbling of the Burial Service ("So also is the resurrection of the dead. It is sown in corruption; it is raised in incorruption," 1 Cor. 15:42). When the narrator says that those who "lower our dear brother down a foot or two . . . sow him in corruption, to be raised in corruption," he borrows St. Paul's language to intensify the moral impact of his reformist point about a sanitation problem of a corrupt society, while grotesquely reversing the apostle's meaning: the dead "rise" only to generate more dying. At the same time he recalls this religious reading of death by retaining the sound of "incorruption" ("in corruption"). Altogether, he pointedly fails to affirm the eloquent testimony of 1 Corinthians 15 to the resurrection, the crux of the Christian faith to St. Paul (see verses 12–17, ". . . if Christ be not risen, then is our preaching in vain. . . . Ye are yet in your sins"). Besides recalling this wider context for the allusion, Dickens' Christian reader would also think of Paul (a favorite saint to the Victorians) as the New Testament's prime example of personal conversion, his own life dramatic corroboration for his creed, as well as for the importance of Christian brotherhood to mediate such individual transformations. (According to Acts 9:17–20, Paul's conversion was not complete until he was taken into the Christian community at Damascus.)

For such readers, then, this conjunction of ironic reversals, depletions, and elisions would draw particular notice to the loss of the Christian framework in which the bid for brotherhood and change of heart would have been more firmly secured. Without any expression of St. Paul's faith, or at least some ringing affirmation of a compensatory creed, the bitter alienation and cynicism of Dickens' narrator then become symptomatic of the larger spiritual crisis toward which his ironic allusions point, a crisis in divine and human relationships marked by the loss of belief in any transcendent power of transformation working through community. It is also a crisis for language no longer secured in human history by the living Logos. The narrative voice, however aware of suffering, is "corrupted" by contempt, like an unconverted Saul; and with no formulas for explaining human misery nor any words at all for hope, his preaching to Victorian sinners is in vain.

The linguistic crisis targeted by and embodied in the religious language of this passage releases farther-reaching ironies than one at first expects. But, some readers might argue, do not the satiric and prophetic voices in this chapter contain these disturbances? To weigh this question, one must consider further what the object of the prophetic satire is. As Dickens rewrites the religious formulas in order to expose the earthly practices that churchly words conceal, he is doing more than continue the Chadband satire on religious hypocrisy, which might be dismissed (and was by indignant Evangelical reviewers) as an irrelevant distortion, an indulgence of the Inimitable's love for grotesquely comic idiolect. In this part of "Our Dear Brother," however, where there is only a generalized "they" to criticize, Dickens can be more attentive to the capacity of otherworldly, idealizing religious language in itself to shroud the facts—here, of pauper misery and public indifference to it. Rather than attacking religious hypocrites, Dickens' skeptical revisions of Prayer Book words forward the attack on the Church pursued elsewhere in *Bleak House*, where "the great Cross on the summit of St. Paul's Cathedral" not only is distant from the unredeemed suffering below, but also symbolizes, as "the crowning confusion of the great, confused city" (19.243), the Babel Church's mere *logoi* that mystify the causes of human misery. In this later, iconographic allusion to the resurrection through the sign of the cathedral's triumphant gold cross, the otherworldly "language" of "St. Paul" is again implicitly presented as mumbo-jumbo that is socially retrograde (just as elsewhere Dickens lets us see the capacities for Pauline formulas to mask some truths from Esther Summerson and impede her growth). And indeed, throughout his career, Dickens pressed beyond the insights of his own satires on characters whose pious words do not match their deeds, to explore the far-reaching implications of experienced gaps between religious idealization, like other abstractions, and human fact—even though Dickens could also ignore such gaps at notorious moments in the fiction. Ironies at the Church's expense do not necessarily amount to a metaphysical critique, of course; but surely Dickens' exposure of the ways that the Church not only fails to act on its beliefs but also "talks nonsense" would be deeply disturbing to the orthodox believer with ears to hear Dickens' parable, in which "civilisation and barbarism wal[k] this boastful island together" (137). If barbarism flourishes with the help of the language of religion, what is regarded as the supreme expression of civilization is in league with the powers of darkness.

The paragraph immediately following these words forms a theatrical segue, in which the controlling author ostentatiously changes the scene while "time passes." Here Dickens abruptly introduces an allegorizing voice that tries to halt subversions of certainty. With "Come night, come darkness"—an allusion to *Macbeth* (see 137, n. 7) prompted by the theatrical mode—the narrator blots out the dread scene, although with the next invocation, "Come, flame of gas," he invites "every passer-by" to "Look here!" at it. In this embarrassingly written paragraph, the odd sense of contradiction—suggesting perhaps Dickens' ambivalence toward the dangerous train of thought he has begun—seems resolved when onto the set shuffles a more hopeful figure, whose Good Samaritan example we priests and Levites passing by are to "look" at. With Jo's secular ritual of respect for the dead Nemo, his attempt to clean up the sanitation and moral pollution problems here by sweeping the graveyard step, Dickens' narrator illumines the darkness as the chapter closes on this tableau. Moving away tentatively from his earlier cynicism, this persona descries "something like a distant ray of light" in Jo's physical and verbal tributes to the "wery good" deeds of *his* Good Samaritan (138)—and the deliberate quotation of Jo's idiom markedly contrasts to the barbaric eloquences of the Church just exposed. With "thou art not quite in outer darkness" (138 and n. 8), the narrator also revises Jesus' wedding feast parable, or a certain reigning dogmatic interpretation of it. In thus doing his own good deed he verbally rescues Jo from those who had earlier put this religiously uninstructed creature aside for his wrong theological answers at the inquest (134), and who have literally deprived this ragamuffin of his "wedding garment" while commandeering all the places at society's feast. Finally, with a suggestion that biblical charity's light is breaking in on himself, the narrator addresses Jo directly as "thou." Such momentary "radiances" cannot be dismissed; they have their effect.

But to argue that this conclusion of "Our Dear Brother" arrests the disturbances of religious certainty here would be to ignore the highly qualifying language in which such allusions are entangled. The "light" descried in Jo is not said to be that of God, but of "reason"; and the verbal rescue of Jo from outer darkness is made with typical restraint. Despite the touches of biblical rhetoric, the refusal to articulate any specifically Christian interpretation remains consistent to the close.

What most powerfully eclipses the glimmerings of religious meaning in chapters 11 and 47, as well as the humanism that tries to replace them, is their larger novelistic context: again and again, rays of light die out in the surrounding gloom. Both passages are amplified by innumerable occasions of the same uses of hollow formula and ironic religious allusion. In *Bleak House* especially, the sheer proliferation of such allusions presses social and ecclesiastical critique, whose ironies might have been contained by a reformist program, toward despair of cosmic order operating in this world where such barbarisms flourish. If in nearly all quarters one finds indifference to biblical values, if it seems that "They dies everywheres" (31.383) without compassion, hope, or meaning, then not only have Bible values become irrelevant to the majority of the populace so portrayed, but the God of the Bible has receded into the fog that lifts only now and then with the arrival of a rescuing text. The spiritual darkness swiftly descending through such long stretches of the novel would seem to foreclose any likelihood that life can be seen *sub specie aeternitatis*, or perhaps understood at all. All we have, then, is the eye of the writer and *his* words; but when he still draws heavily at crisis points upon the cadences of Scripture in his nostalgia for origins and secure values, he creates unintended effects with a borrowed Word that has lost its basis in experienced historical fact. The ironic tensions thus created are not resolved. Meanwhile, the very desperation with which this Victorian writer so often shores up the ruins of a barbarous civilization with biblical fragments testifies to the problematic status of both holy and human words in the nineteenth century for building the new Mythus.

The manifold functions of scriptural allusion discussed here illustrate the essential complexity of Dickens' art. If his allusions can offer some of the cues, simplifications, and closures that Victorians, especially, needed in order to read their novels at all, his revisions of the Bible also provide occasions for hermeneutic instability—from the momentary stimulus to revise a judgment to far-reaching dislocations of meaning—that invite readers to reconstrue the ancient wisdom for the present time. Biblical allusions then become strategies for complicating the act of reading and sometimes help to generate the secrecy of the text, thereby challenging the prevailing norm of interpretation (as preached by Carlyle) that art should reveal "the Divine Idea of the World" at the bottom of appearances.[65] We risk trivializing the Victorian public, those avid readers, if we assume that they wanted no more than confirmation of their world views or conventional inspiration for living. Dickens also gave his readers experiential extensions of their lives and occasions for imaginative play, from the sheer facetiousness of "Piljian's Projisses" to that play of the mind over experience and tradition which made nineteenth-century novels of the highest rank instruments of discovery—even discoveries that full disclosure may be impossible, appearances impenetrable, the Divine Idea a fiction. The advantage to the writer of using unstable allusions is the satisfaction of having challenged his audience "To Think" rather than "Be Thought For" (as a *Household Words* article put the choice),[66] while casting into a form of words his own perplexed sense of his world and expressing his fundamental ambivalence toward authorities of all kinds, including the sovereign Word.

4

TO ASSESS the *status* of Dickens' biblical allusions is to consider them in relation to each other and to other things. In this final stage of introduction to the biblical Boz, it will be helpful to survey the grid of relationships in which his allusions are involved, organizing more schematically some of the issues already raised and bringing in other dimensions of my subject not yet discussed. Literary allusions are enmeshed in two different but intersecting structures of relationships:[67] they are part of the order of words (however indeterminate) that constitutes a literary text, with its implicit or more overt links to previous texts as well as to an experiential world of facts, feelings, events, leading ideas, world views, language, and other conventions (the mimetic axis of the grid); and literary allusions are enmeshed in a structure of communication between a writer and his or her readers (the rhetorical axis). Each of these two headings generates its own particular textual and contextual concerns. Some of the multiple ways of looking at literary texts that this grid produces provide the varying angles from which I examine Dickens' biblical allusions, although not with the same distribution of attention in every chapter of this book. It would have been far simpler, of course, to have looked at these allusions in only one way—to see them, for example, as a kind of metaphor. But the principal assumption behind this study's method is that by shifting perspectives on a subject one can grasp it, if never completely, in its multidimensionality. Surveying those perspectives here will map the broad terrain of this book, which considers literature both as representation and as communication, while disclosing the eclectic theoretical rationale behind these readings of Dickens.

As part of a literary structure, allusions may be considered purely as a feature of style—as verbal embellishments in the text, for example, or as a species of local metaphor. The Bible gave Dickens not one but many styles to import directly, mimic, or otherwise adapt imaginatively (if sometimes also ponderously) for his fiction. Identifying the main biblical voices in each novel and observing some of the plays Dickens makes with the diction, syntax, cadences, and figures of his imported words will be indispensable in each chapter. But an exclusive focus on such stylistic features might lead us to assume that Dickens' allusions achieve merely local effects, to be consumed (in Herman Meyer's homely phrase) like "raisins in the cake."[68] In the mature works this is rarely the case. Dickens' scriptural allusions form larger configurations in the text: they contribute to the networks of interlocking images, allegorical designs, and symbolic patterns that have attracted much critical attention (for example, the Flood archetype and baptismal water in *Bleak House*); they also form the subtextual strata, chains of harmonic and disharmonic verbal echoes, and contrapuntal patterns of rival meanings that will receive emphasis here.

My treatment of style and structure as multiform and often dissonant is grounded in a sense of Dickens' historical context. Mikhail Bakhtin has identified the indispensable condition for the development of the novel as the historical emergence of "a contradictory and multi-languaged world" being shaped by centrifugal forces in eighteenth- and nineteenth-century life.[69] This cultural condition of "heteroglossia" enters a novel through its throng of social voices, each carrying its own belief system into the work. In a mediocre novel, Bakhtin argues, such voices will be merely random, but in a work of novelistic art the language systems represented will be "dialogized," in his jargon—orchestrated, interrelated, and sometimes in local passages stylistically intercut. These voices "know about each other (just as two exchanges in a dialogue know of each other *and are structured in this mutual knowledge of each other*). . . . A potential dialogue is embedded in [the discourses of the novel], one as yet unfolded" (emphasis added).[70]

In the expanded soundscape of *Dombey and Son*, for example, a range of voices from the past (such as phrases from the Prayer Book, Dr. Watts' hymnody, fairytale conventions) contend with each other and with the voices of the dynamic present (the impersonal idiom of the managerial class, metaphors and speech rhythms from railway culture, the bitter logic of the displaced poor, and so on); and through all these voices representing competing social worlds and value systems Dickens weaves the cryptic, nonhuman murmurings of the waves, also multivoiced but speaking first of an eternal world that "rolls round" this one of Past and Present (1.9). Dialogism in *Dombey* serves to remind us that the Victorian universe in Dickens is often a soundstage of voices "contending in boundless hubbub," in Carlyle's terms, with Vox as its God (*CME* 28.32–33; *LDP* 192). In Dickens' frequent use of it, the Tower of Babel story in Genesis 11 becomes an archetypal expression of his finely tuned sense of the contemporary scene; but he also wants to understand what these voices say to one another, how interactively they modify each other's values and claims. In *Bleak House*, for example, he uses this "hubbub" for what Bakhtin calls "the orchestration of his themes and for the refracted (indirect) expression of his intentions and values"[71]—an expression that dialogism, most obviously present in the strategy of double narration, keeps dynamic and unstable.

Dickens' multilanguaged historical context bears upon his treatment of biblical allusion in several ways. First, style: In a novel like *Dombey and Son*, the noisy presence of all the other, nonreligious languages and the world views they represent creates centrifugal pressures not only on the stylistic unity of Dickens' fictional world, but on the univocity of the Word. Gifted as a parodist and mimic, tuned in to the polyphonic scene, Dickens cannot hear just one biblical voice. Moreover, because a unitary Word is inadequate to meet the variously challenging words of its nineteenth-century context, a separating out of the differently cadenced messages in the Bible tradition seems inevitable in order to provide a more flexible lexicon of "words in season." (The fracturing of the Great Code helped to make possible this freely ranging exploitation of whatever parts of the tradition came to hand for particular uses, whether they agreed with each other or not.) Biblical allusions in dialogue with their pressuring contexts and with each other turn out to be multivocal, incompletely merged, competing, sometimes contradictory. They can also be at times no more than the "dead quotations" Bakhtin dismisses (bits of authoritative discourse that have no artistic relation to the dialogic life of their fictional world),[72] although as we shall see the didactic voices in Dickens cannot be adequately explained in Bakhtin's terms.

Second, structure: Using some slippery terminology of his own, Bakhtin describes "the language of the novel" as "the system of its 'languages.'"[73] If we take his second "language" here as any interrelated and consistent set of distinctive usages, and if we refuse to read "system" as either hierarchy or organic totality, Bakhtin's description can usefully be applied to Dickens: we shall find that while the larger patterns which sets of allusions make in a work (or to which they contribute) may each have their own integrity and constitute a "language," these patterns will not necessarily be interrelated harmoniously in the novel's "system." Rather, while these allusive structures will sometimes converge with or complement each other, at other times they will come together only tangentially, diverge, undermine, or overthrow one another.[74] Structuring allusions enter a field of many intersecting and diverging lines of force—sometimes even a battlefield of the sort Bakhtin's militarized terminology suggests. Like the diverging Bunyan and Good Samaritan parables in *Oliver Twist*, or the "battles of biblical books" in Esther's narrative to be discussed, Dickens' patterns of allusion are dialogically multiple and embedded in the novels' formative tensions—tensions that critics have increasingly found essential to understanding Dickens' work.

That *biblical* allusions should lead such a pluralistic life in his fiction inescapably means that his religious messages and moral judgments cannot be read as monological. Here the didactic parabler's narrowest purposes give way to the tolerance, the democratizing impulses, and the imaginative curiosity ("to find out what it's all about, and what it means," *DS* 21.248) that impel the mimetic life of Dickens' fiction. Whatever his other professional reasons for peopling large canvasses, Dickens' novels were his chief expressive means of entering into important cultural dialogues of his day. Although hardly in the manner of a Mrs. Ward, his major fictions (far more profoundly than his speeches) carry on the debate of essential questions through representations of Victorian voices. As I have suggested, these "voices" do not simply coincide with individual characters' idiolects but come into the text in many ways. It is partly through religious and other kinds of allusion that various world views, ideals, values, and even competing interpretations of Scripture are championed, questioned, condemned, and entertained. The heterogeneous ideas and modes of consciousness that Dickens' borrowed words thus import into his fiction become involved in a dialogical play of viewpoints that resists easy resolution, even when he tries to foreclose the issues with fairytale endings or biblical rhetoric. Such diversification no doubt helped to broaden Dickens' appeal—so that nominal Anglicans and devout ones, Unitarians and secular rationalists, all claim him for their own. But it also makes the "religious" dimension of his works, even his code of ethics, far more elusive than they have been taken by some to be. At times that indeterminacy reflects Dickens' sensitive response to many-sided issues; on other occasions, as in *The Old Curiosity Shop*'s range of attitudes toward death and immortality,[75] textual elusiveness seems to reflect the equivocation of a man who wants to be consoling but has no settled belief.

Complicating this account of novelistic dialogue is the fact that ideas are not served up raw in fiction but come encoded in received modes of representation. Some attention is given here to the popular conventions that mediate Dickens' uses of biblical ones, such as the melodramatizing and gothicizing of Scripture texts in *Bleak House*. Dickens' use of iconographic signs from religious pictorial art comes up especially in the chapters on *Dombey*, *Little Dorrit*, and *Our Mutual Friend*, and in remarks along the way about the novels' original illustrations, which Dickens so closely supervised and approved. As we shall see, on some occasions these popular conventions—self-consciously indulged to the point of parody—call attention to their own artificiality and thus tend to reduce the biblical conventions they mediate to the status of unreliable, if necessary fictions. Dickens' use of conventions his readers knew and needed is not only a question of mimesis, of course, but of communication. Here is one of the places where the two axes of the grid clearly cross, compelling us to shift perspectives on our subject.

As one element in the structure of communication between a writer and his readers, allusion can be considered contextually, first, in light of the author's attitudes, intentions, and motivations (public or private, conscious or unconscious). Apart from Dickens' frequent expressions of respect for the New Testament, we have little extratextual information about his religious intentions and none about his literary aims as an alluder to the Bible. The indeterminate texts to be explored, however, will prompt occasional speculation about Dickens' internal dialogue of faith and doubt, as well as the dynamics of his relationship with Thomas Carlyle, a chief reader for whom Dickens wrote and a "biblical" influence. Allusion may also be considered contextually in terms of the history of literary response to a work and its wider impact. Because we have no evidence of real readers' responses to so particular a literary strategy as biblical allusion, only more general contemporary assessments of Dickens' religious language and of the moral suasion his works have been thought to exercise in his culture will come into the argument. A third contextually related issue, concerning the problems of "reading" dramatized and thematized within these novels, will be taken up at the close of this chapter.

Turning to textual issues, we can consider allusion on this communications axis in two ways: as a form of the author's controlling rhetoric, or as an occasion in the text for reader collaboration in the production of meaning. Without attempting to settle all the questions that arise when more than one theoretical construct is being applied to a literary work, I would like to explore here the mutual usefulness of these two apparently antithetical ways of viewing allusion for reading Dickens, especially since both address matters outside Bakhtin's usual range of discussion.

Whatever their context, whatever qualifications are attached, biblical allusions are peculiarly laden with "ideology," especially in Victorian texts. Given Bakhtin's little sympathy for "pedagogic" and authoritative voices in the novel that are univocal, single-minded, and historically nonspecific, that put forward "truth" as abstract proposition and precept,[76] he would probably dismiss many of Dickens' biblical allusions (as indeed do many Dickens critics) as irrelevant to, because unengaged with and even opposed to, the abundant dialogic life of his fiction. They are "rhetoric" in a pejorative sense, failed attempts to effect closure in a dynamic text. In coming to terms with Dickens' scriptures, we must confront the fact that, as the first sort of parabler I have described, he does use stable biblical allusion in some privileged ways. Here the broader, more appreciative understanding in Wayne Booth's earlier work on the "rhetoric of fiction"—all the means a writer uses to convey a world view to his audience—is especially useful in reading Dickens as a popular Victorian novelist with messages to deliver to his public. As we shall see, they are not always single-mindedly propositional or handed down from on high, but sometimes issued with the authority of an orchestrator of multiplicity who appreciates the historic life of language, where precept must be related to specific character and event to be heard. In this broader view, plot, for example, can also be a form of biblical allusion, although as scriptural ideals become involved with these other "rhetorical" strategies, in an elaborately detailed work *they* become entangled in caveats and qualifications that attenuate the power of the Word.

Even where Dickens' moral aesthetic works least qualifiedly and most high-handedly through biblical allusion, those readers who cannot value it aesthetically can appreciate it culturally as language directed to a concrete context which, many felt, needed a newly Authorized Revision of Scripture. Here Barry V. Qualls' work on "the novel as book of life" helps richly to explain why and how Victorian novelists, inheriting Carlyle's amalgamation of the Puritan and Romantic traditions, wrote with special urgency their own form of "biblical romance" (Qualls' improvement on Northrop Frye's too-secular "secular scripture"), in which they guided their readers to set their own lives under the eye of eternity like the lives in the story.[77] Looking at biblical allusion in Dickens, who consciously "imitat[ed]" the "ways of Providence" in his art (to Wilkie Collins, 6 October 1859, D 3:125), will require some attention to these insistent authorial purposes conceived in response to needs the writer shared with his audience.

But, as Qualls also recognizes, such rhetorical overtures become problematized in a cultural context where the writer can no longer appeal to an unbroken biblical standard, assume unanimity among his readers, interpret contemporary life coherently, or act with clarity and equanimity on writerly intentions perfectly known. (As Terry Eagleton puts the latter problem, "An author's intention is itself a complex 'text' " open to interpretation,[78] although the same can be said of the reader's reception and the culture in which intentions and receptions arise.) Where such uncertainties emerge—where, for example, one seemingly "stable" biblical allusion is contradicted by another—we must look beyond appreciative or dismissive theories of the author's controlling rhetoric to explain the workings of allusion.

As a poetic device, allusion obviously requires not only a writer to devise it but also a reader to recognize and activate it for it to produce literary effects at all. Its relevance to the immediate novelistic context is always implicit; in Bakhtin's terms, its dialogue with the voice(s) in that context is "as yet unfolded." How, then, does the reader unfold the dialogue within the text, an act that naturally involves the reader as a dialogist *with* the text? The interpretive possibilities of any Dickens novel proliferate further if we understand this historically actual reader as himself multivoiced, in Bakhtin's terms, because he is a social being, capable of hearing out and producing multiple interpretations to varying degrees, whether he is a nineteenth-century ideologue of some persuasion, a Victorian anxiously self-conscious about the dialogue of the mind with itself, or a post-Freudian likely to be less alarmed by the multiplicities within personalities and a more critical appreciator of the polyphonic Dickens world. Thus defined as multiple, how does Dickens' reader confront a biblical allusion embedded within the dialogues of the work: what shall she or he "do" with it, within the author's constraints on interpretation?

Although Bakhtin does not address the phenomenology of dialogical reading in the "Discourse" essay, some of his foundational earlier writing on the relationships between authors and their heroes, and between people in everyday life, stresses the necessary distance between the "I" and the "other," two consciousnesses that can help to "author" one another only if they do not fuse. This notion of "the absolute aesthetic need of one person for another"[79] points toward a conception of the reader as not entirely within the orbit of the controlling author, but as necessarily to some degree an "outsider" if the various consciousnesses within the work are to be "created" for him. Bakhtin's conviction that true learning is dialogic, not pedagogical, allies itself with a basic assumption of reader response theory, upon which I have drawn selectively in paying special attention to reading the biblical Dickens (with periodic checks into actual responses these five novels have evoked).[80] While Wayne Booth's reader is persuaded to grasp a core of norms everywhere implicit in the work interpreting its events,[81] Wolfgang Iser's reader is a more active participant in the production of meaning, impelled by the paradox of the text—its cues to interpretation and its inexhaustibility—to build provisional illusions of consistency. In *The Implied Reader*, two general descriptions of what texts do to encourage this participation are particularly relevant to the reading of Dickens' biblical allusions. First, texts' omissions and gaps provide occasions for interpretive expansions the reader can perform as he seeks to establish connections and stabilize meaning—not because stable meanings are necessarily the best ones, but because this is one thing readers need to do. Because there is always a gap between the alluding text and the text alluded to, even stable allusions require some imaginative work on the part of the reader to "reconstruct a fuller text," although the play of interpretive possibilities will be circumscribed rather sharply. Further, while there are many different local ways Dickens' allusions stimulate reconstruction, the hardest work they call for is the effort to harmonize, or weigh against one another, the throng of religious and nonreligious voices in one fictional world. Although Iser and Bakhtin may make strange theoretical bedfellows in other ways, the latter's "heteroglossia" creates precisely those gaps which stimulate the productive interpretations of Iser's reader.

Second, Iser discusses the ways that texts thwart or negate a reader's expectations, forcing him continually to adjust the configuration he forms as he proceeds through the text. Here we are usefully reminded that reading allusions, like all reading, is a temporal process; and the fact that an allusion may be qualified by what comes after opens even "stable" ones to reinterpretation. Iser identifies allusion as one element in the writer's "repertoire of [the] familiar" which is then defamiliarized by various textual strategies with the effect of "over-magnification, trivialization, or even annihilation of the allusion."[82] An allusion may be inserted into an incongruous situation, for example; but it may also become estranged from its original import by a subsequent, antithetical allusion which alters the schema that the first one had invited the reader to form. In such cases, allusion becomes itself a literary strategy of defamiliarization, generating unexpected associations that the reader must somehow incorporate into his revised hypothesis of the text.

Such heuristic procedures are not only descriptive of the phenomenology of reading; as Harry Levin writes in *The Gates of Horn*, they are central in the European tradition to which Dickens belonged, a tradition in which the novel contributed to the bringing-out of truth by fostering that ongoing revision of hypotheses characteristic of nineteenth-century science.[83] Iser's parallel argument, based on the assumption that reading is a process of discovery, is that

Victorian novelists turned their co-creating readers into critics of the prevailing ideologies and of themselves.[84] Although Dickens as "Mr. Popular Sentiment" (in Trollope's phrase) could do precisely the opposite, my application of this line of argument is that he also invites his readers to become biblically oriented critics of Victorian ideologies and, sometimes surreptitiously, revisers of biblical and liturgical traditions as well.

Reader response theory is valuable because it helps us see how many of Dickens' scriptural allusions are more imaginatively engaging than the sort of authoritative religious language Bakhtin dismisses, and more dynamically open to interpretation than the controlling rhetoric Booth describes, offering readers a constructive role to play in the creation of new meanings for their time. Allusion can then also be understood in relation to Dickens' larger fictional purposes and his most characteristic moral intentions toward his public. In *Household Words* he once ridiculed the worst sort of authorial tyranny, when he described the zealous writer of a new work on spiritualism ("the sans-culotte of the Spiritual Revolution") as using his own book like "a Clown in a Pantomime," knocking "everybody on the head with it who comes in his way."[85] As "Conductor" Dickens often wanted to come out strong, to "strike a blow" at some abuse or other; but in his letters, the memoranda of a working novelist and editor, he frequently spoke of readers as co-creators whose intelligence and independent judgment are to be respected,[86] and, most important, whose imaginations are to be nurtured. The address to his readers in the first number of *Household Words* (30 March 1850) is his most famous declaration of these literary intentions: the journal would "tenderly cherish that light of Fancy which is inherent in the human breast" and "show to all, that in all familiar things, even in those which are repellant on the surface, there is Romance enough, if we will find it out."

Weighing the rhetorician's need to "show to all" against the necessity for readers to "find it out" was one of the chief challenges of Dickens' art. To him, as to the Victorian sages John Holloway has discussed, to know through experience, to feel the truth of a commonplace (George Eliot), is to decipher world and heart by exercising the imagination, "King over us" (Carlyle), a power of knowledge "inherent in the human breast" (Dickens).[87] To the limitations of this liberal humanist ideology Dickens was not, I think, completely blind; but he persisted in teaching that through imaginative reading, wisdom could be learned for human uses. In *Dombey and Son* he illustrates the wrong way of inculcating the tradition in Mr. Feeder, B.A.'s "barrel-organ" teaching, which reduces the poets' fancies and the sages' lessons to "a mere collection of words and grammar" (11.121). The boys at Blimber's Academy do not imagine that which they know. For Dickens, meaning is not a content poured into waiting vessels but a creation; and if the "lessons of the sages" or the Bible writers are to find their proper significance for modern times, they must be interpreted through an imaginative and personal revaluation.

How challenging that process can be we will see in Dickens' critical treatment of Victorian modes of consolation in *Bleak House*, or the doctrine of renunciation in *Little Dorrit*. If considered in their dynamic multiplicity rather than from the standpoint of their endings, Dickens' mature texts are not the "dangerous" kind Iser warns against, which, by encouraging the uninterrupted formation of illusions, "offer nothing but a harmonious world."[88] When this "uncomfortable writer"[89] stimulated his readers to do more than passively consume pathetic effects or contemplate a Victorian ideal, he was striving to transform them as finer readers of themselves, their world, and England's condition. Whether they are finding Romance or finding it out, the collaborators in Dickens' audience are offered the role of a broadly sympathetic, morally imaginative, and critically alert implied reader so common in his writing that we must sometimes remind ourselves that it *is* only a fiction. The difference between this idealized figure and the typical Englishman as Dickens often angrily described him in letters of the 1850s suggests precisely why he believed this "Reader" had to be created as a redemptive persona in his culture. At the same time, his knowledge of real readers as opposed to the ideal discoverer of Romance, even biblical romance, gave impetus to the darker parables Dickens tells which foster that spirit of critical inquiry no imaginist can afford to be without.

Given these intentions and practices, some aspects of reader response theory are arguably appropriate for Dickens' case, as he might have described it himself. Nonetheless, several tendencies in Iser's accounts of the reading process limit his capacity to explain the instabilities in Dickens' uses of allusion. Especially in *The Implied Reader*, Iser treats the intentions of Victorian novelists as though they were always in command of them, deliberately implanting in their works "cunning" devices to elicit the "right" kinds of participation.[90] To some extent this description fits the enlarged, confessedly problematized, but nonetheless didactic purposes of major nineteenth-century writers such as George Eliot.[91] It is by no means always so clear, however, where Dickens is in command or even aware of his own disruptive ambiguities—or where they are primarily self-expressive, rather than sagelike ruses to effect his readers' reconstruction. Indeed, such socially "useful" ends may be thwarted altogether when the participatory strategies Iser identifies issue in the subversion of all certainty rather than lead to new clarity, as Dickens' unstably ironic biblical allusions can do. On the other hand, a different social benefit than any Iser seems to consider arises from Dickens' dialogical imagination as it produces that democratization of the text Bakhtin so highly values. The Dickens of this study is not Bakhtin's favored Dostoevsky, but these writers shared much; and while their respective commitments to Christianity as expressed through their fiction differed in accent, intensity, and details of dogma, both novelists stretch the moral and existential imaginations of their readers by allowing a full range of voices, including the antireligious and the amoral, to have their say. If the cost in the fiction of this "genial Dickens" is a loss of certitude and a subversion of his own moral aesthetic by what has been loosely termed his verbal "exuberance," the twofold gain is delight in human diversity and readerly practice in tolerance, quite apart from the impetus to "correct" some voices or to re-form outworn ideology as a new myth for the times: a tolerance broader than that Dickens so much admired in the liberal churchmen of his day (and did not find in the increasingly one-note Carlyle).

Iser's account of the beneficial heuristic effects of reading novels requires one further qualification. In Dickens the critique of a prevailing ideology (such as the false messianism of *Little Dorrit*'s capitalists) may go forward on the strength of another set of conventions (the "prophetic" denunciation of capitalism); one set collapses only to disclose another taking its place; and even Dickens' revisions of biblical conventions proceed in some conventionally Victorian ways. It is not necessary to call up deconstruction's intertextual scene of "endlessly shuttling allusion,"[92] or to concede this alluder's hopeless enthrallment with the cultural preconceptions built into his imitative language, to see that his ability or even willingness to disconfirm habitual modes of thought was, like that of all writers, limited. *Contra* the fashionable dismissal of "the author," however, if affirming the view that each of us is a multiple social being, this book celebrates the many authoring Dickenses whose very manipulations of biblical conventions display a remarkable imaginative freedom from old preconceptions, allegiances, even the public persona of "Charles Dickens." And that freedom testifies to powers of origination stimulated by the very "textuality" of this "author." The Inimitable was original precisely because of the ways he was multiple, with a headful of voices (styles, patterns, conventions, literary texts, ideologies) that he orchestrated and combined in so many forms throughout his career. Although of course he did more imaginative things than invent biblical allusions, his uses of Scripture are "original" in these entirely characteristic ways.

Moreover, we can appreciate Dickens' revisions of Bible texts even as we see how they also signal a vast cultural shift in which he was caught up, which he could not yet have completely understood and in some ways stoutly opposed. With this last in mind, we can now consider a final definition of "allusion." Although Dickens consciously rejected "the interpretations and inventions of

Man" in Bible criticism, his allusions are always in some sense a mode of interpretation—not only a lens through which Dickens sees things in his world, but also a means of looking back at Scripture itself. Dickens recalls tradition into the present not merely to repeat it but to re-envision, re-accent, simplify, complicate, imitate critically, defamiliarize, dethrone, or otherwise rewrite the sacred text. T. S. Eliot took it as axiomatic that tradition is "altered by the present as much as the present is directed by the past";[93] and we can see the tradition only through a reconceptualization particular to our time. For an author writing in Carlyle's "mean days that have no sacred word," the Bible becomes not precisely a standard of eternal verities, nor yet only a repertoire of the familiar, but a Code itself discordant that is already being reinterpreted in Dickens' play of allusion.

The related contextual issue along the rhetorical axis of my scheme concerns the fact that Dickens thematizes the subjectivity of knowledge and interpretation from *Dombey* onward. Some of his biblical allusions, here, are as much a part of the problem as in another author or era they might have been its solution. In general, as preformed chunks of literary material with well-known contours, Scripture allusions call attention to themselves and thus to the formulated quality of religious statements. In a time when meaning, as Iser puts it, "is no longer an object to be defined, but is an effect to be experienced,"[94] some of Dickens' scriptural formulations call attention away from their status as Truth-bearing language, and toward their own creation of effects—or to the novelist's rhetorical strategies and the reader's work of interpretation. Especially as Dickens discovered the vast extent of the kingdom called "fiction," the ways (as an *All the Year Round* essay put it) "we are all partly creators of the objects we perceive,"[95] he came to see that a religious reading of events is at least partly and perhaps wholly a human interpretation—a necessary and possible one, he says in *Dombey*, for "all who see it" (16.191). Further, by giving his readers indeterminate allusions, Dickens offers them occasions to sense the vicissitudes of interpretation and to experience their own processes of reconstruction. This sense need not be formulated as it would be by a literary critic already self-conscious about what is, after all, her professional work; any reader's uneasy impression that a passage is dark, that a character's moral outlines are uncertain despite his biblical associations, that an allusion might mean one thing or quite another, registers the fact that the message has been received. Hence Dickens' efforts to create a public that might redeem the time are complicated, even thwarted, by the darker parables he tells about our incapacities to penetrate the secrecy of the text.

From the complex of mimetic and rhetorical, textual and contextual concerns sketched out here comes my hypothesis to cover Dickens' paradoxical case. To put it simply, biblical allusions in his fiction work both to control indeterminacy and to contribute provocative instabilities. Stable and unstable allusions, implying different perspectives on the world reflected in the work and on the Bible itself, cohabit Dickens' major novels in dialogic play: they seem, in Bakhtin's terms, even to "know about each other" and to be structured in relation to each other, as well as to other voices in each fictive world, where dialogue is still going on when "the story is done" (*OMF* 4.13.845) whatever provisional clarities have emerged along the way.

The need for several angles of critical vision in this study will soon become evident from the many forms scriptural allusion takes, slipping like the protean Dickens himself through the theorist's grids and classifications with wonderful dexterity. Because the elusive play of meanings in which his biblical allusions are engaged is the object of my pursuit, I begin with Dickens' second novel. While even *Pickwick Papers* cannot be said to offer only a "harmonious world" of concordant allusion, its disturbing interpolated tales largely enclose their own monologic spaces in the text. It is rather in *Oliver Twist* that a dialogical relation between Dickens' two kinds of "parable" begins to emerge—and to pose those problems of interpretation that become absorbing in his later work.

2

Early Biblical Boz:
The Case of *Oliver Twist*

George Cruikshank

OLIVER TWIST AT MRS. MAYLIE'S DOOR
(George Cruikshank)

All things in parables despise not we
Lest things most hurtful lightly we receive;
And things that good are, of our souls bereave.

John Bunyan, "The Author's Apology for His Book," *The Pilgrim's Progress*

ALTHOUGH *OLIVER TWIST* is not a religious novel, it is a book, as Steven Marcus puts it more precisely, "conceived under substantial pressure of the Christian sentiments and language which were the received culture of Dickens's time."[1] Already in this early work these pressures, meeting counterforces in this same culture, were generating the tensions that distinguish Dickens' work and that impelled him toward the complexity of his later fiction. On the one hand, it has been argued that allusions to Christian texts make sense of this novel, providing what Erving Goffman calls a "frame" for understanding. Yet the religious framework also makes "nonsense" of *Oliver Twist* and calls attention to its own literary and moral inadequacies. Moreover, much of this early novel's potent social vision menaces, even ruptures, the constructive religious frame, with its promise of closure on interpretation. In his later fiction, Dickens anticipates the menace with more subtly elaborated, and more genuinely dialogical, biblical designs than anything attempted in *Oliver Twist*. As later chapters will show, he encapsulates doubt and hermeneutical instability in familiar models from the darker biblical books, he employs the Bible's own poetry of mutability, and he registers tensions in the novel through counterpointed scriptural allusions. Studying how Dickens uses religious texts in *Oliver Twist* can help us to define some of the problems, so evident at the beginning, which Dickens' later complex novels were designed not to solve, certainly, but to entertain and explore in more imaginatively satisfying ways.

In several senses *Oliver Twist* is a simple early case of Dickensian biblical reading. In his use of *The Pilgrim's Progress* we see Dickens experimenting with the technique of a unifying subtext, although his revised version of this Puritan classic confers only a spurious order on his fictional world and for many readers creates more problems than it solves. In this novel some of the key Bible texts for Dickens' entire work begin to establish their importance, although formal allusions to the Authorized Version are few and scattered; they have not yet become resonant poetic devices, means of weighting social prophecy, or tools of critical interpretation. Dickens' extensive use of ironic biblical allusion is adumbrated in *Oliver Twist*'s satire but only in a limited way, producing stable ironies whose meaning is immediately evident. Moreover, the religious allusions are apparently chosen to chime with each other but are not quite consonant. And if the Dickens of *Oliver Twist* is aware of contradiction in his work, which he defends in the famous "streaky bacon" passage, he seems unconscious of its problematic status and masks the hermeneutic instability it creates from his readers, perhaps also from himself, with the affirmations of his religious rhetoric. (In the later fiction, where interpretive uncertainty becomes self-consciously engaged as theme, Dickens also comes to expose religious rhetoric as a strategy of evasion.) The central problem in which the others are rooted has already been suggested: in *Oliver Twist*'s relatively simpler fictional world, the religious design—along with the conventions of melodrama and satire we already see Dickens assimilating to it—is undermined by a social vision that is "Radicalish" (in the word of one Victorian reader)[2] in exposing the failure of received conventions to explain evil and justify suffering. Not surprisingly, given the pressures of this radical vision as well as the inadequacies of its religious counterweights, in *Oliver Twist* we see the early signs of a problem with Christian ideas in Dickens' fiction that Alexander Welsh's work has explored: they are "inescapably there and yet finally elusive."[3] After identifying the sources of those ideas in *Oliver Twist* and the kind of religious frame they make, the discussion will track that elusiveness and its implications for allusion in this early Dickens text.

1

STEVEN MARCUS has placed *Oliver Twist* within the English parabolic tradition of morality plays, homiletic tales, and Bunyan.[4] In fact, *Oliver Twist* is three parables—two of them religious stories in Dean Stanley's sense whose dual operation in this novel is apparently meant to but does not quite produce a clear, univocal message. The most prominent is the fable Bunyan claimed to write "in parables" like his Master: Dickens announces it in the novel's subtitle, "The Parish Boy's Progress," and recalls it in a running headline for chapter 8 ("The Young Pilgrim's Progress," added in 1867),[5] where "Oliver Walks to London, He Encounters on the Road, a Strange Sort of Young Gentleman" when the hero is nearly "dead upon the king's highway" (46). This echo of Bunyan's "such robberies [of faith] are done on the King's highway" (171) calls to mind the other story engaged in *Oliver Twist* as a subtext with wide relevance: the parable of the Good Samaritan. The motif of providential rescue is there in Bunyan's allegory as well as in Jesus' exemplary tale; but the latter's predominance in *Oliver Twist* requires the redefinition of the Bunyan hero as a passive sufferer for Good Samaritans to assist—a redefinition that attenuates the spiritual impact of the revised Puritan classic and clouds the "truth within a fable" Dickens would, like his precursor, convey (B 37). (Here is an early instance of Dickens' privileging one religious subtext, which modifies the perspective of another.) On the other hand, the Good Samaritan subtext is relevant to more of Dickens' novel and, within its own limits, is more imaginatively engaged by Dickens as parabler.

A literary allusion is a medium of vision, as Herman Meyer describes it, "permitting another world to radiate into the self-contained world of the novel."[6] *The Pilgrim's Progress* as subtext invites the reader to see behind the adventures of Oliver's story an archetypal struggle between the forces of good and evil for the hero's soul. Yet since its "other world" is two centuries removed (and in signal ways alien to Dickens' temperament), the Bunyan text must be revised for a later time. One way Dickens secures spiritual issues in a set of nineteenth-century conventions is to assimilate this Bunyan design to melodrama; its signs also gesture toward a subsurface Manichean battle, and in its plot a moral universe among men is at length vindicated.[7] While Bunyan defends his use of parable to convey spiritual truth in "The Author's Apology for His Book," Dickens' famous apology opening chapter 17 argues for the natural truth of melodrama's conventional aim to "present the tragic and the comic scenes, in as regular alternation, as the layers of red and white in a side of streaky, well-cured bacon"; such "sudden shiftings of the scene," besides, are "sanctioned in books by long usage" (102), and although Dickens did not name it in his 1841 preface, *Pilgrim's Progress* is one of those books. Superficially, with its dramatic changes of fortune, Bunyan's story lends itself to melodramatization—not surprisingly, since melodrama's roots can be found in the same morality tradition that Bunyan drew upon. Alternating between radical peril and dramatic rescue, his hero's journey is "sometimes up-hill, sometimes down-hill," as Honest says; "we are seldom at a certainty" about the soul's destination (B 332) until the glorious end. Dickens exploits this apparent uncertainty with melodramatic suspense: Which way will Oliver go?—toward the "tragic" hell of urban crime and poverty or the divinely "comic" heaven he dreams about and miraculously discovers on earth in the society of Mr. Brownlow and the Maylies?

But of course Dickens' Oliver is not Bunyan's more active wayfaring Christian, nor a Christian in any other orthodox sense. If the borrowed paradigm suggests that life is a stage on which the drama of salvation is enacted and the faithful matured as well as tested by adversity, Dickens actually precludes any real moral drama, undercuts this paradigm, and belies the notion of "progress" in his subtitle.[8] For his hero already embodies the "incorruptible" goodness that Christian seeks (B 42), as the preordained "principle of Good surviving through every adverse circumstance, and triumphing at last" (1841 preface, xxv).[9] In consequence Oliver is what Bumble calls him, "a artificial soul and spirit" (7.42), not the "human boy" even Chadband in *Bleak House* finds Jo. At this stage in his career, Dickens apparently needed an unsullied image of his child-self as well as proof definitive of a God who takes care of his own, in what he already knew was "a world of disappointment: often to the hopes we most cherish" (51.338). Thus he embodies a Romantic version of Puritan election in his innocent child, while stoutly rejecting what was the logical counterpart for many of his contemporaries—the predestined damnation voiced by the gentleman in the white waistcoat and Mr. Grimwig (Oliver's "A bad one!" 41.262). As Dickens' melodrama drives toward the revelation of the hero's pure identity and the expulsion of evil in a public spectacle, Oliver must remain a passive victim of the inexorable logic of the plot in order to prove God's all-powerful providence.

Bunyan's allegory also starts with the premise of election; but his story has brought comfort and inspiration to generations of embattled Christians because his hero enacts their struggles in ways that Oliver's so obviously preordained goodness never allows him to do. Unlike the episodic mishaps of the static Oliver, Christian's plot of spiritual growth takes him through the entire Puritan psychology of conversion; and even after he loses his burden at the foot of the Cross and receives assurance of his election, he must beat back an army of spiritual temptations, wrestle for the truth of Scripture texts, and hold onto the promises of eternal life. Oliver, in contrast, dressed in rags and with no burden on his back but the unmerited curse of his illegitimacy and poverty, runs from Dickens' City of Destruction crying for physical survival, the first thing needful for his "Good" to survive; instead of the truth Christian seeks, the utterly lonely Oliver wants only an arbor to rest in and a family identity. In this beginning, Dickens is already setting the scene for his Good Samaritan parable, which requires Oliver not to fight the good fight of faith but to lie in literal and figurative ditches awaiting rescue, "a poor outcast boy . . . alone in the midst of wickedness and guilt" (20.124–25).

Through Sloughs of Despond, Valleys of the Shadow of Death and Valleys of Humiliation, up Hills of Difficulty, and into Vanity Fairs (for Oliver, a Rag-Fair), both protagonists travel; both are met by allegorical personages and confront demons at hell's mouth. But Christian does heroic battle with creatures like Giant Despair who personify his inner doubts, while Oliver's enemies are strictly external menaces, and he seems never seriously to be tempted. Resting in an arbor at the Maylies' country retreat, he momentarily loses his "scroll" (his proof of election) like Christian sleeping, when the evil of Fagin and Monks at the window impresses itself on his consciousness; but it is only a moment, before all traces of them and their influence vanish. This disappearance is the more incredible because the reader *is* powerfully impressed by the real menace of the evil characters—as the Bunyan subtext would require, with its lesson that we must never underestimate the powers of darkness. It is, significantly, in the context Dickens has himself created that the notion of Oliver's inherent goodness seems as much a piece of folly as the self-delusion of Bunyan's Ignorance, who has stifled his conviction of sin because his "heart" has told him he is good (185). Bunyan knows better: Ignorance misses entering the Celestial City by a hair's-breadth; Oliver, on the strength of Dickens' new Pelagian heresy, finds himself already in.

Because being spiritually saved is not enough, Dickens diverges even further from the Bunyan model in his final disposition of affairs. Turning away from whatever divine grace has been implied in Oliver's deliverances, Dickens lands his hero at length in Bunyan's eschewed Village of Morality under the care of Legality and his son Civility to "live by honest neighbours, in credit and good fashion" (B 50). Ordering this ending, Dickens becomes Mr. Worldly-Wiseman, "the eternal bourgeois trying to tell a social inferior which way he should go."[10] As bourgeois rewards of being good replace Christian ones and the "inheritance incorruptible" becomes the father's money and the father's name, Oliver's intimations of the heavenly are realized in Brownlow's "little society, whose condition approached as nearly to one of perfect happiness as can ever be known in this changing world" (53.348). Dickens' last phrase is disingenuous; we have left that world behind for another Eden, like Pickwick's final retreat. The other heaven, after all, is "a long way off; and they are too happy there, to come down to" earth, as Oliver says (12.69). If in this Dickens retreats from affirming the "Heavenly Home" that was Christian's reward, the Victorian writer's earthly paradise is curiously deathlike nonetheless[11]—like Meagles' country home in *Little Dorrit*, "Devilish still" (1.16.188). Cruikshank's last plate, "Rose Maylie and Oliver," is appropriate to this deathlike close of their stories: in a church reduced to its function as mausoleum, the two gaze solemnly at Agnes' memorial stone, their faces grown too old (as Dickens himself noticed) as though their lives are already over. (The picture also resembles the preceding illustration of Fagin's death cell, with stained glass replacing his gaol window.) We have arrived at the other pole of Oliver's predetermined "claustral universe,"[12] where the novel's obsessive fears of suffocation, which J. Hillis Miller has noted, are associated not only with baby farms, chimney sweeping, hanging, and the close

ROSE MAYLIE AND OLIVER
(George Cruikshank)

dens of thieves,[13] but also with the stifling domestic interiors, funereally per-
fumed with flowers, of the Maylie household—and with the church, a place of
the dead. In the irreversible logic of events, this is the artificial Elysium where
Oliver, victim as much as beneficiary of his predestination, has no choice but
to go.

If Dickens attenuates the power of his Bunyan model by eliminating or displacing much of its spiritual drama, in depositing his hero at this House Beautiful he misses another form of dramatic tension and progression in *The Pilgrim's
Progress*. Dayton Haskin has argued that Bunyan presents a drama of interpretation in which Christian, a lonely figure burdened with a Book whose texts initially menace his peace of mind and render him impotent, must "lear[n] to
interpret for himself, making his way through the wilderness of the world."[14]
Growing in his understanding of Scripture at the House of the Interpreter and
later at the House Beautiful, Christian becomes ever more adept, even playful,
at quoting a saving and clarifying text for the situations that arise on his journey,
and correcting the misinterpretations of the tempters put in his way. Bunyan
would foster a similar growth in his reader. Arguing in the "Author's Apology"
for "The use of parables; in which lay hid / That gold, those pearls, and precious stones that were / Worth digging for" (35), Bunyan assigns to his reader
the "travail" of puzzling out readings, that the burden of interpretation
eventually lighten and reading become a source of "delightful things to see"
(37), comfort, and self-knowledge.[15] Enticing his reader at the threshold of his
story into the serious textual play, Bunyan concludes his catalog of the many
pleasures to be found in this work with a challenge to his participating reader:

> Would'st read thyself, and read thou know'st not what
> And yet know whether thou art blest or not,
> By reading the same lines? O then come hither,
> And lay my book, thy head and heart together.
>
> (37)

When Oliver Twist comes to his House Beautiful, like Christian he reviews
his adventures, receives religious instruction, and glimpses the Delectable
Mountains that will be his by the tale's end. Having been earlier prepared at
Brownlow's House of the Interpreter—where he had been ministered to by "soft-
hearted psalm-singers" (16.98) and an old woman with "a small Prayer Book
and a large nightcap" (12.70)—Oliver now can "read a chapter or two from the
Bible: which he had been studying all the week." Rather than bringing the
multiple delights and puzzles Bunyan celebrates, however, reading the Bible is
for Oliver "the performance of [a] duty," which makes him feel "more proud and

pleased, than if he had been the clergyman himself" (33.202). Clearly Oliver is not "pleased" by the pleasures of the text, for no imaginative engagement is required, no difficulties of interpretation arise; learning to read the Bible is assimilated rather to his pleasure of acquiring a higher station in life, even that of the clergyman. Never puzzling over the application of the right texts to life situations, Oliver also never cites any specific verses; the text Oliver's narrator often comes closest to quoting for him is not from Scripture at all but Wordsworth's *Intimations of Immortality* ode (see 30.184, 32.201). Goodness in his world seems as transparently readable as the words of the Book, provoking nothing but a blank of reflection in this artificial soul.

In this early novel, like Oliver, Dickens is not wrestling with the simple biblical texts he chooses for his story; and in his interpretation of Bunyan's classic, founded on shoals of Scripture texts, he smooths all the rough places in their theology and dispenses finally with its Christian message. Nor, with one important exception, does he impose on his readers the burden of interpretation that becomes the serious play of allusion in his later books. Passively we are to receive the Bunyan parallel in the subtitle, without inquiring too far into it; no labor is required to dig out the meaning of other religious allusions, such as the association of Monks and Sikes with Cain (46.296, 48.306–7) or the use of "Pharisee" for the religious hypocrite (294). Like Oliver, we too can be complacently "proud and pleased" with these confirmations of our common heritage, rather than challenged to read for ourselves. In the early Dickens, the reading and application of Scripture is in general unproblematic—or meant to be.

The important exception anticipates, on a small scale, some of the more interesting ways Dickens uses the Bible in his later fiction. If his readers are challenged at all to more active critical reading of themselves and their world, it is not through the Bunyan fable but the parable of the Good Samaritan. One of the few of Christ's parables that sets forth a clear moral for earthly action, and thus appropriate for a Victorian fable that ends in the Village of Morality, this story radiates into the world of Dickens' novel to illuminate where duty lies. At the same time, Dickens' depiction of much social suffering draws attention to the darker places in Oliver Twist's world and in human nature, insoluble enigmas Good Samaritans address in vain. Thus, unlike the Bunyan melodrama, which expels evil with the triumph of good on earth, Dickens' application of Jesus' parable does not solve all the problems it illuminates and is unevenly matched against the forces of the third, darker "parable"—in Kermode's sense—that *Oliver Twist* also tells through its nightmarish visions of the Victorian urban hell.

From a pragmatic point of view, it might seem perfectly obvious why Dickens used the parable of the Good Samaritan: at a time when he was trying to build up his public, he appealed to biblical knowledge the most commonly shared among his readers, thereby gaining credibility while he "flattered their moral feelings" (as Humphry House writes more generally of the religious Dickens and his public).[16] But such an analysis slights both Dickens' serious intention and the biblical story itself. Some consideration of what Jesus' parables are and how Dickens acts as parabler in his Master's tradition will be useful at this point.

Jesus' parables were heuristic devices adapted to specific audiences of his day: through the experience of a story, he intended to make his hearers see a new reality, moving "from 'what is' to 'what might be.' "[17] While the story of the Good Samaritan in Luke 10:25–37 is not metaphorical like most of Jesus' parables, like others it is both dialogical and dialectical. Usually Jesus' teaching stories emerged out of debate; this one begins in Jesus' dialogue with a "certain lawyer" who "tempt[s] him, saying, Master, what shall I do to inherit eternal life?" and, when Jesus urges him to love God and "thy neighbour as thyself," asks further, "And who is my neighbour?" Out of such dialogues the parable emerges, engaging the hearers' ordinary social categories, prejudices, pious beliefs, and conventional expectations at the outset of the tale. But as the parable begins to reveal the kind of story it is, John Dominic Crossan writes, the listeners draw back: "I don't know what you mean by that story," they think, "but I'm certain I don't like it."[18] The dialectical thrust of the parable is to overturn the story the hearers expected to hear, often with polar reversals (poor become rich, rich become poor) that revolutionize the way reality is perceived. Turning on a surprise, the parable draws in the hearers as critical participants; through their participation, the kingdom "comes" in the transformed hearts of those who have ears to hear—or they reject the parable and effectively exclude themselves from the kingdom.

Although the Good Samaritan parable does not illustrate this process as clearly as the Prodigal Son story, for example, Jesus does transform the expectations of his hearers on several key points. In expanding the definition of the "good neighbour" as the one "that sheweth mercy" to the outcast (v. 37), Jesus removes all limits on the duty of love—something his hearers were quite unprepared to accept. Jesus does not exclude the pious priest and the Levite, whom the audience would expect not to help since handling a dead man would have made them ritually unclean, from the injunction to act charitably toward anyone in need. Most tellingly, in making the good neighbor one despised by the Jewish community, to whom "Good Samaritan" would be "a contradiction in terms . . . the impossible, the unspeakable,"[19] Jesus forces those who would "Go and do . . . likewise" (v. 37) to acknowledge the integrity of the traditional enemy and even to identify with the outcast-hero of the story. Entering the

radically new world of these unforseen relationships, the hearer enters the kingdom the parables proclaim.

With its implicit social criticism, its exposure of the legalism and hypocrisy
of religious officialdom, its dramatic counterpointing of indifference and spontaneous generosity, and its challenges to conventional seeing—both of the
wretched and of those who imagine themselves charitable—the Good Samaritan
parable is just the sort of story Dickens would have felt impelled to recast again
and again for new nineteenth-century conditions. Throughout his career, like
Matthew Arnold using "lines and expressions of the great masters" to discover
"the truly excellent,"[20] Dickens used his Master's moral example story as a
touchstone for distinguishing the truly virtuous—those who *act* upon their
faith—from pretenders to virtue.[21] He does so when Esther Summerson and
John Jarndyce (but not Harold Skimpole) befriend Jo, shivering against a window "like some wounded animal that had been found in a ditch" (*BH* 31.384).
Dickens' strategy, however, was not only to embed such little parabolic moments
in his narrative, which may merely call up stock responses by themselves, but
so to detail and populate his novel that his readers might newly see the "vast
outlying mass of unseen human suffering" as well as reconceive their conventional duties. As Dean Stanley observed in his memorial sermon, it was this
"dramatic power of making things which are not seen be as even though they
were seen" that made Dickens the parabler "the advoca[te] of the absent poor."
By combining pathetic and horrific social documentation with the Good Samaritan story, Dickens wanted to recall his readers to a fresh sense of what the
officially current values of a Christian country should mean in the actual urban
setting. The desolate parish boy is his test case.

If Oliver is a pawn in the Bunyanesque spiritual melodrama, he is equally
passive in this second parable; but his being little more than an "item of mortality" (1.1) throughout the story is a mark of his desolation in itself impressive,
quite apart from the other reasons Dickens needed him to remain such a blank.
Oliver comes into the world with his mother's legacy, "the old story"—*she* "was
found lying in the street" (2), rescued by the parish only to die giving birth in
the workhouse. Although Oliver lives, his rescue by these bogus Samaritans is
hardly the happy conclusion of the parable, which turns into a satiric version of
itself. Dickens drives his stable satire home by having Bumble explain the
emblem on his "very elegant button": "The die is the same as the porochial
seal—the Good Samaritan healing the sick and bruised man. . . . I put it on, I
remember, for the first time, to attend the inquest on that reduced tradesman,
who died in a doorway at midnight." "Died from exposure to the cold," Sowerberry adds, "and want of the common necessaries of life" because "the relieving

officer had——" ("refused him," the reader adds silently, readily completing Dickens' point; 4.21–22). When the beadle calls the troublesome Oliver "a dead-weight; a millstone, as I may say; round the porochial throat" (21), he condemns himself, as Dennis Walder has observed, by echoing Christ's words, "But whoso shall offend one of these little ones which believe in me, it were better for him that a millstone were hanged about his neck, and that he were drowned in the depth of the sea" (Matt. 18:6; the board also decides to send Oliver to sea, 23).[22] To "offend" the little ones is to sin not only by cuffing and starving them in the workhouse, but also, as Dr. Arnold explains in one of his sermons on this favorite theme, by "leading them into evil" or hindering them from doing right[23]—as this "porochial" gang would Oliver, were he not under the protection of a Higher Power.

Dickens assimilates other biblical satire to this central situation, in a parish where the practice of baby farming has caused more than one infant to be "summoned into another world, and there gathered to the fathers which it had never known in this" (2.4). When Oliver is apprenticed to the undertaker, he "Forms an Unfavourable Notion of His Master's Business" (title, chap. 5)—"business" hardly spiritual, though concerned with one of the Four Last Things. Here Oliver meets another charity boy named Noah (who "could trace his genealogy all the way back to his parents"), a cruel survivor in whom all the violence of the world before the Flood seems concentrated against the outcast boy "everybody lets . . . alone" (27). The subject of taunts and even prayers against "the sins and vices of Oliver Twist" (3.14), Oliver is only "half-baptized" by the parish (6); it is no wonder he is considered demonic by those who have failed to complete the ritual of exorcism.

The Samaritan type—especially satirical—was widespread in nineteenth-century literature.[24] Dickens often used it: in *Hard Times*, a "deadly statistical clock" proves "that the Good Samaritan was a Bad Economist" (2.12.164), echoing a similar conjunction of ideas initiated in *Oliver Twist* (see 55.22). In *Little Dorrit*, the workhouse is "appointed by law to be the Good Samaritan of [the] district" (1.31.357). In *Our Mutual Friend* as Betty Higden dies in her flight from the workhouse, the narrator comments: "It is a remarkable Christian improvement, to have made a pursuing Fury of the Good Samaritan; but it was so in this case, and it is a type of many, many, many" (3.8.569). In *Martin Chuzzlewit* the satire receives an additional twist: General Choke looks on "at the prospect" of the Eden Land Corporation swindle on poor Martin, "like a good Samaritan waiting for a traveller" (21.419). This is the reverse of the "regeneration of man" that the United States is said to stand for in this novel: the return of the Samaritan figure to the status of enemy, or his degeneration into the band of thieves one falls among. The commonness of this kind of transformation is illustrated by a lead article *Household Words* ran for 14 March 1857, in which Henry Morley decried what was thought a scandal involving the Secretary of the Samaritan Institution, "who stood by one of the way-sides in a great city, and made application to the rich for food and drink, that he might give them to the poor, but maintained his own kitchen therewith, and sent away unaided and uncomforted many a neighbour who, even in the very house of that Samaritan, had fallen among thieves."[25]

In Dickens' later fiction, the satiric and ironic biblical allusions accumulate to expose the inefficacy of the religious models themselves in a culture where "civilisation and barbarism walked this boastful island together" (*BH* 11.137). But in *Oliver Twist*, the satire appeals to Scripture as the still-recognized ground of order against which modern practices are judged. Thus, despite his inventiveness with these biblical texts, Dickens' satire is an art of closure, allowing his reader some imaginative engagement with Scripture but directing that play toward stable moral interpretations. When we later meet the serious counterparts of these Samaritan pretenders, who treat Oliver "with a kindness and solicitude that knew no bounds" (12.68), we are in the even less imaginative realm of the "type." Cruikshank drives the point of the parable home by hanging a religious print of the Good Samaritan over Brownlow's fireplace in his illustration, "Oliver recovering from the fever." After Oliver has been left by the housebreakers badly wounded and "lying in a ditch" (25.155; compare Fagin's "Poor leetle child. Left in a ditch," 26.160), Cruikshank pictures "Oliver Twist at Mrs. Maylie's door" "half dead," a wretched subject indeed for rescue. In every respect these goodly Samaritans counter the bad ones; and unlike the parish authorities, they teach Oliver to pray so that now, with his child's eloquence, he can offer up praise of his benefactors, echoing their own (as Mrs. Maylie says, "may mercy be shewn to me as I shew it to others!" 27.184).

The problem with these types, of course, is that they evoke no critical participation from the reader but merely call up appropriate responses;[26] and a sentiment automatically induced makes no parabolic impact on conventional ways of seeing. Nor do Dickens' respectable Samaritans challenge the hearer to new and surprising identifications. Where the New Testament subtext does become more provocative to the reader's moral imagination is precisely on Jesus' most disturbing point: the identity of the rescuer as outcast, whom the hearer is bid to imitate. In counterpoint to the ideal behavior of the Maylies and the "respectable old gentleman" Brownlow, Dickens also offers the unstable example of the thieves who take Oliver in.

On his way to London, Oliver nearly falls "dead upon the king's highway"

OLIVER RECOVERING FROM THE FEVER
(George Cruikshank)

And when he saw him, he had compassion on him, and went to him, and
bound up his wounds, pouring in oil and wine, and . . . brought him to
an inn, and took care of him. (Luke 10:33–34)

when he is "roused" by a boy "surveying him most earnestly" (8.46–47). Although this "young gentleman" is dressed like a parody of the respectable grown-up male rescuers Oliver will come to know, and his mode of discourse confesses itself "playfully ironical" (49), the Dodger is as spontaneously generous as it is possible for an Artful lad to be, buying food and offering Oliver free lodging in London with "a 'spectable old genelman as lives there, wot'll give you lodgings for nothink, and never ask for the change; that is, if any genelman he knows interduces you" (48–49). Despite the ironic play anticipating the thieves' duplicity soon to be revealed, surely no reader can be insensible to the impact of this aid and comfort upon the lonely Oliver, the Dodger's "new pal" (50). Cruikshank's famous illustration, "Oliver introduced to the respectable Old Gentleman," may contain stable irony in its title but visually it is unstable: there is the devilish Fagin with the boy-sized pitchfork by the fire, but there is also the food and drink, warmth, comfortable smokes, and companionship Oliver has craved. The real attractions of this underground society offset Dickens' efforts to make it a demonic inversion of the other respectable old gentleman's world;[27] indeed, to some readers, like J. Hillis Miller, the thieves' self-conscious parodies of this daylight realm instead "bring into the open the inauthenticity of what is imitated."[28] Unlike Bumble's unconscious parody of Good Samaritanism, the criminals' deliberate equivocal imitations make them hard to judge and may subtly call in question the righteous rescuers of the tale, even if their sentimental form of goodness is not in itself enough to subvert our belief in them.

"Mr. Fagin," who sometimes falls into biblical cadences as cover for his identity as the "Old Gentleman" of folklore, soon turns out to be the Bad Samaritan most to be feared. Like the workhouse authorities, he reads Oliver "a long lecture on the crying sin of ingratitude" and lays "great stress on the fact of his having taken Oliver in, and cherished him, when, without his timely aid, he might have perished with hunger." Fagin also does not fail to follow this with another parable, "the dismal and affecting history of a young lad whom, in his philanthropy, he had succoured under parallel circumstances, but who, proving unworthy of his confidence, and evincing a desire to communicate with the police, had unfortunately come to be hanged at the Old Bailey one morning" (18.109). The effect of these parables is not to transform but to transfix Oliver, his blood running cold. When Sikes falls ill, Fagin poses as Good Samaritan again, but Sikes knows better and punctures the pose. In this underworld, mutual aid is subject to the thieves' Golden Rule, as Fagin explains "the catechism of his trade" (18.114): each must look out for number one, but "You can't take care of yourself, number one, without taking care of me, number one," for "a

George Cruikshank

OLIVER INTRODUCED TO THE RESPECTABLE OLD GENTLEMAN
(George Cruikshank)

Mr. Fagin laid great stress on the fact of his having taken Oliver in, and cherished him, when, without his timely aid, he might have perished with hunger. (*OT* 18.109)

regard for number one holds us all together, and must do so, unless we would all go to pieces in company" (43.276). Still, this ambiguously self-interested kind of Samaritanism is a way of surviving, offering more comfort and expressing more social energies than the cold indifference of the parish authorities or the hostility of the "good citizens" Oliver meets.

It is good enough to evoke Nancy's curious loyalty to the band: "there are many of us who have kept the same courses together," she explains to Rose, "and I'll not turn upon them, who might—any of them—have turned upon me, but didn't, bad as they are" (46.295). It is her commitment to their culture and its rules warring with some contrary sentiments of her "woman's heart" that makes her an equivocal Samaritan, even though the Bunyan parable would have her, more simply, be the "Soul of Goodness in Things Evil" (1867 running headline for chapter 16).[29] She tends Bill in his illness with all solicitude, but she also risks bruising for Oliver's sake. Early on she saves him (with a "God Almighty help me" on her lips; see 16.98–100); later, even while pointing out what she has borne for his sake, she delivers Oliver up to Bill Sikes (with a "God forgive me!" this time, 20.125) as his accomplice in the robbery. It is this sequence that leads to Oliver's being left for dead in a ditch by the fleeing housebreakers. Nancy's curiously indifferent, even brutal response to this reported plight is meant to shock: "The child is better where he is, than among us . . . I hope he lies dead in the ditch, and that his young bones may rot there" (26.160). Nancy, too, looks out for Number One: "I can't bear to have him about me. The sight of him turns me against myself, and all of you." While helping the indigent is easy for the Maylies, Nancy represents the Samaritan ensnared in a morally ambiguous place—not simply "right or wrong," as Dickens says of her in the 1841 preface (xxviii)—caught between conflicting imperatives of help, and between them both and her own need to survive.

2

IN NANCY'S CASE we see how the simple moral lesson of the Good Samaritan parable begins to run aground in *Oliver Twist*, given Dickens' attempt to apply it to the realities of a social scene too complex and indeterminate to fit his understanding of the Bible's scheme. H. M. Daleski has identified this general problem with Dickens' contradictory, unstable book in his argument that *Oliver Twist* is really "two novels"—its story-plot "affirm[ing] a moral belief in virtue triumphant" is inconsistent with the imaginative social problem novel.[30] Daleski does not observe that the other moral story Dickens tells, the Good Samaritan parable, is meant to unite these two worlds of Bunyan and the city: charity is the virtue triumphant that is to solve the social problem. But like the revised Bunyan plot, the use of Jesus' parable confers only a spurious unity on Dickens' novel and is inadequate to contain the potential chaos of his social observation—of the third, dark parable he is constrained to tell.

Dickens' "two novels"—in general, the religious tale with its two diverging parables and the realistically detailed story of poverty and crime—arose out of contradictory intentions voiced in his 1841 preface. (These rival commitments determined the dynamic shape of his fiction for years to come, not as mutually exclusive poles of his novels, but as "dialogized" oppositions; as we shall see especially in *Little Dorrit*, while the religious framework often seems to license the darker explorations, these in turn make the transcendental and moral affirmations urgently necessary.) Dickens first proclaims to his readers that he wanted to draw "a lesson of the purest good . . . from the vilest evil" and has set Oliver amid criminal "companions" in order to prove that Good can triumph over the most "adverse circumstance" (xxv). But as he describes his "aim" (he uses the singular) in depicting these companions' "miserable reality," he already begins to create sympathy for figures who are not merely pawns in a moral fable or proofs of Oliver's election, but people grounded in social concretions Dickens claims to know well (from "long ago" having "tracked [them] through many profligate and noisome ways," xxviii): he aims "to paint them in all their deformity, in all their wretchedness, in all the squalid poverty of their lives; to shew them as they really are" (xxvi). The rest of the preface abandons altogether the initial point of discussion—the "lesson of the purest good"—for self-defense against the charge of having portrayed so much vice. He concludes by discussing Sikes in his "circumstances" "becom[ing], at last, utterly and irredeemably bad" (but no agent of the Devil here) and the equivocal case of Nancy: "It is useless to discuss whether . . . [she] seems natural or unnatural, probable or improbable, right or wrong," he declares, for her portrait is "TRUE" (xxviii). This preface thus makes a telling circuit: the novelist introduces himself as one committed to absolute values and closes by confessing his deeper interest in particular conditions and in what is "a contradiction, an anomaly, an apparent impossibility, but . . . truth" in all its moral awkwardness and murky circumstantiality.

Oliver Twist, then, has its divergent roots in both an explicit moral intention and a commitment to circumstantial truth-telling that declines to name the moral. In her introduction to the Clarendon edition, Kathleen Tillotson traces the novel's most important antecedents to Dickens' 1834–35 sketches (such as "The Old Bailey"), his professional reporting of the police courts and Parliament in

1834–36, and the period in his early life when criminality impinged upon poverty for this "small Cain":[31] "I know," Dickens memorably told Forster, "that I have lounged about the streets, insufficiently and unsatisfactorily fed. I know that, but for the mercy of God, I might easily have been, for any care that was taken of me, a little robber or a little vagabond" (*Life* 1:23–25). This often-quoted passage expresses both the personal experience behind the circumstantial truth-telling of *Oliver Twist* and its need for a moral pattern illustrating "the mercy of God" if also some reason to question God's providence. While one implication of this statement is that the religious patterns in Dickens' thinking cannot be summarily dismissed, the other is that they maintain a precarious hold in fictions directed by his most passionate drive to tell the dark parable. This uneasy coexistence can be observed in the incompletely dialogized relations between *Oliver Twist*'s three parabolic stories, which sometimes seem to know about each other and at other times do not.

The tale of social observation subverts the Bunyan fable because while the latter requires the exclusive moral coordinates of Good and Evil, the Saved and the Damned, the former shows that these structures of belief are as rotten as the tottering houses of the poor. The victims of starvation so starkly presented in Dickens' opening chapters belie these conventional categories of the moral life: these creatures are neither good nor bad,[32] although they already suffer the torments of the damned. With such conditions as theirs in mind, James Anthony Froude's Markham Sutherland in *The Nemesis of Faith* wants to minister to the poor but will preach "no hell terrors, none of these fear doctrines": "No, if I am to be a minister of religion, I must teach the poor people that they have a Father in heaven, not a tyrant. . . . What! am I to tell these poor millions of sufferers, who struggle on their wretched lives of want and misery, starved into sin, maddened into passion by the fiends of hunger and privation, in ignorance because they were never taught, and with but enough of knowledge to feel the deep injustice under which they are pining; am I to tell them, I say, that there is no hope for them here, and less than none hereafter?"[33] Neither can the conventional message of Virtue Tried by Adversity inform a social vision adequate to these horrors, for as many Victorian sermons on Joban patience could illustrate, this moral formula fosters indifference to suffering and, with its injunction to endure unto the end to be saved, vitiates the will to change the conditions that cause distress. The larger general problem with this set of moral ideals in the Bunyan subtext is the inadequacy of applying standards of individual morality to systemic, institutionalized evils. But from such monstrous wrongs, neither can individual acts of Good Samaritanism save—the rescue from "vice and infamy" of one small boy is the right moral gesture of a certain philanthropic sort, but hardly a social program.

With the triumph of charity in the first Brownlow rescue, the Samaritan narrative tries to banish Oliver's past wretchedness and his voices of temptation as "a long and troubled dream." But the eerie reality of this dark parable is what we most remember (in contrast to the bland dreamworld of bourgeois respectability).[34] Stretching to all points of the compass, suddenly looming up in the narrative's path, menacing the borders of the happy episodes, the "neighborhoods" (if such they may be called) of the poor compel the reader's imagination like a recurring nightmare:

> A great many of the tenements had shop-fronts; but these were fast closed, and mouldering away: only the upper rooms being inhabited. Some houses which had become insecure from age and decay, were prevented from falling into the street, by huge beams of wood reared against the walls, and firmly planted in the road; but even these crazy dens seemed to have been selected as the nightly haunts of some houseless wretches; for many of the rough boards, which supplied the place of door and window, were wrenched from their positions, to afford an aperture wide enough for the passage of a human body. The kennel was stagnant and filthy. The very rats, which here and there lay putrefying in its rottenness, were hideous with famine. (5.30–31)

"You'll get used to it in time, Oliver," says the undertaker. "Nothing when you *are* used to it, my boy" (33). But that is precisely what Dickens as dark parabler refuses to let us do: we must see this world invisible to conventional minds over and over again. Near the end of the book the narrator conducts his reader to yet another such locality, "the filthiest, the strangest, the most extraordinary" of all, Jacob's Island:

> To reach this place, the visitor has to penetrate through a maze of close, narrow, and muddy streets, thronged by the roughest and poorest of water-side people, and devoted to the traffic they may be supposed to occasion. The cheapest and least delicate provisions are heaped in the shops; the coarsest and commonest articles of wearing apparel dangle at the salesman's door, and stream from the house-parapet and windows. Jostling with unemployed labourers of the lowest class, ballast-heavers, coal-whippers, brazen women, ragged children, and the very raff and refuse of the river, he makes his way with difficulty along, assailed by offensive sights and smells from the narrow alleys which branch off on the right and left. . . . Arriving, at length, in streets remoter and less-frequented than those through which he has passed, he walks beneath tottering house-fronts projecting over the pavement, dismantled walls that seem to totter as he passes, chimneys half crushed half hesitat-

ing to fall, windows guarded by rusty iron bars that time and dirt have almost eaten away, and every imaginable sign of desolation and neglect. (50.320–21)

How these passages operate parabolically is more complex than at first appears. The signs Dickens bids us read are enigmatic, inviting interpretation of their latent meaning. Ostensibly, the precise detailing of social reality here would seem to teach a simple moral lesson for those who have eyes to see: "every imaginable sign" points to "desolation and neglect"; hence, we must not neglect the poor. Repeatedly erupting in the narrative, what such scenes come to register, however, is Dickens' discovery that a dark, unstable parable has replaced this more transparent one.

At first the narrator seems to promise parabolic clarity by taking his reader in hand to "penetrate through a maze": he will make this outsider an insider by showing him the shocking sights, challenging his conventional ways of seeing, and bringing him into a new sense of the real. Following this parabolic program, these two passages move again and again from "appearance" to "reality": what look like shop fronts are in fact "fast closed"; what at first appear to be people, with occupations and sexual identities, lose all human definition, becoming assimilated to their physical environment ("refuse of the river," mere "offensive sights and smells"); what look like ruins "falling into the street" are really homes; the signs of human entrance and exit are merely places of disappearance, for no one appears in this scene but the rats, "hideous with famine," who have metonymically replaced the humans. Even metonymy is an illusion, for it has a literal meaning after all: the contiguity of rats and people in this close neighborhood menaces human life; bearing disease, a community of rats literally replaces the other one. By moving from appearance to reality in a series of surprises, Dickens defamiliarizes the familiar terms in which his reader normally sees and thinks ("house," "shop," "human"), inviting him to reflect on his ordinary processes of interpretation and giving him a new vision of what is really here.

But this is not the new world and unforeseen relationships in which Jesus' parables terminate: we are left with "what is," not with "what might be." Moreover, Dickens' detailing the surface of the enigma does not "penetrate" it (320).[35] This is the crux of interpretation through which the Dickensian observer moves, turning this parable from a moral example story into a dark enigma or even, perhaps, a mere muddle. Promised he will "penetrate through a maze," the visitor finds only, when he does come to Jacob's Island, an even more bewildering labyrinth of slums; this locale, as Kermode describes obscure narratives, is "a treacherous network rather than a continuous and systematic sequence"[36]—like Dickens' text as contrasted to the clarifying story it had promised to be. The visitor remains an outsider, seeing without perceiving, and so does the narrator: for such scenes are incomprehensible, like the seven ragged paupers, "dumb, wet, silent horrors," which Dickens described to Forster as "sphinxes set up against that dead wall, and no one likely to be at the pains of solving them until the General Overthrow" (*Life* 2:131). Even here, while Dickens seems to suggest there is an answer if only someone took the "pains," these sodden bundles of rags seem more like a muddle than a riddle, and they dramatize a dark parable indeed to the would-be parabler, rebuffing the Samaritan and shutting out this interpreter on the outside of their meaning.

Dickens' reference to the "General Overthrow" reminds us of what is lacking in these passages from *Oliver Twist:* the apocalyptic and prophetic readings of the later fiction, which attempts to place such "horrors" into an apprehensible biblical design.[37] Over such scenes in this early work, however, no God of mercy or judgment presides; starved innocents and good-hearted prostitutes as well as brutal criminals like Sikes are indiscriminately driven to death by the social forces that have made them what they are. Dickens' dark parable in *Oliver Twist* thus explodes religious categories as well as theories of political economy, literary conventions, and familiar ways of seeing: none of the received formulas can make sense of such anarchic "desolation."

Dickens' literary maneuver in this dilemma is to reinvent one of the old categories in a new genre of urban gothic, which does not so much contain or domesticate the "horrors" of his observation as deepen the impact of the dark parable. Gothic conventions express these places' ambiance of brooding fear: their claustral interiors, labyrinths, dim passageways, and rickety platforms over the abyss; their tangle of criminal urges and illicit loves; their scenarios of menaced impotence; their dire portents of grand catastrophes, the imminent collapses of inherited structures; and over all the specter of mortality. Paradoxically, although the outsider cannot penetrate the latent meanings, the effect of urban gothic is to draw him into these nightmare visions; they fascinate, appall, attract the voyeur, and will not be banished by daylight consciousness. Yet they yield no answer. Inside yet outside, the urban observer discovers himself suffocated by a mystery to which even his now-sharpened consciousness has no clue; like the victim in a gothic thriller, he is "buried alive," conscious yet impotent, acutely aware of a social plight that is also a hermeneutical plight, yet equally aware that there can be no simple rescue by Good Samaritans or providential hands, and no way to read the scene for the efficient solution the reformer in Dickens wants. *Oliver Twist*'s pictures of urban poverty mediated by gothic conventions register this moment of obscure discovery, when the moral parabler himself is darkly parabled; the discovery darkens further still in the later books when Dickens has lost all faith in political remedies, and social evils are engulfed in a deeper human condition of irremediable error from which it would seem that no God can save. In *Oliver Twist* urban gothic is already providing Dickens with an expressive medium for the metaphysical anxiety that attends his thwarted social outrage; and the former undermines the practical intentions of the other in urban descriptions that seem, finally, primal scenes of life's vast incomprehensibility, as viewed by the "small Cain" Dickens once was. The writer's acute sensitivity to whatever is "a contradiction, an anomaly, an apparent impossibility, but" *true* is surely rooted in his early experience of "a thing so anomalous" as his blacking-warehouse life (*Life* 1:25). But even to invoke this familiar autobiographical reading is merely to add to the mystery, not to exhaust the latent sense of these Jacob's Island parables.

In the face of this chaos, Dickens' two Christian patterns not only seem like frail, wishful counterweights but also fail to present together a unified message of hope. The Bunyan fable requires a view of life that the Good Samaritan parable rejects and the darker social vision menaces. These mutually cancelling moves destabilize the novel's themes of punishment and mercy, which continue to be generally problematic in the later books. Illustrating the difficulty here is *Oliver Twist*'s equivocal treatment of conventional formulas for hell and the damned.

Dickens' contradiction is focused in a passage in chapter 46, where Nancy, meeting secretly with Rose and Mr. Brownlow, is impelled by "a fear that has made me burn as if I was on fire" (293) to do a good deed for Oliver's sake. Yet on the next page she exposes the cruelty of fire-and-brimstone preaching, and Mr. Brownlow, the Samaritan touchstone, confirms her rejection of it: "Your haughty religious people would have held their heads up to see me as I am tonight, and preached of flames and vengeance. . . . Oh, dear lady, why ar'n't those who claim to be God's own folks as gentle and as kind to us poor wretches as you?" (294). From the early workhouse scene in which Oliver is prayed against as the Devil's agent, Dickens shows in this novel the link between belief in hell and lack of compassion; as the Unitarian minister Henry Giles put it in the Liverpool debates of 1839, "it was not until there was a hell without hope, that there was a heart without mercy."[38] Yet in *Oliver Twist* Dickens employs these conventions—whether they are only metaphorical it would be hard to say, though they seem more literal here than anywhere else in Dickens' work[39]—and he cannot quite dispense with the moral sanction of hell. It was, as Fitzjames Stephen said, "an essential part of the whole Christian scheme"[40] much debated in the nineteenth century, but unquestioned in Bunyan's work except by infidels, for whom the mouths of hell that mine his landscape have been prepared. Dickens translates this landscape into the fires that break out in oaths (Sikes' favorite, "burn my body"), eyes (there is "a fire in the eyes of both" murder-bent Bill and Fagin in 47.302), the thieves' blazing hearth, and the "broad sky" that "seemed on fire" to which Sikes awakens after his crime (48.308). Even poor Oliver, whom we know to be no devil except what the workhouse officials have constructed in the evil imaginations of their hearts, is motivated by this moral sanction when he discovers his new cohorts' true occupation, "felt as if he were in a burning fire," and takes to his heels (10.60). These conventional usages, probably reinforced by Dickens' enthusiastic reading of Defoe's *History of the Devil* while writing *Oliver Twist* (see letter to Forster, 3 November 1837, P 1.328),[41] bring into the novel a genre of sermon his Victorian readers knew only too well, such as C. H. Spurgeon's scarifying "Turn or Burn": "O, sirs, you may think that the fire of hell is indeed a fiction, and that the flames of the nethermost pit are but popish dreams; but if you are believers in the Bible you must believe that it can not be so. Did not our Master say: 'Where their worm dieth not, and their fire is not quenched?' You may say it is a metaphorical fire. But what meant he by this: 'He is able to cast both *body* and soul into hell?' . . . and do you not know that our Master said: '. . . Depart, ye cursed, into everlasting fire, prepared for the devil and his angels'?"[42] When Fagin "crackled with the fever that burnt him up" on his last night alive (52.344), Dickens loudly signals to his reader, with the sermon rhetoric he otherwise abhorred, his thief's infernal fate; what is hypocrites' canting fiction in Nancy's redeemable case becomes the fact of just punishment for this incorrigible old criminal.

The notion of hell embodies the idea of retributive justice, cosmic or institutional. As Geoffrey Rowell observes, the idea of eternal revenge lent support in the nineteenth century to unenlightened theories of punishment in this world, against new ideas of reformation and deterrence put forward by the Utilitarians.[43] The *Spectator* reviewer of *Oliver Twist* (24 November 1838) concluded that "the tendency of the work is to show that nature and habit cannot be eradicated by a sentimentality which contents itself with substituting a penitentiary for a gallows."[44] Its melodramatized Bunyan plot, driving toward the destruction of all the evil characters, aligns the novel with the unenlightened even as it argues for a providential universe. "Let no man talk of murderers escaping justice," the narrator of this plot intones, "and hint that Providence must sleep" (48.308). Despite the sympathy Dickens creates for the haunted murderer's state of mind,[45] he is hoist with his own petard at last in a conclusive act of poetic justice. Fagin likewise will "swing in six days from this, by G——!" (50.322)—the curse reminding the reader that behind the state's justified punishers of crime lurks the Divine Avenger who will destroy both soul and body in hell. If we suspect, as A. J. Duffield did, that the idea of hell expresses "the same spirit that says in the politics of our day that the foundation of the English throne is the English workhouse,"[46] we see the contradiction into which this kind of rhetoric is leading Dickens. The sympathy with the gallows-haunted that he expresses in his 1841 preface turns in the novel into relief that malefactors can be apprehended, as Oliver's friends gather forces with the law near the end of the book, and the workhouse becomes the providentially appointed place for Bumble's end. With his assertion in the preface that some "natures" are "utterly and irredeemably bad," Dickens anticipates his own later harsh positions on flogging and hanging[47] and lines up with such of his antagonists as Fitzjames Stephen as well as his later mentor, Thomas Carlyle, whose hatred of criminals was part of the Puritan legacy he shared with Bunyan.

In "Turn or Burn," Spurgeon aimed to refute "the cry of the age . . . that God is merciful, that God is love" but not justice.[48] Dickens' parable of the Good Samaritan dramatizes this cry; and in tandem with it, his darker parable works against retributive notions of punishment in conventional hells or prisons. J. Hillis Miller points out that when Dickens revised his 1841 preface for the 1856 Charles Dickens Edition, he changed the remark on Sikes being "utterly and irredeemably bad" to "utterly and incurably bad"—as Miller says, "evidently to remove the theological implication of 'irredeemably.' Dickens did not want to deny God's power to redeem even those who are apparently hopelessly evil."[49] The God of Jesus' parable is "that Being whose code is Mercy, and whose great attribute is Benevolence" (53.350), one who also accepts the "penitent confession" of Oliver's father and saves his child from the consequences of his parents' illicit love, if not the wretched mother (51.332). This is the God of whom Rose speaks to Nancy when she holds out hope to this prostitute-thief: "It is never too late for penitence and atonement" (40.257). Although what the social parable tells us about conditions of vice lends some natural truth to Nancy's retort that it may be "God's wrath" driving her hopelessly back to Bill (258), Dickens steps in as Good Samaritan at the last moment—in lieu of the God who does not save her from Bill's hand—with the "mercy" she prays for from "her Maker" (47.303). God's mercy for the penitent sinner is a prominent theme of The Life of Our Lord and of Dickens' testimonial to what the Bible meant to him, in Dombey and Son: it is "the eternal book for all the weary, and the heavy-laden; for all the wretched, fallen, and neglected of this earth . . . the blessed history in which the blind, lame, palsied beggar, the criminal, the woman stained with shame, the shunned of all our dainty clay, has each a portion, that no human pride, indifference, or sophistry through all the ages that this world shall last, can take away, or by the thousandth atom of a grain reduce" (58.692). This testimony also suggests how thoroughly mediated by the parable of the Good Samaritan Dickens' view of the New Testament was, with his emphasis on "the shunned of all our dainty clay." Again, it is his touchstone—even for determining biblical truth from those falsehoods, the hell-doctrines Spurgeon cites from the same book.

Supporting this general view, Dickens' circumstantial social observation led him, if not to a God of Mercy, then to the merciful humanitarianism of those who would understand and intervene in the conditions of the poor—or of anyone "fallen." In an age of raised historical consciousness about causes and conditions, so finely wrought into George Eliot's novels for example, one standard Victorian response is to defend the "creature of circumstances." Thus Markham Sutherland exclaims to his correspondent: "Oh, Arthur! when a crime of one of our fallen brothers comes before ourselves to judge, how unspeakably difficult we find it to measure the balance of the sin; cause winding out of cause, temptation out of temptation; and the more closely we know the poor guilty one, the nature with which he was born, the circumstances which have developed it, how endlessly our difficulty grows upon us!—how more and more it seems to have been inevitable, to deserve . . . not anger and punishment, but tears and pity and forgiveness."[50] Rose similarly rationalizes Oliver's plight to her aunt before they have proof that he is no thief: "But even if he has been wicked, . . . think how young he is; think that he may never have known a mother's love, or the comfort of a home; and that ill-usage and blows, or the want of bread, may have driven him to herd with men who have forced him to guilt. Aunt, dear Aunt, for mercy's sake, think of this, before you let them drag this sick child to a prison, which in any case must be the grave of all his chances of amendment. . . . have pity upon him before it is too late" (30.184). Even in the account of Sikes' death, arranged by Dickens' Bunyan parable with such nice poetic justice, there is pity mingled with the horror as we see him literally thrown against the backdrop of Jacob's Island and all the forces that have produced him, personified in the anarchic mob that wills his death. It is perhaps even this kind of pity that places us momentarily in the deranged mind of the impenitent Fagin in his last hours— giving Oliver's "God forgive this wretched man!" (52.347) some slight force, more at least than we might have expected, in a scene where otherwise Dickens is busily investing his Devil with signs of his damnation.

But if the social parable works in tandem with Jesus' story to lend pity to these scenes, it also shows us the inexorable forces that oppose both Good's victory and the ministrations of Samaritans. Nancy's efforts to secure a home for Oliver may confirm both parables, but her life reflects ironically upon the Bunyan

pattern of Good Triumphant; as Daleski writes, she is "an Oliver whose goodness does not save her from the streets."[51] Her eleventh-hour rescue for the
heavenly streets belongs to the melodramatic plot; it freezes the vital and conflicted woman we knew from the more realistic story in a final tableau of moral
rectitude we find incredible, given that earlier scene when she had refused
Rose's offer of salvation with a convincing mixture of pride, rationalization,
loyalty to the gang, self-denigration, courage, fear, and desperation. This more
complex Nancy, struck down by a stronger hand than Sikes', "disappear[s] from
the earth [in] this moment" of salvation (see 56.296–97). What Dickens does
with the religious rhetoric invoked at Nancy's death is to still forever the ambiguous voices his novel has raised—what is "a contradiction," neither right nor
wrong but true to his more complex conception of life in the darker parable. And
this story is guided by no ideal design, like the celestial carpet in Italo Calvino's
parable "Cities and the Sky 1"; it resembles, rather, this modern parabler's city
of Eudoxia, "a stain that spreads out shapelessly"[52] from its impenetrable center in Jacob's Island horrors. Nancy may urge Rose to "Thank Heaven" for
having friends to care for her in her childhood, but in doing so the unhappy
woman only calls attention to Heaven's negligence toward her in this "disap-
pointing world," which "ain't the shop for justice" (43.282)—a world where
children in and out of the workhouse die, where Brownlow's fiancée was never to
be his wife, and where even "The Soul of Goodness in Things Evil" has no
impact at all on those around her. The precise message of this story, as Howard
Schwartz says of modern parables, "never fully arrives, though the emotional
response it evokes makes it clear that the message has been sent."[53]

3

Transitional Dickens: Biblical Schemes and New Worlds in *Dombey and Son*

LET HIM REMEMBER IT IN THAT ROOM, YEARS TO COME!
(Hablot K. Browne)

The earth was made for Dombey and Son to trade in, and the sun and
moon were made to give them light. Rivers and seas were formed to float
their ships; rainbows gave them promise of fair weather; winds blew for
or against their enterprises; stars and planets circled in their orbits,
to preserve inviolate a system of which they were the centre. . . . A.D.
had no concern with anno Domini, but stood for anno Dombei—and Son.

T HE NASCENT SENSE in *Oliver Twist* that contemporary actuality was
outstripping the Bible's scheme has become far more pressing by the
time of *Dombey and Son*. The influx of new worlds began with Dickens'
deeper interest in exploring the human interior; his novel, as he outlined his
intentions to Forster in the famous letter of 25–26 July 1846, would probe the
demon-ridden struggle of an "obstinate natur[e]" suffering catastrophic reverses
and follow the dynamics of his internal change (P 4:590). New complexities also
erupted from the outer world in which this sharply topical novel of the Railway
Era is set, a new world that had released enormous social energies but had also
radically depleted older conceptions of life, of community, and of the relation
between human beings and the God of the Bible.

More emphatically, consistently, and imaginatively than in Dickens' earlier
works, *Dombey and Son* uses a wide range of biblical, liturgical, and other
kinds of quasi-religious allusion, language, and iconography to help contain
and interpret this influx of disruptive psychic and social realities; like the Carlyle of *Past and Present* (1843), although with some different accents, Dickens
measures the present by traditional values. Nonetheless, despite these advances
in Dickens' creative adaptation of the Bible tradition, and its firmer integration
into the texture of this work than in *Oliver Twist*, the incursion of newly discovered worlds disrupts *Dombey*'s moral and religious formulas offered as valuation or comfort. If, as Steven Marcus says, *Dombey and Son* is "the first of
Dickens's novels in which a strong religious impulse can be felt,"[1] his efforts to
reconceive the traditional wisdom for the present time are finally elusive, despite the energy with which he makes the attempt. To consider how and why they
are elusive will help us to anticipate some of the problematic aspects of biblical
allusion in the later Dickens.

1

ON 3 JULY 1870, J. Panton Ham preached a memorial sermon in the Essex Street Unitarian Chapel, Strand, that hailed Dickens as "a moral instructor by means of parables, and an imitator of the Great Preacher." Anticipated by Dean Stanley by several weeks, this memorialist was perhaps not original, but certainly he spoke for thousands of readers who admired Dickens as one who had "exalt[ed] virtue and degrad[ed] vice," and whose "parables of wisdom, truth, and love" had done more than those of "any other man to humanise society."[2] Mr. Ham took as his text Matthew 13:34–35, where parable is understood as disclosure ("I will open my mouth in parables; I will utter things which have been kept secret from the foundation of the world"), and held up as his chief exhibit an extract from the forty-seventh chapter of *Dombey and Son* (wherein the "good spirit" takes "the house-tops off . . . and show[s] a Christian people what dark shapes issue from amidst their homes," 540). *Dombey* was an appropriate choice, for Dickens was particularly determined to unify his novel of 1846–48 around a parabolic design, doing "with Pride what [*Martin Chuzzlewit*] had done with Selfishness" (*Life* 2:19) in Forster's words, but with more "constructive care" (*Life* 1:274). As Dickens added social elaboration, this parable on human nature grew into a topical Carlylean parable on Mammonism in the England of the 1840s. In both stories, religious allusion guides the reader through complications of plot to see the unambiguous outlines of the carefully constructed—yet collapsible—moral design.

In the parable of Pride and its proverbial fall, adumbrated on the allegorical monthly covers, Dombey is presented in the first chapter as a man who has reversed the order of creation (and revised Genesis 1), usurping the Creator's role in making over the earth as a place exclusively "for Dombey and Son to trade in" (2; see epigraph), and rewritten Christian history as "anno Dombei—and Son." Proud Dombey is regularly associated with Lucifer (see 26.305), but in the moral drama of sin, curse, retribution, and regeneration, Dombey's specific trespass is not to reject God; it is to "rejec[t] the angel" Florence and "t[ake] up with the tormenting spirit crouching in his bosom" instead, the demon Pride (20.238). He "as should have loved and fended of her, treated of her like the beasts as perish," says Cap'en Cuttle (56.657), applying to Dombey's situation Psalm 49:20: "Man that is in honour, and understandeth not, is like the beasts that perish." Declaring he "will incline mine ear to a parable" and "open my dark saying upon the harp," the psalmist addresses those who trust in riches for their immortality and foretells the fall of the House of Pride:

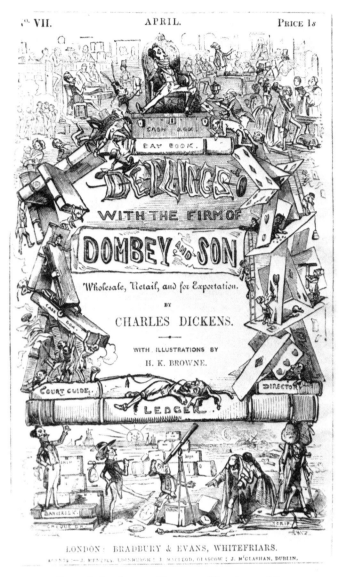

N.º VII. APRIL. PRICE 1s.

DEALINGS WITH THE FIRM OF DOMBEY AND SON

Wholesale, Retail, and for Exportation.

BY

CHARLES DICKENS.

WITH ILLUSTRATIONS BY

H. K. BROWNE.

LONDON: BRADBURY & EVANS, WHITEFRIARS.
AGENTS:—J. MENZIES, EDINBURGH; J. M'LEOD, GLASGOW; J. M'GLASHAN, DUBLIN.

Cover design for monthly parts of *Dombey and Son*
(Hablot K. Browne)

And the rain descended, and the floods came, and the winds blew, and beat upon that house; and it fell: and great was the fall of it. (Matt. 7:27)

"Pride shall have a fall, and it always was and will be so!" observes the housemaid. It is wonderful how good they feel, in making these reflections. (*DS* 59.694)

Their inward thought is, that their houses shall continue for ever. . . .

Nevertheless man being in honour abideth not: he is like the beasts that perish. . . .

Like sheep they are laid in the grave; death shall feed on them; and the upright shall have dominion over them in the morning. (vv. 4, 11–14)

Just as the House of Dombey and Son is doomed, so death feeds on the house he inhabits and funerary urns on the bookcase "preached desolation and decay, as from two pulpits," while "the chimney-glass, reflecting Mr. Dombey and his portrait at one blow, seemed fraught with melancholy meditations" (5.44)— making the house one brooding parabolic sign of the master's state, a sign he ignores (see 8.80).

Like other biblical figures who bring down retribution on themselves, Dombey surrounds himself with people who will cause his downfall. Major Bagstock, "an overfed Mephistopheles" (20.233), lures Dombey on to a disastrous marriage. The manager Carker, consistently allied with beasts of prey and the Devil in the guise of the gentleman, lurks behind a tree like some "monster of the ancient days before the flood" (27.321), when "the wickedness of man was great in the earth" (Gen. 6:5). Carker has a portrait resembling the third in this diabolical trio: "Perhaps it is a Juno; perhaps a Potiphar's Wife; perhaps some scornful Nymph" (33.398). The story of Potiphar's wife and the Jewish slave Joseph provides all the ingredients for one stage of Dickens' plot to humble Dombey: the dissatisfied wife of the master, sexual temptation crossing class boundaries, the foiled seduction, and revenge, all in the context of a business relation between a master and his slave promoted to overseer (see Gen. 39). (Characteristically, the Old Testament writer treats more directly the sexual dynamics, while Dickens sees more deeply into the psychology of class and economic relationships.) Dickens' transformation of this Bible story's basic counters, however, prevents any simple identification of the wife figure as villain, for his characters take on double roles and irony complicates them. It is Carker, anticipating the means of *his* revenge against his arrogant employer, who pictures Edith as Potiphar's wife (he owns the portrait) and himself as an already corrupted Joseph, as much seducer as seducee (if overtly as virtuous as that hero of faith). Edith, who has led the manager on in order to effect *her* revenges, turns out in the event to be the righteous Joseph, fleeing the scene of temptation but leaving a garment behind (see Gen. 39:12 and Edith's veil in 54.642). In both versions, the wrathful master puts the betraying servant out of the way, although God saves Joseph while a providential justice strikes down the wicked Carker, even as it operates through this episode to bring down the master as well.

An even more ominous iconographic sign of Edith's danger to Dombey is offered the attentive reader of Phiz's ironically titled illustration for the Dijon episode, "Mr. Carker in his hour of triumph": as Michael Steig has pointed out, Edith's pose, its mirror-image in the large painting behind her, and another over the fireplace visually repeat the theme of Judith slaying Holofernes.[3] This legendary Jewish heroine, forever the type of the castrating woman, is celebrated for delivering her native city by entering the camp of Nebuchadnezzar's general and beheading him in his drunken sleep. While Edith surely menaces the swelled head of Dombey, her pride-drunk enemy, Carker is the more appropriate Holofernes figure, toward whom her swordlike arm (and concealed knife) is pointed in the illustration: for his is the enemy camp she enters under false pretenses, and his the sexual interest she exploits in order to rout him.

As so often in Dickens, biblical allusion and iconographic recall of this sort, like the association of Mrs. Merdle with Judith in *Little Dorrit*, adumbrate plot developments and provide implicit moral commentary on characters without helping us see *into* them. The Potiphar's wife parallel, one of the more complex allusions in *Dombey*, may be an exception: fraught with sexual background for Edith's story, it hints more about "what devil possesses" Dickens' thwarted heroine than the melodramatic vindication of her virtue in this scene would allow us to see. "Their name is Legion," she tells Carker darkly (54.640–41), multiplying devils and echoing the Gadarene demoniac of Mark 5:2–13, who dwells in tombs, pulls at his fetters as Edith plucks at her bracelets and her marriage "manacle," and rends himself (see 47.539).

In the moral plot, these allegorically simplified figures are pawns of destiny, destroying Dombey's marriage and undermining his firm. Ironically, however, the most powerful force of retribution issues from Florence, Dombey's "better angel," who is necessary in the moral plot to show us that he has a conscience and to act as both scourge and reward. Florence's all-giving love causes her father the bitterest suffering: "How few of those who stiffened in her father's freezing atmosphere," the narrator tells us, "suspected what a heap of fiery coals was piled upon his head!" (24.292). Dickens surely intends the pious reading of Romans 12:20; but as a covert strategy of revenge, St. Paul's formula for overcoming evil with good could hardly be more effective, acquitting the innocent inflicter of these punishments to boot.

For long stretches of the novel, however, Florence does not overcome evil with good; to all appearances, the faithful daughter like Mrs. MacStinger does "a thankless thing, and cast[s] pearls before swine!" (23.275), and, as the Sermon on the Mount warns (contradicting Romans 12), others do "turn again and rend" her (Matt. 7:6). When Florence steals up to seek a blessing from the

MR. CARKER IN HIS HOUR OF TRIUMPH
(Hablot K. Browne)

Smite by the deceit of my lips the servant with the prince, and the prince
with the servant: break down their stateliness by the hand of a woman.
(Judith 9:10)

dozing, wounded father after an accident, the narrator intervenes on both their behalf: "Awake, doomed man, while she is near! The time is flitting by; the hour is coming with an angry tread. . . . Awake!" (43.509). St. Paul likewise exhorts his readers, "now it is high time to awake out of sleep: for now is our salvation nearer than when we believed. The night is far spent, the day is at hand: let us therefore cast off the works of darkness, and let us put on the armour of light" (Rom. 13:10–12). In this chapter the apostle proclaims the law of love, the opposite of Dombey's "creed" (46.537), and urges Christians to assume their duties to the community, which for Dombey must begin with his own family. But Dombey does not awaken to Florence or the biblical voices and Time treads on, bringing the downfall of his house built on sand. In recording this change, the narrator calls up, besides the traditional shipwreck emblem, Jesus' story from the Sermon on the Mount using imagery of seashore and weather, while the language borrows the epigrammatic terseness of parabolic prose: "The sea had ebbed and flowed, through a whole year. . . . the ceaseless work of Time had been performed, in storm and sunshine. . . . Through a whole year the famous House of Dombey and Son had fought a fight for life . . . [but] its head . . . would not listen to a word of warning that the ship he strained so hard against the storm, was weak, and could not bear it. The year was out, and the great House was down" (58.680). "And the rain descended, and the floods came, and the winds blew, and beat upon that house; and it fell: and great was the fall of it" (Matt. 7:27).

Penned up in his "ruined house," Dombey comes face to face with his sharpest retribution, the knowledge of the banished daughter's faithful love: "he always knew she would have been true to him, if he had suffered her"—but he did not suffer the little child to come unto him; and "he was as certain that [love] was in her nature, as he was that there was a sky above him; and he sat thinking so, in his loneliness, from hour to hour. Day after day uttered this speech; night after night showed him this knowledge" (59.702). In this adaptation of Psalm 19:1–2—"The heavens declare the glory of God; and the firmament sheweth his handywork. Day unto day uttereth speech, and night unto night sheweth knowledge"—it is not God's glory of which the "sky above" assures Dombey, and days and nights speak; it is the handiwork of a woman's love, which will convert and cleanse him "from secret faults" as the psalmist promises the Lord will do (see vv. 7, 12–13). Again biblical allusion associates Florence with divine powers, although she seems less God's agent than his replacement. While she never reads the Bible to Dombey, in her intuitive grasp of spiritual processes Florence will fulfill the promises of all the hopeful biblical texts associated with his parable; she is the text incarnate in which the story of his life is to be rewritten. Florence brings him out of all the fearful "intricacy of his brain" (703) in the simplicity of her love, which the Lord makes wise (Ps. 19:7). Then "the upright shall have dominion" over the rich man "in the morning" (Ps. 49:14), when a "glorious sunshine . . . crept in with Florence" and, his night far spent, he casts off the works of darkness: "Oh my God, forgive me, for I need it very much!" (706; see illustration on chapter title page). Whether or not it is God who hears his prayer, Dombey finds his forgiveness in Florence and is restored to a Christian community where Love has prevailed over Pride.

With such insistent biblical associations, *Dombey and Son* has invited parabolic interpretation from Dickens' day to our own.[4] Yet it is also as parable that the novel has not satisfied. Although as Forster reports Dickens had such "a nervous dread of caricature" that he sent his illustrators to living models of the merchant-prince (*Life* 2:23–24), many reviewers still found Edith melodramatic, Dombey unnatural, and the pair "blocks of painted wood," while *Blackwood's* judged Dombey's final undocumented transformation "out of all nature."[5] Typically, it was the exaggeration of "both natural goodness and natural wickedness" fostered by the parabolic design that offended; and, ironically, the parable casting Dombey "as a human soul threatened with damnation and struggling to resist an overpowering call to be saved," in Julian Moynahan's words, does not interest us in him as a soul.[6] At the same time, while even Forster conceded that Dickens' power was "even yet not fully developed in its higher and more ideal tendencies," he found in *Dombey and Son* "the subtler requisites which satisfy imagination and reflection"; and a writer in the *Revue de Deux Mondes* hailed Dickens' "mind of great depth and uncommon extent" and called the man "a philosopher and a thinker."[7] Such a range of critical response suggests that Dickens' thoughts about Dombey are not contained by the biblical and moral patterns he employs.

For one thing, reductive moralizing is one of Dickens' targets—witness Mrs. Pipchin's cautionary lessons "of a violent and stunning character" (to which Paul responds flatly, "I don't believe that story," 8.86, 89), Dombey's lecture rising to heights of "moral magnificence" on Edith's marital duty (40.474), Edith's and Carker's speeches on Dombey's pride, or the "solemn and religious" court that preaches duty to Alice Marwood (34.411). In chapter 47 (discussed below), Dickens declares his contempt for those who would "hold forth on . . . unnatural sinfulness"; we must rather "think a little," as Dickens had begun to do in *Oliver Twist*, of the conditions in which sin is "conceived, and born, and bred" (540). Although there are far too many passages in *Dombey and Son* that luxuriate in what F. R. Leavis has called the "lush unrealities of high moral insistence,"[8] many others use language in more subtle ways to pay exact attention to the circumstances under which the "long train of nameless sins against the natural affections and repulsions of mankind" (540) is perpetuated in Dombey's life. Throughout the novel, in the speech patterns of toadying servants, employees, and relatives, Dickens registers a most precise sense of those conditions that foster Dombey's blindness to the dangers of his pride, so that when Mrs. Skewton simpers, "We are dreadfully real, Mr. Carker; are we not?" (27.325), we feel with a shock the inadvertent truth of the remark—vividly real is the whole range of dreadfully false estimates that surround Dombey. In the presence of this thicker sense of circumstance, Dickens' incorporation into the novel of reductive versions of his moral read as self-parody. The paintings at Warwick Castle call attention to the limits of the allegoric method for presenting complex personalities: "A churchman, with his hand upraised, denounced the mockery of such a couple coming to God's altar. . . . Ruins cried, 'Look here, and see what We are, wedded to uncongenial Time!' Animals, opposed by nature, worried one another, as a moral to them" (27.328). The downstairs servants in the Dombey mansion provide an ongoing "chorus" of moralizing remarks[9]—"How are the mighty fallen!" sighs the Cook, joined by the housemaid, "Pride shall have a fall, and it always was and will be so!" But the narrator also complicates such parabolic reading by revealing these readers' complacency: "It is wonderful how good they feel, in making these reflections; and what a Christian unanimity they are sensible of" (59.694).

That Dombey does not fit into the outlines of the Christian scheme we sense, too, whenever Dickens peers into the murky depths of this man's soul, as in the railway journey sequence. At such moments the reader, though he might have traveled more simply along the older lines of transportation, gets on a modern train of thought like Mr. Toodle's: "I comes to a branch; I takes on what I finds there; and a whole train of ideas gets coupled on to him, afore I knows where I am, or where they comes from. What a Junction a man's thoughts is, to-be-sure!" (38.449). Or, to consider another figure the novel proposes, like Sir Barnet Skittles "in his voyage of discovery through the social system" (compared to the widening vibrations of sound), Dickens "go[es] on travelling . . . through the interminable fields of space" in the interiors of his characters to a remarkable degree, and "nothing but coming to the end of his moral tether could stop" him (24.287)—and it did stop Dickens, of course, at some obvious points. While Dombey is learning his lesson from the parable of life, the writer and the reader are learning many other things that they cannot put a name to or shape within a religious design, and these discoveries challenge the "contracted sympathies and estimates" (47.541) of the old moral fables despite Dickens' need of them.

Following out the train of circumstance that formed a Dombey took Dickens into the wider social world of the 1840s, a world of the *Communist Manifesto* and the managerial revolution, the new money men and new horrors of urban poverty exposed by the new railway system. "It was a world," the narrator observes with heavy sarcasm when Dombey goes bankrupt, "in which there was no other sort of bankruptcy whatever. There were no conspicuous people in it, trading far and wide on rotten banks of religion, patriotism, virtue, honour" (58.680). Dickens focuses *Dombey and Son*'s critical representation of this morally anarchic scene by reaching for the biblical cadences and insistent religious reference of a new voice, which he had tried out in *The Chimes* (1844)—the voice of Carlylean prophecy. Carlyle's social criticism gave Dickens, to borrow Kathleen Tillotson's words and Matthew Arnold's, an " 'Idea of the World' which protects Dickens from being 'prevailed over by the world's multitudinousness.' "[10] That idea Dickens did not yet have in *Oliver Twist*. Biblical texts used in Carlylean ways by the prophet of *Dombey* add rhetorical force to his pronouncements while they serve as means of interpreting the contemporary scene; but no more than his parable of Dombey's fall and regeneration do these other biblical usages finally order the disruptive facts Dickens finds there.

In *Past and Present* Carlyle sets out to "rede the riddle of Destiny" for England. The paradox this sage propounds is that "England is full of wealth," yet "In the midst of plethoric plenty, the people perish" (*P&P* 1.1.7, 6, 1), like little Paul wasting away amid the sumptuous garnitures of the Dombey mansion. Like that sage old child, Carlyle inquires, What is wealth?—"what can it do?" (8.77)—for from all appearances, it does *not* do. Because the English have "forgotten to *live* in the middle of" their riches, "It is an enchanted wealth; no man of us can yet touch it," like the Midas of old fable (1.1.5). Dickens sets his Midas of Commerce into a parodic fairytale world, where, in the "enchanted circle within which the operations of Dombey and Son were conducted" (20.239–40), the head imagines that his young heir "had a charmed life, and *must* become the man . . . for whom he planned and projected, as for an existing reality, every day" (8.76). But Dombey's enchantment by money prevents the living realization of his fondest wish. Carlyle's answer to why a Dombey cannot touch his wealth is that "a whole Nation, as our Fathers used to say, has 'forgotten God;' has remembered only Mammon, and what Mammon leads to!" (3.1.144). The heart of the trouble is not economic but spiritual, although it has profound socioeconomic consequences, "threatening all modern things with frightful death. . . . There is no religion; there is no God; man has lost his soul" (3.1.137). In Dickens' Carlylean parable on the love of money as the root of nineteenth-century evils, this religious malaise, spreading the kingdom of death through all social relations, is brought home in ironic biblical and liturgical allusions that point the fatal blasphemy of the "sumptuous Merchant-Prince[s]" of his age (*P&P* 3.2.147).

If we return to Dombey's revision of Genesis 1, we see that imagining "The earth was made for Dombey and Son to trade in" is not just the sin of a private egoism but a wider recreation of the world that puts the art of making money at its center instead of God—a reconception worthy of an era of unprecedented mercantile expansion, when capitalist entrepreneurs could identify their own activities with the operations of Providence. [11] As one of the new supreme masters of time as well as space, Dombey also revises "anno Domini" to honor the lord of trade—Mammon, inseparable from his own name. And when A.D. becomes "anno Dombei—and Son," Dickens drives home the fact that the son of this new earthly deity, with his high destinies, has replaced as a center of worship the Son of God. With an irony appropriate to a stable parable, Mammonism, by "threatening all modern things with frightful death," makes "the boy born to be the Son" and the "Boy born, to die"[12] synonymous. Thus is Dombey's egoistic project of achieving immortality through money—and Son— foiled by the death-forces unleashed by his own form of worship.

"We have no Faith left, positively," screeches Mrs. Skewton in a ghastly simulacrum of Carlyle's manner (27.327). In *Dombey and Son*, it is especially by exposing these Mammonists' perversions of Church ritual that Dickens illustrates Skewton's "How dreadfully we have degenerated!" (as one who cannot even remember "the Garden of what's-its-name" and who is "turning of the earth, earthy" should know [20.241 and 40.477; cf. I Cor. 15:47]). That he does not do this in defense of the Established Church is evident enough from his detailed picture of the moldy and almost congregationless Church Visible in which Florence and Walter are married (see 56.663–64). Like other spots Dickens visited in his *All the Year Round* essay, "City of London Churches" (5 May 1860; *UT* 97–109), this "shabby pile" is a familiar emblem in his writings for the empty shell the Church had become, another "rotten bank" with worthless currency. It is not in the name of the institution but for the sake of those values it has cherished, attached to the common experiences of life, that Dickens deplores the depletion of religious rituals associated with birth, marriage, death. In a novel where the rhythms of time and nature are continually evoked, the Book of Common Prayer is a kind of Everyman's guidebook through "the tides of human chance and change" (58.680), gathering little communities of celebration or consolation, reminding all of their common source and end, setting human affairs under the eye of Eternity, and gracing these occasions with the solace of familiar poetic language to uplift mind and heart. Set off against

Cap'en Cuttle's earnest, if absurd, allusions to this cultural treasury, the novel's revised edition of the Prayer Book for Mammon worship measures the depletion of the common, a whole society's amnesia about its divine origin and end, and the fatal loss of soul from the language of the new pagan rituals.

The money fetish, Carlyle wrote, demands a monstrous sacrifice of humanity and community, confounding older ideas of social relations: "We call it a Society; and go about professing openly the totalest separation, isolation. . . . We have profoundly forgotten everywhere that *Cash-payment* is not the sole relation of human beings; we think, nothing doubting, that *it* absolves and liquidates all engagements of man" (*P&P* 3.2.146). Dickens' account of Paul's christening in chapter 5 is brilliantly conceived to expose this liquidated social world. While Holy Baptism is a sacrament profoundly communal, normally taking place in the Sunday worship service and celebrating the child's entry into the earthly Christian community as well as the kingdom of God, in *Dombey* not only is no regular congregation gathered, but the participants in the mechanical ritual enact their parts in "the totalest separation." Through the whole day, narratively constructed to move from one anticlimax of social and familial expectation to another, nothing but "the same bleak fellowship" (48) prevails. The ritual soon enough over, its culmination is the clinking of coin—the clergyman, the pew-opener, the beadle, the sexton, all are "remembered"; and the ritual of cash-payment is repeated on a more genteel plane with the exchange of gifts afterward, including Dombey's magnificent bestowal of a place at the Charitable Grinders' school upon a child of Richards' (whose relation to her employer is "a mere matter of bargain and sale," 2.14).[13] The main event is the meal at which the party seems "to be gradually resolving itself into a congealed and gelid state, like the collation round which it was assembled," which looks "more like a dead dinner lying in state than a social refreshment" (5.51, 48).

Forster says somewhat evasively that by 1841 "whatever realities had gone out of the ceremony of christening [for Dickens], the meaning still remained in it of enabling him to form a relationship with friends he most loved" (*Life* 1:146).[14] This human bonding is the chief reality that has evaporated from *Dombey*'s Mammonist baptism, but allied values (related to "the great origin and purpose of the ceremony," 48) have been lost as well. In its image of mutual Christian help in building up the good life, the ritual of baptism offers what no self-made Colossus of Commerce would want in this world created for Dombey and Son to trade in, as Dombey reveals in his attitudes toward the sponsors, so carelessly chosen, and their vows. At the close of the ceremony when the priest exhorts these parties to promise that the child will be taught the prayers and creeds, Mr. Dombey is "seen to express by a majestic look" at Mr. Chick "that he would like to catch him at it" (48). Not for his son is the vow "obediently [to] keep God's holy will and commandments, and walk in the same all the days of thy life" (*BCP* 296), the source of Cuttle's fatherly counsel to Walter ("Walk fast, Wal'r, my lad; and walk the same all the days of your life. Overhaul the catechism for that advice, and keep it!" 9.102). Well might this Lucifer figure set himself in opposition to a service that calls upon the sponsors to "renounce the devil" and "the vain pomp and glory of the world" (*BCP* 295), especially given the "cold pomp of glass and silver" waiting at home to complete and confirm an empty ritual. When the godfather offers a toast to little Paul, Dombey appropriates it as a tribute to his own position: " 'Mr. John,' said Mr. Dombey, with severe gravity, 'my son would feel and express himself obliged to you, I have no doubt, if he could appreciate the favour you have done him [by your toast]. He will prove, in time to come, I trust, equal to any responsibility that the obliging disposition of his relations and friends, in private, or the onerous nature of our position, in public, may impose upon him.' " This is the soulless language of the new pagan rituals—"eloquence indeed!" sighs Tox (49)—that has replaced the meta- phorically rich and inspiriting idiom of the liturgy, not one word of which we ever hear in this scene. Clearly the "son and heir" (46) has not been baptized "in the Name of the Father" of all, to become "an heir of everlasting salvation" (*BCP* 294); he has rather been ritually dedicated, even sacrificed, to the usurper of divine rights who seeks to immortalize the paternal Paul in this naming cere- mony for Son.

While he was writing this sharp religious satire, Dickens had to remind him- self "of the possibility of malice in christening points of faith, and put the drag on as I wrote" (to Forster, 3 October 1846, P 4:628). He does not draw upon the whole baptismal service for his satire; certain "points of faith" served his liter- ary ends more than others, and in his implicit revision of Prayer Book ritual we can see what he does find important there. In Christian theology baptism is a symbolic drowning, an identification "with Christ in his death" that sin might be washed away (*BCP* 299). A typical verse on baptism in *The Christian Year* makes these associations:

> What sparkles in that lucid flood
> Is water, by gross mortals ey'd:
> But seen by Faith, 'tis Blood
> Out of a dear Friend's side.[15]

Dickens dispenses with this doctrinal framework but keeps its "essence," the archetype of spiritual rebirth, important yet problematic throughout his fic- tion.[16] Besides some silly byplay with parodies of the rebirth theme,[17] the serious irony Dickens develops with this point of faith in *Dombey* is that Paul is baptized into a death—nothing more. The funereal imagery begun early in chapter 5 climaxes at the baptismal party's point of entering the church, a "chill and earthy" place like the grave (47). In unison with the mourning vestiture of the nursery group, Paul cries until he is "black in the face"—the right shade to wear at a ceremonial induction into death worship. Significantly, in a novel "full to overflowing of waves whispering and wandering; of dark rivers rolling to the sea, . . . and golden ripples," as one skeptical reviewer of 1848 put it,[18] we *see* no sacramental gestures with the water of regeneration in Dickens' narrative account of this prominent christening scene.

To Dickens this innocent child, of course, does not need the washing of regeneration so much as Dombey himself. With its Gospel taken from one of Dickens' favorite texts ("Suffer the little children to come unto me, and forbid them not: for of such is the kingdom of God. . . . Whosoever shall not receive the kingdom of God as a little child, he shall not enter therein," Mark 10:13–15; cf. *BCP* 293), the baptismal rite only calls to mind how far Dombey and all his worldly-wise kind are from the kingdom in their so very grown-up world. But Dickens' literary power in so impressing upon us this frozen gentleman's resistance to any kind of renewal renders his final rebirth into a second childhood incredible, in a seashore scene awash with wishful simplification. Harriet Carker may affirm Dickens' belief in "a GOD above us to work changes in the hearts HE made," but Mr. Morfin conjures up Dickens' other knowledge of a business world that renders such divine work impotent: "But we go on . . . in our clock-work routine, from day to day, and can't make out, or follow, these changes. They—they're a metaphysical sort of thing. We—we haven't leisure for it. We—we haven't courage. They're not taught at schools or colleges, and we don't know how to set about it. In short, we are so d——d business-like" (33.402). Morfin's special theme is that the modern transformation of the structure of daily living—in which habit ensures that "One don't see anything, one don't hear anything, one don't know anything"—has deadened the moral sense and left no chink for the in-breaking of the Transcendent.

The fault, however, does not lie only with Dombey or his world—and here the Prayer Book satire becomes unstable. Church rituals cannot renew the weary spirit or recall the erring soul to life because they, too, have become routine. The church where Paul is christened is a baptism-mill, a marriage-mill, and a funeral-mill, where one rite comes hard on the heels of the next and where the ministrants merely "trea[d] the circle of their daily lives" (31.379), gathering coin at each round. It is not just the Dombey set that is being satirized in a chapter like "The Wedding," for in a Mammon-worshipping age, the Church too has become unfeeling, and its rituals—organs of forgetting rather than remembering the dead, marital duty, or God's commandments—only encourage the general spiritual amnesia. The danger, therefore, that Dickens' satire courts is not too much silliness in things liturgical—such as Miss Tox murmuring responses from the Gunpowder Plot at the christening—but, precisely as he put it, "malice in . . . points of faith." As Dickens learned from objections to his early sketch, "The Bloomsbury Christening" (a "trifling with a sacred ordinance and exposing it to ridicule," according to one clergyman),[19] even the description of perversions of religion can easily become an attack on religion itself—so corrosive is the power of irony to "eat into the most solid-seeming structures."[20] As the central religious expression of the Church of England, the Book of Common Prayer shifts, under the pressure of Dickens' ironic vision in *Dombey and Son*, from a stable standard of value to a destabilized text no longer commanding unquestioning belief (although an object of doubt rather than direct attack cannot be said to signal Dickens' despair of religious values). Dickens' readers might see the potential of the Prayer Book to order and uplift human experience glimmer in *Dombey and Son*, but the light dims, perhaps goes out.

What is even more striking in this novel is the radical attenuation or total absence of Prayer Book language on the occasions for its use. Here one must make distinctions between stable satiric effects, such as those Dickens achieves with "The Wedding" (chap. 51), and disruptive ambiguities such as those that emerge at the burial of Paul. The marital ceremony drives on in an abbreviated, "modern" railway style that suggests the parties' inattentiveness to the meaning of the rite and their weary, mechanical agreement to "be jined together in the house of bondage," as Cuttle says on another occasion (50.588). All that is verbally omitted from the ritual defines what is lacking in this union, while making starkly more evident the blasphemy of what is primarily left of the service—the vows themselves (see 51.373). But even these words are presented indirectly, without quotation marks, and the effect is further to depersonalize the ceremony for the reader as for the distanced bride and groom; like other rituals in *Dombey*, this one is finally only reported, not experienced. At the close of the chapter Dickens uses the vows again to drive home his parable on "the mockery of such a couple coming to God's altar"; he leaves the "solemn terms" echoing in our ears but already turned against themselves by the man mimicking them, Carker, who will put these bonds asunder (see 380). The final emphasis is on "until death do them part." Like all the Mammonist rituals, this wedding too turns into a funeral, for the Dombeys' "marriage way" will be "a road of ashes" (47.539) leading for the fallen Edith to a condition she calls "the grave" (61.729).

With Paul's burial, the effects of Prayer Book omissions are more disturbing. Just as there is no baptismal ritual described or quoted at the christening, so Paul's rite is not narrated at all—we move almost directly from the funeral procession toward "the sound of a church bell" to the next paragraph beginning, off-handedly, "The service over, . . ." (18.203). Or rather, in place of the burial rite's hopeful promises, we have Dickens' intercessory words: ". . . the sound of a church bell. In this same church, the pretty boy received all that will soon be left of him on earth—a name. All of him that is dead, they lay there, near the perishable substance of his mother. It is well. Their ashes lie where Florence in her walks—oh lonely, lonely walks!—may pass them any day" (203). The phrase, "All of him that is dead," echoing the *Times* obituary formula "all that is mortal" and coyly intimating that there may be more, is all that remains of the rite's "I am the resurrection and the life" (John 11:25; *BCP* 363). The reconciliation that the Burial Service verses are meant to foster becomes, here, an unconvincing "It is well" followed by the outburst that does not believe it, "oh lonely, lonely walks!" Again, the satiric design only partially explains what Dickens is doing here. On the one hand, Florence will be lonely because there is for her no "sad community of love and grief" (205), which the Burial Service intends to gather for the bereaved; the absence of its language and of this consoling community is, in terms of the Mammon parable, a mark of her world's emotional malaise.[21] Nonetheless, what is so surprising about Dickens' own version of the Burial Service here is that, even as he tries to inject some meaning into the hollow forms, his words are barren of the quasi-Christian consolation he does give his readers elsewhere, especially at Paul's deathbed. In contrast, the emphasis in this burial scene is on the "earth" in which Paul's remains are laid, "the perishable substance of his mother," "Their ashes," and "lonely," unconsoled meditation upon these grim last things. The Order for the Burial of the Dead has become the disorder of grief without hope, morbidly feeding on itself. And of course, this was precisely the charge some reviewers, who *could* read "the death of little Paul Dombey with a heart unmoved and an eye tearless,"[22] flung at Dickens. If Dickens dwells on such scenes "with a kind of fawning fondness," as Walter Bagehot discerned,[23] it is perhaps because for him, as for others in the "whole nation" that was "flung . . . into mourning" by Paul's death,[24] the rituals of the Church and the Bible in which these rites are rooted no longer had the power to order feeling and inspire hope. At this point the Mammon parable's omission of the religious formulas becomes Dickens' inability to say them, and satire turns upon itself to reveal a vacancy in the novelist's own heart.

2

DICKENS' stable ironic uses of the Book of Common Prayer in *Dombey and Son* derive from a cultural perspective given most powerful recent expression in *Past and Present*. From this and other of Carlyle's writings, Dickens was also tutored in the voice of the Victorian prophet, particularly on the theme of "Two Nations." The paradox Carlyle proposes to interpret at the outset of this work drives him to consider not only what wealth is but what it means to be poor, "in the money sense or a far fataler one" (1.1.1). To Carlyle's credit, his preoccupation with spiritual inanition does not entail, as it did for other Victorian preachers, disregard for the physical conditions of impoverishment.[25] Like Dickens in *Oliver Twist*, Carlyle invites his reader on a tour ("Descend where you will into the lower class . . .") of misery "hidden from all but the eye of God" for which "there was literally never any parallel" (1.1.3). But the unknown, what threatens to be unspeakable, Carlyle brings under literary control through the use of conventional images, allusion (there is something "of Dante's Hell in the look of all this," 1.1.2), and the apocalyptic rhetoric that makes the dark parable readable even as it intensifies the moral impact of the lesson. Dickens hardly needed Carlyle's help to see the concrete misery of the poor; but what we find in Dickens' writings after he met his mentor in 1840 and began to listen to his preachings are the distinctive biblical cadence and the setting of these horrors under the eye of Eternity that is ever Carlyle's way. Moreover, it was a way Dickens found useful, if not completely adequate, for encapsulating in a reassuring design the perils of the present that were also so intimately an expression of his childhood sorrow and anger, his own suffering "hidden from all." In *Dombey and Son*, we begin to see the first fruits of a literary relationship that, becoming uneasy after 1850, had a shifting influence on Dickens' uses of the Bible for the rest of his career.

Dombey and Son is a social novel primarily in registering the effects of wide changes on family relations and the buried life of feeling, rather than in working out a large-scale Two Nations design. But the sense of unprecedented misery outdoors periodically interrupts the sequence of indoor scenes of domestic misery to suggest the radical contrasts being generated in the larger *Dombey* world. Dombey himself experiences such an influx of the social chaos on his railway journey after Paul's death. While he "glimpses" the Old England from his carriage window, his vision climaxes with the shock of the new, until "smoke, and crowded gables, and distorted chimneys, and deformity of brick and mortar penning up deformity of mind and body, choke the murky distance. . . . It was

the journey's fitting end, and might have been the end of everything" (see
20.236–37). Although here, as elsewhere in *Dombey and Son*, Dickens emphasizes the subjectivity of vision in the "ruinous and dreary" obsessions of a bereaved, bewildered man, Dombey's nightmare is real enough as a vision of the
world entrepreneurs like him were making. When Dickens tries to order
Dombey's disorder by calling upon him to "Awake, doomed man!" (43.509),
probably more directly than Romans 13:11 he is echoing Carlyle's cry to the
Captains of Industry: "Awake, O nightmare sleepers; awake, arise, or be forever
fallen!" (4.272).[26] Against the facts, what "might have been the end of everything"—social life, human dignity, the moral sense, reason itself—Dickens
elsewhere too asserts the apocalyptic paradigm in which an unprecedented new
world threatening to become no-world can have meaning here and now.

The need for a way to read England's public riddle and Dickens' private one
was pressing indeed in *Oliver Twist*'s nightmarish visions of the "homes" of the
poor, but at certain points in *Dombey* that urgency is intensified in its visions of
the utterly homeless. With her different perspective, Harriet Carker "often
looked with compassion . . . upon the stragglers who came wandering into London, by the great highway hard-by. . . . Day after day, such travellers crept
past, but always, as she thought, in one direction—always towards the town.
Swallowed up in one phase or other of its immensity, towards which they seemed
impelled by a desperate fascination, they never returned. Food for the hospitals,
the churchyards, the prisons, the river, fever, madness, vice, and death,—they
passed on to the monster, roaring in the distance, and were lost" (23.404–5).
Again a naturalized apocalypse impends, in which humanity is swallowed up by
"the monster"—Death to Dombey, "the town" and all its Dombeyian values
here. Harriet's way of dealing with this anarchy is to rescue one poor wayfarer
and, on her deathbed, read to her "the eternal book for all the weary, and the
heavy-laden; for all the wretched, fallen, and neglected of this earth . . . read
the ministry of Him, who, through the round of human life, and all its hopes and
griefs, from birth to death, from infancy to age, had sweet compassion for, and
interest in, its every scene and stage, its every suffering and error" (58.692).
Nothing like this appears in *Oliver Twist*; it suggests Dickens' deepened appreciation for the New Testament by 1846–48 and the particular Good Samaritan
emphasis of that appreciation, as I have argued. Carlyle's idiom is notably longer on Old Testament judgment than on what Victorians thought of as New Testament compassion; or rather, apocalyptic warning was his more typical way of
expressing his compassion for poverties of body and spirit he saw around him.
In *Dombey and Son* we find both the appropriation of this Carlylean rhetoric and
a more fervent advocacy of those other biblical values exemplified in Harriet

Carker's New Testament charity: both are needed, lest her Bible be nothing more than what Charles Kingsley called "an opium dose for keeping beasts of burden patient while they are being overloaded—a mere book to keep the poor in order."[27] A detailed comparison of two parallel passages from *Oliver Twist* and *Dombey* will set forth more concretely these two lines along which Dickens was moving in his use of biblical language. It will help further to suggest how, in its changing context, Dickens' Bible is becoming unstable in the later novel.

The context for the first passage is Oliver's recital to the Maylies as he lies badly wounded, but recovering under their care, the "weary catalogue of evils and calamities which hard men had brought upon him." Dickens' narrator precipitously interrupts this history almost as though he cannot hear another word of it, and must point its moral: "Oh! if, when we oppress and grind our fellow-creatures, we bestowed but one thought on the dark evidences of human error, which, like dense and heavy clouds, are rising, slowly it is true, but not less surely, to Heaven, to pour their after-vengeance on our heads; if we heard but one instant, in imagination, the deep testimony of dead men's voices, which no power can stifle, and no pride shut out; where would be the injury and injustice: the suffering, misery, cruelty, and wrong: that each day's life brings with it!" (30.186). In his sequence of parallel conditional clauses, Dickens makes his typical double appeal first to fear, then to pity; as in the *Dombey* passage below, he conjures up a storm cloud of the nineteenth century that is entirely of men's making, and although he suggests that vengeance belongs to the Lord, he assumes that social evils can be mended by human acts of "thought" and "imagination" leading to better deeds. While the same strategies and ideas are present in the *Dombey* passage, two differences will prove significant: one is that biblical allusion is minimal here—the reference to pouring "after-vengeance" recalling the pouring out of the vials of God's wrath in St. John's vision (Rev. 16); the other is that while the *Oliver Twist* appeal is apparently addressed not to anyone like the respectable characters in the dramatic scene but to villains elsewhere, Dickens' appeal in the following passage is prompted by the subject of the rich man's vices and is addressed directly to "a Christian people."

The context for the *Dombey* passage is the question, prompted by new evidence of "Mr. Dombey's master-vice," of whether it is "an unnatural characteristic": "It might be worth while, sometimes, to inquire what Nature is, and how men work to change her, and whether, in the enforced distortions so produced, it is not natural to be unnatural" (47.539). Unlike the impassioned outburst prompted by Oliver's "weary catalogue," the tone here is restrained, rational, proposing "to inquire." That spirit of discovery is still limited by the desire for moral closure; here the narrator is confident that given time he can unravel the paradox he has proposed. The subject, not metaphysical evil but the social production of vice, promises to be treated with the novelist's more mature awareness of causes and conditions, which began in *Oliver Twist*.

Significantly, he first takes up the vice of the rich man, "prisoner to one idea . . . who has never risen up upon the wings of a free mind . . . to see [Nature] in her comprehensive truth!" A vast confidence—it is also Carlylean—is implicit in this understanding criticism of Dombey, for it commits the writer to conveying that "comprehensive truth" of "Nature's own Laws" (1.2.13) rather than the partial estimate, which can be "monstrous delusion." With this introduction, Dickens passes on to consider false estimates of the poor's vices in very much the way that Carlyle, in his opening paragraphs of *Past and Present*, shames "the idle reader of Newspapers," who mutters, over a pauper crime report, "Brutal savages, degraded Irish," without understanding (1.1.4). Dickens writes:

> Alas! are there so few things in the world about us, most unnatural, and yet most natural in being so! Hear the magistrate or judge admonish the unnatural outcasts of society. . . . But follow the good clergyman or doctor, who, with his life imperilled at every breath he draws, goes down into their dens, lying within the echoes of our carriage wheels and daily tread upon the pavement stones. Look round upon the world of odious sights. . . . Breathe the polluted air . . . offended, sickened and disgusted. . . . Vainly attempt to think of any simple plant, or flower, or wholesome weed, that, set in this foetid bed, could have its natural growth, or put its little leaves forth to the sun as GOD designed it. And then, calling up some ghastly child, with stunted form and wicked face, hold forth on its unnatural sinfulness, and lament its being, so early, far away from Heaven—but think a little of its having been conceived, and born, and bred, in Hell! (539–40)

Here Dickens incorporates *Oliver Twist*'s parabolic journey into evil, with himself for conductor (in the guise of "the good clergyman or doctor"). Here the "deep testimony" is made not by the voices of dead men or rapid authorial generalization but by the witness of "every sense" to the offensive reality of this "foetid bed." Not until Dickens has piled up this empirical evidence does he strategically remind the reader that "GOD designed" the creatures who live here, for "natural growth." Quickly then he moves to expose the hollowness of religious language so far off the mark ("hold forth on its unnatural sinfulness, and lament its being . . . far away from Heaven"). He thus closes with the same contrast with which he began this paragraph—between ignorant, complacent judgment (see Matt. 7:1ff) and speech informed by thoughtful experience; and he

will end the whole passage by exposing the "contracted sympathies and estimates" he has tried to expand in this unwonted tour.

His next, even more disturbing train of ideas leads back from the poor to the
rich. For those who say "I don't believe it!" denial is fruitless:

> Those who study the physical sciences, and bring them to bear upon the health
> of Man, tell us that if the noxious particles that rise from vitiated air, were palpable
> to the sight, we should see them lowering in a dense black cloud above such
> haunts, and rolling slowly on to corrupt the better portions of a town. But if the
> moral pestilence that rises with them, and, in the eternal laws of outraged Nature,
> is inseparable from them, could be made discernable too, how terrible the revela-
> tion! Then should we see depravity, impiety, drunkenness, theft, murder, and a long
> train of nameless sins against the natural affections and repulsions of mankind,
> overhanging the devoted spots, and creeping on, to blight the innocent and spread
> contagion among the pure. (540)

The "dense and heavy clouds" that are "the dark evidences of human error" in
Oliver Twist receive in *Dombey* scientific support before biblical confirmation is
brought in at the end of this paragraph. The "after-vengeance" is no mere poetic
justice but actual contamination, physical and moral, of those respectable folk
who, Dickens now asserts, are responsible for these conditions. Declaring the
poor but also possibly apostrophizing the rich as "Unnatural humanity!" he
clinches his argument with an allusion to the Sermon on the Mount: "When we
shall gather grapes from thorns, and figs from thistles; when fields of grain shall
spring up from the offal in the by-ways of our wicked cities, and roses bloom in
the fat churchyards that they cherish; then we may look for natural humanity,
and find it growing from such seed." Like Jesus in Matthew 7:16 ("Do men
gather grapes of thorns, or figs of thistles?"), Dickens appeals to the "eternal
laws" of nature that declare a corrupt tree cannot bring forth good fruit (v. 18).

Further, while the subject of Jesus' parabolic utterance is the false prophets,
whom "Ye shall know . . . by their fruits" (v. 16), Dickens warns against a
certain kind of Victorian false prophecy that would "hold forth" about "the
unnatural outcasts of society" without changing the conditions of their production. To counter such false estimates, this prophet then unveils his own "terrible
revelation" of what will befall a people not known for their good deeds (just as
Jesus warns that the fruitless tree will be "cast into the fire," v. 19): "Oh for a
good spirit who would take the house-tops off, with a more potent and benignant
hand than the lame demon in the tale, and show a Christian people what dark
shapes issue from amidst their homes, to swell the retinue of the Destroying Angel
as he moves forth among them!" Here the apocalyptic note in *Oliver Twist*'s

"after-vengeance" is now fully sounded: the Destroying Angel of Revelation is already here, bringing not the end of the world but social and physical death, which for Dickens may be "the end of everything." Moreover, the "tremendous social retributions" no longer proceed "slowly it is true" as in *Oliver Twist*, but in 1846 come quickly and are "ever coming thicker!" With an eschatological urgency Rev. Melchiesedeck Howler might relish, Dickens announces that the time is at hand for Englishmen to repent their neglect. An earthly heaven "should" (the conditional is significant) follow the good spirit's revelations: "Bright and blest the morning that should rise on such a night: for men, delayed no more by stumbling-blocks of their own making, which are but specks of dust upon the path between them and eternity, would then apply themselves, like creatures of one common origin, owning one duty to the Father of one family, and tending to one common end, to make the world a better place!" (540–41). Here, with a somewhat confused echo of the motes and beams parable of the Sermon (Matt. 7:3–5; cf. 7.74) turning into a *Pilgrim's Progress* emblem, Dickens makes his final appeal by rendering explicit the religious reasons for not neglecting the poor, bringing in *Dombey*'s themes of the Father as origin and dust as end of all. Although "eternity" is mentioned, the final emphasis is typically on this world as the "better place." At this point we hear Harriet Carker's "eternal book for all the weary" urging us to charitable deeds, even as Carlyle in the penultimate paragraph of *Past and Present* urges his readers "To make some nook of God's Creation a little fruitfuller, better, more worthy of God; to make some human hearts a little wiser, manfuler, happier. . . . Sooty Hell of mutiny and savagery and despair can, by man's energy, be made a kind of Heaven; . . . the everlasting arch of Heaven's azure overspanning *it* too, and its cunning mechanisms and tall chimney-steeples, as a birth of Heaven" (4.8.298). Carlyle's prose also enacts a familiar Victorian stylistic movement: a typical contraction ("some nook . . . a little fruitfuller . . . a little wiser") is followed by an inspirational expansion, but the apocalyptic rhetoric calling for some far-reaching salvation scheme only belies the inadequacy of individual good deeds for bringing about the earthly paradise. The belief that the "growing good of the world," in George Eliot's phrase, begins in the "nook," the home, the charitable deed, is an article of Victorian faith that assumes far more than it proves. Nonetheless, this limited individual change is the solution toward which *Dombey and Son* moves, an end so out of keeping with the profound social and spiritual malaise that has been portrayed and a solution literally removed, too, from the novel's scenes of neglect. But here, in the midst of *Dombey*'s perplexities, Dickens' prose takes a final, perhaps surprising turn to conclude the inquiry of chapter 47 into the "comprehensive truth." In contrast to that final reign of domesticated Christianity in Sol Gills' back parlor, and countering Dickens' hope that his readers *can* "make the world a better place," he returns to the darker facts of the blind rich and the "perversion of nature in their own contracted sympathies and estimates; as great, and yet as natural in its development once begun, as the lowest degradation known" (541). With this vehement ending, Dickens makes an already implied point explicitly damning and flings the fruitless hearer who would not heed the parable into the fire along with the "unnatural outcasts of society."

I have dwelt upon this passage from *Dombey and Son* at such length first to illustrate how Dickens, from this point in his career, will draw increasingly upon biblical models and language with confidence and poise as one whose public role has grown. He speaks now as the Victorian sage—in John Holloway's terms, as one who would awaken the Christian conscience of his readers by conducting them through an experience toward what Newman called real assent. As sage Dickens does this by redefining and revivifying religious and other common terms (such as "unnatural") that have masked the facts, while making readers physically and morally see what they had been blind to before.[28] Biblical truisms, implicitly redefined by their creative application to the contemporary context, become organs of seeing and judging that the social critic of *Oliver Twist* did not have at his command. The confidence of the prophet and confidence in the Bible would seem to go hand in hand here: in the words of the Unitarian preacher who used this chapter to exemplify Dickens as parabler, the "imitator of the Great Preacher" will decipher his significant paradox, read the reader and the times, reinterpret Scripture, and so tell comprehensive truth.

This line of biblically based social prophecy becomes increasingly problematic in Dickens' later books, where he was attacked for "setting to work to illustrate some enigma which Thomas Carlyle perhaps, or some such congenial dreary spirit, . . . has left rather darker than before."[29] I have also dwelt upon the *Dombey* passage because in it we begin to see the changing context in which biblical allusion becomes at once more explicit and more importunate (although not as desperate as it would become in the Carlyle of 1850). Despite the benevolent wishes for a better world, the tone of the passage is bitter; the biblical allusions are flung at a public that, as Carlyle said, kisses its closed Bible (*LDP* 314). Biblical values are appealed to, yet they are evidently not operative in this landscape of corrupted "Christian" homes. Indeed, the very religious expressions of Dickens' hearers are proof of their kinship with the most degraded. The repetitions in this passage (much longer than what is quoted here) and the making explicit what might have remained implicit anticipate a readership that has not ears to hear.

Moreover, although Dickens neatly dovetails the findings of science with Jesus' knowledge of corrupt nature, his nineteenth-century "scientific" understanding of causes and conditions subtly puts the biblical world view in question. His emphasis on "eternal laws" only calls attention to the cruelty of a Father's world in which these laws "naturally" operate to God-born creatures' earthly damnation. The feeling of tautology in the whole passage, which circles around the same ideas and envisions the same pestilential cloud pouring out its vengeance again and again, suggests the quandary into which Dickens is driven by his causal "inquiry": how does one begin to change the conditions in which good citizens' "contracted sympathies"—perpetuating the scenes of neglect in which vice and misery are bred—are themselves bred? Indifference breeds misery, more misery breeds more indifference, until by the operation of "eternal laws" there is scarcely a "natural" sentiment or norm by which to judge these things and "all distinctions between good and evil" are utterly confounded (539). The need for a change of heart amid the tangled web of temporal conditions is the novel's central theme, and its great crux—most pressing but unresolved here.

This darker part of the "comprehensive truth" Dickens forcefully communicates but does not fully explore; ironically, for him as for the indifferent moralizers he assails, religious language serves finally to enforce closure on inquiry. Again and again such rhetoric comes to his rescue. At the first climax of his thoughts on the evil power of social conditions (ending with "and find it growing from such seed," where the s sounds hiss his contempt), his outburst comes, "Oh for a good spirit. . . ." The yearning for some goodness amid these evil scenes is felt also in Dickens' insistence that the hand showing us our vice is "benignant" rather than a Destroying Angel obliterating our faith in human nature. Dickens' final emphasis is on people's nearly infinite capacities for "fiction," their ability to manipulate perception to their own desire. This condition of "vice," gift or curse of "nature" to all human minds, can perhaps be combated by a more powerful moral imagination, such as the popular novelist's in *Dombey and Son*. But the final effect of his darkly imagined meditations on unnatural human nature is malignant, not benignant; and no revelation of the poor's miseries ever dawns for any major character in the story, not even blessed Florence and Walter. It is as though Dickens could not bring about, even if only in fiction, the social transformation he so desired and had abandoned the attempt. Perhaps it is for these reasons that Carlyle himself dismissed this novel: "Dickens writes a *Dombey and Son*, Thackeray a *Vanity Fair*; not *reapers* they, either of them!"[30] Carlyle believed "Every man that writes is writing a new Bible; or a new Apocrypha; to last for a week, or for a thousand years," for "he that convinces a man and sets him working is the doer of a *miracle*."[31] Despite Dickens' biblical insistences, the miracle he would work in his readers is thwarted by his baffled knowledge of human vice; and he leaves the riddle he would read rather darker than before.

With the influx of new worlds in *Dombey and Son*, Dickens' biblical framework has become intensely necessary, yet remains impotent to dispel the unease these forces have provoked. This is the changed context in which much of the religious allusion in *Dombey* must be considered. Biblical language is a participant in a complex social dialogue in Dickens' mature novels, where many voices contend for mastery (including the false religious cries Dickens corrects in chapter 47). Bakhtin reminds us that in the multilanguaged world of the novel as in everyday dialogue, "every word is directed toward an *answer* and cannot escape the profound influence of the answering word that it anticipates."[32] That is why it is not very useful to call Dickens an apocalyptic prophet or a "New Testament Christian" without specifying the context in which he tries to make his witness. The borrowed scriptural formulas reflect, in their very reformulation, the pressures of the fictional world in which they are found. In *Dombey and Son* they are already anticipating hostile or indifferent answers in ways that mark a striking development from *Oliver Twist*. In chapter 47, the religious words are piled up defensively in response to the voices that deny their relevance and truth. Throughout the novel, the sheer number of ironic religious allusions has sharply increased, and as they accumulate, we sense a destabilization process under way: the efficacy of the Bible and Prayer Book standards Dickens also calls upon to judge the irreligious times is being gradually and ineluctably undermined. This ebbing of biblical authority from the novel is only confirmed by the withdrawal of the good characters from the complex contemporary scene they cannot transform, over which their idiom holds no sway.

3

IN *DOMBEY* as in *Past and Present*, the urgency to formulate some "infinitely deeper Gospel, . . . daily and hourly corrective, to the Cash one" (*P&P* 3.10.189) is strongly felt. Carlyle turns to the Gospel of Work; Dickens, to a Romanticist religion of divine intimations and to various forms of "essential Christianity." But while he can call for vigorous social action in chapter 47, in the rest of the novel he makes surprisingly little positive application of the Bible to that "moral and social restitution" of the larger community which was the essence of Christian action for such as Dr. Arnold,[33] whom Dickens immensely admired. Contracted into smaller communities of feeling, the witness of Word and deed in the Midshipman group, in Paul's life and death, and in the characterization of Florence forms Dickens' alternative gospel—one that largely fails. Anticipating the hostile answering word, the Christian and quasi-religious allusions associated with these characters opposed to money worship seem merely to quail from its pressures and, instead of articulating a robust Christian faith or projecting a powerful visionary language, retire murmuring dreamily to themselves. The efficacy and solidity of these religious words are further diminished by the several ways they call attention to their status as fictive creations; and they do this in a novel that repeatedly dramatizes the subjective processes of interpretation and symbolization.

The supremely funny *Pickwick Papers* had at its core a divine comedy that culminated in the reign of something like the kingdom of heaven on earth.[34] In "the little society of the back parlour" at the Midshipman (32.383), Dickens tries to recreate this earlier embodiment of Gospel values. Lord Jeffrey's praise of *Dombey*'s "delightful children"—"how deeply do we feel that 'of such is the kingdom of Heaven'"—expresses Dickens' evident intention with the whole Midshipman company. But whereas *Pickwick* had evoked a chorus of affirmation and delight, *Dombey*'s central expression of its positive values did not satisfy its readers in at all the same way. Even Lord Jeffrey reading the novel could not help expressing his sense of all that is left out of its picture of innocence, for he adds in his letter to Dickens, "how ashamed [we feel] of the contaminations which *our* manhood has received from the contact of earth"; he also "wonder[s] how *you* should have been admitted into that pure communion, and so 'presumed, an earthly guest, and drawn Empyrial air,' though for our benefit and instruction."[35] His remarks recall Dr. Arnold's candid admissions about the Sermon on the Mount, which "cannot be read by any good man without the strongest feelings of shame and humiliation for the contrast between the picture of Christian principles there drawn, and the reality which he sees around him."[36] The instability of the *Dombey* text, however, comes partly from its internal increase in realism: because the novel shows us the actualities environing the good Midshipman, we become more aware of the charmed circle's fictive status. Abandoning Dickens' more complex Carlylean sense of society, this nautical group is as simplified in its internal organization and as isolated as an artificial community aboard ship; it also embodies the romantic dream of sailing away from the shores of a corrupt European civilization to some happier primitive (albeit Christianized) isle (cf. Paul, 14.160). Instead of an informed, vigorous, faithful party formed in opposition to Mammonism, therefore, what we find in the Midshipman group is, in Julian Moynahan's withering phrase, "an ark commanded by a plurality of sweet old Noahs and floating on a fathomless sea of sentiment"[37]—and the bumpers of old Madeira with which they toast their faith. Dickens' alternative society scarcely knows what it opposes; and their use of religious texts only serves the dream, while calling attention to the artificially constructed nature of their world.

That the Midshipman's gospel ark is kept afloat on the resolute principle of *not* "see[ing] around" (or into) itself we note in the typical way, for example, that Captain Cuttle reads the Sermon on the Mount—with the greatest complacency: "although he was accustomed to quote the text, without book, after his own manner, he appeared to read it with as reverent an understanding of its heavenly spirit, as if he had got it all by heart in Greek, and had been able to write any number of fierce theological disquisitions on its every phrase" (39.456). Like the Dickens who wants the Sermon (and his Bible) as a simple, readable text,[38] Cuttle can preserve its "essential" simplicity only by denying the difficulties of applying religious formula to contemporary facts. (This complacency becomes "maniacal" in his approval of the Dombey marriage ceremony; see 51.371–74.) The Captain's allusions throughout the novel are meant to signify, like the sacraments, "what you may call a out'ard and visible sign of an in'ard and spirited grasp" (23.277; see *BCP* 327), but the little irony of his mispronunciation is that he grasps little of use for the actual world. If religion is (in Forster's version of Dr. Arnold's definition) "a system directing and influencing our conduct, principles, and feelings, and professing to do this with sovereign authority, and most efficacious influence,"[39] Cuttle's religion anchored in key texts of the marriage service and the catechism clarifies little of what principles should guide action in the novel's more complex world. His constant theme of undiscriminating loyalty (so embarrassing to Walter at Dombey's), in which he confuses the Order of Matrimony with the old nautical saw about not deserting the ship ("I'll stand by, and not desert until death doe us part," 23.277), is useful to Florence seeking asylum at the Midshipman from a Dombey world. But if we are to take Florence as victim seriously, we can see only that this confused girl, trying to suppress "the still small woice of a wownded mind!" (563; cf. 1 Kings 19:12) because her father has rejected her, needs more than the Captain's complacent "balsam" or his counsel (most ironic in her case) to "Love! Honour! And Obey!" (4.35). She needs a fuller emotional response than his artificial constructions can express and, according to at least one Victorian reviewer, clearer principles on which to act.[40] But she will get neither at the Midshipman, and that is why Dickens brings her there—to dissolve her demons, rather than resolve her problems, in its baptismal baths of sentiment.

If Cuttle's Prayer Book suggests its inadequacy for addressing real human

problems, his reductive Authorized Version nourishes his infinite capacity for
idealization. Walter is "a lad of promise—a lad over-flowing . . . with milk and
honey" (10.111; Exod. 3:8). Walter's exaltation of Florence Cuttle wholly commends with a confused recollection of Psalm Forty-two: "The wery planks she
walked on was as high esteemed by Wal'r as the water brooks is by the hart
which never rejices." Here Cuttle turns into a jejune text what is actually a *de
profundis* psalm, in which the singer laments, "As the hart panteth after the
water brooks, so panteth my soul after thee, O God . . . Deep calleth unto deep
at the noise of thy waterspouts: all thy waves and thy billows are gone over me"
(vv. 1, 7). Despite the nautical images, Cuttle forgets all this (except in acciden-
tally implying that poor Florence has walked the plank); and elsewhere his
typical response to shipwreck is glib affirmation. At a point when all the Midshipman plans "lay drifting, without mast or rudder, on the waste of waters," he
is so buoyant on the billows as to versify for Toots one of the Bible's most
disturbing statements of faith: "Cap'en Cuttle is my name, and England is my
nation, this here is my dwelling place, and blessed be creation—Job" (32.383,
387; cf. Job 1:21). Upon reading the newspaper account of the *Son and Heir*'s
wreck, Toots in contrast breaks out into a highly individualistic lament that it is
a Job's world: "Somebody's always dying, or going and doing something uncomfortable in it. . . . It's a great deal worse than Blimber's" (390). Cuttle's reaction
to this "Job's-news" is at least not self-conscious, ponderous allusion; but his
spontaneous memorial on the "dozen Wal'rs that I know'd and loved" is nothing
but idealization, and his quiet reading of the Burial Service later to "commi[t]
Walter's body to the deep" (396) is an act of honoring the dead rather than of
affirming the resurrection faith, as the ritual is meant to do. This simple reading
closes the episode and forecloses the issues Toots' lament has raised.

    While we are to admire Cuttle's good fellowship as his activated creed, his
patching together of the liturgical with the nautical, the Holy Book and Dr.
Watts with the *Beggar's Opera* and popular ditties, forcibly draws our attention
to the devaluation of religious language by the Midshipman's chief
spokesman.[41] Thus, to counter the selfishness of the Mammonists (see
Bagstock, 20.239; cf. Ps. 78:65), Cuttle gives us the popular drinking song,
"May we never want a friend in need, nor a bottle to give him," which he
solemnly attributes to "the Proverbs of Solomon" (15.176). Like all his allusions, his religious formulas are fictive creations—"beautiful quotation[s]" to
him (23.277), but still only too like the classical allusions at Blimber's Academy, "a mere collection of words and grammar, . . . [with] no other meaning in
the world" (11.121). Appropriating the authority due to Solomon Gills' biblical

name, the Captain is a comic caricature of self-appointed Christian "wisdom"—
his manner "the very concentration and sublimation of all philosophical reflection and grave inquiry" (15.178). But he is not one of Dickens' wise fools: he is
the foolish fool who thinks that because he has the authoritative words at hand,
he has the wisdom. Unlike the writer of Proverbs, he often "wants a word in
season" (15.181; cf. Prov. 15:23). Cuttle maintains a maniacal complacency by
this system of preserving traditional language for its own sake—a cargo of dead
quotations stowed away in his enormous head—regardless of its application
(often remote indeed) to duty in the situations he so pointedly yet so ineffectually
"improves."

Setting the tone of the Midshipman group, Cuttle's habit of absurd idealization and his comic reductions of religious texts to the level of other, banal texts
obviously lighten these characters as counterweights to the Mammon worship-
pers. In his simplicity, Cuttle believes "that all books" are "true" (39.456), but
the novel's more intricate psychological worlds demand more subtle and less
credulous acts of interpretation. In Dickens' other embodiments of virtue, Paul
and Florence, he indicates the importance of that subtlety, yet abandons it for
the simplifications of his moral and religious designs.

With the death of little Paul, Dickens not only dramatized in fiction but
created in fact that "sad community of love and grief" (18.205) so lacking in the
Dombey world. It is clear from Dickens' 1848 preface that he wanted to create
for himself a sense of intimacy with his readers as well,[42] for he commends their
"unbounded warmth and earnestness of their sympathy" with his work and goes
on rather immodestly to assert his role in creating that response (see xxi). While
later readers did not share so readily in this community, the reason for its creation as an answering word to its society was evident: as Walter Bagehot explained, "the unfeeling obtuseness of the early part of this century was to be
corrected by an extreme, perhaps an excessive, sensibility to human suffering in
the years which have followed."[43] If there "was urgent need to paint such a man
as Dombey,"[44] there was equally the need for a son.

What still interests those of us who can read of Paul's death "with a heart
unmoved and an eye tearless" is what F. R. Leavis has called Paul's "*enfant
terrible* disconcertingness."[45] He is the wise child with a preternatural, instinctive knowledge of evil from his early experience of it as a "little Dombey,"
half-baptized if not fully inducted into a culture of death. Gazing into the fire
"with an old, old face . . . with the fixed and rapt attention of a sage" (8.77) or a
revolutionary, "entertaining" not "complicated worldly schemes" like his father
but "Heaven knows what wild fancies," which find expression at length in his

PROFOUND COGITATION OF CAPTAIN CUTTLE
(Hablot K. Browne)

Thereupon the Captain put his iron hook between his teeth, as if it were a hand . . . with an air of wisdom and profundity that was the very concentration and sublimation of all philosophical reflection and grave inquiry. (*DS* 15.178)

blasphemous question, "Papa! what's money?"—this pathetic victim of the
money culture is a locus for Dickens' critical values in complex ways the good
Midshipman group cannot be (especially ending as they do on a high note of
capitalist expansionism). But with Paul's death, given all the pressures Dickens
felt to make of it an occasion for communal feeling, the writer transforms his
contaminated victim-critic into an unsullied ideal. Here Dickens draws upon
biblical and popular iconographic allusion to associate his "Master Paul"
(15.184) with Christ and to create for his readers a pictorial religious pamphlet
of the pious dying child who converts all those around him, as well as other
consoling pictures.[46] The last moment of Paul's critical vision occurs when he
sees a "figure" unmoved and silent by his bed: when he asks Floy, "What *is*
that?" and she answers, "There's nothing there, except Papa!" Paul "looked *it*
in the face, and thought, was This his father?" (16.188–89; emphasis added).
In this moment, Paul instinctively spurns the worship of this objectified Mam-
mon-idol, who has made nearly all human relations into Martin Buber's "I-it."
But in the dying scenes that follow, Paul becomes the voice and visionary agent
of an otherworldly reconciliation. No longer seeing in a glass darkly but face to
face, Paul awakens to the reality of a kingdom in this world: "then Paul woke—
woke mind and body—and sat upright in his bed. He saw them now about him.
There was no grey mist before them, as there had been sometimes in the night.
He knew them every one, and called them by their names" (190). Like the Good
Shepherd of John 10:1–5, who "calleth his own sheep by name and leadeth
them out," Paul is the true leader whose voice even the black sheep know; and
with the authority of the dying beloved, he leads his father to receive a little
child—the outcast Walter—not in Christ's name (Mark 9:37) but in his own:
"Remember Walter, dear Papa. . . . I was fond of Walter!" (191).

    The chapter closes on a series of religious tableaux cast into traditional ico-
nography as well as Romantic images of growth that vaguely intimate hopes of
immortal life:

> Sister and brother wound their arms around each other, and the golden light
> came streaming in, and fell upon them, locked together.
>
> "How fast the river runs, between its green banks and the rushes, Floy! But it's
> very near the sea. I hear the waves! They always said so!"
>
> Presently he told her that the motion of the boat upon the stream was lulling him
> to rest. How green the banks were now, how bright the flowers growing on them,
> and how tall the rushes! Now the boat was out at sea, but gliding smoothly on. And
> now there was a shore before him. Who stood on the bank!—. . . .
>
> He put his hands together, as he had been used to do, at his prayers. . . .
>
> "Mama is like you, Floy. I know her by the face! But tell them that the print upon

the stairs at school, is not Divine enough. The light about the head is shining on me as I go!" (191)

Haloed by the "golden light" of these tableaux, Paul's visage—now no longer the "little image" of a Mammon-god (8.77)—blends with Christ's image in two pictures earlier planted in the book, the "portrait on the stairs" at school that earnestly "seemed to gaze at him" alone until he was out of sight, and another print "where, in the centre of a wondering group, one figure that he knew, a figure with a light about its head—benignant, mild, and merciful—stood pointing upward" (14.163). Moving like Cap'en Cuttle's imaginary ship on high seas, "head on, to the world without end, evermore, amen" (49.576; see *BCP* 5), Paul also enacts the familiar voyage to eternity of Tennyson's "Crossing the Bar." Dickens' novel of 1848 and Tennyson's poem of 1889 share the same configuration of conventional images, from the mystic "clear call" of the sea and the smoothly gliding boat that lulls to sleep, to the denial of any "sadness of farewell" for one who is going "home" and the vision of the figure on the bank— to Tennyson "my Pilot" and "that Divine and Unseen Who is always guiding us,"[47] but to Dickens, a "figure" left unnamed, either because it is too obvious to need naming or because its identity is uncertain to the author himself.

The very vagueness of Paul's visionary experience of dying unto life seems then to call forth the narrator's final heavy-handed interpretation in an emblematic passage invoking the whole sweep of Bible narrative, from Genesis to Revelation (see Rev. 6:14): "The golden ripple on the wall came back again, and nothing else stirred in the room. The old, old fashion! The fashion that came in with our first garments, and will last unchanged until our race has run its course, and the wide firmament is rolled up like a scroll. The old, old fashion— Death! Oh thank GOD, all who see it, for that older fashion yet, of Immortality! And look upon us, angels of young children, with regards not quite estranged, when the swift river bears us to the ocean!" (191). When Paul was first fading, Dickens had begun to call him "old-fashioned" (Miss Blimber's word for this "singular" child, 14.155). Paul's singularity as a child who "dream[s] about such cu-ri-ous things" (8.79) and sees leering faces in the patterns of carpet and wallpaper is almost Quilpish; it allies him with an even older fashion than Christianity, with the traditions of grim folktale and "book[s] of necromancy" that he studies in "Mrs. Pipchin, and the cat, and the fire, night after night" (89). But all the ghoulish reading of this "old man or . . . young goblin" (79) has been banished at his deathbed, when Paul is called upon, like the Midshipman group through Cuttle's quotations, to preserve the traditional Christian language. In Dickens' closing paragraphs, the ambiguous possibilities he has

PAUL AND MRS. PIPCHIN
(Hablot K. Browne)

Paul . . . went on studying Mrs. Pipchin, and the cat, and the fire, night
after night, as if they were a book of necromancy, in three volumes.
(*DS* 8.89)

played with in the term "old-fashioned" are stabilized into a message: to the worldly contemporaries he implicitly addresses and answers, the "older fashion" of "Immortality" may seem a mere eccentricity of belief, but it is a tradition worth preserving, the biblical images insist, for its reconcilement of new-fashioned worlds to Time's "deeper operations" in human affairs (1.1).

Despite Dickens' efforts to close this scene hopefully, several things work to undermine the stability he would achieve for Paul's vision, beginning with the troublesome word "fashion," which will not settle down into one meaning even here. To a rationalist like William Kent, the word rings false; it would "be more appropriate in the mouth of a sceptic for a term to satirise the belief in a future life."[48] As I have suggested, Dickens seems to anticipate this interpretation by trying "dialogically" to engage the religious skeptic's dismissive term and to reappropriate it, although in doing so he also reminds us that the opposing view of immortality exists (and leaves doubters like Kent unmoved). Even to the less skeptical reader, who might appreciate the stable irony Dickens tries for by insisting upon a "fashion" that is unchanging, his choice of words ("came in with our first garments") might remind that belief in immortality can be only an adopted convention, clothes put on for an occasion of great need—comfort for which we are to "thank GOD" if we are among those "who see it." And this qualification, which sounds the note of the theologically tolerant Dickens, again more forcefully recalls that there are other, possibly valid opinions about immortality. If Dickens is expressing his belief in the afterlife here as many readers have thought, it is a remarkably coy affirmation, hedging its absoluteness by invoking other voices and, further, by going out of its way to display the fictive ("fashioned") quality of religious language. The literary self-consciousness of the last two paragraphs, with their plays upon words, rhetorical parallelism, and emblematic devices, calls attention to the fact that if these figurative expressions console it is not necessarily because they speak truth, but because they are aesthetically and emotionally satisfying. In the preceding scene, the insistent pictorial emphasis, of which the dying Paul is so much aware, and the self-consciously poetic prose contribute to the impression that religious belief is a matter not of objective reality but of subjectively experienced effects. Most of all, this sense of the fictive is achieved by presenting Paul's vision as the projection of a dying imagination and then re-emphasizing the element of subjectivity in the final paragraph's important qualifying clause, "Oh thank GOD, *all who see it*" (emphasis added). The more one examines its language, the child's death scene followed by the narrator's artfully fashioned interpretation of it comes to be little more than a dream of literary order assuming religious proportions, while behind and through it all a less than orderly chorus of other voices can be heard.

Even John Forster, who greatly admired the life and death of Paul Dombey, responded to these fictive qualities, although he did not object to them: "It is a fairy vision to a piece of actual suffering; a sorrow with heaven's hues upon it, to a sorrow with all the bitterness of earth" (*Life* 2:30). But a "fairy vision" can carry on no dialogue with "all the bitterness of earth." Other Victorians reacted more strongly against the self-consciously literary quality of this death and re-birth scene. The *North British Review* regretted the "affectations of style," anticipating the later reaction of R. H. Hutton (1870), who dismissed the feeling of Paul's death scene as the "pathos of the Adelphi Theatre . . . feasting on itself."[49] Dickens places his Paul at the center of a wondering group, which expands from the child's friends and relations to take in Dickens' readers, who are to emulate the company that gathers round Paul when he leaves Blimber's for good: "Once, for a last look, he turned and gazed upon the faces thus addressed to him, surprised to see how shining and how bright, and numerous they were, and how they were all piled and heaped up, as faces are at crowded theatres" (14.171). But this "seemed . . . always a dream, full of eyes" to Paul, like the picture of a Christ whose penetrating glance does not rivet the mind on divine things but only draws Paul's attention to himself as the object of the look. Paul likewise calls our last look to the light "on me, as I go!" It is therefore not only the fictive qualities of the conventions Dickens draws upon but, as with Cuttle's quotations, a certain solipsism that hampers Dickens' efforts to revive "old-fashioned" belief, which would draw the believer away from self toward God. If Dickens' appreciative readers were not aware of this, it is because, as he insists, "There were some immunities . . . attaching to the character" of Paul "enjoyed by no one else" (14.156); and these immunities—from criticism as well as from "the bitterness of earth"—are secured by the conventions in which his death is framed for Victorian consumption. In Dickens' performance with these conventions, the iconographic tradition and New Testament allusions are not the organs of vision he supposes, but tinted lenses like Mrs. Skewton's "Rose-coloured curtains" (37.444), masking from the view of surrounding admirers the fact of their own self-contemplation and the ironic placement of all such egoism by the inexorable advance of "Death!"

If Paul is an unsatisfying locus for Dickens' positive values, what about Florence, whose suffering and imputed powers command so much more of the book? Paul's disconcerting question, "Floy, are we *all* dead, except you?" (16.189), poses the central issue for Florence as a religious figure. If she is entombed in an abstract religious design, her suffering will not be felt and the hope she represents cannot convincingly save others enmeshed in the real world; on the other hand, if she is alive, she will be in dialogue with that world, possess an interiority that wrestles with its temptations and its power to inflict suffering, and win her hope, realize her love for others, even in the teeth of her despair. While Forster and other Victorians viewed Florence as alive in this sense, "a brave young resolute heart [who] . . . works out her own redemption from earth's roughest trials" (*Life* 2:33), this "*grown-up* female angel" (in Jeffrey's phrase)[50] is in fact both dead and alive; and the uncertainties of her characterization, which embodies conflicting roles, lessen her efficacy as a salvific figure for the novel.

The most convincing of these roles comes to life when this girl-child not "worth mentioning" (1.2) realizes her plight (see 24.291–92) and when she wanders desolately through the deserted mansion, an emblem of her empty life and "wownded mind." In such moments, Dickens produces without theatrical orchestrations that community of feeling for her so lacking in her Dombey world; he also thereby effects that implicit criticism of it which her very existence embodies, as her father knows. But Dickens wants her for more than an implied attack on Mammonism; he wants a realization of the living gospel. Instead of creating a human Florence who works out her salvation with diligence and religious faithfulness, however, he makes her an even more elaborated Christ-figure than Paul, beginning with her *via dolorosa* on "bleeding feet along that stoney road which ended in her father's heart" (28.336), where she is crucified and yet remains the loving mediatrix who will preside over his redemption. These religious codes, coupled with the even more extensive fairytale conventions Dickens weaves into her story, create a circle of immunity around Florence (despite the "bleeding feet" and "stoney road"), protecting her from the conditions of vice and the operations of natural law he so insists upon elsewhere in the novel. As a result, not only is the reader's identification with her pathos short-circuited, but her religious role becomes infantilized in ways that nearly prevent her from having any credible salvific power over *Dombey*'s grown-up world. At the same time, given Dickens' interest in Florence's interior processes, he also subtly places her religious outlook in question by suggesting in several ways its essential subjectivity and its status as the product of need. Here again, as his Christ-figure turns into a more ordinary victim whose very quasi-religious hopes are part of her pathos, we see Dickens' desire to explore the human interior breaking the constraints of his religious design. While he will more convincingly embody a living gospel in Little Dorrit, in *Dombey and Son* he seems at least beginning to discover some limitations of such heroines, even as he also strives here to make those limits endearing, and more, the paradoxical sources of Florence Dombey's strength.

Steven Marcus sees operating through the legitimate yet long-suffering Florence, who does not get the miracle she longs for until the end, a conception of grace Dickens had revised since *Oliver Twist* to accord with his advanced understanding of those miserable childhood days when Providence did not intervene to save him.[51] Nonetheless we feel this Presence intervening in the very qualities with which she has been supernaturally endowed that make her "an angel" (32.388) to all appreciators. She can read Dombey's murky soul (see 20.237), has inexplicable problem-solving powers (12.139), can dispel anxiety with a word (19.222), and can make even the stony Edith weep, as when Florence's touch "was like the prophet's rod of old, upon the rock. [Edith's] tears sprung forth beneath it, as she sunk upon her knees" (30.366). In a moment of self-conscious iconography like Paul's, Florence imagines her own "pure love" as a Pentecostal fire, "the sacred fire from Heaven, [which] is as gentle in the heart, as when it rested on the heads of the assembled twelve, and showed each man his brother, brightened and unhurt" (18.208). Dickens' humanized Pentecostal image also suggests the "spirit of love and truth" Florence represents, a Victorian figure of Christian wisdom (biblically founded in John 14:15–17 as well as in older Wisdom texts) through which writers like Dickens, as Alexander Welsh has documented, relocated the sphere of the Comforter's influence to the home and the deathbed.[52] This is the ideal; other dimensions of Florence's plot and character tell a different story.

In *Dombey and Son* one senses the beginnings of a seriously ambivalent attitude toward such ideals. Like Captain Cuttle preserving traditional language in allusion, or Paul in iconographic quotation, Florence preserves in her own heart a conserving love and loyalty that outlasts all changes of fortune (see 19.220); and for others she is a precious relic, a talisman to be treasured against an evil day and the temptations of the world. The very allusion to her name is a sign of inward and spiritual grace; her father, naturally, never alludes to her. Besides their conventional attractiveness, Dickens needed to believe in such icons; as Forster explains of Mary Hogarth's idealized image, "Through later troubled years, whatever was worthiest in him found in this an ark of safety; and it was the nobler part of his being which had thus become also the essential" (*Life* 2:402). On the other hand, Dickens must have in some sense known that he was creating a character in the "Mary Hogarth" of memory and that the hope of angelizing women was a male fiction. ("Wot's the good o' callin' a young 'ooman a Wenus or a angel, Sammy?" Sam Weller's father had asked in *Pickwick*. "You might jist as well call her a griffin, or a unicorn, or a king's arms at once, which is werry well known to be a col-lection o' fabulous animals" [33.540, 542].) In *Dombey and Son*, Dickens both dwells on the Midshipman males' processes of fictionalization, subjecting them to gentle criticism, and follows their lead. Walter is indefatigable in building up his own romantic sense of self-importance through idealizing Florence; Cuttle thinks of this pair "until they both seemed to his homely fancy to be dead, and to have passed away into eternal youth, the beautiful and innocent children of his first remembrance" (39.456). Yet while Cuttle's airy castles are gently mocked, Dickens encloses the happy pair in precisely such an unchanging design on their marriage day (narrated in present tense), when "the childish feet of long ago, did not tread such enchanted ground as theirs do now" (57.674–75).

But this is only the climax of Dickens' efforts throughout the novel to slip the implications of Florence's more realistic story through imposing the conventions of fairytale. Dombey's house may be under Carlyle's "baleful Fiat . . . of Enchantment" in many descriptive passages, but with her white magic "Florence bloomed there, like the king's fair daughter in the story," living "within the circle of her innocent pursuits and thoughts, and nothing harmed her" (see 23.266–68). That these self-consciously flourished conventions of the female Angel and the enchanted Princess are fictive we realize the more sharply because Dickens has written into his novel a psychologically credible standard of comparison. In chapters 47, 48, and 49, where Florence passes from the world of this darker story into the ideal one, we can see how this basic ambivalence in her characterization destabilizes our belief in her religious faith and uncomplicated virtue.

The scene of Florence's flight from her father's house is powerful because of its dangerously unfixed moment of flurry, anguish, and violence, and because of the appalling truth Florence *sees* there: "she looked at [her father], and a cry of desolation issued from her heart. For as she looked, she saw him murdering that fond idea to which she had held in spite of him. She saw his cruelty, neglect, and hatred, dominant above it, and stamping it down. She saw she had no father upon earth, and ran out, orphaned, from his house" (47.557). But when Florence passes into the magic circle of the Midshipman ("as safe here as if you was at the top of St. Paul's Cathedral," 48.563), the virtue of this "wandering princess" becomes as unreal as the evil of a "good monster in a storybook": "Unlike as they were externally . . . in simple innocence of the world's ways and the world's perplexities and dangers, they were nearly on a level. No child could have surpassed Captain Cuttle in inexperience of everything but wind and weather; in simplicity, credulity, and generous trustfulness. Faith, hope, and charity, shared his whole nature among them. An odd sort of romance, perfectly unimaginative, yet perfectly unreal, and subject to no considerations of worldly prudence or practicability, was the only partner they had in [Cuttle's] character" (49.572). Having watched Florence pass through the nadir of "the world's perplexities and dangers" and seen her most "fond idea" murdered, we cannot accept her association with such "simplicity, credulity, and generous trustfulness." Most damaging of all to Dickens' religious design, he implies by the association with Cuttle that Florence's "faith, hope, and charity" are born of her "inexperience of everything," whereas St. Paul impresses on his readers that true charity "suffereth long" (1 Cor. 13:4)—as Florence's love does do in the other story. By setting his account of her virtues here into the framework of the "story-book," Dickens not only unnecessarily infantilizes these virtues (reversing 1 Cor. 13:11, he reverts to "childish things"); he also suggests their fictive nature by conjoining them with Cuttle's "odd sort of romance, perfectly unimaginative, yet perfectly unreal." Elsewhere too Dickens intimates that his heroine's faith is but a dream, woven into the fabric of other dreamy fantasies.

In her thinking about supernatural things, Florence never matures very far from Polly's improvised story about heaven (3.20),[53] for the bereaved child will repeat this consoling story to herself in later life over and over again. Revolving around her own need and its satisfaction are her "solemn wonderings and hopes, arising in the dim world behind the present life, and murmuring, like faint music, of recognition in the far-off land between her brother and her mother: of some present consciousness in both *of her;* some love and commiseration *for her:* and some knowledge *of her* as she went her way upon the earth. It was *a soothing consolation to Florence* to give shelter to these *thoughts*" (23.269; emphasis added). In contrast, Cleopatra's more disinterested wonderings about "a previous state of existence"—her "curiosity to find out what it's all about, and what it means" (21.248)—reveal none of this solipsism. Of course, Mrs. Skewton has no problems of the heart like the outcast child, and she creates her own ghastly fictions of immortality on earth. Like them, Florence's fancy of heaven is a self-servicing mechanism through which she escapes the very real powers of death around her; and her faith is so completely woven into the whole fabric of her desire for "soothing consolation" that we cannot judge its truth. In a "current of . . . pensive fiction," she imagines how "her kind father . . . told her of their common hope and trust in God" (23.268–69); and after she meets Edith, she begins "to hope that she would learn, from her new and beautiful Mama, how to gain her father's love; and in her sleep that night, in her lost old home, her own Mama smiled radiantly upon the hope, and blessed it. Dreaming Florence!" (28.343). Is the maternal angel in heaven, too, only a "pensive fiction" arising out of need? Dickens does not say. All he knows is that "Dreaming Florence" has "ministering thoughts" (23.268), as other characters have rescuing texts.

Their unreality and incompleteness is exposed most tellingly in Florence's extraordinary nightmare of chapter 35, where her knowledge of evil and her suppressed anger at her father collide with her dream of heaven. In this dream she images the mission impossible Dickens has imposed upon her as salvific heroine, "seeking her father in wildernesses," up "fearful heights," and through symbols of the unconscious ("deep mines and caverns") when all at once she sees her archantagonist, who "had never loved her to the last," lying dead, and she falls "upon his cold breast, passionately weeping." This intolerable discovery is short-circuited, as are other dark discoveries in this novel, by divine intervention: "Then, a prospect opened, and a river flowed, and a plaintive voice she knew, cried, 'It is running on, Floy! It has never stopped! You are moving with it!'" (35.427). But the River of Life pulls *her* toward death—punishment for her sins?—as well as toward the beloved dead. Then up comes reality again in the form of Edith "upon the brink of a dark grave, and . . . pointing down" (not upward) to reveal "what!—another Edith lying at the bottom." That Florence has many such oppressive dreams shows us she does not live in an enchanted circle where "nothing harmed her." Just as Cuttle's allusive conflations of the sacred and the profane devalue his religious language to the worth of commonplace fictions, so the placing of Florence's religious intimations within ordinary psychological processes makes her faith seem nothing more than an imaginative projection against the pressures of evil that are also within her own heart—despite Dickens' other efforts, like Walter's, "to garner up her simple faith, inviolate" (19.222).

The fact that Florence's faith in "that higher Father who does not reject his children's love" (43.506) seems but an expression of her earthly need does not discredit her as a character; it adds sharply to her pathos. If it diminishes her stature as a Christian heroine, so does the actual content of her visions. Commenting on Florence's typical prayer to "GOD . . . to let one angel love her and remember her" (18.208), which echoes the narrator's "look upon us, angels of young children" in chapter 16, the *North British Review* saw ominously hanging over this scene "the darkness of a miserable pantheism, . . . a highly-coloured view of *heathen* feeling—of what man's griefs *might have been*, if the Gospel had not been sent into the world. . . . poetry and sentiment are not religion, and most miserable substitutes for it. . . . He, then, who writes as if the Gospel had never spoken of Him 'who is touched by the feeling of our infirmities' is no neutral, but an enemy cruising under a neutral flag."[54] To this Christian reader, Paul's pious deathbed evidently did not convert Florence any more than Dombey. The untutored girl, who never reads the Bible or refers to Christ, will never be a Harriet Carker reciting the history of the Master of all healing to the oppressed. Given Florence's centrality in the novel, her pantheistic romanticism could even quietly undermine the other pious heroine's specifically Christian

faith—just as in *Oliver Twist* we find one religious subtext rivaling another—
were it not for one important fact: Florence's natural religion leads her to
Christlike acts of forgiveness that embody in daily living the lessons of the
divine history Harriet reads. This embodiment, however, is as problematic as
Florence's visions. Dickens wholly endorses her idealized role as supernaturally
gifted mediatrix for her father; but in the later scene with her stepmother, he
places Florence's desire for reconciliation naturalistically as a simple, childlike
wish ignorant of the difficulties with which hearts are changed and of any supernatural transforming Power. In this later scene Dickens does not discredit Christian forgiveness, but he does suggest that in the real world, reconciliations after
such pain are more likely to resemble Edith's with Dombey at a distance, than
like Dombey's with Florence and the universe.

Florence's good offices as mediatrix must be seen against the novel's modestly
complicated backdrop of the forgiveness theme; it reaches from bogus acts of
forgiving (see 1.7; 46.536) to a variety of Christian models, each with its attendant qualifications. When Harriet Carker learns that a way has been opened for
her brother to repay the firm he has wronged, there is "Such a look of exulta-
tion" on her face as "on angels' faces, when the one repentant sinner enters
Heaven, among ninety-nine just men" (58.686; cf. Lk. 15:7); but the cost of this
restitution is her other brother's death. Through Harriet's ministrations Alice
forgives her mother on her own deathbed, echoing St. Paul's resurrection faith
("We shall all change, Mother, in our turn," 691; cf. 1 Cor. 15:51);[55] similarly,
Edith forgives her mother on the eve of the wedding (30.365) and again when
Mrs. Skewton is near death (41.490). These offers of forgiveness by Harriet and
Edith do them good; but neither does any good for their unrepentant mothers,
who are dead to virtuous example. The compassionate narrator holds out the
possibility of "remorse" even for Carker when a "transcendent" and "divinely
solemn" sun rises on his last moments, but in the remorseless plot this potential
victory is literally swallowed up by Monster Death (55.652–53).[56]

The simple Gospel paradigm tellingly runs into complications, however, in
Florence's late reunion with Edith, each "looking at the other over the black gulf
of the irrevocable past" (61.725). In a spirit of moral simplicity, Florence ea-
gerly tries to put words of forgiveness into Edith's mouth that Edith refuses to
say: "You wish well to him, and would have him happy. I am sure you would!"
she urges. "Oh! let me be able, if I have the occasion at some future time, to say
so?" Edith at length replies, "with her dark eyes gazing steadfastly before her"
into the night outside:

> "Tell him that if, in his own present, he can find any reason to compassionate my
> past, I sent word that I asked him to do so. Tell him that if, in his own present, he

can find any reason to think less bitterly of me, I asked him to do so. Tell him that, dead as we are to one another, never more to meet on this side of eternity, he knows there is one feeling in common between us now, that there never was before."

Her sternness seemed to yield, and there were tears in her dark eyes.

"I trust myself to that," she said, "for his better thoughts of me, and mine of him. When he loves his Florence most, he will hate me least. When he is most proud and happy in her and her children, he will be most repentant of his own part in the dark vision of our married life. At that time, I will be repentant too—let him know it then—and think that when I thought so much of all the causes that had made me what I was, I needed to have allowed more for the causes that had made him what he was. I will try, then, to forgive him his share of blame. Let him try to forgive me mine!" (728)

Although the language is stilted and repetitive, calling attention to its own constructedness, there are more nuances here in this carefully adjusted statement of "Relenting" (the chapter's title) than are dreamt of in Florence's philosophy—or are found in Edith's earlier idioms of melodramatic morality. When she yields nonetheless, it is under Florence's natural influence as the beloved child of two warring parents, not through her supernatural powers. Florence's presence has not transformed her stepmother's nature nor elicited the "unconditional surrender" that the unyielding religious design requires of her father.[57] Ironically, while Florence's natural intervention with Edith turns her from a melodramatic heroine into a more credible character, the daughter's divine mediation with her father turns him into a soggy cardboard regenerate—a victim of religious machinery Mr. Weller had called "some inwention for grown-up people being born again" (*PP* 22.379).

It is partly by contrast with Edith's case, but more generally because of the final loss of all Dombey's complexity that we see in his transformation the imposing of a fictive design. When Florence returns to him "Of all the world unchanged" and forgiving (59.705), the narrator signals to the reader that Dombey will be saved by drawing upon the traditional mirror emblem: instead of the "wasted likeness of himself" in his suicidal reflections, Dombey sees in the glass "his own [self]" again (704–5). Further, in Dombey's one Christian confession ("Oh my God, forgive me, for I need it very much!" 706), he illustrates Dickens' remark in a letter to David Dickson that "every man who seeks heaven must be born again, in good thoughts of his Maker" (10 May 1843, P 3:485). But the working out of Dombey's rebirth does not fully bear out even this "essentialized" Christian design nor the implications of the mirror emblem for new being. From Dombey's moment of reconciliation with Florence, he becomes a mere shadow of his former self, as though the Divine forgetting can mean only obliteration of personality. Ill and repentant, he feels "a sympathy with shad-ows. It was natural that he should," the narrator moralizes. "To him, life and the world were nothing else" (61.720; cf. a parody of this idea and echo of *Hamlet* 2.2.274–75 on p. 729). The otherworldly religion Dickens had criticized in chapter 37 as socially irresponsible he wholly endorses here, even as he physi-cally removes Dombey from the world of work in which this converted magnate might, like Carlyle's Captains of Industry, have done some good even in his declining years. Now all "the intricacy of his brain" (59.703) is washed away in his new birth to become merely simplemindedness. In this state, he believes only in the Florence who ends up "praying to him" (705); and, rather than being "born again" as a man, he merely becomes her (just as the impish Paul dis-solves upon merging with his Pilot on the other side). Although Florence has been credited as Dombey's destroyer,[58] of course it is not she who enfeebles him any more than Bill Sikes murders Nancy's more complex self. It is the author yielding up his characters to the fatal embrace of conventions unimaginatively employed and perhaps no longer found deeply credible, in order to rescue his story from its influx of worlds, worlds not easily renewed by the sacramental element.

4

IF THE HUMAN religious voices in *Dombey and Son* articulate no satisfying re-sponse to the novel's welter of worldly voices, what about the interminable des-cant of the waves throughout the story? Addressing his "Christian Reader" in *Past and Present*, Carlyle declares that even if the notions of heaven and hell "have got a fabulous or semi-fabulous character"—as they have in *Dombey*—"an *Infinite* has [not] vanished or can vanish from the Life of any Man. . . . Came it never, like the gleam of *preter*natural eternal Oceans, like the voice of old Eternities, far-sounding through thy heart of hearts?" (3.2.145). Carlyle's oceans speak a univocal Word to universal Man; at times Dickens seems to imply that "the dark and unknown sea that rolls round all the world" (1.9) carries but one message, the testimony of Cuttle's "almighty element" to a "world without end, evermore, amen." Throughout the soundscape of *Dombey and Son*, however, the paradoxical water symbolism speaks with many "voices" (the plural is always used)—of separation and reconciliation, of beginnings and endings, of the mysterious land on the other shore and the secrets sunk in the depths of the human heart.[59] The waves are also multivocal to the characters, each revealing in his or her interpretation of their mystery individual powers of

Frontispiece for *Dombey and Son*
(Hablot K. Browne)

mind, moral states, preoccupations of heart. David D. Marcus is right to argue that the sea does not represent a "permanent moral center in the midst of the flux of experience"; rather, Dickens' dramatizations of how people variously see it show us that its symbolism is the creation of their perceiving minds.[60]

At the beginning of chapter 41, "New Voices in the Waves," the narrator invokes the symbol through the device of personification:[61] "All is going on as it was wont. The waves are hoarse with repetition of their mystery; the dust lies piled upon the shore; the sea-birds soar and hover; the winds and clouds go forth upon their trackless flight; the white arms beckon, in the moonlight, to the invisible country far away" (483). As each human character confronts this non-human world of natural processes, some kind of humanization is always necessary. To Paul, the waves, first the voice of his child's consciousness of death, eventually speak of "another country opposite" where reunion with his dead mother beckons to his desire. As Florence sits pensively by the water, she hears Paul's "little story told again . . . and finds that all her life and hopes, and griefs, since . . . have a portion in the burden of the marvellous song" (483). Florence's harmonic interpretation of the "hoarse" sea as a "marvellous song" reveals one strategy by which she lives in an unresponsive world, as David Marcus has observed.[62] On other occasions, her sea thoughts register her preoccupation with death as the only way to the life she craves of peace and reconciliation (see 24:294–95). Such thoughts modulate to happier ones when she and Walter are married: here, the waves whisper "of love, eternal and illimitable, not bounded by the confines of this world, or by the end of time, but ranging still, beyond the sea, beyond the sky, to the invisible country far away!" (57.679). And in the birth of her son at sea, Florence hears a message (Shakespearean rather than biblical) of potential rebirth that teaches her to come back to her father (59.706).

Meanwhile—through all their various interpretations by Toots, Mr. Feeder, Mrs. Skewton, and Dombey himself—the waves are "hoarse with the repetition of their mystery; the dust lies piled upon the shore; the sea-birds soar and hover; and winds and clouds go forth upon their trackless flight. . . ." If there is a religious impulse emerging in *Dombey and Son*, it is less because Dickens is concerned with the challenges that pride and Mammonism present to rebirth than because he explores the possibilities of imputing higher meaning to the "chances and changes" of human life in an indifferent universe.[63] Dickens may wish that the waves preserve the old-fashioned language of transcendence; but in the context of his whole story they speak more certainly of the inhuman world they literally represent—the world of fate, circumstance, and natural process. Only by the human imputation of a Paul, a Florence, or a Dickens do the waves "answer" with the message of immortality the intractable word they also speak of mortality, piling up "dust" on the shore.

By calling attention to human modes of symbolization, the figure of the waves repeatedly reminds the reader that these mortal conditions include the laws of the human mind; that is, they also remind of the fated precariousness of the inner world, with its tensions between each person's irrevocable limit and his irrepressible urge to surpass those constraints in order to shape the "trackless ways" of the world outside the mind into patterns of meaning. Dickens' awareness of this imagination of control through the making of fiction, conditioned for each mortal by the givens of personality and circumstance, inevitably destabilizes *Dombey and Son*'s presentation of his characters' religious impulses, their ideas about the Transcendent, and their human uses of biblical texts. Yet although Dickens is becoming more aware that religion, if not God, is a human creation, he presents its fictions like some others as at once unstable and necessary—whether Cuttle's quotations, Paul's visions, Florence's dreamy faith, the narrator's apocalyptic rhetoric, or Dickens' moral parables that work out "the fulness of the time and the design," *his* design (62.731). Otherwise the world would be what the nonreligious Feenix declares it, "the most unintelligible thing within a man's experience" (61.726). As Dickens continues to explore the workings of human consciousness in his later fiction, his awareness of moral problems arising from the subjectivity of all human interpretation remains in tension with his persisting desire as moral parabler for the legible, objectified design. That tension is a source of specifically literary complexity in these novels because of the centrifugal pressures it exerts on the Dickens "world," multiplying styles and generating divergent narrative lines—even as in this book Florence and Paul inhabit several different religious and nonreligious stories, each with its own proper language. In the darkest novels, *Bleak House* and *Little Dorrit*, where this tension becomes acute, Dickens is drawn to those parts of the Bible that express hermeneutic uncertainty of the sort he is already suspecting in 1846–48 in all religious expressions—even though he continues to use them, down to his reprise of *Dombey*'s death and rebirth motifs in *Our Mutual Friend*.

Among the religious voices sounding in *Dombey and Son*, there is much that is merely conventional, unselfcritical, diminished, and contradictory; these traditional voices fail to equal the challenging words they anticipate in the godless babble of the present time, or for that matter the novelist's own realistic language of humanist exploration. Julian Moynahan is finally right to argue that this novel's vision is "neither genuinely religious . . . nor genuinely secular."[64] Yet something more commands attention here than a confused creed or a sentimental poetry trying to mask its failures of belief. Speaking of the limits of Toots' intelligence, the narrator observes that "Ideas, like ghosts (according to the common notion of ghosts), must be spoken to a little before they will explain themselves; and Toots had long left off asking any questions of his own mind" (12.140). Although the Dickens of *Dombey and Son* might like to preserve his faith inviolate, an unquestioned certainty like the Eternal Facts of Carlyle's universe, in this book the novelist in transition writing about change has begun to ask questions of that faith and the elusive human mind which creates it. In the later fictions, it is chiefly in such dialogues of the writer with himself—Dickens' internal heteroglossia—that his interest as a "religious" novelist resides.

4

Biblical Reading
in the Later Dickens:
The Book of Job
According to *Bleak House*

CONSECRATED GROUND
(Hablot K. Browne)

"Hope, Joy, Youth, Peace, Rest, Life, Dust, Ashes, Waste, Want, Ruin, Despair, Madness, Death, Cunning, Folly, Words, Wigs, Rags, Sheepskin, Plunder, Precedent, Jargon, Gammon, and Spinach. That's the whole collection . . . all cooped up together, by my noble and learned brother."
"This is a bitter wind!" muttered my Guardian.

T HE EAST WIND in *Bleak House* has a traditional as well as a topical location:[1] it blows from the Book of Job, the story of "the greatest of all the men of the east" who is at once a victim of the "great wind from the wilderness" (Job 1:3, 19) that made his household bleak[2] and a source of his own desolation, "fill[ing] his belly with the east wind" (15:2) in the futility of his complaint. Grounded in historical anguish, in Israel's experience of exile, the Book of Job is even more important for *Bleak House* than the mythic Genesis and Apocalypse texts most often identified with this historically topical and autobiographical novel.[3] Providing a matrix of resonant images and themes, a model of literary strategies, and a resource for formal literary allusions, the Book of Job nourishes the "poetic and prophetic Genesis"[4] of a new phase in Dickens' writing. And just as this Old Testament book engages critically with other parts of biblical tradition, so it establishes in *Bleak House* the mature reflective context in which the mythic Bible stories less problematic in Dickens' earlier books (as well as other Scripture texts) are now implicitly subjected to reinterpretation—newly, on biblical and not only secular grounds.

For many readers, of course, such scripturally sponsored reinterpretations of received religious ideas need not be ultimately disconcerting: on this reading, *Bleak House* with its Joban subtext provokes readers to reconsider conventions of order they have inherited, while encapsulating this questioning in a conventional model of doubt and faith (with its familiar language and finally triumphant structure) which Dickens' audience could understand and accept. How far this reading applies to Esther Summerson's "Progress" I shall be considering. Yet when this biblical book is seen as itself unstable—structurally divided, stylistically protean, crisis-ridden—Dickens' Joban subtext cannot be expected to provide a reassuring design resolving the discords of *Bleak House*. Rather, in my reading of both the Bible and Dickens' text—also stylistically multivoiced, discontinuous, riddling—Job's internal debates brought into this Victorian novel help to generate its unresolved dialogical tensions between religious and irreligious points of view. Caught up in that dialogue, the novel's many other scriptural allusions cannot function either as authoritative texts, however much these are wanted; but they gain from their engagement with other voices a newly authentic resonance in Dickens' fiction. Ironically, then, his most radically skeptical and hermeneutically uncertain novel turns out to be his most richly biblical, not just in sheer numbers of Scripture allusions but in the quality of his imaginative engagement with Old and New Testament tradition. For these reasons, *Bleak House* becomes a particularly interesting locus for studying the instabilities of scriptural interpretation for author and reader in the elaborated works of Dickens' maturity.

The aim of exploring this dense, enigmatic text to locate some of the dialogical tensions in which Dickens' Scripture becomes entangled poses peculiar problems of method. To consider fairly the affirmations and questionings in the novelistic discourse of *Bleak House* would require a much larger discussion than can be mounted here; and not all the important biblical allusions can be treated. To make the reading both representative and directed, this chapter will therefore take a somewhat different form than previous chapters. After discussing the general importance of the Book of Job for the Victorians and for *Bleak House*, in order to establish its cultural context and make up for critical neglect of this pervasive Joban material, I will give extended close readings of two key chapters (1 and 32) in which allusions, echoes, and underpatterns from Job are typically engaged in the serious play of viewpoints that we find in the anonymous narrator's part of the novel. An inescapable dimension of that interplay is Dickens' use of various stylistic and narrative conventions to mediate his biblical allusions (such as parody, satire, gothic), mediations present throughout his writing but given special attention in this chapter. Turning then to Esther's narrative, with its analogues to the Book of Esther and its New Testament language, I will trace the ways incursions of the Joban into her discourse create fundamental tensions—"battles of biblical books"—that link her account with the darker narrator's story. Following a common line of argument about *Bleak House*'s double narration, Peter K. Garrett has observed that the novel "articulates radically different and irreconcilable visions of the world, presenting precisely what Bakhtin describes, a dialogical opposition of 'independent and unmerged voices and consciousnesses.'"[5] But Esther's narrative is not simply "radically different." It bears signs of affinity to the other teller's account and records her induction into his world. Thus the dialogical interplay of voices is also present within her story, which exhibits (and tries to conceal) an internal heteroglossia that destabilizes even the religious heroine's biblical texts. However carefully Dickens tries to separate his religious and skeptical voices, these two narrators "from opposite sides of great gulfs, have, nevertheless, been very curiously brought together" (16.197) to form *Bleak House* out of common nineteenth-century experiences. For these experiences many Victorians found the Book of Job a compelling interpretive model.

1

MUCH READ AND often quoted in the nineteenth century, the Book of Job provided a resonant paradigm of loss and gain for Dickens as for other Victorian writers. In his "Hero as Prophet" lecture, Thomas Carlyle hailed the book's paradigmatic quality when he praised its "Sublime sorrow, sublime reconciliation; oldest choral melody as of the heart of mankind" (*H* 49). Tennyson called it "the greatest poem of ancient and modern times."[6] The book spoke to a wide range of Victorians seeking to understand the meaning of suffering: meditating on Job 10:2 ("Show me wherefore thou contendest with me"), the Baptist preacher Charles Haddon Spurgeon counseled that "Afflictions are often the black foils in which God doth set the jewels of His children's graces, to make them shine the better. . . . *real growth* in grace is the result of sanctified trials"—a common interpretation Esther Summerson uses when she writes, in her last efforts at theodicy, "The sorrow that has been in [Ada's] face . . . seems to have purified even its innocent expression, and to have given it a diviner quality" (67.769).[7] From his different theological camp, James Anthony Froude could echo Spurgeon's meaning in an 1853 essay: rising into the "high faith" of self-sacrifice, Job is seen "treading his temptations under his feet, and finding in them a ladder on which his spirit rises."[8]

But the peculiar relevance of the Book of Job for Victorian readers had to do not only with its assertions of faith, but more specifically with the problematic context for those assertions. In an 1859 essay, Ernest Renan argued that Job was written out of an "incurable trouble" which afflicted defenders of traditional theology when the Semitic nomads came into contact with profane civilizations; in this cultural setting, when nothing had become more obvious than the happiness of men without God and the suffering of the righteous, "the old patriarchal theory, based exclusively upon the promises of the terrestrial life, became insufficient."[9] Froude likewise read the book as the product of a period of religious transition, recording "the first fierce collision of the new fact with the formula which will not stretch to cover it," and he observed a similar cultural disjunction in the mid-nineteenth century: "what Job saw as exceptions" to the formula of punishment and reward in this world "we see round us everywhere. It was true then, it is infinitely more true now, that what is called virtue in the common sense of the word, still more that nobleness, godliness, or heroism of character in any form whatsoever, have nothing to do with this or that man's prosperity, or even happiness." Yet out of such a "fierce collision" of Hebrew old clothes and new facts came a biblical poem that, Froude ventured, may "one day . . . be seen towering up alone, far away above all the poetry of the world." In this essay Froude praised a Job "given over into Satan's hand to be tempted" who, "though he shakes, . . . does not fall." It is not the author's piety alone, however, but the passion of his faithful querying that Froude so evidently admired: "In the writer of the Book of Job there is an awful moral earnestness before which we bend as in the presence of a superior being. The orthodoxy against which he contended is not set aside or denied; he sees what truth is in it; only he sees more than it, and over it, and through it."[10]

This faithful challenge to traditional authority by new "seeing" of experience is reflected in the literary strategies of the Book of Job and, as I shall argue, of *Bleak House*. Although considered one composition, the biblical book is divided into two literary modes. Its prologue (chapters 1–2) and epilogue (42:7–17) form a prose fairytale that embodies a doctrine of poetic justice: the patient, righteous sufferer who has been made poor is restored to riches; Job's end is greater than his beginning. The biblical scholar Paul Scherer calls this frame-story a "folk tale at the crossroads," however, for the author shows his reader that this "time-worn story just isn't so, as you have heard it all your life" by inserting thirty-nine poetic chapters between prologue and epilogue that expose perplexities of suffering and belief from the perspective of wide human experience.[11] Samuel Terrien nicely observes that Job's reader, therefore, has "the impression of two literary hands—indeed, two literary worlds" in the text: "The prose narrative suggests to our imagination the haunting strains of the nursery tale, with its villain and its happy ending, whereas the poetic discussion has the ring of grim history." The first hand "writes about somebody else" with the craft of a superb storyteller, while the second "writes about himself" in "the voice of introspective authenticity."[12] Implicit in this sequentially multiperspectival book is the notion of corrective structure, with its sense that "the possibilities of experience are always vaster than our efforts to account for them";[13] in working through its sequences of discourse, the reader must make and remake his sense of the text, reconstruing the meaning of Job's plight as the debates multiply views of it, down to his final discovery of his "deliverance from his own story" in his restitution.[14] If the Book of Job is a paradigm of loss and gain, then, it is not simply the U-shaped pattern Northrop Frye calls romance, for the whole is more than its memorable folktale frame; its less shapely literary strategy is first to call its own initial conventional structure into question, and then through the subsequent reconstructions of the middle to deepen the sense of historical loss and human complexity while making that much more dramatic, even melodramatic, the book's final vision of gain.

Bleak House recapitulates the general movement of Job from curse to blessing in that its much-tried heroine of faith, who also "shakes [but] does not fall," confirms this providential design. But within this pattern, East Wind, plague, desolated habitations, enigmatic persecutions, interminable debates, nightmare, suicide, and a grim poetry of mud, dung, and darkness—the motifs of the Joban middle before folktale reasserts the pattern of fulfilled desire—embody in both of Dickens' narratives the author's "incurable trouble," his faithful querying of the traditional wisdom in which his heroine strives to believe. From the opening pages of *Bleak House* (discussed below), all are "born unto trouble" (Job 5:7), like Skimpole "born in the same scrape . . . 'a son in difficulties'" (6.73). Evil and innocent alike are "destroyed from morning to evening: they perish for ever without any regarding it. . . . they die, even without wisdom" (Job 4:20–21), an observation Jo also makes—"They dies everywheres. . . . in their lodgings . . . down in Tom-all-Alone's in heaps. They dies more than they lives, according to what *I* see" (31.383). This is the "modern theology" Ruskin lamented in *Bleak House:* the dramatized idea that even by "the will of Providence," "the appointed destiny of a large average of our population is to die like rats in a drain."[15]

The problematic qualities of *Bleak House* are not only, however, a matter of such thematically resonant imagery and plot detail but, more fundamentally, of literary techniques shared with the Joban author that prevent any reading of the novel as a univocal text. Just as the Book of Job is traditionally seen as an interpretive act, "An exposition of the book of Providence,"[16] so *Bleak House* seems to be Dickens' attempt to write his own "book of Providence" that would account for the panoramic suffering which piles up, like Job's dung-heap and London mud, in the opening paragraphs.[17] But neither the author of Job nor Dickens can finally compose theodicy, the rational accounting of God's ways to men that Summerson attempts most pointedly in "The Close of Esther's Narrative."[18] Adopting Joban modes of interpretation, Dickens can but multiply readings of the human condition, only one of which is Esther's providential "Progress"—demonstrating the truth of Froude's dictum that "the facts of moral experience do not teach their own meaning, but submit to many readings according to the power of the eye which we bring with us."[19]

Dickens' is ever a mobile eye; what particularly solicit our attention here are the ways his specific literary strategies of multiplying readings are analogous to those Job's author uses to make his book faithful to the vagaries of history and to the range of tonalities he sounds in the human spirit. To summarize: First, in the construction of his narrative Dickens repeatedly disrupts and revises conventions (including the Job story itself), challenging formula by his vision of complicating facts. Second, he presents his story primarily through two viewpoints ("two literary hands"), which are multiplied and qualified by a range of lesser Joban characterizations echoing aspects of Esther and the anonymous narrator. Third, he uses debate as motif and device to present many attitudes toward the enigma of suffering. Most important for the readings to follow of chapters 1 and 32, Dickens engages in these three related strategies with a disconcerting stylistic virtuosity that is also characteristic of the Joban author. These commonalities of technique might be merely coincidental, were it not for the many allusions to the Book of Job that appear in *Bleak House,* indicating how deeply Dickens has entered into the preoccupations and vision of this biblical book, without wholeheartedly adopting its final faith. To recall Froude on Job, implicit in the whole approach Dickens takes is his urgent questioning of the forms of authority in his culture at a latter day of "collision" when religion, as Carlyle declared in *Sartor Resartus,* and the Bible itself, had "been smote at . . . needfully and needlessly; till now it is quite rent into shreds."

First, *Bleak House* dramatizes many disjunctions between justifying traditional formulas and the facts of actual living and dying in the nineteenth century. The revision of formula proceeds apace on many smaller occasions in the narrative, but on the large scale, we can see it in the way the overarching design of *Bleak House* recapitulates in vestigial form the Book of Job's self-corrective structure. Dickens opens with a parodic Chancery version of Job's courtroom scene between God and Satan, and he closes the novel with a folktalelike abundance of reward for Esther Summerson's faithful life (if not the vision of God vouchsafed to Job); thus, the folktale frame of Job begins and ends Dickens' book, although it has already been ironically reconstrued in his first chapter and is not quite completed in the last. But in chapter 3, Dickens reopens the narrative from a different point of view, as does the biblical author in his third chapter, where Job's anathema pronounced against an innocent's birth day is like the curse against Esther Summerson's; she is persecuted by the forces of Victorian legalism as Job is by Satan and the legalistic comforters with God's consent. And thereafter throughout the novel, not only folktale but all sorts of other conventional patterns (such as Genesis and Apocalypse myths, formulas of consolation, proverbs, received accounts of the social order, inherited literary modes) are disrupted and questioned on many occasions as new facts arise in incident, lament, and debate. It is not necessary to trace these processes of disruption through the novel; as the following readings of characteristic strategies in chapters 1 and 32 will show, it is as though Dickens saw "more than" and "through" the conventions of order he also needed in his equivocal inquest into divine, social, and poetic justice.

This penetrative and expansive seeing proceeds not only as a matter of narrative structure, but also through Dickens' experiments in multiple points of view. Here the division of Job into its prose and poetry sections, its "two literary worlds," is relevant although not in any simple equation to Dickens' two narrators. The dual impulses Samuel Terrien detects in Job invade *both* sections of Dickens' novel: the "grim history" that dominates the impersonal narrative becomes part of what Esther must learn to tell, even as she discovers some of the dangers of placing "nursery tale" frames around her experience. On the other hand, Dickens' distanced storyteller writing "about somebody else" also sounds the note of "introspective authenticity," not directly like Esther but indirectly through recurrent settings and images that evoke the biblical experience of the depths. While this narrator sometimes adopts the cynical view of human possibilities characteristic of the Adversary in Job's folktale prologue, a satanic figure who walks "to and fro in the earth" to spy out men's wrongdoings (Job 1:7), the nameless teller is also the bitter elegist of human losses in the middle of Job's book—impatient, rebellious, unconsoled.

The inherent instability of the dual narration is increased not only by the many voices of the anonymous persona but also by Dickens' characterization of Esther Summerson, whose account reflects some of Job's shifting points of view, as I shall show, making it harder to take her quite as the saintly Christian she is often misunderstood to be. Dickens, although no orthodox typologist, uses what George P. Landow calls a "privileged . . . divinely instituted signifying system" to associate his heroine with Job the patient and with Queen Esther as types of Christ and his Church;[20] but the divinely ordered world his typology evokes is called into question by Summerson's further identification with Job the rebel. No more than he, is she purely the hero of faith who can say with absolute conviction, "the Lord gave, and the Lord hath taken away; blessed be the name of the Lord" (Job 1:21), even though Esther tries repeatedly to affirm a faithful acceptance of her losses. As I will argue, for most of her narrative she is "full of confusion" (Job 10:15) in seeming "guilty and yet innocent" (3.20) like the afflicted but righteous Job.

The shifting attitudes of Esther and the nameless narrator are echoed and modified by lesser Joban characterizations that turn up in both narratives. The delusions of the apocalyptically expectant Miss Flite, a patient Job whose whole family has been wiped out, implicitly modify our opinion of Esther's hope for reunion with Woodcourt in heaven. (The list of Flite's birds in my epigraph also follows the order of events in Job.) The persecuted, bankrupt Mr. Jellyby, whom Esther likes "very much" (50.603) when he sits with his head against the wall like mute Job on his dung-heap—opening his mouth, shaking his head, groaning again (see 30.373–77)—intensifies, and with black humor parodies, Esther's own "Sad patience, too near neighbor to despair."[21] Reflecting the dangers of the nameless narrator's anger when it becomes all-consuming are Caddy Jellyby and, more seriously, the rebellious Gridley. He cries out to the court and is not heard (Job 30:20), is a "standing jok[e]" like Job mocked (15.192; cf. Job 21:3), will accuse his persecutors "before the great eternal bar!" (193), and threatens to "give up the ghost" if he must remain silent (see Job 13:19): yet he dies anyway, raging against his fate. Richard Carstone illustrates the folly of being "impatient" (60.722) with Providence (Jarndyce) misread as nemesis. In Richard, Gridley, Caddy, and Mr. Jellyby, the suicidal longings of Job (Jo's "Wishermaydie," 46.557) emerge to express the subversive impulses Esther quickly represses, only to effect another form of death in life.[22] Skimpole, Sir Leicester Dedlock, Jobling, and Snagsby parody Joban attitudes. These examples of Dickens' many variations on the essential types of Job the patient and Job the rebel not only illustrate the scope of the disaster, echoed by uncounted anonymous sufferers, but provide a spectrum of attitudes toward human loss "according to the power of the eye" in them. So do Dickens' exemplars of false comforting; and here, Jo, Esther, and the brickmakers provide test cases in Dickens' trial of certain conventions of his readers, Victorian modes of consolation.

"Driven to and fro" (Job 13:25), hunted and witnessed against (10:17), terrified by recurring nightmares (7:14) of mysterious ladies and of his life, "dwell-[ing] in desolate cities, and in houses which no man inhabiteth, which are ready to become heaps" (15:28), Jo is a victim who can make "nothink" of his condition; his "words," like his abbreviated Joban name, "are swallowed up" (Job 6:3). The suspicion of a loving friend somewhere (Nemo, the ur-Job behind them all and truly "a father to the poor," 29:16) hovers over Jo's disjointed discourse like a guardian angel, just as his biblical counterpart is haunted by the image of a loving God (see 7:21): but so often in *Bleak House* that compassionate being is absent, dead, or cannot be named. Like Job, Jo voices his belief that the wicked must be punished, but equally he protests his innocence and truthfulness—thus forcing upon our attention the inadequacy of the retribution theory to explain why he and Nemo suffer the calamities of the wicked: "His remembrance shall perish from the earth, and he shall have no name in the street. He shall be driven from light into darkness, and chased out of the world. He shall neither have son nor nephew . . . nor any remaining in his dwellings. They that come after him shall be astonied at his day" (Job 18:17–20; see also illustration on chapter title page). Yet retribution theology is the kind of "comfort" Reverend Chadband offers in his discourse on Jo's troubles as the natural result of his heathen condition, "the seal of indifference and perdition being set upon his eyelids" (25.322; cf. Job 16:16, "on my eyelids is the shadow of death").[23] While ironically it is Chadband who asks the key Job question of this truncated human specimen—Why is he without anything? (see 320)—he "overwhelm[s] the fatherless" (6:27) with his doctrine of deserved calamity, like the militant religionists in Job's book. So does Aunt Barbary, falsely comforting the young Esther with the wisdom teaching of her time that "Submission, self-denial, diligent work" (3.19) is the way of salvation. Like one of Job's comforters whom Froude calls a "Calvinist of the old world,"[24] Barbary preaches the doctrine that "filthy is man, which drinketh iniquity like water" (Job 15:16); she, too, worships what Martin Buber terms the "great ideological idol"[25] that repays duty and infidelity according to a strict moral calculus, without provision for the forgiveness in which Dickens strove to believe. Completing this satirical triad is the expert in charity, Mrs. Pardiggle: monotonous and inflexible like her biblical types, come to "poll-pry and question according to custom" (8.99), she overwhelms the childless brickmakers with the nongospel that their losses are for their own good—a doctrine they refute in the despairing Joban manner. Social and economic facts challenge the Pardiggle formulas—as well as the cultural fact that forcing Bible study upon the poor without offering practical help is a form of "rapacious benevolence" (93). Given his sensitivity to these facts, the nondogmatic Dickens might well have appreciated the Book of Job as "the grandest lesson that has been given to intemperate dogmatism," in Ernest Renan's words, "and to the pretensions of the superficial mind which has become imbued with theology."[26] This part of the Joban subtext gives precedent for Dickens' unequivocal condemnation of his religious hypocrites: these "physicians of no value" are all "forgers of lies" (Job 13:4).

Throughout *Bleak House*, a third Joban strategy by which truth is pursued through many viewpoints and formulas are overturned or made provisional is the setting of such sufferers and comforters as these in the midst of debate; debate in *Bleak House*, moreover, is neither communication nor dialectic, as the counter-catechizing of Mrs. Pardiggle by the contentious brickmaker illustrates. The refutation of others' doctrines is compounded in the Book of Job by his colloquies with himself and his complaints directed against a silent God. These poems are filled with forensic imagery; in the biblical psalm of lament, the defendant must establish his innocence against his enemies, adversaries in court.[27] Like a Chancery suit, the cycles of debate in Job double back on themselves and "multipl[y] words without knowledge" (35:16); the successive speakers harangue in monologue rather than forward truth through dialogue; and "From one end of the poem to the other," as Renan observed, "the question in dispute is not advanced a single step."[28] Indeed, as my students will testify, this biblical book "in course of time, become[s] so complicated, that no man alive knows what it means" (1.7), like the Jarndyce suit. What is thematically important for *Bleak House* is that the middle of the Book of Job is one long inconclusive contention about authorities: specifically, the wisdom of the past, Holy Scripture, dreams and visions, concrete experience, documents, spoken testimony, language itself—the familiar objects of *Bleak House*'s questioning. The biblical speakers' words are a texture of revisions, cross-references, and allusions; they quote, misquote, reverse one another's formulations, making a windy wilderness of "Gammon," Flite's Anglo-Saxon word related to the commonplace, "You are making game of me."[29] "Mock on," Job defies his comforters (21:3), but he also mocks and reverses himself, exposes the inadequacies of Scripture (see Job 7:17–18 on Ps. 8:4), and anxiously improvises his position in a kind of theological no-man's-land to which his very honesty has exiled him.

It is finally this anxious improvisation, this perpetual invention and reinterpretation of phrase and theory, that most of all multiplies readings of the human condition in Job and in *Bleak House*. The biblical writer has often been praised for his stylistic virtuosity, running "the whole gamut of tones";[30] his hero wrestles most immediately not with the silent God but with his own and others' language. By voicing many alternate versions of his story, he may seem dextrously to escape final strangulation in any one account; but it is also his peculiar plight to keep on talking this intellectually provisional and emotionally mercurial poetry without relief and without clarification, stopping only when the comforters interrupt him and God's whirlwind of questions finally swallows him up.

Chiefly through his impersonal narrator, Dickens approximates this stylistic flexibility by his control of poetic, fantastic, reportorial, satirical, parodic, prophetic, and other modes—all adopted by what W. J. Harvey has called a "vast, collective choric voice brilliantly mimicking the varied life it describes."[31] Each style taken up in chapter 1, like the various narrative modes to be discussed in chapter 32, implies a different reading of human facts and qualifies the reader's acceptance of the other interpretive modes, one displacing the next. Even in Esther's narrative, to which I will return in the last section of this chapter, stylistic shifts are a strategic means of survival to keep the speaker from being subdued to what she works in, succumbing to the troubling realities she knows;[32] attending to her anxious dialogues of the mind with itself, her ambivalent evaluations of others, her blindnesses, self-deceptions, genuine malaise of unknowing, and flashes of faith and hope, the reader is troubled to determine the meanings of her story—to decide where, for example, her covering a multitude of sins by charity ends and evasion by scriptural quotation begins. One has the impression that, like the great nineteenth-century writers Wolfgang Iser describes, Esther makes her providential account "with a view not to interpreting the meaning of the events but to gaining a position outside them—to regarding them, as it were, from a distance. The commentaries, then, strike one as mere hypotheses, and they seem to imply other possibilities of evaluation than those that arise directly from the events described."[33]

This verbal maneuvering for an account that is definitive and saving lies at the heart of *Bleak House*'s hermeneutic instabilities: from its stylistically indecisive first chapter, a primary challenge to the reader will be how to interpret not the events but the many voices guiding his reading of those events—a continuous challenge raising over and over again, in quieter and more theatrical ways, the novel's crisis of authority that also moves Job's pleas to hear the one unequivocal Word of his God. In drawing his reader from the start into the vicissitudes of interpretation and the insufficiency of language, Dickens enters most deeply into the dark spirit of the writer who produced this philosophical poem; and as we shall see, the novelist's handling of biblical material, even of the Joban subtext, partakes of its dubieties. If he is thereby challenging his Victorian audience to reformulate the "ancient wisdom" for the present time in these "mean days that have no sacred word," as Carlyle wrote, *Bleak House* never definitively establishes the new Mythus so much wanted to reconcile the discontinuities that, even through his biblical allusions, Dickens has exposed.

2

BLEAK HOUSE opens on an existential scene more deeply piled with error than "mountains of costly nonsense" from Chancery suits, or the national "dung-mountains" Carlyle had recently attacked in his 1850 "Downing Street" pamphlet (*LDP* 107). Biblical echoes and references in this opening set Dickens' novel into an eternal perspective that includes but extends beyond social analysis; an antigenesis regressing in time, the first paragraph moves backward from flood to fall to creation ("waters . . . but newly retired from the face of the earth," the "general infection of ill-temper," "if the day ever broke," 1.5). From such allusions, critics have assumed that the novel is set in the "mythic times . . . of Genesis."[34] But civilization has grown much older. The state of things opening *Bleak House* belongs to Genesis mythology as seen from the later viewpoint of the Book of Job, with its discussions and revisions of this and other material in the earlier books of the Old Testament.[35] To adapt an observation from Iser, the Genesis archetype may be familiar, yet in this textual location it "seems different, for its component parts have been altered, its frame of reference has changed, its validity has, to a degree, been negated"[36] in the presence of the Joban subtext so well suited to the Victorian times of Dickens' newspaperlike facts. As one set of allusions is thus mediated, and defamiliarized, by another, the effects are to place in question the biblical creation story (and the nineteenth-century scientific revision of it to which the narrator refers), as well as to *remind* us that Father Noah is absent from this scene: there is no righteous survivor whom "God remembered" (Gen. 8:1) and whose name means "to console";[37] only "chance people" happen to have survived, stranded on bridges in choking fog (5). Nor without sun can there be any rainbow, the sign that history is embraced in God's purpose and that the genealogies will continue: only the haggard haloes of gas lamps and an entire populace, the just and unjust "indistinguishable" in suffering, better not born.

But if Noah is not here, the other "righteous" one associated with him in Ezekiel 14:14, whose name means "to mourn"[38]—alas, he is here, although indistinguishable as a human figure, his state of mind blended with the elements, his dung-heap the city mud. As cloud and darkness envelop the opening scene, Job's curse of his day descends upon all England: "Let the day perish wherein I was born, and the night in which it was said, There is a man child conceived. Let that day be darkness; let not God regard it from above, neither let the light shine upon it. Let darkness and the shadow of death stain it; let a cloud dwell upon it; let the blackness of the day terrify it . . . let no joyful voice come therein" (Job 3:3–5, 7). Like foul cosmic weather, the Joban mystery of suffering in *Bleak House* lies in its inexplicable givenness from the beginning. Set in Job's time and space, the novel is in William Axton's words "suspended between the Deluge and Armageddon,"[39] but with the disappointment of a flood that failed to cleanse the earth, and expectations that are mere parody of human wishes—stranding the reader like Job between his folktale prologue and epilogue, awaiting the "incomprehensible judgment" (7). *Bleak House* is generated from such poetry; it is the first of Dickens' midcareer, midlife novels set explicitly "in the middest," and its yearning for beginnings and for ends are the hopes and fears of this inbetween time.[40]

Even as Dickens' evocative weather reporter is drawing into his prose some of

the Joban poetry his contemporaries found so moving, already in the first paragraph another narrative voice is subverting these yearnings for elegiac expression. A fantasist playfully uplifting the ends of sagging sentences with imaginative speculations entertains us with the possibility that we might escape the
sticking elements. His performances, too, draw upon the Joban subtext: the
Bible's "brother to dragons" (Job 30:29) is overwhelmed by meeting the
Leviathan, "king over all the children of pride," in God's whirlwind speech
(41:34), but Dickens' imaginist makes it a pet to "play with" (41:5) by mate-
rializing a Megalosaurus on Holborn Hill;[41] deftly, too, he metamorphoses the
Job who "went mourning without the sun" (30:28) into sootflakes "gone into
mourning . . . for the death of the sun" (5). Anticipating the comic parodist
soon to appear, he makes even *de profundis* into low comedy with all the jostling
and losing of footholds, groping and floundering among the sons of men.

By the fourth paragraph, the new voice of an editorialist-prophet has emerged
to take us out of the cosmic fog and into the realm of certain moral judgments
about the causes of affliction. With "the raw afternoon is rawest, the dense fog is
densest," we begin to descend into a different kind of extremity; the underlying
elegiac poetry becomes a litany of prophetic curses for England, Job's anathema
directed outward to social conditions, with cadences like the "woes" of the
prophet Habakkuk:

> Well may the court be dim, with wasting candles here and there;
> Well may the fog hang heavy in it, as if it would never get out;
> Well may the stained glass windows lose their colour and admit no light of day
>   into the place.
>
> (6; cf. Hab. 2:6, 9, 12)

The frame of reference for "let that day be darkness" has changed. With the
narrator's first full-blown editorial phrase—"Chancery, most pestilent of hoary
sinners . . . in the sight of heaven and earth"—we have shifted to another part
of the Joban subtext, the prophetic message of the comforters threatening wickedness with calamity, and to the related formulas of Old Testament prophets
("Sword, famine, pestilence") for the scourges of God upon idolatrous Israel.
The presence of a "pestilent" institution in the heart of England is a judgment
against a whole society that tolerates these "leaden-headed old obstruction[s],"
like idols, "in [its] sight" (5–6). The message turns apocalyptic: "pestilence"
will come with the Antichrist, the "beginning of sorrows," the darkening of the
sun (see Matt. 24:7–8, 29 and Luke 21:11ff).

At the end of paragraph 6, the prophet launches his attack on the source of
evil: "This is the Court of Chancery; which has its decaying houses and its

blighted lands in every shire; . . . which gives to monied might the means abundantly of wearing out the right; which so exhausts finances, patience, courage, hope; so overthrows the brain and breaks the heart" (6–7). Here "Jarndyce and Jarndyce has stretched forth its unwholesome hand to spoil and corrupt" many (8), as Satan challenges God to do in Job 1:11 ("put forth thine hand now, and touch all that he hath, and he will curse thee to thy face").[42] But Dickens has significantly altered his Joban subtext for his present editorial purposes. In the Bible all that Job has and is has been "blighted" with God's leave—God's is the might which "destroyest the hope of man" (14:19); in contrast, in this phase of Dickens' first chapter, the terrors of God have become the blight of the powerful false god, the Law, with the Lord High Chancellor as antichrist. We are no longer in a "chancery" world of accidental living and dying "without any regarding it" but in the Court, where a watchful human judge conducts his fellow countrymen to the bar. With the simple moral coordinates of the prophet (rich/poor, mighty/weak, wicked/virtuous), the double-barreled clauses and phrases, the prose like an editorial machine rumbles on to its final outburst that flings his antagonists into Dante's hell, counseling patience with fiery impatience: "Suffer any wrong that can be done you, rather than come here!" (7).

This chapter had opened with a darker vision, and against such awareness no legal reforms can save: so it is swallowed up in the righteous ire of the Victorian prophet, licensed by another part of the biblical subtext. As pain that had been alluded to obliquely becomes pain firmly contained by the overbearing biblical insistences of the editorial voice, and the inward gnawing of damp November cold turns its violence outward, we observe the most characteristic movement of the anonymous narrator in *Bleak House:* the forcible suppression of awareness of one kind of desolation by stylistic shifts that compel the reader's attention to other, more legible kinds of violence. Still, this voice insists that the "hoary sinne[r]" is white with years of evildoing unregarded by "heaven"; the "leaden-headed old obstruction" sounds immovable despite efforts of rhetorical levitation; and the present tense verbs imply a lack of expectation that the end will come as in the days of Noah (see Matt. 24:37–39). Despite the confidence of his apocalyptic warnings, therefore, this reiterative prophet only underscores the "perennially hopeless" (8) state of England, and we return, if we follow these implications of style, back to the frustration of Job's lament: "Behold, I cry out of wrong, but I am not heard: I cry aloud, but there is no judgment" (19:7).

Soon enough this lament finds voice in the court. In the next paragraph, the Man from Shropshire "complain[s] in the bitterness of [his] soul" (Job 7:11) to the godlike figures at the bench, but his "voice of sonorous complaint" (7) is unregarded and "there is no judgment" (see also Job 30:20). The Book of Job contains warnings against the vehemence of the victim; Job's judges find his rebellious words "violent" in the way Old Testament prophets frequently used the word—he violates divine rights.[43] Job "addeth rebell on unto his sin," Elihu admonishes, "he clappeth his hands among us, and multiplieth his words against God" (34:37). In *Bleak House* the failure of Gridley's vehement prophetic rhetoric leads to his death, an ambiguous suicide by words: "if a man speak, surely he shall be swallowed up" (Job 37:20). As for the other anonymous court attendant in chapter 1, Miss Flite's madness is exacerbated by the feeble awareness that her apocalyptic language is failing to assure the Judgment she awaits. Although she is one of the novel's Joban orphans, whose whole family has been wiped out, she also falls victim to the same sort of rhetoric Dickens' prophet indulges in this chapter and is one of those "confounded because they had hoped" (Job 6:20).

No joyful voice comes into this court, but meantime comedy with harsh satirical point appears, to "enlive[n] the dismal weather a little" (7). In the first of the novel's Job parodies, the Lord High Chancellor sits near Temple Bar, England's bar of heaven, "with a foggy glory round his head, softly fenced in with crimson cloth and curtains, addressed by a large advocate with great whiskers and an interminable brief" for the trial of the pawns below. This primal conspiratorial scene between a mock-god and the adversary[44] is from Job's first chapter, revised through the Dantean climax of the paragraph to evoke a satanic enclave in hell. Without adequate lighting—for these false "sitting" and "rising" suns have no light of "Truth" in them to shed on the proceedings (7, 6)—our Lord Chancellor "look[s] for light, but [has] none" (Job 3:9) as he "looks into the lantern that has no light in it" and "can see nothing but fog" (6). While Jesus warns the auditors of his Little Apocalypse to "look up . . . for your redemption draweth nigh. . . . Watch ye therefore" (Luke 21:28, 36), this modern-day antichrist is blind to his own demonic nature and England's doom.

While the Joban subtext persists, its significance shifts with Dickens' mutations in style. "The earth is given into the hands of the wicked," Job laments: "he covereth the faces of the judges thereof; if not, where, and who is he?" (9:24). In his self-delighting performances, Dickens' parodist-narrator is not concerned with Job's question or the outraged editorialist's complaint. Rather, maliciously he relishes the "groping and floundering" of the mighty in their slapstick version of the destructions God threatens to the wicked, who will "meet with darkness in the daytime, and grope in the noonday as in the night" (Job 5:14). In contrast to the prophet-narrator, the parodist makes the Joban court proceedings into a Punch and Judy show, in which comic effigies go "trip-

ping one another up on slippery precedents, groping knee-deep in tech-
nicalities" (6); he sticks their wigs in fog banks and reduces men to "maces, or
petty-bags, or privy-purses . . . in legal court suits," dressing them in puns (7).
Like Job threatening to be "no more" (see 7:8ff), these puppets pop up, drop
down, vanish from sight. They are talking heads, complaining of each other's
windy speeches: "'Mr. Tangle,' says the Lord High Chancellor, latterly something restless under the eloquence of that learned gentleman. . . . 'Have you
nearly concluded your argument?' 'Mlud, no—variety of points—feel it my duty
tsubmit—ludship'" (9). "Should a wise man utter vain knowledge, and fill his
belly with the east wind?" asks Eliphaz. "Should he reason with unprofitable
talk?" (15:2–3). Wallowing in words, running up Chancery costs by making
unprofitable talk pay, the High Court someday too may be "swallowed up."

The satiric point of the first parody does not prevent this voice from breaking
out into pure facetiousness in his final parodic play of chapter 1, when he toys
with Job 7:8–10, a passage in which the speaker desires to die: "The eye of him
that hath seen me shall see me no more. . . . As the cloud is consumed and
vanisheth away: so he that goeth down to the grave shall come up no more. He
shall return no more to his house, neither shall his place know him anymore." A
"very little counsel, with a terrific bass voice, arises" to deliver an address "like
a sepulchral message" to the court, then "drops, and the fog knows him no
more. Everybody looks for him. Nobody can see him" (10).[45] Indeed, the whole
foggy court "vanisheth away" in a final flourishing parody of the sudden death
threatened to the wicked ("the Chancellor . . . has dextrously vanished. Everybody else quickly vanishes too"), before the prophetic editorialist comes on for a
final appearance. He begins strongly: "If all the injustice [the Court] has committed, and all the misery it has caused, could only be locked up with it, and the
whole burnt away in a great funeral pyre—." But with the pause this voice
suppresses itself: "why so much the better for other parties than the parties in
Jarndyce and Jarndyce!" These might be the words of a socially conscious member of the Bar who has burst out eloquently at his club but instantly covers these
impolitic sentiments with a commonplace urbanity, turning all into a joke and a
jingle. Armageddon is chatted away, made merely fanciful ("If," "could only")
after all. Shall we trust *this* champion of justice? We may look for the fiery
prophet of an earlier paragraph, but his place knows him no more. If a man
speak, surely he shall be swallowed up.

Or he can swallow himself up. The self-reflexive structure of this chapter's
final sentence, suppressing itself in the very form of its expression, portends one
characteristic way violence will be done in *Bleak House*, as effective as the more
overt suppression of dissent by the bailiffs who arrest Gridley for contempt.

Even if the concluding oracle were taken for a false prophecy in its conflation of personal desire with a higher moral will, the syntax would itself be truly "prophetic." For in this generating chapter, Dickens has taught us to read a certain kind of movement that will recur throughout *Bleak House:* people have popped up and disappeared,[46] strong words (Gridley's, Mr. Tangle's) have been "crushed" (9), voices have come forth and faded away or done two things at once—one style overlaps another, undermining it in the play of the text. A fanciful mode trifles with the tones of the elegiac poet; an editorialist's formulated rhetoric contains the darker messages of the Joban subtext; the comedy of parodist and puppeteer casts doubt on the earnestness of the Victorian prophet; the presence of biblical cadences makes the satire of "Chizzle, Mizzle, . . . Drizzle" (9), even of "Jarndyce and Jarndyce," jingle like false tunes. As the editorial voice modulates into the comic parodist, he emulates the violence of the satanic powers toward their pawns by making the court characters into pawns of his own; as satirist, he makes a morose joke out of the unpleasant pleasantries which the court people make out of Jarndyce and Jarndyce. Are these the stylistic gestures of poetic justice, prophetic in intent? Or does the protean narrator like the lawyers merely make "a pretense of equity with [a] serious [face], as players might" (6)? In these imitative, reflexive, and self-canceling moves, what word shall we trust? As the kaleidoscope of style turns from serious to comic modes and halfway back again, which transaction with the biblical subtext is the definitive model of interpretation?

The uncertainties of reading unresolvable at the end of chapter 1 are perfectly in keeping with the Joban novel Dickens is generating. In his kaleidoscopic discourse, Job at times insists he has the "right words" (6:25), speaking with an authority that surpasses the traditionalists, yet he admits his words are those "of one that is desperate, which are as wind" (6:26). From speech act to speech act in *Bleak House*, which way is the wind blowing? Each of the novel's many storytellers makes untrustworthy formulations; like the successive narrators of chapter 1, for example, Esther Summerson and Harold Skimpole both wear verbal disguises, make inappropriate merry jokes, editorialize to silence expressions of pain. The text into which *Bleak House*'s reconstructing reader has been drawn forces him through these originating transformations of style to participate in the novelist's problems—given the untrustworthiness of language as a vehicle for expression and evasion—of *how* to read the meaning of suffering, and of *whether* it can be read in any of the shifting biblical terms Dickens invokes.

Through all its permutations, the Joban subtext persists. Its disturbing undertone intimates why the narrator's writerly ways of expressing, enclosing, for-

mulating, evading, or momentarily transcending the violence of life are inadequate, can never be final. The general disaster proceeds whether Job complains
or remains silent: "Though I speak, my grief is not asswaged: and though I
forbear, what am I eased?" (16:6). Dickens' victims write incessantly for their
causes and harangue the air, yet nothing uttered can fully express, explain, or
reverse the persistence of human affliction, kindred mystery with the fog and
mud. To recall another recurrent allusion in *Bleak House:* all flesh is grass.[47]
Thus even if a man speak, surely he shall be swallowed up. The end impends
over all writerly beginnings.

Biblical allusions seed Dickens' first chapter with threats and promises of
poetic moods to continue and events to come—clues disguised, diverted, or
suppressed by stylistic fancywork. In the "other world" behind the world of the
story-text toward which allusions can gesture ambiguously—is it really beneficent? malevolent? indifferent?—something seems to be going on, something not
consistently attended to, that may come out at any moment, or at a later, appointed time.

3

THE DESTRUCTION of the wicked is a favorite theme of the Old Testament prophets, Job's comforters, and nineteenth-century melodrama. In the prophetic tradition, the formula "the appointed time" refers to the eventual triumph of God's
justice over the death forces of history, as in Habakkuk 2:1–3: "And the
Lord . . . said, Write the vision, and make it plain upon tables, that he may run
that readeth it. For the vision is yet for an appointed time, but at the end it shall
speak, and not lie: though it tarry, wait for it; because it will surely come." But
in the Book of Job, this tradition of retributive violence is profoundly questioned
by the poetic articulations of Job's *de profundis,* a theme the biblical prophets
also sound when God's historical intervention tarries.[48] When God seems absent, Job cries for Everyman's "appointed time" in a different context, longing
for death ("O that thou wouldest hide me in the grave") as an escape from his
uncertainty of a Providence that would dispense cosmic and personal justice
("O . . . that thou wouldest appoint me a set time, and remember me!" 14:13).
Both interpretations of this recurrent phrase in *Bleak House*[49] lie behind
Dickens' title for chapter 32, which narrates a meaningless suicide in an atmosphere pregnant with prophetic expectation. (In its instability of meaning, "The
Appointed Time" resembles "In Chancery" as well as other chapter titles, such
as "Covering a Multitude of Sins," that can be read in divergent ways.) Chapter

32 maintains the interpretive ambivalence of chapter 1 as it fulfills and continues the different times with which the novel began, which its first chapter had appointed: the *kairos* of Old Testament prophecy when fulfilment is nigh (suggested as well in the barren grape vine of Job 15:32–33 framing the monthly cover design) and the *chronos* of the interminable middle in a chancery universe, where death is longed for but lacks transcendent meaning. We come to a predicted climax of justice in this structurally central chapter of *Bleak House*, yet we are still "in the middest," preoccupied with the injustices of mortality and uncertainly awaiting the "incomprehensible judgment."

As elsewhere in the anonymous narrative, biblical reading is made further unstable by the conventions through which allusions are mediated. While in chapter 1, a plenitude of suffering was ambivalently expressed and contained through stylistic modulations, in chapter 32 Dickens shifts narrative modes as well as styles, ranging from melodrama and gothic to comedy of manners and blasphemous parody. Again the significance and force of the Joban subtext (and related Bible allusions) shift as one frame of reference replaces another and as facts disconfirm formula, making our readings unstable despite the fulfillment of the prophecy ending chapter 1 in Krook's "funeral pyre" (10). With this decisive end, valorized by biblical sources, Dickens mediates one account of human suffering through melodrama, which Peter Brooks has called "the expressionism of the moral imagination"; the *raison d'être* of melodrama is "to 'prove' the existence of a moral universe which, though put into question, masked by villainy and perversions of judgment, does exist and can be made to assert its presence and its categorical force among men."[50] But there are also other accounting methods guiding our interpretations of this middle chapter. With the introduction of the gothic mode, we are induced suspensefully to wonder not so much which explanation of Jobling's "horrors" is the true one, but whether it is possible to do any rational or moral account-keeping at all, as melodrama does. The surplus of mystery that gothic generates finds its biblical precedents too in a now-familiar Joban poetry drawn upon in chapter 32. The *de profundis* theme replayed through gothic conventions[51] puts an end to the light comedy of manners that is also here; indeed, it turns the comic impulse inside out toward blasphemous parody. This parody barely contains within a familiar New Testament story the most radically disturbing violence of all and unleashes a surplus of dark meanings that spill over into adjoining and subsequent chapters in Esther's providential narrative. Despite the forward thrust of "The Appointed Time" toward revelation and further apocalyptic prediction, the reader who has not only been amused by this chapter but has attended to the vicissitudes of biblical reading here is left, as Froude concluded of Job's baffled reader, with

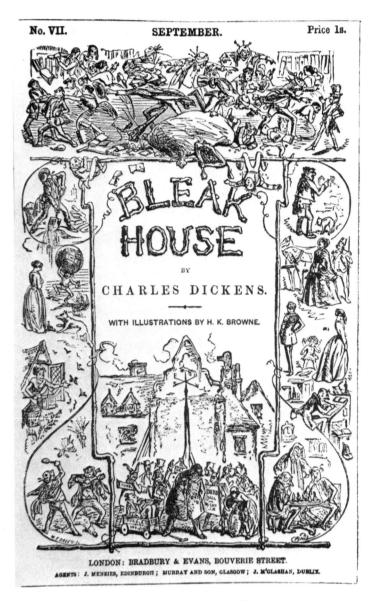

No. VII.   SEPTEMBER.   Price 1s.

BLEAK HOUSE

BY

CHARLES DICKENS.

WITH ILLUSTRATIONS BY H. K. BROWNE.

LONDON: BRADBURY & EVANS, BOUVERIE STREET.
AGENTS: J. MENZIES, EDINBURGH; MURRAY AND SON, GLASGOW; J. M'GLASHAN, DUBLIN.

Cover design for monthly parts of *Bleak House*
(Hablot K. Browne)

And [the wicked man] dwelleth in desolate cities, and in houses which no
man inhabiteth, which are ready to become heaps. . . . His
recompence . . . shall be accomplished before his time, and his branch
shall not be green. He shall shake off his unripe grape as the vine.
(Job 15:28, 31–33)

"the mystery of the government of the world"—although not merely to acquiesce in it like the Job of 40:4, Calvin's exemplar (but hardly Dickens'), laying his hand upon his mouth.[52]

In the melodramatic structure of chapter 32, as Jobling and Guppy await the midnight hour when Krook will hand over the love letters in which lurid secrets of identity are to be revealed, the climax is suspended in nightmarish anticipation while evil forces literally "in the air" (32.393) have full play for a time. Ominous physical signs intensely charge the surface of the narrative: suppressed documents, disguised identities, a secretive villain-figure, plotting and conspiratorial vows, a deadline dictating the inexorable logic of events, extreme occurrences, and hyperbolic language. Such familiar conventions from melodrama, as Peter Brooks observes, gesture toward "the true drama that lies behind,"[53] a Manichaean battle in which the wicked shall at last be expelled in a public spectacle. In *Bleak House* violent texts from Job and the Old Testament prophets clarify the meaning of this mysterious subsurface drama and give it moral weight; they also justify the narrator's final acts of retributive violence through words.

In the Book of Daniel, the prophet is promised that "at the time appointed the end shall be" (8:19); the Antichrist, a terrible ruler who "shall cause craft to prosper," shall at last "be broken without hand" (8:25).[54] The repetition of this formula in Job 34:20—"in a moment shall [the wicked] die, and the people shall be troubled at midnight, and pass away: and the mighty shall be taken away without hand"—has special nuances for the end of Dickens' chapter. In Job 20 there is an even more explicit scenario for Krook's end, its physical and moral causes, and its aftermath for the survivors. Zophar's speech about God's terrors for the wicked opens with a picture fitting for both the Lord High Chancellor in court fog and for the dustman Krook, the inevitable fall of the first being implicit in the existence of his lowly counterpart: "Though his excellency mount up to the heavens, and his head reach unto the clouds; Yet he shall perish for ever like his own dung: they which have seen him shall say, Where is he? He shall fly away as a dream, and shall not be found: yea, he shall be chased away as a vision of the night. The eye also which saw him shall see him no more; neither shall his place any more behold him. . . . His bones are full of the sin of his youth, which shall lie down with him in the dust" (Job 20:6–9, 11). "The old man's not there," says Tony Jobling. Although "on one chair back, hang the old man's hairy cap and coat," Krook's place knows him no more; they may "Look!" but do not see him (402). As a character who bears the signs of the stage villain although ironically he is not villainous, the mysteriously motiveless and drunken Krook seems to be even more what Brooks figuratively calls a "conveyor of evil" because he is literally "inhabited" by corruption;[55] he will be destroyed by all he has physically consumed. Zophar's wicked man has secretly "swallowed down riches" but "God shall cast them out of his belly. . . . There shall none of his meat be left": "God shall cast the fury of his wrath upon him, and shall rain it upon him while he is eating. . . . All darkness shall be hid in his secret places: a fire not blown shall consume him; it shall go ill with him that is left in his tabernacle" (20:15, 21, 23, 26).

Krook's bizarre demise by a "fire not blown" is grounded as much in biblical as in the scientific sources Dickens defended to George Henry Lewes. But it is also the conventions of melodrama that require "Spontaneous Combustion and no other death"[56] as a theatricalized metaphorical gesture carrying the essential idea: the internally corrupting system must swallow itself up in God's appointed time. As the conventions require, moral evil is nominalized in this "old Boguey downstairs" (396); and it must be publicly recognized as "evil" (403) before it can be expelled. But what kind of evil does Krook represent? In melodrama the sign must be made unmistakably legible, yet Dickens' witnesses flee in silence at the end. The vortex created by their exit then whirls onstage the professional *prophētēs*, "one who speaks for another" by charismatic seizure.[57] This narrator arrives to generalize in the framework of moral law the significance of Krook's charred bone: "The Lord Chancellor of that Court, true to his title in his last act, has died the death of all Lord Chancellors in all Courts, and of all authorities in all places under all names soever, where false pretences are made, and where injustice is done. Call the death by any name Your Highness will, attribute it to whom you will, or say it might have been prevented how you will, it is the same death eternally—inborn, inbred, engendered in the corrupted humours of the vicious body itself, and that only—Spontaneous Combustion, and none other of all the deaths that can be died" (403). Calling kings of all sorts to account for violating their covenant with truth and justice, seeking through his public utterance to form his people's conscience, this Victorian prophet reads the bit of "wood sprinkled with white ashes"—a nonverbal prophetic sign[58]—as a call to repentance, one unmistakably readable even for those who would "run away" from the signs of "evil" they recognize. "Write the vision," says the Lord to Habakkuk, "and make it plain upon tables, that he may run that readeth it."

With this rhetorical climax, the kairotic moment—tarrying since the prophetic voice of chapter 1 had indicated, half-jocularly, the direction of events— now arrives, not only in an emblematic death on a "funeral pyre" but also in language. With injustice expelled in Krook's demise, Dickens' narrator now does justice through speaking words of judgment. In the passage quoted above, where the doubling and tripling of almost every element consolidates one unequivocal declamation, the sudden downfall of all unjust authorities seems already to have happened. As with the prophetic word in the Bible, speech becomes act of God, while effecting melodramatic peripety; superseding the speechlessness of the fallible witnesses—more, their refusal to *do* justice—this narrator's oracular language becomes exemplary deed. With his strident rhetorical rhythms, he seeks to enact in the reader that culminating "moment of astonishment," in Brooks' phrase, when the force of a moral universe among men is recognized. In so aggressively flourishing his powers, the narrator may seem as violent as those he denounces; but just as the prophetic word is "power of God" transmitted through his servant, so Dickens' persona assumes the prerogatives of one who is simply obedient, not violent—answering the Lord's summons in the subtext to make the vision of the "appointed time" plain, while satisfying the demands of melodramatic structure for conclusive moral legibility.

Dickens' use of melodrama in chapter 32 is not just the strategic move of a popular entertainer, but an appropriate conventional response to a historical situation in which the Bible's language of threat and promise had come into question, but had not yet been abandoned as a literary and moral resource. In Peter Brooks' account of the context in which this theatrical mode came to have special resonance, the rise of melodrama signaled cultural anxieties analogous to those I have noted in the period of Job's composition (and that the dramatic climax of this book had addressed). With the silencing of the Logos, Brooks argues, melodrama emerged as a central theatrical form to make a moral universe again speak clearly for wide audiences in need of such a word. In this context, Dickens' use of melodrama in *Bleak House*, while it draws on biblical precedent, is also predicated on the ebbing of biblical authority; the old prophetic *logoi* must be rewritten through the human words of an author attuned to his readers' wants and the popular conventions that would answer them.

But as the following rereading of chapter 32 will disclose, even Dickens' text confesses that a melodramatized Scripture no longer quite serves. Brooks also notes that there was a point beyond which melodrama could no longer adequately contain the cultural trouble at heart which called it forth. In the strained surface of some later Victorian fictions (notably James'), he observes the great effort required "to perceive the image of the spiritual in a world voided of its traditional Sacred, where the body of the ethical has become a sort of *deus absconditus* which must be . . . brought into man's existence" by imaginative force[59]—even by rhetorical violence of the sort that erupts at the end of "The Appointed Time." Dickens' melodrama in chapter 32 finally becomes as strained as that rhetoric, pressing its own theatrical conventions toward parody of themselves. Even more to the point is the fact that their mediating presence here inevitably trivializes the biblical traditions in which this theatrical mode is partly rooted. Dickens' scriptural allusions then become unstable in spite of—or because of—his melodrama's insistence on moral certainty. Further, the reader's sense that the prophetic-apocalyptic words Dickens draws upon can no longer be taken with complete seriousness is exacerbated by another set of conventions operating in this chapter. These displace the melodramatic ones and reveal their own biblical affinities with the poetic middle of Job's book.

As Dickens' authoritative cadences at the close of chapter 32 overthrow false authorities, the awareness of a greater violence than even theirs is diverted but not removed from the reader's mind. For through the other narrative mode also present in this chapter, Dickens has fostered the subversive possibility of a moral chaos where there are no authorities at all in which to believe and to anchor one's language. This chaos, the empire of death, impinges on the reader's consciousness through the destabilizing gothic tale Dickens tells in chapter 32. Significantly, its biblical subtext, centered in Job 7, makes a different transaction with the fictional context than do the prophetic allusions that give moral weight to Dickens' melodrama: rather than elucidating the charged surface, these other Scripture texts undermine moral certitude and unleash a black humor that would be anathema to the Victorian prophet.

Jobling's midnight announcement suggests the alternate and subversive source for Dickens' chapter title: "It's the appointed time at last. Shall I go?" (402). The appointment he and Guppy keep, however, is not with melodramatic or prophetic closure but with death, Everyman's appointed time (Job 7:1, 14:14). To convey this theme, Dickens loads chapter 32 with the paraphernalia of gothic: in its atmosphere of brooding fear, there are macabre and portentous happenings, incredible rationalist explanations for them, hints of lurid crimes and pacts with the powers of darkness, ghostly noises, a devilish cat (descended from Hoffmann's), melting flesh, and a scenario of live burial in the charnel house of Krook's shop. Some of these derive from melodrama, but George J. Worth is right to argue of *Bleak House* that melodramatic device has limited importance in a novel which refuses to define good and evil clearly;[60] gothic, on the other hand, shrouds horrific meanings in obscurity to intensify undefinable perils of body and soul. Further, for the reader the actual effect of the melodramatic strategy of delay is to throw the weight of this chapter more on the anxieties of the witnesses (comic types only too ripe for the pleasures of suspense and horror) than upon the prophetic emblem of Krook's death. What "happens" in the course of this episode coincides with the time of trial we expect in the middle of melodrama's structure; but, "tr[ied] . . . every moment" (Job 7:18), the anxious witnesses discover that their extremities do not really come to resolution. Instead of the clarification of "this evil place," their gothic narrative unleashes ineffable forces that draw them ineluctably into a place which no Victorian prophet can exorcise, from which melodrama cannot rescue them, and from which they cannot escape in any language. Significantly, the experience culminates in gripping silence, curing Jobling and Guppy of their light-comedy talk.

To appreciate the displacement of other conventional formulas in the impact of the gothic tale, we have to see these two superstitious characters first as figures in a comic mode familiar in Dickens' fiction. As his diminutive name suggests, Tony Jobling is a lower-class comedy-of-manners Job, first encountered in chapter 20; by chapter 32, he becomes a more darkly humorous Job figure when he takes on the role of replacement for the dead Nemo. In chapter 20, in another parody of Job's folktale prologue, Jobling is waiting in the lower regions of Kenge and Carboy's for the illustrious Guppy, whose name ("little fish") identifies him as a comic God-sign.[61] Like God over Job, Guppy has "se[t] a watch" (7:12) over Jobling through the aid of the "sagacious Smallweed," lest Tony become "disgusted with waiting, and mak[e] an untimely departure" (246) like his suicidal precursor. Dressed as a gentleman come down in the world, Jobling announces "bitterly" that he has "got the sack!" (250) and asks in his half-jocular way the questions of God's providence and human vocation that turn up repeatedly in *Bleak House*: "What am I to do? How am I to live?" (249). Companion to the "owlish" Smallweed (246; cf. Job 30:29), Jobling spurns false comforting. But he accepts the bounteous feast they lay out for him and experiences a comic fairytale renewal through consuming enormous mouthfuls in a physical act of "coming of age fast" (248).

But this fairytale resolution, like others in *Bleak House*, is deceptive; Jobling has yet to come of age through his grimly comic experience "in the Downs" (396). By chapter 32, having taken over Nemo's rooms and vocation as lawwriter, Jobling has begun to age inwardly in the "perplexed and troublous valley of the shadow of the law" (391). Dickens' allusion to Psalm 23:4, carrying forward the legal satire's antipastoral theme,[62] incorporates an echo of Job's death wish (see 10:21–22) which is more directly appropriate to the morbid atmosphere being built up here through the gothic themes that drive deeper than the satire. Indeed, the Joban mood of Psalm 22 ("My God, my God, why hast thou forsaken me?") has succeeded Psalm 23 in this shadowy place where no comforters prepare a table for Jobling now. Still, Dickens' play on the *de profundis* psalm (to reappear more directly at the end of this chapter) is mediated by his comedy of these characters' superstitious ignorance: Jobling calls his godforsaken state "the horrors" (394).

Job's horror is his longing for his appointed time in that morally ambiguous middle which melodrama's Manichaean structure would exclude. The gothic fascination with death in "The Appointed Time" is not only the wages of Jobling's and Guppy's sins of injustice through the law, however deathly its powers according to the legal satire; rather, the preoccupation with mortality develops out of the ambiance of ambiguous guilty victimage established through gothic, which threatens to spread a wider moral and psychological chaos ultimately associated with "KING DEATH!" (33.413). Near the beginning of chapter 32, Dickens generalizes his characters' condition through another ominous weather report: on this "fine steaming night," which will "give the Registrar of Deaths some extra business," the confidence of the sanitary-reform prophet concerned with unwholesome air is invaded by the unease of the gothic narrator, who does not know what is wrong: "It may be something in the air—there is plenty in it— or it may be something in himself that is in fault; but Mr. Weevle, otherwise Jobling, is very ill at ease" (393). Afflicted by this uncertain internal something, Jobling walks "down and up, and down and up" between his room and the street door; a "wearisome nigh[t is] appointed to" him (Job 7:3; cf. "I never had such a night in my life!"), although "Nothing has been the matter" that he can name (396). In fact, even more than his hiding from his creditors at Krook's place under the false name of "Weevle," his becoming wee-evil as an agent for Guppy's unexplained stratagems has made a conundrum of his moral life. As the two converse secretively, Jobling finds that Weevle's "light vivacious tone of fashionable life . . . sits so ill upon him tonight, that he abandons that and his [false] whiskers together"—like Job shedding his garments, sitting down in the dung to mourn—and "appears to yield himself up, a prey to the horrors again" (399).

Even though his partner tries to the end to remain godlike, aloof, a patron dispensing comforts, Guppy too becomes inducted into a gothic nightmare *de profundis* that displaces simpler comic formulas for his identity and makes him a guilty victim. At once he is confronted by dark signs he cannot brighten by his "light-comedy tone" (401); and, falling into Jobling's tone of "injured remonstrance," he becomes as defensive as a god charged with injuring his servant "without cause" (Job 2:3): "far be it from me, I am sure, to wound even your feelings without a cause!" (397). Meanwhile macabre, unreadable happenings interrupt their voluble comic colloquy over who is at fault. As Krook's vapor falls, Guppy's "skin . . . become[s] loathsome" (Job 7:5), and as he vigorously scrubs his hand, the guilty appendage of the law, he is as bewildered as Job wondering why God does not pardon him (7:21). When Jobling descends the stairs at the appointed time, Guppy "tries to compose himself, before the fire"; but like Job seeking his couch in vain, he too is terrified by visions (7:14) when

Tony rushes back "so horribly frightened . . . that his terror seizes the other, who makes a rush at him, and asks loudly, 'What's the matter?' " (402). Bereft of his comic name, Guppy as "the other" is seized by the fact of the ineffable into an anonymous brotherhood of terror.

As this gothic tale unfolds, a simpler plot is being played out with another parodic underpattern from Job's prologue that aligns these characters with his persecutors: Weevle plays a little-satan to Guppy's little-god as both plot against the rag-and-bottle king downstairs. With his disguise of a "cheap tight velvet skull-cap" and whiskers "out of all proportion" (393), Weevle resembles the "large advocate with great whiskers, [and] a little voice" identified with the Adversary in chapter 1; his ambulatory restlessness ("down and up") also mimics the movements of the spying Satan who comes "from walking up and down" in the earth (Job 1:7). To complete this scenario, Krook himself is also a demonic Job-figure, one who becomes his own ash-heap even before these conspirators have a chance to get at him.[63] Krook's association with Job does not really complicate our view of him, although it subverts the melodramatic logic of chapter 32 that would cast him as pure villain. But the playing of double roles by Jobling and Guppy—as both the superhuman victimizers in the folktale and little Jobs in the middle—underscores their condition as guilty victims: they are people who do themselves harm while victimizing others who are harming them in this predatory world, where "every one is either robbing, or being robbed," or both at once (393).

Admittedly, as this little Job parody suggests, the guilt into which the gothic nightmare of chapter 32 is inducting these two characters is partially explicable: their conspiracy to get the letters from Krook is somewhat crooked and self-serving, especially because they pretend to be "doing the deceased a service" (400)—the same burial service of indifference "Our Dear Brother" had when he died. In terms of the prophetic narrator's logic, for their sins of lovelessness and injustice they must suffer the foul "rain" of God's wrath in Krook's dropping vapors, for "it shall go ill with him that is left" in the house of the wicked man (Job 20:26). Neither do these conspirators get what they are after, for when the Smallweeds move in, Krook's "goods . . . flow away in the day of . . . wrath" (Job 20:28).

Still, their appointed time is not just with the *kairos* of divine justice. Despite the appropriateness of these Old Testament formulas to Dickens' legal satire, the whole atmosphere of chapter 32 is charged with something that neither prophetic nor comic modes here can rationalize, contain, or transcend: the acute awareness that death impinges. To convey this Dickens employs the arch-motif of the gothic imagination, the experience of being buried alive—the "loss of mobility and of identity"[64] but not consciousness. On this "close night" in the "troublous valley of the shadow," Jobling, dressed in a skull-cap for death, is as restless as though he were being buried and has already begun to lose his identity when he appears as "Weevle" ("a worm, and no man," Ps. 22:6), while the astonished Guppy becomes "the other." In the claustral spaces of chapter 32 as the plot closes around them, their "appointed time" arrives. When at last "they go down, more dead than alive" into Krook's "suffocating" shop (402), their heads are anointed with a nauseous oil (Ps. 23:5) and their hearts melt "like wax . . . in the midst of [their] bowels" (Ps. 22:14), for they discover not only the fact of the dustman's demise but their mortal fraternity with such as Krook: they are "flesh of his flesh," and even though alive, "shadow of his shadow" (25.324).

Guppy and Jobling also make the novel's central discovery of a Joban theme, the radical opposition between language and death, in their speechless recognition of Krook as dust—not as an emblem for anything. Their "moment of astonishment" is that time not when evil or virtue speaks its name, but when men are made speechless in the midst of ordinary, even comic, talk, by death's arrival. Such interruptions return throughout the chapter. Later in the Sol's Arms, "they find it difficult to put a name to anything quite distinctly" (33.405)—an ongoing state of affairs that is the natural result of their encounter in Krook's shop. Jobling and Guppy "go down" in search of written answers, the letters that will prove Lady Dedlock's identity; what they find instead is an illegible sign, a thing on the floor. For their discovery that man the talker, *homo significans*, is unreadable, mute dust, there is no name but "O Horror" (403). Their peripety from cockney loquacity to speechlessness is a savage action: it catapults them out of the shop, "Striking out the light and overturning one another into the street" (403). They have lost their names and faces in Dickens' final tableau, which does not stabilize moral relations like the telling tableaux of melodrama; with the discovery of radical illegibility in their world, their human identities vanish as the light goes out. The next words in Dickens' text are only an anonymous cry, relayed indirectly by the narrator: "Help, help, help! Come into this house for Heaven's sake! Plenty will come in, but none can help." "Be not far from me," cries the psalmist in 22:11, ". . . for there is none to help." Godforsaken, dying without even the help the psalmist calls upon, man becomes less than human: a disembodied cry in the dark, not even in quotation marks, perhaps not heard.

This apocalyptic moment of human disappearance is paradigmatic in *Bleak House*: since chapters 1 and 2, figures have been dropping out of sight, protests have been quashed, the mourning voices have been submerged, styles have arisen and subsided, narrators have vanished into thin air. At the horrific crux of chapter 32, there comes a typical kind of "help": shepherd, guardian, watchman, interpreter—all traditional names for the prophet—now steps in promptly with his professional interpretation of the gothic nightmare. Like Job's comforters silencing his laments with their prophetic theories of retribution, authoritatively Dickens' narrator tries to put an end to these morbid imaginings by providing (in the words of an Isaac Watts hymn he earlier parodies) "some good account at last" (392). Yet even when such "help" in suppression arrives to make the preoccupation with disappearance disappear, the extremities that have been unleashed by the gothic persist in undermining even this narrator's stance. His obsessively repetitive denunciation of "all" failed "authorities in all places under all names soever, where false pretenses are made, and where injustice is done" does not preclude the suspicion that Authority itself has failed in justice. Haunting, too, in this narrator's final outburst is the repeated opposition between naming and death: "*Call* the death by any name Your Highness will, *attribute* it to whom you will, or *say* it might have been prevented how you will, it is the same death eternally . . . all the deaths that can be died" (403; emphasis added). These significant lexical choices, in this telling syntactic frame, give continued expression to Dickens' *de profundis* in the face of our "appointed time." "They perish for ever without any regarding it": whatever the legible causes of Krook's demise and England's peril, "the same death eternally" reigns.

If Dickens' reformist social critique is belied by his universal concern with the inevitable here, there is yet an important subterranean connection between the prophetic narrator's righteous condemnation of his society and the discoveries of Jobling and Guppy. They come face to face with the horror of mortality; the narrator's final words forcefully impress upon the reader the incapacity of his civilization, in its present state, to give death meaning. Like the empty burial service celebrated for "Our Dear Brother" that raises no resurrection hope and testifies shamefully "to future ages, how civilisation and barbarism walked this boastful island together" (11.137), this culture with all its proper forms of language, rituals, and conventions, "all names soever," can avail nothing finally against the beast in the human that feeds on other human flesh, or against nature's reduction of everyone to dust without spirit. The *Bleak House* world from its failed Deluge onward is "filled with violence" (Gen. 6:11) of nature and of men: to report it, to be a witness, is to be covered with the loathsome stuff, no matter how authoritative the teller, no matter what stylistic shifts are tried for a time. Expressive or silencing, the verbal and narrative modes of "The Appointed Time" provide no answer to the Joban preoccupations that grip this novel, although Dickens' playfulness with these modes affords some relief. Indeed, the energy of his inventions seems even to mock—perhaps *needs* to mock—the novel's *de profundis* poetry as morbid overreaction, although it persists. Because that playfulness also persists in maintaining Dickens' distance from these "horrors," his range never reaches the "sublime expression" that made the Book of Job, even in its "cry of the soul,"[65] an inspiration to his contemporaries, "a noble Book; all men's Book!" in Carlyle's words, "one of the grandest things ever written with pen" (*H* 49).

The Book of Job works toward a brilliant epiphany: "but now mine eyes seeth thee" (42:5). The faithful speaker anticipates this later moment in the famous credo, part of the Anglican Burial Service, that erupts as a flash of hope amid an earlier lament: "For I know that my redeemer liveth, and that he shall stand at the latter day upon the earth: And though after my skin worms destroy this body, yet in my flesh shall I see God" (19:25–26). To St. Jerome, these passages uttered by Job as a type of Christ proved the hope of the resurrection against Origen's heretical view (which Dickens seems to have shared) that Jesus was not the divine Son of God. It was just this kind of typological proof-texting that critical work on the Bible in the nineteenth century had exposed; and Froude uses this passage to illustrate how doctrine had been built upon doctored translations of the biblical text.[66] *Bleak House*, divided on this resurrection faith as on other fundamental themes,[67] both makes its assertions of faith and allows them to be placed in question.

In its middle chapters, resurrection emerges as a central concern. In chapter 31, Charley and Esther recall the Gospel stories—like that of "the ruler's daughter raised up by the gracious hand upon her bed of death" (389)—upon which Victorian formulas of religious consolation so important to Dickens in *The Life of Our Lord* were founded. The exchanges of comfort here between these sisters of Job the patient are uncriticized in their immediate context, but they bear traces of a problem to which Froude points in his essay: "no doctrine [is] in itself so pure" that it can resist the pressure toward reducing "the once living spirit . . . into formulae."[68] Merely by being recalled in tag-phrases, such stories assure Esther "that we might know our hope to be restored in Heaven!" (389)—where she also plans to meet Alan Woodcourt in her glorified body. Adept at inspirational repression, Esther we know can grasp at religious formulas to save herself from troubling facts she wants to ignore; such conventional closures for her life nearly lose her to the Jarndyce marriage. Calamity befalls her after this exchange of comforting, and at the end of the chapter she is "blind." Her generalized hope, her "last high belief in the watching Angel" (390) is then obliterated in the vivid imagery of the nameless narrator's next chapter, which opens with an allegory of blind deity, "bleared Argus with a fathomless pocket for every eye and an eye upon it," and the figure of a guardian night-porter "with a mighty power of sleep" (392). As chapter 32 proceeds to challenge consolatory formulas, its morbid fascinations and finally its death without help wash back over the reader's memories of the last, hopeful chapter, and chaos rises again.

This savage backward subversion of hope climaxes at the end of chapter 32 when the comedy of which the witnesses have been cured is redirected in a dark parody of the Easter story—the closest Dickens comes to the blasphemy of Job. For Jobling and Guppy, this is the final account through which the chapter's repressed contents find surreptitious expression. The "horror" of Krook's death is after all not his disappearance, but his reappearance as charred bone. As the witnesses descend into the sepulchrous shop, no creature greets them at the door but a devilish cat; no heavenly messenger reassures them with the tidings, "he is not here: behold the place where they laid him" (see Mark 16:1–8), as they look at Krook's empty place and behold the foul abandoned garments. "The old man's not there," whispers Jobling, and again, "he is *not* there!" But on the third dawning of consciousness, when they hold up the light as though in some parody of religious pictures, Krook is resurrected: "O Horror, he is here!" From this they "run away" like the disciples who "fled . . . trembled and . . . amazed" from Jesus' tomb in silence (Mark 16:8). Job's resurrection credo is inverted, for with their own eyes and even on their flesh they have witnessed a demonic epiphany.

4

ERNEST RENAN summed up his interpretation of the Book of Job with an assertion of high Victorian faith: "The march of the world is enveloped in darkness, but it tends toward God."[69] Among the English Victorians, it is Arnold and not Dickens who pursues this as a line of thought; yet in Esther Summerson's "Progress" this divine tendency is implicit—a goal perceived through the gloom more in nineteenth-century terms than in the Bunyanesque formula of seventeenth-century faith to which her first chapter title alludes. Its difficult beginning shadowed by a death curse, enveloped by the darker witness of the nameless narrator, Esther's story moves through mortal spiritual conflict toward fuller enlightenment in a providential world even though she sees herself in a glass darkly to the end.[70] As I have suggested, Dickens' identification of Esther with the unstable Joban subtext complicates our reading of her simply as a Christian type; for this and other reasons her reader, too, sees darkly, even as he perceives the tendency of Esther's narrative toward God.

Up to its fairytale-like conclusion, Esther Summerson's story is a pious but conflicted approximation of the *Bildungsroman*. With its task of achieving a more mature self from which to write her spiritual autobiography, her "Progress" is more subtly elaborated and less shapely than Little Nell's version of the pilgrim journey: Esther's is a provisional forward movement toward deeper understanding through many setbacks, descents into false guilt, and authentic encounters with evil, mitigated and redeemed by guardian-angel rescues as well as by Esther's gradual discoveries about herself and about this world which, she believes, the other world "sets . . . right" (65.763). Up to her final chapter, which begins the fairytale resolution with Jarndyce's gift of two hundred pounds, Esther grows toward modest maturity through a narrative pattern that bears partial resemblance to a familiar process in Victorian fiction: myths of identity and society are shattered by disruptions—by Esther's encounters with the incongruous, with what does not fit her picture of herself and the world—as she is gradually the most unevenly educated through her trials. [71]

Because Dickens makes her so explicitly a religious woman, it might be expected that Esther's biblical texts simply set these worldly trials *sub specie aeternitatis*, bringing a stability of outlook to the ordering of her narrative and thus to the whole of *Bleak House*. While it is true that her religious mythos generally counters the other narrator's chaos, Esther's Bible quotations, echoes, and subtexts are also problematic, occasioning interpretive dissonances that signal the tensions of her provisional "progress" through a Joban world. Behind this claim is the assumption that Esther as inscribed in her language is more complex[72] than the lineaments of the Christian ideal she does embody in the faithful and charitable actions so important to Dickens. This complexity is reflected in her allusions because Esther Summerson is one of Dickens' "good people" who are inducted into the depths. As an 1864 article in *All the Year Round* posed the issue Dickens had long been addressing, and struggled with most successfully in establishing the authenticity of his religious heroines in *Bleak House* and *Little Dorrit:* "why is all art to be restricted to the uniform level of quiet domesticity? . . . Whenever humanity wrestles with the gods of passion and pain, there, of necessity, is that departure from our diurnal platitudes which the cant of existing criticism denounces . . . The mystery of evil is as interesting to us now as it was in the time of SHAKESPEARE; and it is downright affectation or effeminacy to say that we are never to glance into that abyss, but are perpetually to construct our novels out of the amenities of respectable, easygoing men and women."[73] Esther Summerson does wrestle with the gods of passion and pain, even if she often will do no more than "glance" into the abyss and—like the "effeminate" authors the article denounces—affecting ignorance in the hope of attaining innocence, tries to construct her narrative of experiences in the depths out of domestic and religious platitudes. Granting this character inscribed in such conflicting language more than the unidimensionality of a Victorian religious icon, I will argue that not a univocal Word but a "battle of biblical books," in three different senses, underlies Esther's narrative. Before turning to the most important chapters for Esther's conflicts, I want to summarize these three forms of dialogical tension and then give some general discussion to what seems to me the central battle of texts.

First and least difficult to interpret is the conflict between Law and Gospel. Esther is a Christian disciple not only in her good deeds but explicitly in some of her sincere biblical citations. Bearing witness to the "broad spirit" of the New Testament in which Dickens professed belief, repeatedly she rewrites in this spirit the narrow letter of Old Testament texts associated with her Calvinist aunt and her self-condemned mother. We see this process of revision most strikingly in the verbal combat of Esther's generating chapter. As though to correct her aunt's vengeful application of Exodus 20:5 ("pray daily that the sins of others be not visited upon your head, according to what is written," 3.19), which also omits the Lord's promise of "mercy unto thousands of them that love me, and keep my commandments" (Exod. 20:6), Esther reads to her aunt Jesus' words in John 8:7 reversing the Law for the adulterous woman ("He that is without sin among you, let him first cast a stone at her!" 21). In an exchange of Scripture texts reminiscent of fundamentalist debates, the aunt cuts off Esther's reading at a place where words of mercy follow ("Neither do I condemn thee: go, and sin no more," John 8:11) and "cr[ies] out, in an awful voice, from quite another part of the book: 'Watch ye therefore! lest coming suddenly he find you sleeping. And what I say unto you, I say unto all, Watch!'" (21). At this apocalyptic moment, when the aunt hurls Mark 13:35–37 like an Old Testament prophet's warning, she is stricken like a shattered idol, and the visitation upon her self-serving bibliolatry comes down.

Esther is thus melodramatically vindicated early in the novel, but the Law-Gospel debate is not over. As I shall show, it continues, internalized, in Esther's dialogues with herself as she strives to unlearn the psychically damaging story about her original guilt of having been born illegitimate—the Law myth that cannot save. This internal battle of the books seems the least problematic in the novel because the New Testament values of forgiveness and charity are presumably stable, there for Esther to realize if only she can. Still, the persistent difficulty she has in believing the Gospel for herself subtly puts in question its power to cast out the demons of legalistic thought and feeling. Thus, until her happy resolution, the very persistence of this tension within the religious voice lends some corroboration to the wider skepticism of the other narrator, whose bleak account of a populace hopelessly entangled in English legal practice is further darkened by his vision of humanity "slipping and sliding since the day broke," as though all are created fallen (illegitimate) and remain unredeemed (1.5).

To ennoble her Christian character and adumbrate certain plot developments, Dickens also associates his heroine with Queen Esther, who risked death to save her people. More attention will be paid to this parallel shortly; let it be said here that Esther Summerson is not just a "pattern young lady" (63.747) modeled after an ideal human type nor, as Michael Ragussis has argued, a clearly readable sign of the "Summer-son,"[74] neatly opposed to the other narrator of Chaos and Old Night. While Dickens associates his Esther with New Testament texts and a Christological queen, he also challenges these identifications in two important ways—the second and third senses in which battles of the books disturb her narrative.

The second is the way Dickens permits alternative interpretations of those Bible passages which Esther quotes naively as though their hermeneutic stability were assured. In doing so Dickens introduces tensions between not "books," precisely, but readings of scriptural passages and of his heroine, with muted irony at Esther's expense. Her favorite New Testament passages often perform a double function: they may speak a gospel that needs to be heard, yet they can also serve unconsciously to "cover a multitude of sins" (1 Pet. 4:8) by perpetuating some crucial evasion that makes it easier for Esther to "forgive" what she has not in fact brought fully to mind. In chapter 8 ("Covering a Multitude of Sins"), Esther's acts of charity alternate with or double as acts of evasion; even with her pious attempt to comfort the brickmaker's wife (whose baby has died) by "whisper[ing] to her of what Our Saviour said of children" (100), Esther in pointedly making one biblical allusion unconsciously avoids alluding to other, unpleasant things. (The unconsoled mother "answered nothing, but sat weeping—weeping very much.") On other occasions of comforting herself, the Bible becomes an aid to her unstable recoveries from those glances into the abyss which periodically draw Esther's attention beyond the "uniform level of quiet domesticity" she associates with God's care. Because her recoveries repeatedly prove temporary, these moments of biblically sponsored suppression become a distinctive note of her narrative; behind them looms the Joban existential anxiety she strives faithfully to overcome. Discerning the psychodynamics of Esther's New Testament usages, the reader enters into Dickens' Victorian understanding of the psychic needs religion serves. That kind of understanding is, of course, mingled with tolerance for weak Esther, although it is laced with cynicism for the novel's satiric religionists such as Mrs. Pardiggle, who satisfies her own need to be a "prominent . . . character" by forcing her piety upon the poor (96).

In arguing more later for some ironic instability in specific New Testament usages in Esther's narrative, I intend to show that an ambivalence toward conventional religious resolutions is detectable in the self-revealing text produced by this fictional author. Of course, behind Esther, Dickens' actual literary intentions and state of personal religious belief are impossible to prove from the novel alone, particularly given his use of the uninterpreted first-person point of view for her story. [75] Indeed, what seems his mimetic strategy of using Bible quotation in ways that reflect Esther's pious but evasive character may more simply indicate his own need to impose religious interpretations on crisis experiences (just as his other narrator imposes divine justice following Krook's death). If that is the case, the irony lies entirely in the skeptical reader's construction of the text and exists at Dickens' as well as Esther's expense.

Thirdly, Dickens challenges Summerson's identification with the Old Testament's Christological queen by involving his heroine with the long-suffering and godforsaken Job, more firmly established in the tradition as a type of Christ (although surely a problematic one). While the Book of Esther forms a reassuring biblical subtext for this Victorian heroine's autobiography, as the discussion will show, the parallels also reveal important limits; and these limits are marked by the corrective presence of a Joban subtext qualifying and deepening the meaning of Esther's queenly "progress." The books of both Esther and Job are necessary to the overall tendency of *Bleak House* to move from curse to blessing, but they coexist for most of the story in dialogical tension as though a struggle between their different perspectives were going on beneath the surface of Esther's narrative. To see what these are, we must look first more closely at the story of her regal counterpart, a stunning Old Testament heroine.

With its similarities to other Persian tales such as Dickens' favorite *A Thousand and One Nights*, its Cinderella motif, its melodramatic suspense and folkloristic plotting, its satire and comic artifice, [76] the Book of Esther is just the sort of Old Testament tale Dickens would have relished. This underpattern for Esther's narrative operates within a moral framework for human action as a fairy story of supernatural deliverance. To adapt Northrop Frye's terminology in *The Great Code* for the "divine comedy" of other Bible narratives, this book's double U-shaped pattern projects its heroine prophetically upward, takes her through a fall into danger, and propels a second, more glorious rise that identifies her personal victory with the redemption of her race. Commentaries popular in Dickens' day, like Matthew Henry's, emphasized Esther's "wonderfu[l] . . . concurrence of providences,"[77] the apocalyptic motif elaborately built into the multiple polar reversals of this tale. While the legal and political evils of *Bleak House* are not redeemed like those in the Book of Esther,[78] its theme of faith renewed in divine Providence amid "the apparent hopelessness of a human history dominated by secular power"[79] is the redeeming substance of Esther Summerson's testimony.

Both Esthers begin their stories in bondage followed by Cinderella-like rises in social station and comfort that show how "God . . . rais[es] up friends for the fatherless and motherless."[80] An orphan and "no one" socially (4.45), the Jewish slave girl earns the people's favor and King Xerxes' notice through her winsome, natural qualities, living up to the name given by her Babylonian captors and derived from Ishtar, goddess of love. Her benefactor Mordecai is a "cousin" who proves so loyal a friend that, according to one tradition, he generously yields to her "better preferment" as Xerxes' chosen queen even though he desires her (like Jarndyce) for his own wife.[81] Dickens' "orphan" heroine is born into a peculiarly Victorian captivity: she is captive not to pagans but to biblical texts barbarously applied in an unchristian spirit, and the slave name bestowed is a euphemism to cover the shame of Esther Summerson's fallen-woman associations. On her chaste Victorian terms, she too obtains "favour in the sight of all them that looked upon her" (Est. 2:15; cf. Woodcourt's "what sacred admiration and what love she wins," 61.731). Hints of royalty already attend her childhood at Windsor, where she says she was "brought up . . . like some of the princesses in fairy stories, only I was not charming" (3.17). Typically, however, Summerson suggests noble kinship while denying the sexual charms of her biblical counterpart. As the stories continue, this sexual denial forms the most striking of several important contrasts between these parallel characters.

Both are raised from their "desolate" positions to do their "duty" (as Kenge proses) "in that station of life unto which it has pleased—shall I say Providence?—to call" them (23). The rise of both heroines is tainted by guilt, however, and complicated by hidden identities. To keep her new social position as the Persian king's concubine, Queen Esther, who knows who she really is, must conceal the Jewish identity that makes her association with a Gentile unclean. When the plot thickens with the king's edict against the Jews and Mordecai's secret appeal that Esther intervene, she delays, fearing for her life if she reveals her Jewish kinship. But the queen cannot escape the pogrom just because she lives in the king's palace any more than can Esther Summerson conceal forever her family connections or avoid the general contagion because she lives in snug Bleak House and a separate narrative, or in her illness escape the fiery ring of the human condition.

Forced to difficult points of choice in their relation to wider communities, both heroines decide to risk self-sacrifice for others, illustrating how "The lives of God's people are so intertwined that none of them can ever find salvation without seeking it for his brothers also."[82] After mourning in solidarity with her people—putting ashes and dung on her head and covering herself with her tangled hair (Apoc. Est. 14:2)—the queen appears before the king as a splendid actress ("her countenance was cheerful and very amiable: but her heart was in anguish for fear," Apoc. Est. 15:5), gradually discloses her kinship, and succeeds in her plea for mercy. Through her mediation, the "appointed time" of death to Jews is transmuted into the appointment of a celebration for life, the festival of Purim (Est. 9:27).

Esther Summerson's sacrificial consideration for others and widening circle of charity cause her to be "held in remembrance above all other people!" (13.163) like the "memorable" queen.[83] But even as Dickens' heroine fulfills her biblical commissions, she is enmeshed in complexities of her own: Even after she learns who she is, she strives to maintain her social and moral position by acquiescing in the suppression of her true identity, with its "unclean" association with Lady Dedlock. While the biblical heroine has political reasons for disguise and puts her physical charms to the service of her nation, Esther Summerson's merely domestic service requires her to desexualize herself. She is not vindicated by playacting but victimized by her subterfuges and incompatible roles, all part of a "communal fantasy" that encourages destructive deceptions.[84] In contrast to the queen who opposes those "unworthily placed in authority" (Apoc. Est. 16:7), Summerson's worst enemies are the demons within that prevent her from establishing her own authority as a coherent person.

Because it lacks this complexity, the Book of Esther is finally an inadequate subtext for Esther's "progress": its characters are Wisdom literature stereotypes,[85] its evils are nominalized in villain figures providentially converted or destroyed, and it does not deal with the psychological and moral dilemmas that Esther Summerson must both report and face in herself, notably the anomaly of guilty innocence. For the Victorian woman who matures to become a "river of good" for others although much more modestly than the heroine of Mordecai's dream,[86] limited growth comes about not through the stark transformations of fairytale logic that empower the Book of Esther's forward movement, and that prevail only at the happy conclusion of Summerson's narrative. Until this ending is imposed, she grows through the more psychologically credible processes typical of realist fiction. For these maturing experiences, in which new facts compel the rethinking of old formulas, the more appropriate biblical subtext is the Book of Job, which offers what Matthew Henry called "more manly meat" for exercising the spiritual senses than the preceding Old Testament books,[87] including the contiguous Book of Esther.

What we find in this darker subtext is no simple set of analogues for Esther's narrative; if Scripture informs Dickens' fictional interpretations of experience, his novel also fosters a rereading of biblical tradition for latter days. The Book of Job according to *Bleak House* is inevitably revised, although it must be remembered that Job's author had also written a self-reflexive critique into his own profoundly dialogical book. Thus Dickens' exposure of some Calvinist uses of Job in *Bleak House* can also be supported from the biblical text, which dramatizes one man's persecution by human acts of misguided religious zeal, as well as by that "indifferent parent," "the universe" (Jarndyce, 6.68). If Esther Summerson's illegitimacy symbolizes the suffering inexplicably given to all who enter the world of a hidden God, a Creator who has abandoned the embarrassment of his fallen creatures, the more immediate (and remediable) cause of her anguish is a puritanical society that locates in her birth peculiar guilt. Tellingly, it is a representative of this religious tradition who first introduces the Joban subtext into Esther's story: treating this living child as "an hidden untimely birth" (Job 3:16), Miss Barbary cruelly transmutes Job's "Let the day perish wherein I was born" (3:3) into the curse upon this nobody's child who should "never [have] been born!" (3.19). Much of Esther's inner warfare is her confused struggle with the opprobrium of this misapplied text; she must throw off this false identification with Job. At the same time, in striving to escape parental injustice and perverted bibliolatry while remaining a faithful servant, she is also like her biblical counterpart more vigorously resisting the misguided sermons of self-appointed religious authorities while striving to hear, understand, and obey the word of his God.

But in both stories that God is largely silent. The most troubling Joban dimension of Esther's narrative is the existential anxiety she feels in such a world as a guilty innocent—an anomalous identity to which religious formulas she knows cannot speak the definitive and comforting word. Both Job and Esther struggle to maintain their belief that God loves them and to assert their honesty and virtue, for both appear to be God's elect, acknowledged for their practical acts of charity. ("I was eyes to the blind . . . a father to the poor," says Job in 29:15–16—a text Dean Stanley used in his memorial sermon on Dickens.) Yet for both, multiple calamities have called this election into question. In the face of her misfortune of being born into a society that condemns illegitimacy as a crime, Esther feels "confusedly . . . guilty and yet innocent" (3.20; cf. Job

10:15); later when she hears her mother's confession, the guilt becomes more intimately her own secret. Although Summerson and Job are worlds apart in some ways, it is this complex state of soul they share—caught between a "psalm of innocence" and a "psalm of penitence"[88] (neither entirely legitimate)—that generates both characters' internal debates and ambivalent utterances from the third chapter of both narratives. And, given God's silence, exacerbating these ambivalences are certain of Job's problems with authority, knowledge, and belief which also preoccupy Esther Summerson and the other *Bleak House* narrator: all three in their distinctive ways reveal the limits of worldly and biblical wisdom,[89] expose the failures of the patriarchs to provide trustworthy counsel,[90] suffer from hermeneutic uncertainty in a world of mysterious signs, and in responding to these uncertainties fall victim to unrealistic expectation (whether of false apocalyptic, prophetic, or fairytale thinking) and to equally unrealistic, impious despair.

Esther's ambivalences are nearly ended, as Job's are definitively, only when the heroine of faith is rewarded after many trials. But her resolution revises Job's in important, timely ways reflecting the several intervening traditions and later perspectives that influenced Dickens' uses of the Bible. Job's debates are ended by his words of utter humiliation, which Calvin admired for its acknowledgment of God's sovereignty: "I abhor myself, and repent in dust and ashes" (42:6). Such a text viewed not in Calvin's transcendent terms but on a humanistic plane is merely neurotic, less a resolution than an abject dissolution of the creatureliness which Calvin in fact celebrated if his puritan followers did not. Esther Summerson is also, of course, a "wrestler of self-denial," as St. John Chrysostom called Job; and as a character partially governed by the conventions of the renunciation story Dickens so often used,[91] as well as a Victorian progressive paradigm, she too is to prove that one can rise on the stepping-stones of her dead selves to higher things. But in Dickens' vestigially Romantic revision of the Calvinist model, Esther must also recover from self-abhorrence in her pilgrimage toward wholeness of self,[92] moving progressively away from the injustice of the birth curse and her own excesses of penitential humility. To the humanist in Dickens, one of the selves Esther must die to is the woman of unnecessary and hurtful renunciations, although as a Victorian heroine she must not renounce all self-denials but come to discern which are needful in the responsible and faithful life.

If one strand of Romantic ideology the Victorians inherited requires the rejection of Job as abject creature, another requires Esther Summerson to confront the *de profundis* of the Joban middle for a time: not to wrestle with supernatural powers like Bunyan's pilgrim (as she thinks), not to acknowledge her sin like Job the penitent, but to confront her psychic demons and the evils inseparable from her living. Here, the novel's humanized baptismal imagery becomes important. Esther's "godmother" had perverted the role of namegiver in implicitly associating the child with accursed Job, for the Order of Baptism is meant to expel the Devil, not bring demonic forces down on the infant's head or insinuate them into her heart. To give herself her authentic name, Dickens' heroine must be rebaptized by undergoing in later life her own experiences of the depths.

These, too, are interpreted "according to *Bleak House*" as a latter-day, Victorian fiction. Esther's two major trials (discussed below) are severe baptisms of fire and water, but they are not different in kind from the rest of Esther's experience; they intensify the paradigmatically Joban encounter with the anomalous that occurs repeatedly in Esther's daily modern life—in court, in church, at Miss Flite's, with Richard Carstone, with Jo, with Jarndyce, and everyone else. Such encounters, in their most terrific and supernatural forms, had been the staple of gothic romance, its mysterious source of menace and mechanism of calamity; and, as we shall see, the gothic of the other narrative does erupt at certain points in Esther's story. But in the Victorian realist novel, with which her narrative is more consistently allied, the confrontation with what is "other," unexpected and unaccounted for, is psychologized and socialized; and more important for Dickens' revision of the Joban paradigm, it is incorporated into a "progress," which assures that Esther's thoughtful encounters with the anomalous, whether terrific or mundane, will bring the wisdom of maturity. Even more important, then, than Summerson's Joban suffering is her interpretation and transcendence of it through her embodiment of the progressive pattern that Victorians like Froude also imposed on the Book of Job. Dickens' heroine of faith matures in understanding with the hopeful motto for reading Job that Matthew Henry appended to his exposition, *"Plus ultra—Onward."*[93]

What sustains her through the *chronos* of the middle when no onward motion toward fulfillment appears is a final Victorian addition to the Book of Job, its resolution in love. Although it is also a source of pain and confusion, Esther's charity signals her ultimate salvation; as Dickens reminded himself in the "mem" for Number 10 (where she is stricken blind), "Esther's love must be kept in view, to make the coming trial the greater . . . and the victory the more meritorious."[94] In this the amorous queen of the other subtext also reasserts herself, still in chaste Victorian form, uniting the previously discordant meanings of "love" in Summerson's experience—sexual love, compassion for other individuals and concern for communal life, and acceptance of her conflicted identity that allows this autobiographer to write her own Joban "Book of Esther."

The readings of individual chapters that follow have more to say about how these two subtexts vie for mastery in "Esther's Narrative" up to the happy ending when the logic of both biblical folktales nearly leaves behind the more realistic story. Taken individually, both scriptural associations authenticate Summerson's religious identity, although in different ways; their copresence in her discourse, in which each subtext implicitly modifies and critiques the other, troubles this identity and complicates the progressive pattern that Esther, her readers, and Dickens would impose. Her modest "progress" labors in fact under double jeopardy, courting the dangers that these two major subtexts for her story each epitomize. With the Book of Esther, Summerson risks the simplifications of magical scheming that effects a world of desire. Thus she is tempted at times to reduce the ways of Providence to patterns that confuse her wishes with the Divine Will (see 50.606) and to believe in a fairytale logic incongruous with her adult experience—the illogic of her advice to herself after Jarndyce's proposal, "you are happy for life" (44.538), or the nonsense of the nursery-rhyme vocation of sweeping "the cobwebs out of the sky" when she cannot cleanse Lady Dedlock's guilt nor rightly order Richard Carstone's life. Dickens' Esther learns at length that some things (like Chancery promises) are "too good to be true" in this world (65.758).

In her internal combat of biblical books, Joban realism qualifies this sort of fantasy; on the other hand, the Joban poetry invading Summerson's narrative poses its own perils, which the firm faith of a Queen Esther would overcome. Summerson risks being consumed by passive self-pity and the submerged anger, deflected toward herself, of one victimized by "a combination on the part of mankind against an amiable child" (Skimpole, 61.729). It is, finally, because Dickens' heroine so narrowly misses embracing "for life" the limited attitudes represented in both biblical subtexts—the easy affirmation and the debilitating despair that are both on trial in *Bleak House*—that her development is not, after all, "a constantly triumphant progression"[95] but a more provisional Victorian pilgrimage. In its qualities of narrative fluctuation, stylistic shifting, and internal dialogue, it bears more affinity to the uncertainly progressing middle of *In Memoriam*, which appeared two years before *Bleak House*, than anything Dickens wrote. Esther's narrative is his "way of a soul."

The major argument of this chapter is that the whole of *Bleak House*, and not just the skeptical narrative, reads as a work written amid Victorian religious anxieties and discords in biblical interpretation. What has been called the novel's "radical dilemma" of "denial and affirmation"[96] the reader experiences as well in the hermeneutic uncertainty of Esther's progress, which brings into its serious play of meanings all three battles of biblical books I have discussed. The scriptural allusions associated with Summerson's major crises in the second half of the novel (in chapters 35 and 36, 57 and 59) mark her alternations between Joban confusion and despair, Joban patience, and queenly hope; the allusions also mirror her internal stresses between Law and Gospel, showing the reader the moral importance of the endangered New Testament values in which Esther struggles to believe, if also, ironically, the emotional attractiveness of religious language to authorize her mechanisms of evasion. Her resolutions of major conflicts, often culminating in a biblical allusion or echo, are for most of the novel unstable and temporary; compulsively, the familiar battles of texts continue to surface in chapter after chapter.

Esther's first "little trial" (35.437) of major importance takes up scarcely more than a page; even more effectively containing the experience than the enforced brevity of the account is the familiar biblical pattern in which Dickens encapsulates her dark night of the soul. Suffering Job's "wearisome nights" (7:3) of guilty complaint and morbid imaginings ("My flesh is clothed with worms and clods of dust," Job 7:5), "full of tossings to and fro unto the dawning of the day" (7:4), she nearly meets the "appointed time" for which he longs (7:1). Unlike a Gridley or a Jobling, Esther reports her "one long night" with tremulous apology as though her "painful unrest" were a bitter blasphemy her Christian reader can scarcely understand or forgive: "I am almost afraid to hint at that time in my disorder—it seemed one long night, but I believe there were both nights and days in it—when I laboured up colossal staircases, ever striving to reach the top, and ever turned, as I have seen a worm in a garden path, by some obstruction, and labouring again. . . . I would find myself complaining, 'O more of these never-ending stairs, Charley,—more and more—piled up to the sky, I think!' and labouring on again" (431). When the terrors of a godforsaken cosmos come upon her, she is "scare[d] . . . with dreams, and terrifie[d] . . . through visions" (Job 7:14); appalled by the condition she shares with all mortals, like Job she "long[s] for death, but it cometh not" (3:21). "Dare I hint," Esther asks timidly, "at that worse time when, strung together somewhere in great black space, there was a flaming necklace, or ring, or starry circle of some kind, of which *I* was one of the beads! And when my only prayer was to be taken off from the rest, and when it was such inexplicable agony and misery to be part of the dreadful thing?" (432). Job's "days are swifter than a weaver's shuttle," and he declares his "eye shall no more see good" (7:6–7). Blind Esther becomes aware of "how short life really was, and into how small a space the mind could put it." "Oppressed . . . by the great perplexity of endlessly trying to reconcile" the disparate images of her life (431), she longs for an end to her confusion about guilt and innocence, with its challenge to the very legitimacy of her existence as a child of God. Esther has always been oppressed by the sense of an ending—

intensified in the apocalyptic images of her fever-nightmare, lingering after her recovery in her consciousness of the lost face, the self others have denied which she also tries to bury. That this loss represents not just a blow to vanity but her new intolerable knowledge of a kind of premature death she has *chosen* is hinted in Esther's internal questioning as she later waits for Ada's return: "Might she not look for her old Esther, and not find her?" she asks (36.455), echoing Job's bolder suicidal addresses to God in 7:21, "thou shalt seek me in the morning, but I shall not be."

Although love is strong as death, countering even the death wish, in Esther's victories,[97] she has not simply been purified by this "little trial"; it has exacerbated the battle of Law and Gospel within. As all the old "pet" names for her "guardian" and his "dear, dear girl" return in full force after her illness (see 35.434–37), Esther embraces not the wisdom of greater maturity but "the childish prayer of that old birthday" in which one finds these two forces of judgment and mercy contending still: in her resolve "to be industrious, contented, and true-hearted, and to do some good to some one, and win some love to myself if I could" (437), there linger vestiges of her aunt's Law sermon on the "Submission, self-denial, diligent work" (3.19) through which Esther might atone for the guilt of having been born.

Capping this regression is the "appointed day" of Miss Flite's arrival (438), leading to Esther's coy admission of Woodcourt's love followed by her immediate retreat from it. Esther is glad to learn the "gentle lesson" of the "poor afflicted creature['s]" greater affliction and "to soothe her under her calamity." But she cannot learn from Flite's literally maddening use of Bible promises—cannot observe, as the reader does ironically, that while she sensibly advises Flite to abandon the old inappropriate apocalyptic expectations of Chancery, Esther deflects her yearning for earthly union with Woodcourt through her own inappropriate expressions of Christian hope, "aspir[ing] to meet him, unselfishly, innocently, better far . . . at the journey's end" (see 437–43). The secret community of feeling between these two patient Joban sufferers—"the mad little woman worn out with curtseying and smiling" and the Little Woman who makes herself "no one" in her deferential cheeriness—is their common anguish, "the sickness of hope deferred" (24.307; Esther, who makes this allusion to Proverbs 13:12, recognizes this sickness in Chancery suitors but does not apply it to herself).[98]

When chapter 36 opens, the recovering Esther is prematurely blessed with a folktale restitution at Boythorn's lovely country house, as though she were "a princess" favored by "a good fairy" after all (444). But the cheerful attempt to produce a "happy ever after" ending breaks down, just as her resolutions to deny the flesh fail because she does love the created world; again and again Esther returns to the "loss" of the old face while striving in conventional ways to count some "gain" from her illness (see 443). After the deeply troubling encounter with Lady Dedlock in chapter 36, Esther's ambivalent response is characteristically reflected in two rival sets of Scripture allusions. Lady Dedlock's remorseful letter prompts Esther to recall the first set of (Old Testament) texts, climaxing with the savage return of her repressed Joban death wish. Later, Ada's and Jarndyce's loving letters inspire Esther to rewrite the legalism that has nearly crushed her; reversing the Joban curse, she takes heart with a New Testament allusion and makes a birth announcement of kinship with the innocent Queen Esther. But for reasons that will appear, these resolutions are unstable and allow the reader to make some ironic observations about Esther's use of religious texts.

To understand how the Law and Gospel, Job and Esther texts remain in tension in chapter 36, we must recall the first time Esther had encountered her mother in Chesney Wold chapel. This truncated recognition scene had been framed by a fragment of a penitential psalm used to open Morning Prayer in the Anglican liturgy: "Enter not into judgment with thy servant, O Lord, for in thy sight——" (18.224). Here Esther interrupts the second verse from Psalm 143 to record her mother's "look"—not God's, for the words of judgment that follow are omitted ("in thy sight shall no man living be justified"). Although Esther does not know it, Lady Dedlock cannot pray David's prayer, for she is another "official representative of all the pomps and vanities" who has not renounced them as the catechism bids in "this wicked world" (see 224 and n. 6).[99] The Joban fate the psalmist fears will become the dark end of her history in the pauper graveyard: he urges, "Hear me speedily, O Lord: my spirit faileth: hide not thy face from me, lest I be like unto them that go down into the pit" (v. 7). What follows Psalm 143:2 in the liturgy is the priest's exhortation to the confession of sins ("we should not dissemble nor cloke them before the face of Almighty God") and the absolution. But the rite in progress falls to the background as Esther's partial memories of "the days of old" (v. 5) surface and the "reader's voice" becomes the stern voice of her "godmother" (225). Just as the psalmist's plea for mercy is left unfinished and the words of absolution remain unheard in the service, so Esther and her mother miss the promises of forgiveness. Nor have they confessed: just as the half-verse brings only partly into the open a statement of guilt, Esther's "scraps of old remembrances" produce only partial confession of kinship. With only haughty evasion for Lady Dedlock and evasive self-subdual for Esther—their characteristic ways of responding to the admonition to be penitent—there can be no peace for the "two troubled minds" that meet privately at last in chapter 36 (449).

In this scene, Lady Dedlock tells Esther she has been wandering in "the desert" without exodus, where "useless remorse" and her own denial of maternal love are the earthly judgment she has brought upon herself (450–52). Here we have a naturalized version of the divine visitation to which Aunt Barbary had alluded in chapter 3 ("pray daily that the sins of others be not visited upon your head"), when she had recalled the first commandment against idol worship ("For I the Lord thy God am a jealous God, visiting the iniquity of the fathers upon the children") but conflated Exodus 20:5 with the theme of Leviticus 18:25, where God threatens to "visit the iniquity . . . upon [the land]" for specifically sexual transgressions. Combining these texts, Aunt Barbary had taken it upon herself to carry out jealous Jahweh's visitation upon little Esther. Now so much later in life, as Esther reads her mother's remorseful confession, she reports that she "could not disentangle all that was about me; and I felt as if the blame and the shame were all in me, and the visitation had come down" (453). Momentarily in chapter 36 she has no New Testament verses with which to combat this virulent legacy of past Law. Crushed by her first full awareness of the web of sins and deceptions in which she has been enmeshed simply by being born, Esther herself pronounces the curse against her birth, not even alluding to her aunt's words but adopting them as her own authentic expression of "the real feelings that I had": "I hope it may not appear very unnatural or bad in me, that I then became heavily sorrowful to think I had ever been reared. That I felt as if I knew it would have been better and happier for many people, if indeed I had never breathed" (453). Esther's parallel sentences moving the curse backward in time recall the regressive form of Job's curse in the deepening of his despair ("Let the day perish wherein I was born, and the night in which it was said, There is a man child conceived," 3:3). Esther reiterates her confession, not with Job's vehemence but with his compulsion: "I was so confused and shaken, as to be possessed of a belief that it was right, and had been intended, that I should die in my birth; and that it was wrong, and not intended, that I should be then alive" (453). "Why died I not from the womb?" Job cries. For "then had I been at rest, With kings and counsellors of the earth, which built desolate places for themselves; . . . Or as an hidden untimely birth I had not been; as infants which never saw light" (3:11, 13–14, 16). Lady Dedlock will flee the desolate place where she has built her deceptive noble position; Esther longs for release in the hiddenness of never having been born at all. If there is providential care in the world, it seems not "intended" for these sisters of Job. [100]

Esther's fantasy of her own evil influence outside any benevolent order next unleashes a gothic influx near the Ghost's Walk, temporarily obscuring her religious hope. But this is an indulgence of fantasy guilt; her descent into the depths is yet to come. With the restoration of the domestic security that does much to sustain Esther's faith, loving letters from Ada and Jarndyce arrive to counter Lady Dedlock's written confession. Now the better memory of a New Testament text expels the darker remembrances of grim Old Testament passages: Esther sees "very well how many things had worked together, for my welfare; and that if the sins of the fathers were sometimes visited upon the children, the phrase did not mean what I had in the morning feared it meant. I knew I was as innocent of my birth as a queen of hers; and that before my Heavenly Father I should not be punished for birth, nor a queen rewarded for it" (454–55). With the recall of Romans 8:28 ("And we know that all things work together for good to them that love God, to them who are the called according to his purpose"), Esther forces closure on her Joban doubts of God's providence. Her remembrance of a rescuing New Testament text also leads to her implicit identification with the queen whose people were nearly punished for their birth but were saved from a genocidal law by a wonderful "concurrence of providences."

For all her eloquence at this climax, however, Esther's struggles are hardly over, [101] for her Romans 8:28 echo may also remind us that the human "conspiracy to make [her] happy" at Bleak House (35.437) has not worked altogether for the good of Dame Durden. The closing tableau of chapter 36 bears out once again the irony of the New Testament allusion. When Esther hears "my darling calling as she came up-stairs, 'Esther, my dear. . . . Little Woman, dear Dame Durden!' " (456), she is "called" to her "purpose" like "them that love God"; but as Ada's pet names imply, this calling is to become only a little woman, when Esther becomes "like a child" in the Madonna-Ada's arms (456). In the context of these infantilizing human providences, therefore, to recognize her birth as "innocent" from inherited sexual fault is also a way for Esther to deny her adult identity; and on a second, skeptical reading, her apparently inspiring association with Queen Esther becomes a disloyal declaration of independence from tainted Lady Dedlock—that very denial of kinship which the biblical queen had to overcome. Esther Summerson must still come to terms with her own fleshly nature and that of the mother she has agreed to conceal with the help of "the providence of God" (449)—a God wanted, the reader notes ironically, to protect from public shame rather than to empower full and open forgiveness.

In these ways do Esther's saving texts only point her unresolved dilemmas. Indeed, if it is in the Christian spirit of St. Paul's Epistle to the Romans that she has meant to rewrite her mother's Law-ridden letter, the terms of Esther's self-deception are also deducible from a central opposition developed in Romans 8 between the carnally and the spiritually minded. Esther chooses the path to "glory" by adopting the mortification of the flesh, seemingly confirmed by her "providential" disfigurement ("if ye through the Spirit do mortify the deeds of the body, ye shall live," 8:13). In this way, as Lawrence Frank has observed of Esther's mechanisms, she "fix[es] herself . . . in a state beyond temptation" and avoids her mother's carnal misdeeds,[102] hoping thereby to secure salvation from spiritual anxiety. As one of "the children of God" (8:16–17), Esther then gains a spiritual parentage to replace the fleshly one she has rejected; and in "the Spirit of adoption" she can "cry, Abba, Father" (8:15) not only to her "Heavenly Father" (454) but also to the aging father-husband in her chaste marriage to John Jarndyce. Ironically, Romans 8 read this way is no rescuing text but authorizes instead that very betrayal of the heart, represented in marriage to an older, sexually impotent man of position, that was to Dickens Lady Dedlock's most serious misdeed.

The "child" Esther becomes at the end of her double crisis in chapters 35 and 36 (456) may have exchanged the nobody's child she rightly disowns for the redeemed child of God, but the woman has not been wholly renewed despite the imprimatur that biblical allusions seem to place upon her resolution of crisis. In the chapters that follow her queenly declaration, what might have been progression is merely a "return" to Bleak House, not the "general new beginning altogether" for which she yearns (38.472; and see Rom. 8:22). Again we hear the burden of the same old Victorian-Calvinist tune: "'Once more, duty, duty, Esther,' said I; 'and if you are not overjoyed to do it, more than cheerfully and contentedly, through anything and everything, you ought to be.'" Until her second baptismal trial in chapter 59, Esther remains captive to the unresolved battle of her texts.

Up to this point, in thus presenting a character whose religion appears to be at once the great resource of her life and her bane, Dickens leaves his reader with a problem of interpretation Froude had identified for the thoughtful reader of modern life: "how rightly to estimate a human being; what constitutes a real vitiation of character, and how to distinguish, without either denying the good or making light of the evil; how to be just to the popular theories, and yet not to blind ourselves to their shallowness and injustice,—that is a problem for us, for the solution of which we are at present left to our ordinary instinct, without any recognized guidance whatsoever."[103] Given the first-person narrative, we are vouchsafed no direct authorial guidance as we strive to read Esther's religious interpretations of events. And yet, if we trust not the teller but the tale, we see that the structure of Esther's narrative, while ridden by spiritual conflict and enveloped in darkness, nevertheless tends toward God in its Victorian version of the Joban pattern: a progress through the depths to love. While the Book of Job does not resolve itself so much in charity as in a manifestation of God's power, the Victorians typically concluded the Joban perplexities—and their literary expressions of these—with love. An act of love which is an act of God is the "one, far-off divine event" toward which *In Memoriam* fitfully moves; it is also the concluding affirmation toward which Froude's essay on Job tends, the affirmation of "a faith which has flashed up in all times and all lands, wherever high-minded men were to be found, and which passed in Christianity into the acknowledged creed of half the world. The cross was the new symbol, the Divine sufferer the great example." As in this historical development that gave Froude hope, the "law of reward and punishment" pronounced upon Job's anguish by his loveless comforters is "superseded by the law of love" in this book[104]—and it sustains Esther Summerson through the major crisis of her life.

Esther's greatest potential for healing comes at her point of deepest extremity with the pursuit, discovery, and public recognition of Lady Dedlock as her mother. Reliving in this crisis the *de profundis* experience of her illness, only to find herself more deeply implicated in human misery than ever before, a matured Esther is now given the grace to rewrite the blasphemies of "The Appointed Time" in the loving spirit of the New Testament—this time, without incurring irony at her own expense. The other narrator had already replayed some motifs from chapter 32 in the scene of Tulkinghorn's death, but there had offered no answer to the question, "What does it mean?" except the unmeaning flourishes of the "paralysed dumb witness" (an unredeemed Roman) on the lawyer's allegorical ceiling (58.585). In Esther's extended crisis narrative of chapters 57 and 59, an allegorical journey into the "abyss" of evil, Dickens conveys the only kind of answer he knows—and a humanistic one—to the question of meaning in the face of death.

In chapter 57, Esther is roused from sleep only to lose her "right mind" (674) that she might enter into the horror of "a dream" (676), a more extended allegory of her inner life than the terrifying visions of her fever. In the extremity of the search after Lady Dedlock, Esther "retrace[s] the way" (678) of her earlier illness, which had left her in irresolution. As before, time becomes "an indefinite period of great duration" (687), stretching back to the beginnings of her selfhood and incorporating all the intervening years of struggle. Now the fearful dreamimages are directly of her mother confronting an Esther who gazes in horror at that which she has been seeking all along in her preoccupation with loss. Like Job foundering in cross seas of internal debate, Esther "torment[s herself] with questioning . . . and discussing" and "long dwelling on such reflections" as are

A NEW MEANING IN THE ROMAN
(Hablot K. Browne)

For many years, the persistent Roman has been pointing, with no
particular meaning, from that ceiling. It is not likely that he has any new
meaning in him to-night. Once pointing, always pointing—like any
Roman, or even Briton, with a single idea. . . . What does it mean? No
light is admitted into the darkened chamber. . . . All eyes look up at the
Roman, and all voices murmur, "If he could only tell what he saw!"
(*BH* 48.585)

impossible to answer because her thoughts of her mother darkly "reflect" herself (59.703). Meanwhile the horses slip and founder in a liquid, labyrinthine landscape that resembles her mind losing direction, "miss[ing] the way" (687) it normally follows in its progress by diurnal platitudes. Instead of the usual evasions, Bucket and Esther drive on "through streams of turbulent water" that rise, and rise again, in a dark baptismal flood.

In the midst of this ritual crisis, Bucket, a benign godfather reversing the gloomy "godmother," renames the plucky Esther "Queen," recalling for the reader her own declaration of innocent birth (704). But while these are necessary "encouraging words . . . under those lonely and anxious circumstances," the pair must plunge ever deeper into the unknown Joban regions where fairytale identities do not save, where Esther is not unambiguously innocent, and where the baptismal immersion becomes a penetrating contamination. "Descending into a deeper complication" of narrow, obscure streets (704), Esther meets new tests of her maturity. At Snagsby's, a crucial stage on the way, Esther becomes a Job figure in several impressive aspects—at once a comforter of the "poor soul" Guster, a fellow sufferer with her trembling and weeping, and an inquirer after the truth though it lead to the unthinkable (712).

Further still Esther travels into "ways . . . deep" with falling sleet, where narrow courts close in and "stained house fronts put on human shapes and loo[k at her]" (712). This weatherbeaten landscape of urban gothic repeats, in its inchoate guilt and liquidity, the place of horrors to which Jobling and Guppy were brought in Krook's shop. Here, in the graveyard pit of Psalm 143 but outside any liturgical framework, Esther meets her "appointed time"; "great water gates seemed to be opening and closing in [her] head, or in the air" (712–13) as her "roarings are poured out like the waters" of Job when "the thing which I greatly feared is come upon me" (3:24–25). Again, as for Jobling and Guppy, in the early morning hours they have descended into a claustral space, where "a thick humidity . . . like a disease" (713) makes everything loathsome to touch and smell. Just as Dickens' earlier witnesses had at first misread the unstable signs of Krook's demise ("he is *not* there!" 402), so Esther uncharacteristically mistakes the signs she sees of her mother's disappearance: "On the step at the gate . . . I saw, with a cry of pity and horror, a woman lying—Jenny, the mother of the dead child" (713). Now Esther finds that words have "no meaning [attached] to them," like the speechless witnesses to Krook's death; nor can Esther, normally quick "to read a face" (64.750), "comprehend the solemn and compassionate look in Mr. Woodcourt's face." "Shall she go?" asks a voice (713; cf. Jobling's "Shall I go?" 402). Esther at last goes down into the burial place to read accurately the sign of her mother's reappearance, not as charred bone but, again, as the merely material form of a human being: "I passed on to the gate, and stooped down. I lifted the heavy head, put the long dank hair aside, and turned the face. And it was my mother, cold and dead" (714). Unlike Jobling and Guppy, Esther does not immediately "run away" from the evil she recognizes, with a maidenly cry of "O Horror" (403): she "r[uns] forward" with "pity and horror" to discover her kinship with the woman she also names "my mother" and with all such "distressed, unsheltered, senseless creature[s]" whom the dead figure emblematizes.

"I pray to Heaven it may end well!" Esther had pleaded at the start of this journey into the depths (675). In her discovery of death by the dead letter, death without the belief in forgiveness that would have saved the woman alive, Esther offers the only help she can, a wordless gesture of love and acceptance. No longer the child cradled in Ada's arms, Esther has become the mourning adult survivor in a pathetic pietà. The chapter ends; there are no further words for this eloquent, chilling tableau, no coda of moral indignation, no easy reassurances of "our hope to be restored in Heaven!", no ironic placing, no authorial "help." In her final gesture before the locked gate, Esther shows she has learned the lesson of a Scripture text important in *Bleak House* which urges the full Gospel and not some cheerful, evasive substitute for it: "the end of all things is at hand. . . . above all things have fervent charity among yourselves: for charity shall cover the multitude of sins" (1 Pet. 4:7–8). For Dickens, apocalypse may never come to right the world, but death unquestionably is here: therefore have love. [105] The narrative blacks out; the reader is left in the enveloping darkness to apply the lesson of the charitable deed to the moments of death in his own life.

The alternating, unstable biblical texts in which Esther's provisional progress is involved ground her suffering and gradual, if flawed, maturity in the common experiences of *Bleak House* which even the comic Guppy and Jobling undergo. (As she says, she "can't be kept out" of the larger story; 9.103.) Her inductions into the depths have the effect of authenticating her charity and making her more humanly convincing than an unrelieved account of a "Saint Summerson" would have done (43.524). Like Job, she moves from knowing herself as "one that comforteth the mourners" (29:25) to recognizing herself as "one who mourns"; afflicted with her own calamity as well as a more mature knowledge of evil, she finally embraces the human condition to which the other narrator has borne witness. As Spurgeon mused on this favorite theme of sermons on Job in the nineteenth century: "A man is never made thoroughly useful unless he has suffering. . . . We must first suffer in our head and hearts the things we preach, or we shall never preach them with effect. . . . Then take heart. Perhaps the

Lord designs thee for a great work. He is keeping thee low in bondage, and doubt, and fear, that he may bring thee out more clearly, and make thy light like the light of seven days, and bring forth thy righteousness 'clear as the sun.' "[106] Although Dickens did not admire preachers like Spurgeon, and other voices in *Bleak House* most effectively protest just this kind of religious rationalization of suffering, the final disposition of Esther's case follows this common line of argument in Victorian theodicy.

Dickens' acts of restitution swiftly follow in a romantic conclusion that imposes the hopeful hypothesis where none would be warranted in a realistically conceived narrative. But Job and Esther Summerson are delivered from the realistic story. Esther cannot rescue "all the deaths that can be died" from illegibility for they lie beyond her ken, and the theodicy in her closing paragraphs is highly selective; but with the deepening of her sense of human loss, Esther has learned the more profound meaning of genuine charity—not to win back love to oneself only, as she so often has said, but to wrest some meaning from the pitilessness of events. And for this maturing of her love that her provisional realistic narrative has forwarded up to this point, Esther is rewarded as abruptly and almost as abundantly as Job.

Then she finds, as Spurgeon promised and Job hoped, that her "age shall be clearer than the noonday," that she can "shine forth" and "be as the morning" (Job 11:17; cf. Apoc. Est. 11:11). This is now her "usual time" (60.717) and the setting for her acts of writing "early in the morning at my summer window" (67.768). In the seventh year of her restoration, this creator can now reconstruct her pilgrimage "even supposing" (770) that, whatever her battles with "bondage, and doubt, and fear," whatever her misuse of texts that kill and of others that would bring life, the end of her Victorian progress will be greater than her beginning. But it is only after the Joban subtext emerges in the drama of her story that Dickens can allow a vision of gain to triumph—and then with a final note that re-engages the dialogical tensions of *Bleak House*, as Esther's last words of romantic hope are swallowed up.

5

The Seer, the Preacher, and the Living Gospel: Vision and Revision in *Little Dorrit*

THE NIGHT
(Hablot K. Browne)

And I saw a new heaven and a new earth: . . . and there was no more
sea. . . . And he that sat upon the throne said, Behold, I make all things
new. And he said unto me, Write: for these words are true and faithful.

Revelation 21:1, 5

The thing that hath been, it is that which shall be; and that which is done
is that which shall be done: and there is no new thing under the sun.

Ecclesiastes 1:9

And the day ended, and the night ended, and the morning came, and
Little Dorrit . . . came into the prison with the sunshine.

I F IN *Bleak House* Dickens' skepticism contends with his will to believe,
Little Dorrit is his most profoundly divided novel, formed of many contradictions left largely unresolved. The opening chapter, "Sun and Shadow,"
presents a paradigm of this contention and its partial resolution, engaging in
dialectical interplay two Theorems of the Universe, both biblical, that contend for
mastery down to the last words of Dickens' text. Dickens found these rival
interpretations of experience in the books of Revelation and Ecclesiastes, to both
of which his novel responds ambivalently; and although the indecidability of this
fictional work has a more complex genesis, it is largely from the interplay of these
two texts within the discourse of *Little Dorrit* that its capacities for supporting
radically different readings arise. Put simply, throughout this novel the transcendent anticipations of the Seer's "Behold, I make all things new" are modified by
the this-worldly pessimism of the Preacher's "there is no new thing under the
sun." We can catch a preliminary glimpse of this formative tension by looking at
the narrative structure of book 1, chapter 1, where Dickens' vision of what time of
the world and what kind of a world it is twice undergoes subtle revision as this
paradigmatic chapter unfolds.

Dickens opens *Little Dorrit* upon an eschatological spectacle of shivering
expectancy in which anyone may read the signs of the End Time. "A blazing sun
upon a fierce August day" has evoked in blistering harbor and fiercely blue sea
the lake of fire in Revelation 20:14; beyond the shade of the church, one
"plunge[s] into a fiery river" of superheated air under "a sky of purple, set with
one great flaming jewel of fire" (1–2). But having called up a vision of Mar-

seilles that portends a demonic apocalypse under a hostile sky, Dickens retreats from this fierce day to the time before the End—from a theorem of radical change and definitive closure to the perspective of an interminable meantime, where hope languishes in shadow. This retreat is managed via a descent into the chiaroscuro of a French gaol, where an assassin awaiting trial revises the light of this "day" to "the light of yesterday week . . . of six months ago . . . of six years ago" (9). Here the *kairos* of apocalyptic, the time of fulfillment, is abandoned for the merely successive *chronos* to which many characters in *Little Dorrit* will succumb—an illusion-ridden waiting time with "no new thing" and with no vision of origin and end to give meaning to suffering "in the middest." Through the dead center of this first chapter, as in the novel's middle chapters with their stylistic approximations of "mists and obscurities" (2.19.632), the play of consciously fictive language sustains living and partly living in the prison, an emblem throughout for "this lower world" (2.30.741).[1] Both this discouraging estimate of human probabilities and the demonic apocalypse with which we began are revised, however, when we ascend at the close of this chapter to watch the "day" die in a picturesque sunset. Closure and eventual clarity are conventionally promised, if faintly, after all, as Dickens shifts our perspective *sub specie aeternitatis:* the End, now, is not imminent cataclysm in a hostile universe or a present impossibility, but an immeasurably distant event in a providential world. The stars (passageway to the city of the divine apocalypse) have come out "in the heavens," and "so deep a hush was on the sea, that it scarcely whispered of the time when it shall give up its dead" (14; cf. Rev. 20:13).

The dominant biblical mode of this chapter and of *Little Dorrit* sponsors what Frank Kermode might call skeptical apocalyptic: in this fictional structure, the End expected by naive apocalypticism has been "disconfirmed without being discredited."[2] In anticipating and then revising the End time, chapter 1 enacts a recurrent dialectical movement in the novel: as expectations of endings or of new beginnings are repeatedly disappointed, we sense that Dickens' narrative is working not to confirm the mythic paradigms with which he begins both book 1 (fire) and book 2 (flood), but rather to modify them through an ironic rhythm of disconfirmation and reformulation. Thus the novel repeatedly moves through cycles of vision and revision. Of the tentative reconstructions *Little Dorrit* makes I shall have more to say; the impetus to disconfirm and revise received myths of the End comes from the skeptical realism of the other biblical subtext even more influential for *Little Dorrit* than Revelation. From the vantage point of wide human experience, Ecclesiastes' central project is to challenge traditional formulas of prophecy and wisdom with his relentless urge to "know" and "see." The uncertainties, injustices, futilities, and illusions of human life that he discovers the Preacher sums up in his own formula: "vanity of vanities; all is vanity," vapor, nothingness (1:2)—the antithesis of the eternal substance promised in the new creation. Throughout *Little Dorrit*, Dickens quietly undermines the hopes that chapter 1 affirms "shall" be fulfilled by showing his readers what he sees as the Ecclesiastian observer: how much of his society, indeed the entire scope of human action, is nothing but "Mist" (the original title of 1.1).[3]

In skeptical apocalyptic, the hopeful pattern, "even when ironized, even when denied," as Kermode says—delayed, misinterpreted, misappropriated for selfish purposes, trivialized, or doubted—is yet not wholly discredited.[4] Ultimately the ironic rhythm of Dickens' novel radically modifies the expectation of a total transformation of reality; but Ecclesiastian disillusion, too, is modestly revised. Kermode argues that a fiction structured to upset naive expectations by acknowledging facts and contingencies gives us the impression that it is "finding something out for us, something *real*."[5] *Little Dorrit*'s dialectical movement of anticipation and revision of belief results in a debilitating uncertainty for some, like William Dorrit, but does carry hero and heroine forward through painful readjustments of perspective to the partial knowledge and modest happiness of their reunion. Although Dickens' larger world is not released from its perpetual contradiction between "Sun and Shadow," the conclusion of the love plot unites and transcends *Little Dorrit*'s two contending Theorems of the Universe in the hopeful (Apocalypse) realism (Ecclesiastes) of the marriage between Amy and Arthur. Nonetheless, the way to even this muted happy ending is very long; the reader must grope her way with the characters amid uncertainty, "the twilight judgments of this world" (2.19.632), only rarely illuminated from above and only for a chosen few. The losses that attend the process of experiential learning accumulate unbearably for hero and heroine, as though to learn is virtually to lose and nothing more. Whatever new birth of being or advance in knowledge is possible in *Little Dorrit* must contend with the bitter awareness that even the noblest motives, aspirations, and actions partake of "vanity" in several senses of the word.

It is because of this awareness that the Book of Ecclesiastes, like the predominant Book of Job in *Bleak House*, is *Little Dorrit*'s primary biblical subtext, if not its secure center; too internally contradictory to be the privileged ground of any discourse, it is all the more a richly literary resource of themes, styles, and method as well as overt allusions for *Little Dorrit*. The Preacher's themes—and his conflicted presentation of them—are the preoccupations of Dickens' ambivalent novel of 1855–57. The central motif of *vanitas, vanitatum* empowers Dickens' confident satire on the Victorian scene, especially the vanity of riches, but it also pervades his more troubled understanding of the wider futility of labor and the vanity of the search for wisdom. "Wisdom"—a repeated word in this novel—is extensively satirized in the folly of Society's self-justifying philosophers; these "fool[s'] . . . multitude of words" (Ecc. 5:3) also illustrates in contemporary life Ecclesiastes' reinvocation of the Babel story (cf. *LD* 1.1.1 and 2.34.802). But wisdom also brings the sorrows of learning through experience for such nonsatirical characters as Arthur Clennam; and Arthur, too, suffers from a heteroglossia of fools' voices, external and internal. Ecclesiastes' questioning of providential order, his sense of humankind's imprisonment in monotonous, repetitive motion, his knowledge that the present repeats the past, his contrary perception that "There is no remembrance" (1:11), his motif of old age and of death leveling all, and his counsel of resignation and patience—all preoccupy the Dickens of *Little Dorrit*. Dickens' style also replays some of the most characteristic features of this biblical writer's mode: his circumlocutions around the same themes, his self-reflexive constructions, his returns to dead ends of thought and feeling, some of his prominent figures, and, most important, his stylistic approximations of chiaroscuro.

These thematic and linguistic affinities will find their places in the lengthy discussion of *Little Dorrit* that follows. What most deeply reflects Dickens' response to his Ecclesiastes subtext, however, is his adoption of its skeptical method. I have emphasized "skeptical apocalyptic" not only because this term juxtaposes in ironic poise the two most important subtexts for *Little Dorrit*, but also because it is the central biblical model for a larger heuristic process Kermode sees in fiction: the subjecting of paradigms of order and received formulas of all sorts to reinterpretation, a project of turning "vision" to "revision" that proceeds apace in *Little Dorrit* on many fronts. I have called Dickens' impetus for revision Ecclesiastian because the "something real" this novel's experience finds out for us, again and again, is the Preacher's one certainty of "vanity"— the insubstantial, the fictive. If there is more in *Little Dorrit*, its substantiality is highly qualified. Dickens' observation to Forster in a letter of 1852, "But *this* is all a Dream, may be, and death will wake us" (8 August; D 2:408) anticipates the Ecclesiastian mood of even the affirmations in *Little Dorrit*, where the final awakening and anticipatory intimations of divine Presence become only a "may be" of hypothetical belief.

The revisionary impulse in *Little Dorrit* is not directed only against the Book of Revelation, although this is the chief rival subtext, suggested in both its destructive and recreative phases in the monthly cover design. Dickens also challenges the formulas of worldly wisdom and the Calvinist beliefs (of Mrs. Clennam) that we would expect him to oppose; more problematically, he questions leading Victorian ideas, Christian ideals, and literary conventions (the mode of satire, the omniscient narrator) that he also draws upon in the same work. The section titled "Confession and Dialogue" will give extended discussion to the ways Dickens is rereading Carlyle (who provided several contemporary subtexts for *Little Dorrit*) through the perspective of Ecclesiastes. Most generally important for the concerns of this chapter, this book of Scripture becomes the dark interpretive lens through which nearly all the other biblical allusions in the novel have been skeptically re-envisioned and re-presented. As I shall argue, some of this revision of biblical formula results in stable ironies; in other cases the Bible standard itself, including Ecclesiastes, is subjected to the corrosions of the Preacher's skeptical method.

One thing this focus on Ecclesiastes will help us to see is that Dickens' challenges to formula in *Little Dorrit* are less decisive than Carlyle's in the *Latter-Day Pamphlets* and less definitive than some critical accounts of this novel would allow. K. J. Fielding's characteristic assertion, for example, that this is the work of a thoroughly disillusioned man "intent on stripping away all false disguises"[6] assumes both a belief in some bedrock reality beneath these illusions and an iconoclastic hostility to "fiction" that we do not find unequivocally expressed in *Little Dorrit*. If sometimes Dickens rips off the mask (as in Casby's unveiling), so often he discovers beneath the illusory formula only the nothingness, the nonsense, the fiction that the Preacher also finds at the inconclusive end of his quest for reality. Furthermore, Dickens knows that fictions, especially hypotheses of religious belief, are necessary in this "ignorant life"; less religiously, he celebrates the fluidity of self-consciously fictive language as a means of survival in the prison world. That affirmation we also find, as I shall argue, in the supremely literary discourse of Ecclesiastes, who takes pleasure in his own language and whose perpetual reconstructions open the text, for all its preoccupation with futility and enclosure, to the play of interpretation.

Dean Stanley heard in Ecclesiastes a "wisdom so refined, so serious, as to belong rather to a modern age, than to that when the book was composed."[7] Listening to what this ambivalent Wisdom text might say to his time and his own life, Dickens reflects in *Little Dorrit* several different readings of the Preacher's book that are kept in dialogical play to the end of the novel. In the three following sections, this chapter will take up in sequence three ways that Ecclesiastes bears upon *Little Dorrit*, depending upon Dickens' angle of interpretation. In each, tension with the vision of Revelation has an important role; at each stage, certain of the novel's other critical contradictions will also be assessed. First,

taken traditionally as admonitory sermon, Ecclesiastes empowers Dickens' satire on Victorian vanities and worldly wisdom, including its false forms of apocalyptic thinking ("Sermon and Satire"). Second, experienced as personal confession, the Preacher's conflicted discourse provides a biblical precedent for the
dialogue of the mind with itself inscribed into Dickens' novel—its subtly staged
battles between ideal and actuality, and between rival philosophies of life including apocalyptic ("Confession and Dialogue"). Third, read for its proverbial
wisdom on work, enjoyment, and patience, Ecclesiastes affirms some of the
values that make living possible in *Little Dorrit*'s lower world, the only world the
Preacher knows; but Dickens also reaches beyond what this biblical skeptic can
see for a more capacious and consoling religious vision, turning more explicitly
than he had yet to Christian wisdom, the Gospels, and apocalyptic themes and
symbols ("Proverbial Wisdom and Living Gospel"). "Skeptical apocalyptic" operates here in the way that Dickens, in this most overtly Christian of his mature
works, is forced not to abandon altogether his favorite texts of promise, but to
modify his account of their efficacy. They are disconfirmed by experience; they
are not wholly discredited. In a fictional universe whose instabilities issue from
an Ecclesiastian skeptical realism, set against the author's yearning to affirm a
transcendent faith, Little Dorrit emerges to become Dickens' most credible religious heroine. Not a supernaturalized mediatrix like the protected Florence
Dombey nor a long-suffering Esther Summerson delivered from her realistic
story, Amy is an Ideal embodied in the Actual, a living gospel—convincing
because she too is a fiction-maker and a fellow sufferer in the illusion-ridden
"middest."

Sermon and Satire

IF ECCLESIASTES belongs to the Wisdom movement like Proverbs, it enters this
tradition as a subversive, even heretical text. Its author, conventionally believed to be King Solomon, writes from a uniquely privileged position to know
wisdom from folly: the insider become outsider, he was, in Matthew Henry's
words, "the wisest of men, [who had] played the fool so egregiously,"[8] and who
now preaches as the reconstructed sage. His repeated assertion is not "it is
written" but "I saw": "I returned, and saw under the sun, that the race is not to
the swift, nor the battle to the strong, neither yet bread to the wise, nor yet
riches to men of understanding, nor yet favour to men of skill; but time and
chance happeneth to them all" (9:11). Relentlessly this cosmopolitan thinker
tests the precepts of the Wisdom teachers, as well as the vision of the prophet

and the assurance of the psalmist, against the teachings of experience and his "own heart" (1:16). With his repeated "this too is vanity," Ecclesiastes discards one form of wisdom after another in a futile search for what is not vanity. Insofar as his book can be read as a sermon, as traditionally it has been, at the heart of the Preacher's public purpose is the urging to disconfirm the accepted paradigms with the facts; but unlike the drive of skeptical apocalyptic, his impulse is to leave them discredited. They are mere words, empty formulas without force of truth.

Even more than Dickens speaks in *Little Dorrit* as the prophet familiar from *Bleak House* or *Hard Times*, he assumes the voice of the Victorian sage, the voice of many days "under the sun" (an Ecclesiastes phrase recurrent in this novel). From the vantage point of "large experience of humanity," Dickens invites his readers to "Come and see what I see!" (2.25.683, 684); but while "Come and see" in the Seer's book is an invitation to envision the four horses of the apocalypse (Rev. 6:1), *Little Dorrit*'s philosophizing narrator appeals rather to concrete seeing, like Ecclesiastes. This commitment to close observation, however, does not simply ground the novel in the solidity of "fact[s] . . . firmly established by experience" (2.13.554). Dickens' experiential vision in *Little Dorrit* issues in two divergent modes of fictional language, the satiric and the novelistic, each with its own view of "the facts." Before I turn to the novel's biblically based satire, some general discussion of these two modes (and their relation to two impulses in Ecclesiastes) is in order. While their coexistence in the Dickens world is a commonplace of criticism,[9] what has not been considered is the pressure their incongruous juxtaposition in one work brings to bear upon Dickens' use of biblical material. Especially in the satire, Dickens' Scripture is a firm ground of order, but it becomes a source of disorder in the novelistic portions of *Little Dorrit*.

In his well-known essay on this novel, Lionel Trilling admired the abstraction that produces satiric counters like Bar, Bishop, and Mrs. General—figures of a sort familiar in Victorian-sage writing from Carlyle to Arnold. But these "great general images whose abstractness is their actuality"[10] would not have such power were they not embedded in a realistic context. Such characterizations issue from the novelist's commitment to experiential truth; they are part of the pragmatic satirist's project Northrop Frye has identified, the deflation of ideas and generalizations—"stereotypes, fossilized beliefs, superstitious terrors, crank theories, pedantic dogmatisms, oppressive fashions" and other fictions—as measured "against the life they are supposed to explain."[11] Dickens was already warming to such a satiric project when, fresh from the Paris Exhibition in October 1855, he wrote to John Forster that "mere forms and conventionalities usurp, in English art, as in English government and social relations, the place of living force and truth" (D 2:700). By 1855, Dickens' longstanding opposition to "mere form" in the arts and to whatever was rigid and fossilizing in government and social relations had deepened with his reading of Carlylean prophecy about the spiritual paralysis of a mechanical age and its hollow idol worship. Just five years before in the *Latter-Day Pamphlets*, Carlyle had launched a violent attack on the "modern" notion that "formulas, with or without the facts symbolised by them, were sacred and salutary; that formulas, well persisted in, could still save us when the facts were all fled!" (*LDP* 294). Reissuing this challenge in *Little Dorrit* and reproducing many particulars of the *Pamphlets* satire, [12] Dickens set out to expose the empty formulas of his time—not only in art, government, and social relations, but also in economics, philosophy, and religion.

Frye observes that experiential wisdom—of the sort Dickens opposes to "mere forms and conventionalities"—implies its own dogmas of circumstantial truth-telling which the satirist may also attack. [13] Dickens subtly calls this wisdom, too, into question in *Little Dorrit*, but not satirically. The other direction his concern with experience takes him is toward a novelistic mode in which Dickens does not disclose "the truth behind appearances" so much as he reveals the inescapably ambiguous nature of "the truth." Knowing that "we are all partly creators of the objects we perceive," [14] Dickens explores more fully in *Little Dorrit* than he yet had the inescapable realm of "fiction," the influence of the imagined and the constructed in human life—of "vanity" in the Preacher's word. Thus, working as moralist, social psychologist, and sociolinguist, Dickens pays extraordinary attention to all those conceptual lenses the characters use for viewing the facts, such as the theories of fate through which they justify their lives as well as the distinctive word choices, syntax, metaphors, and other figures with which they construct their views of themselves and the universe. Much of this "fiction" is the product of a particular culture—a culture in Carlyle's view (to some extent Dickens') given to "Jesuitical" lying and worship of hollow forms. But beyond Carlyle, Dickens sees the problem of the imagined as a fact of the human condition, as inescapable ("nobody's fault") as the nature of the mind and the inherent abstraction of language. One of *Little Dorrit*'s chief instabilities, therefore, and the most important sign of Dickens' revising the received wisdom of Carlyle, is the discrepancy between its two views of fact: between the satiric rhetorician's unequivocal appeals to "fact[s] . . . firmly established by experience," which follow the Carlylean program for the writer, and the novelist's disquieting attention to the infirmity of the facts given the vast kingdom of the fictive, which the *Pamphlets* had declared damnable untruth.

The coexistence of *Little Dorrit*'s satiric and novelistic modes creates the novel's closed-yet-open structure: with its exposure of human vices and call to virtue, the satire tends to exert an internal "pressure toward order"[15] (except in a sense I shall discuss later), whereas the novelistic reportage of the infirm facts opens *Little Dorrit* to indeterminate readings. This fundamental aporia reflects Dickens' response to two voices in his dominant Scripture subtext. The sermonic Ecclesiastes authorizes the satirist's project by providing both a general model of critical method and particular content of social criticism still relevant in Dickens' time. Here the skepticism of Ecclesiastes provides the lens through which other biblical allusions are viewed ironically; the satire's ironies are stable and do not erode the authority of Scripture as a source of norms. But there is religious search as well as moral design in *Little Dorrit*. For this search, the influential subtext is not the sermonic but the confessional Ecclesiastes (introduced more fully in the third section below). In his multivoiced discourse, the Preacher also confesses his disquieting response to his own critical project, a confession of personal emptiness and futility in a Universe of Nothing. It is to this dimension of the Ecclesiastes subtext that the novelistic mode in *Little Dorrit* responds. In the large tracts of the book lying outside its satire, this more fundamental skepticism provides the interpretive means through which other biblical allusions are destabilized and the Bible's authority as a source of ideals is most subtly put in question. The third and fourth stages of this chapter will take up these issues in detail; here the discussion will anticipate the later argument by calling attention to places where the satiric mode, with its stable biblical allusions, is invaded by the indeterminacies of novelistic inquiry, and the readability of allusion begins to break down.

At a time when his work was being challenged by Thackeray's in the literary marketplace, *Little Dorrit* is Dickens' earnest Carlylean answer to *Vanity Fair*. "Like an Archbishop discoursing on Vanity" (1.27.316) but with a playfulness that distinguishes satire from sermonic denunciation, Dickens draws upon the scriptural tradition for an array of clever parodies that aim to deconstruct the accepted paradigms of Victorian worldly "wisdom." His chief strategy of mock-apocalyptic is supported by parodic versions of Bible characters, of Jesus' kingdom parables, of Wisdom literature, even of the Preacher's doctrines and his method of revising proverbial lore (see Fanny, 2.14.572; Meagles, 2.9.510–11). The extensive involvement of *biblical* allusions in this satiric rhetoric points to Dickens' perception by 1855–57 that political and social ills were but symptoms of a deeper spiritual malaise: what Carlyle called "an enormous Life-in-Death!" (*LDP* 320) was depleting his culture's formulas of their "living force and truth." Even so, that malaise does not infect Dickens when he is posing as satirist; for this persona the Bible's formulas are not vanity but sources of eternal value against which modern theory and practice are judged.

Exposing the operating principle of that "boiling-over old Christian" Christopher Casby, Pancks formulates the central doctrine of economic and social life early in the book: "What else do you suppose I think I am made for? *Nothing*. Rattle me out of bed early, set me going, give me as short a time as you like to bolt my meals in, and keep me at it. Keep me always at it, I'll keep you always at it, you keep somebody else always at it. There you are, with the Whole Duty of Man in a commercial country" (154; emphasis added). Like Carlyle's "Whole Duty of Pigs" in the "Jesuitism" pamphlet, Pancks' bitterly humorous revision of Ecclesiastes 12:13 ("Fear God, and keep his commandments: for this is the whole duty of man")[16] discloses the irreligious meaning of the Victorian doctrine of work done in obeisance to Mammon. This creed leads to "vanity"—Pancks' "Nothing"—in several senses of the word: work is monotonous, empty, obsessively self-concerned, and stimulates the imagination of gain, for nothing but "a dream cometh through the multitude of business" (Ecc. 5:3). It is this vain dreaming that Dickens most clearly targets in his biblically grounded satire on a commercial society.

In their vanity of "Riches," Mammon-worshippers indulge many "new polite reading[s]" of Scripture, but most extensive is their appropriation of the Bible's most powerful dream in order to enhance capitalist ideology with the fiction that riches are the ultimate apocalypse, the transforming energy that ushers in heaven on earth. As its central symbol, "the name of Merdle" is not simply "the name of the age" (2.5.469) but the name of the New Age—the Plornishes' "Golden Age revived" (2.13.556–57), which arrives with the influx of money: "O ye sun, moon, and stars, the great man! The rich man, who had in a manner revised the New Testament, and already entered into the Kingdom of Heaven" (2.16.593). Pointing to the "travesty of Psalm 148:3 here ('Praise ye him, sun and moon: praise him, all ye stars of light')," Alexander Welsh identifies Merdle as Dickens' antichrist figure, one who blasphemes the name of God and is worshipped for this blasphemy (see Rev. 13:4–6).[17] Although Antichrist makes war with the saints and such as Merdle make the poor poorer, his apparent miracle-working power deceives "rich and poor, free and bond" (see Rev. 13:7–16; Dan. 7:21); all "find an unfathomable excuse and consolation in allusions to the magic name" (2.13.555). That their allusions are sometimes biblical makes their blind worship the more blasphemous (see 2.16.593 and Acts 5:15; 1.21.244 and 1 Tim. 6:10). In Revelation all "wonde[r] after the beast" because one of its heads has a deadly wound that appears to be healed (13:3). Merdle-worshippers ignore what they know of his "complaint," for in the name of the proverb "money answereth all things" (Ecc. 10:19) they choose to believe that "The magic name of Merdle . . . no doubt will suffice for all" (2.12.546). Like those without ears to hear Jesus' stories, the "high priests of this worship" have the parable of Merdle "habitually in their view" and sit "at his feasts," yet they ignore the "signs" that this capitalist is no messiah (2.12.539; cf. Matt. 16:3) but rather one "possessed by several Devils" (2.24.683). Nor is he the sage— "the wise and sagacious"—they habitually name him (1.21.245). More than "a Midas without the ears" (1.21.241), a revision of fable borrowed from *Past and Present*, Merdle is Dickens' parodic latter-day Solomon ("what a rich man!") turned fool, as in the Preacher's sermon.

In *Little Dorrit* Ecclesiastian realities (or nothings) disconfirm the apocalypse of Riches. One of the biblical codes through which Dickens mediates his portrayal of Merdle is the formula of the rich man who destroys himself—a particular theme of the Preacher's, who warns of "a sore evil which I have seen under the sun, namely, riches kept for the owners thereof to their hurt": "All his days also he eateth in darkness, and he hath much sorrow and wrath with his sickness"; although "he begetteth a son, . . . there is nothing in his hand. As he came forth of his mother's womb, naked shall he return to go as he came" (see 5:10–17). The restless, dissatisfied Merdle hints at the vanity of his money-getting to Mrs. Merdle; his "indigestive" eating at barren messianic banquets is one of its symptoms. To Ecclesiastes the vanity of labor for the rich is that although a man want nothing, "yet God giveth him not power to eat thereof" (6:2). Such deprivations anticipate the sudden end of his "riches . . . by evil travail" (5:14) when Merdle's body is found naked and empty-handed in the bath. Nor can the stepson Sparkler, whose head has "nothing" in it, carry on the magic name.

In these Ecclesiastian disconfirmations, the Preacher's play upon the radical contrast of "abundance" and "nothing" is translated into Dickens' satire on Riches as Poverty. One of its subsidiary motifs is fraudulent verbal wealth, the "multitude of words" that comes with "multitude of business." Rhetorical inflation makes especially ironic Dickens' parody of Jesus' parable of the rich man and the needle's eye (Matt. 19:23–24): "Mr. Merdle came home, from his daily occupation of causing the British name to be more and more respected in all parts of the civilised globe, capable of the appreciation of world-wide commercial enterprise and gigantic combinations of skill and capital. For, though nobody knew with the least precision what Mr. Merdle's business was, except that it was to coin money, these were the terms in which everybody defined it on all ceremonious occasions, and which it was the last new polite reading of the parable of the camel and the needle's eye to accept without enquiry" (1.33.386;

cf. *MC* 25.474). When the climax comes, the Dickensian Preacher deflates all the worldly formulas of Merdle's greatness with the simple fact of forgery and robbery: "He, the uncouth object of such widespread adulation, the sitter at great men's feasts, . . . he, the shining wonder, the new constellation to be followed by the wise men bringing gifts, until it stopped over a certain carrion at the bottom of a bath and disappeared—was simply the greatest Forger and the greatest Thief that ever cheated the gallows" (2.25.691). Dickens' heaping-up of "adulation" in this longer passage is an inverted equivalent of flyting, extravagant invective, by which he aims to achieve the legendary magical effect of primitive satire: the driving out of evil with the incantations of his fatal wit.[18] The whole effect of the passage turns also upon its production of a kind of bathos in which verbal riches perish by evil travail. Such exaggeration as flyting and bathos require, however, drives out the more complex, nearly novelistic effects Dickens achieves elsewhere in Merdle's story—as when, at the end of his "desperate" argument with Mrs. Merdle, he "looked out of nine windows in succession, and appeared to see nine wastes of space," peers into the "gloomy depths" of carpets "in unison with his oppressed soul," and goes "sighing to bed" (1.33.390). Here Dickens is connecting the suicidal Merdle with the confessional dimension of the Ecclesiastes subtext, in which the Preacher is driven to hatred of life by his discovery that all is vanity (2:17). Such passages also unite Merdle with widely separated characters, even with Amy Dorrit despairing in her first full awareness that life in Riches is waste.

But Dickens as satirist at the end of chapter 25 of book 2 must simplify all this[19] and conceal his simplification with the help of other authoritative Bible texts. In order to enforce his lesson, Dickens enlists the sweeping vision of St. John, ironically, in this constriction of novelistic seeing. Merdle's reversal is polar and total: as in the fall of Babylon, "in one great hour so great riches is come to nought" (Rev. 18:17) and the false messiah is acknowledged as antichrist. The plummeting of this "new constellation" recalls the fall of the great star called "Wormwood": it also poisons the waters into which it falls, "and many men died of the waters, because they were made bitter" (Rev. 8:10–11; cf. 2.26.691, "on the deep was nothing but ruin")—the aftermath we experience in the bitterness of Pancks and Clennam. The "sun, moon, and stars" by which Merdle was worshipped have now gone out, as John predicts in the latter days.

But just as Ecclesiastian vanities have disconfirmed the false apocalypse of Riches, the presence of this skeptical subtext undermines Dickens' attempted apocalyptic reversal of falsehood for truth. In titling his next chapter "Reaping the Whirlwind," Dickens recalls the prophet's warning—"they have sown the wind, and they shall reap the whirlwind" (Hosea 8:7)—only to disconfirm its implicit promise of divine justice.[20] The innocent women and children among the "legions . . . desolated by the hand of this mighty scoundrel" (26:690) are not vindicated, and notably Arthur Clennam is a "just man" who "perisheth in his righteousness" (Ecc. 7:15). As Ferdinand Barnacle's later speech to Clennam in debtor's prison implies, the "verdant hope" the whirlwind might have brought for "repentance" and renewal is itself undermined by the sheer persistence of human vanity (see 2.28.717–18, 690). "There is no remembrance of former things" (Ecc. 1:11) for the populace at large, who do not learn from their experience of Merdle. We are left only with Ferdinand's "hopeful confession of his faith" in "humbug"—debilitated slang for "vanity"—and the Preacher's vision of the injustice done upon earth (8:14).

Some have the wisdom to admit that the millennium has not arrived in Society (see Mrs. Merdle, 1.20.237), yet the apocalyptic fiction must be kept up even when it is disconfirmed; "Jesuitism" reigns where it is still believed that "formulas, well persisted in, could still save us when the facts were all fled!" Thus the widowed Mrs. Merdle "came out of her furnace like a wise woman, and did exceeding well" (even without the angel in Daniel; 2.33.781). The story of William Dorrit's days of vanity is structured to expose similar anticlimaxes as well as the need to conceal them with empty formulas of belief. Yet from the beginning his story is complicated by the fact that he is one of those Dickens characters who moves from the satiric to the novelistic mode, often within subtle shifts of language, and sometimes seems to inhabit both at once. This mixture of modes complicates the way we read the biblical texts for Dorrit's story. Even as the satire exposes his apocalypse of Riches, as well as his presumptuous roles as messiah, prophet, and sage, its stable standards of judgment yield to the unstable sympathy created for Dorrit by Dickens' novelistic attentions, which are grounded in the extra-sermonic dimension of the Ecclesiastes subtext confessing "nothing" in which to believe. The pity of Dorrit's belief in almost nothing but his insubstantialities leads his story away from the providential ordering of the satire into uncharted moral and spiritual territory, forcing the reader to give up conventional judgments against blasphemy and to feel even for the condemned. As the novelistic mode fosters indeterminate readings of Dorrit's story, it quietly undermines the authority of the satiric biblical allusions so wittily and, it would seem, so tellingly arrayed against him.

Book 1 ends in a rush of mock-eschatological suspense: Dorrit is climactically rescued when the Book of Life—Pancks' notebook—is opened to reveal his name therein ("That man's your Father of the Marshalsea!" 1.32.379). Pancks buys into this fantasy of a premature millennium, proposing a celestial banquet in the prison. Amy's thankful prayer for her father's release echoes the eschatological hope of 1 Corinthians 13:12 ("For now we see through a glass darkly, but then face to face"): "I shall see him, as I never saw him yet. I shall see my dear love, with the dark cloud cleared away. . . . O father, father! O thank God, thank God!" (1.35.406). Dorrit, who has been accustomed to laying "his hands upon the heads of their infants" on Sundays and holydays (1.19.214), travestying Dickens' Jesus the lover of children, rises to the occasion of his greatness to adopt emptied formulas of messiah and prophet. When "the final day" arrives—"the day" is ever arriving yet not arriving in *Little Dorrit*—like a modern Isaiah promising glory to suffering Israel, Dorrit circulates among the prisoners "and seemed for their consolation to walk encircled by the legend in golden characters, 'Be comforted, my people! Bear it!'" (1.36.417). But the prophet's apocalyptic truth of justice and theophany— "Comfort ye, comfort ye my people, saith your God. . . . Every valley shall be exalted . . . And the glory of the Lord shall be revealed" (Isa. 40:1, 4–5)—is a mere "legend in golden characters," to this unbeliever a verbal fiction. Nor can he hear the prophet's warnings in this appropriate chapter of Isaiah against the idolatry that will be Dorrit's downfall; Isaiah's God "bringeth the princes to nothing" (v. 23), and his "whirlwind shall take them away as stubble" (v. 24) as the Merdle "whirlwind" will sweep away Dorrit's wealth.

The mutually confirming biblical allusions behind Dickens' "satire on family pride" (1.20.225) make its points unmistakable, especially at the end of book 1. Book 2 opens with a richer mingling of effects, enlarging the scope of interpretation. Here Dickens uses biblical allusion both to judge the false millennium of Riches[21] and to create sympathy for a man whose vain hopes for transformation retain some vestige of the yearning for higher being. In the brilliantly orchestrated opening of book 2, Dickens revises the order of biblical events offered in the first chapter of book 1 (which had opened with an imminent *dies irae* but had closed with heavenly promise); playing with the sequences of his own narrative as well as biblical time, shifting from night to day to night again in a mystifying chiaroscuro, he scores his satiric points within a structure of narrative ambivalence that involves the reader in what it mimics, Dorrit's state of soul fluttering between dread and hope. The general effect of these indeterminacies is a darkening of vision, for neither Scripture's promise nor its threat seems certain; and biblical associations generalize Dorrit's case to embrace the condition of all humankind.

The ominous opening line of book 2 portends old Dorrit's journey toward death: ". . . Darkness and Night were creeping up to the highest ridges of the Alps" (419). Yet it is only a hint: in the next two paragraphs shifting to earlier in the day, heaven seems to have arrived both in the fragrant "vintage time" of the valley (see Rev. 14:15–20) and in the visionary beauty of this "bright day," when "Shining metal spires and church-roofs, distant and rarely seen, had sparkled in the view" (419). But as this "day" dies, the promising heavenly visions seem "solemnly to recede, like spectres who were going to vanish" (as Dorrit's hopes will recede in book 2). The narrator loops back to the ominous time of the opening line, with "the ascending Night came up the mountain like [the] rising water" (420). With the Genesis archetype, Dickens portentously invokes the return (just as the line returns) of the Deluge, recalling the biblical threat that the end will come as in the days of Noah. This apocalyptic recall now invites us to reread the beneficent "vintage time" of the second paragraph as a warning emblem of that day when the grapes shall be cast into God's winepress (see Rev. 14:19–20).

As we follow this prose, now hopeful, now ominous, Dickens teaches us repeatedly to revise our perceptions of material abundance and spiritual certitude—the whole opening of book 2 is an implicit lesson in point of view. But it also destabilizes the Victorian reader's easy biblical condemnation of William Dorrit. In the opening paragraphs Dickens does not simply evoke *dies irae* images to portend God's judgment on the rich; instead, seeming to promise and then withhold paradise, promise and then withhold punishment, he imitates in these confirmations and disconfirmations the structure of Dorrit's uncertain spiritual state and prompts our indeterminate response to him. Further, when the vision of disaster returns, it seems vastly disproportionate for the puny pilgrims turning and winding slowly up the steep ascent as though up the circles of a frozen hell, which matches in its sensory intensity and rhetorical amplification the fiery hellscape opening the novel (see 420). Again innocent and evil alike are beset by the elements.

Just when we think the travelers have met more than their just deserts, the narrator saves them for yet another false heaven and rescues the impending moral disorder for the certainties of satiric judgment. This heaven evokes the iconography of religious painting: "At length, a light on the summit of the rocky staircase gleamed through the snow and mist," and the convent of the Saint Bernard appears, like a secular church, to be "another Ark float[ing] away upon the shadowy waves" (420). A table is laid for the hungry wayfarers next to a beneficent fire, and by the end of the chapter this parody of the world of God triumphs when they seem to secure their—social—salvation by writing their own names in the Traveller's Book.

Ridden by a sense of his own impending end, yearning for substance yet dimly aware of his own insubstantiality, Dorrit succumbs to Ecclesiastian mist: "Up here in the clouds, everything was seen through cloud, and seemed dissolving into cloud. . . . as if the whole rugged edifice were filled with nothing else, and would collapse as soon as it had emptied itself, leaving the snow to fall upon the bare mountain summit" (420–21). "Seen through cloud," through the Preacher's ironizing vision, the ark of abundance and security Dorrit seeks is "nothing else" but vanity. The paradisal feast that follows becomes disenchanted when we hear that the Ecclesiastian monotony of what is "always the same, always the same"—confinement—is still on Dorrit's mind (430). Although he desires to "sweep that accursed experience off the face of the earth!" (2.5.464), there is no new thing under the "bright morning sun" that reappears in chapter 3, when the "new sensation of breathing" the mountain air "was like the having entered on a new existence" (439). This is all "delusion" helped by the impression, again mock-apocalyptic, that "the solid ground itself seemed gone" in Dorrit's denial of reality.

In book 2 he also tries to banish "the last point of the old standing-ground in life" for Amy (2.3.451). As a result, ironically the saintly female who has been the novel's earthly ground of being and a moral touchstone becomes a spokeswoman for Ecclesiastes' antireligious vision. From her newly insubstantial "position" of having no one to care for in the world of the rich, "all she saw appeared unreal . . . all a dream." But Amy, who only partly is carrying on Dickens' satire here, does not only reject the vanity of wealth; she becomes herself as bereft of hope as the confessional Ecclesiastes in Vanity Fair and suffers from "the unreality of her inner life as she went through its vacant places all day long." When with Amy we reach Italy's wasteland, "where there seemed to be nothing to support life, nothing to eat, nothing to make, nothing to grow, nothing to hope, nothing to do but die" (453), we have reached that point where satire collapses because, as Frye writes, "its content is too oppressively real to permit the maintaining of [a] fantastic or hypothetical tone."[22] The exaggeration here is not satiric; it realistically sounds the depths of Amy's quiet despair amid the "usual nothings" of Society (2.6.475).

The breakdown of satire has been felt since book 1 in the pitiable collapses of old Dorrit's speech; we glimpse through the fissures of his syntax the weakness, partly caused by an economic plight not his fault, that makes him more than an object of ridicule. But Dickens' complex comic-pathetic effects are heightened precisely because Dorrit so consciously assumes the tones of patriarch and sage, whose voices in the Bible carry authority only in that they remain unbroken. In book 1, the metaphoric description of old age in Ecclesiastes 12 provides a subtext for a favorite theme of Dorrit's homilies: the infirmities of Frederick (see 19.218–19) and Nandy (see 1.31.367–68). Both Ecclesiastes 12:3–7 and Dorrit's second homily proceed by cataloging similar points of physical breakdown; both speak in allegoric code (Dorrit's asides on Nandy's failing faculties are displaced expressions of his own); and both end with the end of "spirit" ("the spirit shall return unto God who gave it," 12:7; cf. 368, "Spirit broken and gone—pulverised—crushed out of him, sir, completely!"). Then, in his own "Spirit. Becoming Spirit," Dorrit says, "I do—ha—extend as much protection and kindness to the—hum—the bruised reed—I trust I may so call him without impropriety—as in my circumstances, I can" (362). Isaiah's "A bruised reed shall he not break" refers to a messianic deliverer of prisoners, and one with God's "spirit upon him" (42:3, 7, 1). In the spirit of a mock-patriarchal patron, Dorrit hopes not to deliver but to be delivered from the "ha—humiliation" of his Marshalsea existence; yet that lofty transcendence is impossible because his spiritual faculties (as he says of Nandy's physical ones) are going. He, not Nandy, is Isaiah's "deaf" and "blind" idol-worshipper "hid in prison houses" and subject to God's judgment (see vv. 17–22).

That judgment delays, however, while in book 2 Dorrit plays the sage on ever higher ground than before to "point [the] moral" of new social occasions "by his wisdom" (see 2.3.442).[23] As this old fool runs up his Castle in the Air that eventually surpasses the towers of Notre Dame (2.17.616), Dorrit builds not only another Tower of Babel but Ecclesiastes' "house of feasting," which C. H. Spurgeon described in a sermon on the theme as "a fantastic structure, very much like those fairy palaces which we fabricate in our dreams with the architect of fancy."[24] But "It is better to go to the house of mourning," the Preacher writes, ". . . for that is the end of all men" (7:2). In "The Storming of the Castle in the Air" Dickens sends Dorrit for correction to the house of mourning with the lurid funeral procession that passes his carriage, exhorting him to remember the common end that levels all social pretensions (2.19.617). Dorrit also builds like other rich biblical fools (and Dombey) who believe "that their houses shall continue for ever" (Ps. 49:11) but "shall carry nothing away" (v. 17) because they construct on no solid foundations (see also the parable in Matt. 7:24–27). Great, then, is the fall of the House of Dorrit, for through his aristocratic and spiritual "slothfulness the building decayeth" (Ecc. 10:18). Ecclesiastes' comparison of the aging body to a house also lies behind Dickens' collapsing castle metaphor, for with the storming of his castle Dorrit physically sickens toward that time when his spirit "return[s] unto God who gave it."

Taken by themselves, the satiric biblical allusions for Dorrit's story would be damning. Yet he is finally judged neither innocent nor guilty. Near his end, Dorrit the believer in false apocalyptic seems to be literally lifted out of the satire and allowed to enter the kingdom that the Preacher never glimpses. As the lines in his face melt away, the "vanity and vexation of spirit" in his life is

visibly erased (see 2.19.631); the magical transformation signals the reintro-
duction of naive apocalyptic's (and Amy's) wishful thinking—or so it seems. But
this transformation is not the last word; the closing passages of chapter 19 work
against both the assurance of clemency Dickens wants and any firm belief in a
forgiving God. The concluding melodramatic tableau is ambiguous: in Browne's
illustration "The Night," beams from another world illuminate only delusion
frozen in death—William enthroned on the bed, Frederick worshipping him; in
the narrative, "William" and "Frederick" are invisible, "equally removed by an
untraversable distance from the teeming earth," their souls "before their Father;
far beyond the twilight judgments of this world; high above its mists and
obscurities" (632). These two different kinds of fools have been handed over to
an utterly transcendent God, so far "removed" that he shows neither a merciful
nor a condemning face. Indeed, "Father"—the name of Frederick's personal
God who "discern[s] clearly and brightly" (631)—seems a linguistic fiction
when applied to a deity whose immeasurable remoteness Dickens stresses.
Ironically, too, this address reminds us of the paternal fictions for which Dorrit
has been judged on earth. In the chapter's inconclusive close, these two souls
and their God vanish. Abandoning biblical stability, the final phrase leaves us
in "mists and obscurities"—words which mute the heavenly promises and remind us that the human is as unknowable as the divine.

Like her father, the Fanny Dorrit of the satire is a mock-wisdom figure who
pretends to yield to "Necessity and time" while becoming her own nemesis. Her
fiction of determinism is "what Society requires"; her marriage to "vanity"—
"nothing. . . . less than nothing" as Merdle's stepson is (2.7.498)—then becomes the apotheosis of worldly wisdom, illustrating the way "the Island Savages contriv[e] these things now-a-days" (2.15.589) in the modern pagan manner of perverting the rituals of the Church. Dickens points Fanny's kind of folly
as blasphemy with his witty parody of the Order of Matrimony in the chapter
titled "No Just Cause or Impediment Why These Two Persons Should Not Be
Joined Together" (578). But even as the satirical play on marriage service
themes and phrases goes on—climaxing in Bunyan's "Slough of Despond"
(589)—the reader remembers how Dickens has novelistically recorded the details of Fanny's smothering of her own spirit, while disguising the nature and
agent of her choices, in her artful manipulations of language. We last see the
married Fanny dressed in black and continuing to wish herself dead in yet
another parody of the Day of Judgment, "The Evening of a Long Day." In *her*
house of mourning, Fanny has reached the dead end of Vanity Fair's illusive
wisdom, gazing at her own image in mourning in the glass (2.24.673). We last
hear *of* her "going into Society for ever and a day" (2.34.801), succumbing to its

delusion of eternal life. But we never *hear* her again, as though she has lost the inimitable voice in which we had caught the accents of a lively human soul at odds with herself. While her father's story fluctuates throughout between the satiric and the novelistic and his fate is finally dissolved in obscurity, Fanny's life shrinks from the novelistic to the satiric, her destiny decided in the caricature she finally makes of herself.

Fanny and her father are not the only characters who set "Folly . . . in great dignity" (Ecc. 10:6). The novel resounds with the fools' chatter of vain, self-serving philosophers who put forward "bad design[s]" that claim to be "expressly religious" ones (preface, p. lix). They indulge much mock-millennial thinking, but its pessimistic counterpart is even more extensive, the many common theories of fate that the characters entertain—Nemesis, Pressure, Precedent, Circumstances, Society, the course of nature, cosmic or economic "ups" and "downs" (2.27.712), Everybody's Fault, Nobody's Fault. In her preacherly discourse on the "hollow and conventional and worldly and very shocking" nature of Society, for example, Mrs. Merdle advises that we must nonetheless "consult it. It is the common lot" (1.20.234). In these caricatures of Ecclesiastes' resignation, the characters mystify identifiable human causes of malaise as natural causes in order to rationalize inaction. But the subtlety of Dickens' response to his Ecclesiastes subtext is expressed through much novelistic reportage that it is not, in fact, "in the nature of man to be perfectly happy" (Bishop, 1.21.247, n. 2). Moreover, in this novel it is difficult to say exactly why natural growth and change, Dickens' official answer to both falsely hopeful and falsely pessimistic thinking, so rarely takes place.[25] Given the vast unknowable, which seems to expand before the searching eye, all the satirist can do is identify some of the more obvious obstacles to change, which in *Little Dorrit* also reflect certain themes of the Preacher's sermon.

Surveying "the evil work that is done under the sun," Ecclesiastes sees "all the oppressions" of the powerful (4:3, 1). In Dickens' satire on the vanity of the governing powers, he uses religious image and biblical allusion to disclose their evil work, although the Ecclesiastes subtext read selectively could also support their false wisdom, and it promises no release from their oppression. The Lords of the Circumlocution Office are first introduced as parody-seers but become parody-sages. They are entrusted with the "bright revelation" about how to govern that is fundamentally anti-apocalyptic, hostile to recreation: "the art of perceiving—HOW NOT TO DO IT" (1.10.100). Knowing that "It is the point of view that is the essential thing" (2.28.716), the Office has invented innumerable ways to make civic labor as vanity, to bring to nothing all "recompense for a man's toil and hope," as Doyce charges (116). This "sagacious master in some handicraft" (112–13) who would serve his nation with his invention is treated like the "poor wise man" in the Preacher's antiwisdom anecdote, who "by his wisdom delivered the [beseiged] city; yet no man remembered that same poor man" (see Ecc. 9:13–16). From the Circumlocution sages' point of view, which has redefined wisdom, discouraging ingenuity like Doyce's *is* a "wise system" since "How to do it must obviously be regarded as the natural and mortal enemy of How not to do it" (2.8.500).

Echoing but negating Ecclesiastes' "that which is done is that which shall be done," the Office responds to public criticism that "it hadn't been done . . . and . . . should be done" by "devis[ing], How it was not to be done" (101). But they do fulfill Ecclesiastes' formula in 1:9 by holding on to precedent; there is no thing new "under the sun or moon" (1.34.390) with the Circumlocution Barnacles in power. Their Whole Duty of Man is to block public action while keeping themselves in office; and they do *this* quite effectively by sheer mystification, like the inscrutable God of Ecclesiastes turning the wheel of existence. At the head of this "politico diplomatico hocus pocus piece of machinery" are "the presiding Idols of the Circumlocution Office" (111), "Sages" who assemble in their "sanctuary"; out of this "awful inner apartment" Clennam sees "an imposing coming of papers," and into it "an imposing going of papers, almost constantly" (110) in the regular cycles of their little universe (see Ecc. 1:5–7). They are likewise the masters of verbal circumlocution, the "sham talking machines, and hollow windy fools!" of Carlyle's *Pamphlets* and Ecclesiastes.[26]

The Office's mystification by religious formula is exposed from several other points of view, each biblical. The skeptical Clennam reverses Jesus' parable of the kingdom and speculates about "the mustard-seed" of misplaced faith "that had sprung up into the great tree of the Circumlocution Office" (1.16.189). Doyce, always "looking into the distance before him as if his grey eye were measuring it" (116), places the Office under the eye of eternity: he has "a calm knowledge that what was true must remain true, in spite of all the Barnacles in the family ocean, and would be just the truth . . . when even that sea had run dry" (186; cf. Rev. 21:1). In the delay of that Day, the narrator names the governing powers simply demonic: they are "Legion" (102; cf. 1.34.396). However, the novel's last word is Ferdinand Barnacle's, who echoes Dickens' complaints against the English people in his letters of this period.[27] Returning us to the disillusion of the Ecclesiastes subtext, this unbelieving Barnacle deconstructs the demonic paradigm by insisting, "our place is not a wicked Giant to be charged at full tilt; but, only a windmill showing you, as it grinds immense quantities of chaff, which way the country wind blows" (2.27.717). His urbane

acceptance of injustice we find in a cryptic passage that undermines the Preacher's own complaints against the oppressions of the powerful: "If thou seest the
oppression of the poor, and violent perverting of judgment and justice in a
province, marvel not at the matter: for he that is higher than the highest regar-
deth; and there be higher than they" (5:8; the Jerusalem Bible translates this
passage: "You will be told that officials are under the supervision of superiors,
who are supervised in turn; you will hear talk of 'the common good' and 'the
service of the king'"). Well-versed in all the official excuses, Ferdinand counsels Clennam to resign himself to the Office's providential arrangements which
are "intended to be, and must be" (716). In the final "hopeful confession of his
faith as the head of the rising Barnacles who were born of woman" (718), the
echo of Job's warnings against such (14:1) implies that the evil of indifference to
the public weal really is in the order of nature. Biblical allusion may verbally
expose the Office's blasphemies, but with no divine order in *Little Dorrit* to
create a better human nature or to punish these sins of omission, the very notion
of blasphemy is but a verbal fiction. If the Theorem of the Universe that Ferdinand Barnacle forwards is true, the satirist's exposures are labor in vain.

The lapse of political hope in Ferdinand's formulaic defense of the system
expresses the larger crisis of belief in *Little Dorrit*'s nineteenth-century setting,
where people of all sorts subscribe to formulas, as "sacred and salutary" "when
the facts were all fled!" In his religious satire, Dickens illustrates Carlyle's
diagnosis of the modern malaise with Mrs. Clennam's case, using her perversions of biblical formulas to clarify the nature of her gross impiety. Yet like
Dorrit, she exceeds the bounds of satire, as her psychological complexity is
further revealed in her engagements with the Bible.

Mrs. Clennam's chief formula is the Calvinist doctrine of election, which,
being empty of religious content to Dickens, is filled with her own "bad passions." Her assumption that it is "a grace and favor to be elected" (1.30.351; cf.
2 Pet. 1:10, 2 Thess. 2:13–14) valorizes the central religious claim she makes
to disguise her jealousy: that "it was appointed to me to lay the hand of punishment upon that creature of perdition" (2.30.753), the rival for Mr. Clennam's
love whom Mrs. Clennam had destroyed many years ago. In exhibiting a self-
appointed religious woman who is continually forgetting to be humbled by the
doctrine of election, Dickens shows us not only the spiritual dangers of this idea
as outlined in the Seventeenth Article of Religion, but the hollowness of the
whole rigid, repressive, and outmoded religious complex of which it is a part—
another "bad design" claiming to be "an expressly religious" one. In portraying
Mrs. Clennam, however, Dickens does not satirize only a Calvinist mythos that
he found abhorrent. Mrs. Clennam also personifies a modern moral and psycho-

logical type of unbeliever Carlyle had dissected in "Characteristics," who "knows she has a system." The self-conscious piety of this paralytic Christian is, in Carlyle's terms, an "unhealthy Virtue," which "consumes itself to leanness in repenting and anxiety" or "inflates itself into dropsical boastfulness and vain-glory" (*CME* 28:7–8)—in either case, obsessed with self. Moreover, her self-consciousness links this otherwise isolated Puritan with other characters in *Little Dorrit*'s Vanity Fair (like Gowan) quite outside the pale of religion. Through them all we see, as John Ruskin wrote in *Modern Painters*, that "It is *only* vanity, never love, nor any other noble feeling, which prompts men to desert their allegiance to the simple truth, in vain pursuit of the imaginative truth."[28] Mrs. Clennam is the chief religious figure in Dickens' exhibition of the subjective distortions that pass for wisdom in a faithless age. But he is not always so certain as Ruskin of where the "simple truth" lies; and it is Mrs. Clennam's link to the novel's theme of perception that creates some sympathy even for her, for we see she suffers in her "vain pursuit of the imaginative truth."

Mrs. Clennam's governing fiction is her reversal of "the order of Creation" by breathing "her own breath into a clay image of her Creator"; and for this "daring, gross, and shocking" act counter to the theology of Genesis, the Dickensian satirist has only invective (2.30.754). Acting as "the disposer of all things" (755), she not only appoints the times of destiny like Ecclesiastes' God but also arranges her own lectionary for the days of her vanity, proof texts that mirror her own supreme being. "Man!" she shouts, "I justify myself by the authority of these Books!"—but her more unguarded remark, "I have justified it to myself" (1.15.176), discloses more nakedly the self-reflexive manner in which this vain woman reads, indeed worships, the glass of her Bible.

While Dennis Walder has suggested the book of Jeremiah as a subtext for Mrs. Clennam's story,[29] we might well look at her more direct manipulations of formulas in Ecclesiastes. With the sage's pride of having sounded life to its depths and found it hollow, she tells Arthur, "The world has narrowed to these dimensions. . . . It is well for me that I have never set my heart upon its hollow vanities" (1.3.34). What we know of *Little Dorrit*'s world confirms her judgment that others live a "life of vanity and pleasure" (1.5.48), but we also recognize that the condition she deplores she has created for herself. All she sees appears to be vanity because her world view is "narrowed," voided of so much (and Dickens' running title echoing her words, "No Tenderness for the World's Vanities," stresses what her life lacks; 1.30.351). The House of Clennam is also manifestly "vacant" (2.17.603); and throughout the chapter in which she is first introduced, the word *nothing* and its equivalents resound, signs that Mrs. Clennam's use of the Preacher's theme is itself another vanity. If hers is, moreover, the novel's most gloomily appointed house of mourning, it is not the place of wisdom in Ecclesiastes 7:2 but "an enormous Life-in-Death!" where her "Consecrated Unveracity" presides (*LDP* 320). In a decaying house that emblematizes her own decadence, like the allegorical house in Ecclesiastes' poem on old age, Mrs. Clennam is oppressed with a sense of the end of all. It is not, however, because she shares his mood of philosophical reflection, but because she fears for herself the Day when "God shall bring every work into judgment, with every secret thing" (Ecc. 12:14).

If Mrs. Clennam exploits certain other of the Preacher's themes as well, especially the determinism of 1:9, she also freely rewrites his text to suit her "imaginative truth." She repudiates the regular changes of season appointed in Ecclesiastes 3, with "All seasons are alike to me. . . . The Lord has been pleased to put me beyond all that" (34–35). On the theme of "There is no remembrance of former things," Mrs. Clennam both revises and follows the biblical text. She wants to be remembered respectfully by Arthur; more than this, she reverses Ecclesiastian formula in her interpretation of the romantic message inside his dead father's watch, "Do Not Forget," which reminds her (as the ghost of Hamlet's father would remind his son in III.iv.125) to remember her revenge for the adultery of long ago. Yet because she deliberately misreads the past and this motto in the watch, which should remind her now to "Make restitution!" (2.30.760) for one of the "daughters of musick" she has "brought low" (Ecc. 12:4), there is after all no remembrance of former things in the lacunae of her deliberately selective memory. The reader's experience of Mrs. Clennam proves Ecclesiastes' pessimism; and all she does "remember," in the gloom of her thoughts and blackout of her repressions, are "the days of darkness; for they shall be many" (Ecc. 11:8).

In a parody of Ecclesiastes' method, she also revises other received formulas to suit what she perceives to be her experience. Her biblical formula for Arthur's upbringing in a penitential but unredeemed state of mind contains several misreadings of Scripture: "I was stern with him, knowing that the transgressions of the parents are visited on their offspring, and that there was an angry mark upon him at his birth" (2.31.769), his illegitimacy. Like Miss Barbary, Mrs. Clennam selectively draws upon Exodus 20:5 ("I the Lord thy God am a jealous God, visiting the iniquity of the fathers upon the children") for a saying that explains her own continuing spiritual unease and justifies her refusal, like this Jehovah, to brook rivals. She misses the relevance of the First Commandment for her own sins of idolatry—she resembles a pagan idol (see 1.3.46)—and she forgets to remember the next verse: "And shewing mercy unto thousands of them that love me, and keep my commandments" (v. 6). This woman

also misreads the sign of God's protection for Cain as an "angry mark," reflecting her own anger. No more than Esther Summerson is Arthur born a Cain; he
has been made one, and he still thinks of himself even in adult life as the
outcast wanderer (see 1.23.260, where he surrounds himself with the iconography of Abel's murder in a child's picture book).

Mrs. Clennam's selective revisions of the New Testament also mirror her own
bad passions. One of her most favored subjective adaptations echoes Philippians 2:12–13: "Wherefore, my beloved, as ye have always obeyed, not as in
my presence only, but now much more in my absence, work out your own salvation with fear and trembling. For it is God which worketh in you both to will and
to do of his good pleasure." Mrs. Clennam, naturally attracted by such a phrase
as "fear and trembling," misappropriates it to justify her harsh upbringing of
Arthur: "I devoted myself to reclaim the otherwise predestined and lost
boy. . . . to bring him up in fear and trembling, and in a life of practical contri-
tion for the sins that were heavy on his head before his entrance into this condemned world" (2.30.755). The Bible's counsel on reverent obedience Mrs.
Clennam has made into the boy's hopeless labor of self-redemption for sins he
has never committed. That the harsh creed has rebounded upon Mrs. Clennam
herself we hear in her cryptic echo of these words from Philippians: "I take it as
a grace and favor to be elected to make the satisfaction I am making here, to
know what I know for certain here, and *to work out what I have worked out here*"
(1.30.351, emphasis added; Arthur echoes her, 2.26.693). To call either
"what" *salvation* would be heresy in St. Paul's sense, as this woman knows but
does not want "to know"; hence the verbal suppressions as well as the deletion
of God, who inspires the "work" in St. Paul.

The ironies of these Bible misreadings would be stable if they only exposed
Mrs. Clennam's bibliolatry as hypocrisy. But they become unstable on several
counts. The more general of these is reflected in the remark of one contemporary
reviewer who was appalled by Dickens' "parade of Bible reading" in this characterization: "Surely it is not to teach us that the diligent reader of it will be full
of 'envy, hatred, malice, and all uncharitableness'; that the only influence of the
Bible . . . will be but to cherish in the reader's mind, thoughts and feelings the
most directly opposed to its whole teachings!"[30] Through Mrs. Clennam,
Dickens makes his strongest attack on those parts of the Old Testament that
were, notoriously, stumbling blocks to many Victorian believers—as Dean
Stanley phrased the problem, "the apparent vindictiveness and cruelty of the
precepts in the Old Testament, compared with the milder spirit of the New."
This fundamental contradiction in the Bible was solved for Stanley (and apparently for Dickens) by the notion of progressive revelation.[31] But in *Little Dorrit*
that contradiction is nakedly on view in the opposed *ethoi* of Mrs. Clennam and

MR. FLINTWINCH MEDIATES AS A FRIEND OF THE FAMILY
(Hablot K. Browne)

And the sun stood still, and the moon stayed, until the people had
avenged themselves upon their enemies. (Joshua 10:13; note the print
above Flintwinch's head)

Amy Dorrit; and implicitly it opens to question a sacred text that lends itself to vengeful uses and misconstructions. Having thus exposed its instability, Dickens tries to resolve the problem by satirizing and finally silencing one party to it, just as his Victorian reviewer excludes much from the "whole teachings" of the Bible.

Mrs. Clennam's Bible misreadings are also unstable in that they create some novelistic sympathy for a woman who victimizes herself in hollow religious language she evidently believes and who does obeisance to a God of Vanity—to "nothing" but an invisible icon created entirely from her own rhetoric.[32] Some of the allusions do not reduce her to a satiric target but help us to appreciate the psychic contortions of a lost soul, as a final example will show. Fending off Jeremiah's probing questions, she selects from different parts of Scripture to construct a rhetorical question that turns out to be a real one: "Are we not all *cut down like the grass* of the field, and was I not shorn by the scythe many years ago; since when, I have been lying here, waiting to be gathered into the barn?" (1.15.177, emphasis added). At first reading she seems to be fusing such passages supportive of her self-image as Isaiah 40:6 ("All flesh is grass"), Jesus' parable of wheat and tares ("but gather the wheat into my barn" at harvest, Matt. 13:30), and Old Testament phraseology used of the patriarchs she invokes as her own precedents (Isaac "was gathered unto his people" in death, Gen. 35:29). But the first and more direct echo is of Psalm 37:2, which would class Mrs. Clennam with evildoers: "For they shall soon be cut down like the grass, and wither as the green herb." Inadvertently such patchworks reveal Mrs. Clennam's equivocal attitude, however unconscious, toward her guilt and virtue; in such passages we hear her mourning in advance the possible loss of her salvation when the day of harvest comes, even in the way she constructs her linguistic defenses against it.

Although allowed her novelistic dimension, Mrs. Clennam is finally engulfed in the satiric design when a series of reversals, founded on biblical models with melodramatic potential Dickens exploits, deposes this woman and her religion with the apocalyptic force she fears. Jeremiah—that "spiritual little dog" (2.30.743, n. 2) with "presentiments" who at first seems a parody-prophet but becomes a real one—first denounces Mrs. Clennam's idolatry and demonism (as well as "that jumping jade and Jezebel" Affery, recalling the woman of 1 Kings who cut off the prophets; 760). As in Revelation and in Ecclesiastes 12:14, all her secrets are finally revealed—ironically, by Blandois, "the devil . . . let loose" (1.11.121) to swindle in Belgium, Italy, and England like Satan "loosed out of his prison . . . to deceive the nations" in the time before the End (Rev. 20:7–8). Terrified by the fall of her house, Mrs. Clennam drops down in the street, becomes dumb, and "lived and died a statue" (772; cf. Ps. 39:9–10 and

Ecc. 5:2). In *his* role as the disposer of all things in *Little Dorrit*, the novelist metes out the just deserts of silence and total stability to a woman who has so abused the potential of biblical and other language for unstable interpretation in her pursuit of fiction.

Dickens' more publicly significant visitation is the fall of the house itself, a place of business for Clennam and Company as well as the temple of her empty religion. Defying Matthew 6:24 ("Ye cannot serve God and Mammon"), this Victorian businesswoman is cousin to those money-worshippers in "Hudson's Statue" who serve "*both* God and the Devil" (*LDP* 260). The house of this evil partnership, like Dorrit's Castle in the Air, decays "by much slothfulness" of spirit and must drop through. But the spiritually decadent Mrs. Clennam (and Jeremiah), like others who refuse to heed the signs of the times, misses the clues of impending collapse—even though the house leans "on some half dozen gigantic crutches: which . . . appeared in these latter days to be no very sure reliance" (1.3.32)—and she is wholly unprepared for the day of destruction: "In one swift instant, the old house was before them . . . another thundering sound, and it heaved, surged outward, trembled asunder in fifty places, collapsed, and fell. Deafened by the noise, stifled, choked, and blinded by the dust, they hid their faces and stood rooted to the spot. The dust storm, driving between them and the placid sky, parted for a moment *and showed them the stars*. As they looked up, wildly crying for help, the great pile of chimneys which was then alone left standing, like a tower in a whirlwind, rocked, broke, and hailed itself down upon the heap of ruin" (772, emphasis added). This whirlwind, which has picked up from a parody Day of Wrath in an "adjacent churchyard" in book 1 (29.337), issues in no harvest of souls; like the Merdle whirlwind, it creates only "ruin." But it serves Dickens' satire on dead religions in its echo of Carlyle's description of the collapse of the Church—"the world-tree of the Nations for so long!"—when its roots have died: "Shaken to and fro, . . . it must sway hither and thither; nod ever farther from the perpendicular; nod at last too far; and,—sweeping the Eternal Heavens clear of its old brown foliage . . . —come to the ground with much confused crashing, and *disclose* the diurnal and nocturnal Upper Lights again!" (*LDP* 332–33). If Carlyle's and Dickens' lodestars remain in place in these moments, we see that solecisms like Mrs. Clennam's religion, vitiated in a materialistic culture, founded on Old Testament texts now discredited, cannot remain forever propped up. The melodramatic collapse of the House of Clennam gestures prophetically toward the failure of the old symbolic structures and enacts the needful destruction of an antiquated Mythus (*SR* 115).

Complementing Dickens' satire on the vanities of wealth and of religion is his exposure of worldly philosophy in Christopher Casby, "the Last of the Pa-

DAMOCLES
(Hablot K. Browne)

For man also knoweth not his time: as the fishes that are taken in an evil
net, and as the birds that are caught in the snare; so are the sons of men
snared in an evil time, when it falleth suddenly upon them. (Ecc. 9:12)

The dwelling place of the wicked shall come to nought. (Job 8:22)

triarchs" who never quotes the Bible but forever seems "to be delivering sentiments of rare wisdom and virtue" (1.13.140). From a purely facetious point of view, Casby's vacantly sagacious locutions mimic the Preacher's circumlocutions of expression, epigrams that revolve (like Christopher's thumbs) around "nothing." If the "nothing" for Casby is money, that too is a Preacherly theme, although Ecclesiastes' contrary counsels to make hay while the sun shines—for example, "In the morning sow thy seed, and in the evening withhold not thine hand" (11:6)—also lie behind the Proprietor's urgings that his Grubber toil on, morning and evening, to get "much more money." For this pair there is a "season" for everything profitable, chiefly "a time to plant, and a time to pluck up that which is planted" (3:2): "Bleeding Heart Yard had been harrowed by Mr. Pancks, and cropped by Mr. Casby, at the regular seasons" (2.32.774). Given his fill of Casby's Whole Duty of Man, Pancks at length replaces this false sage's wisdom and his "golden rule" with his own more authentic preaching when he breaks out as a spokesman for the vanity of labor as mutual exploitation in a commercial country. Pancks is more than a preacher; he becomes a Dickensian satirist, who sets the formulas of received wisdom about the Patriarch against the actuality of his "moral game" and then, shears in hand, literally deconstructs him (778–80).

While Casby is only a "Booby" of a sage, Dickens has placed in *Little Dorrit* a more formidable and most articulate philosopher of Nothing who is a match for Mrs. Clennam on the world's hollow vanities, and who represents more nakedly the dead end of the disbelieving age. With Henry Gowan (and in the shadows, Miss Wade), Dickens satirizes the folly of Ecclesiastian "wisdom" put to self-serving uses by the intelligent, well-educated moderns who are the advanced thinkers in the book. But in contrast to Dickens' exposures of deterministic thinking elsewhere, the satiric mode yields to novelistic treatment for these younger, more dangerously alive characters. Through their stories (among other ways), the confessional Ecclesiastes subtext becomes a seriously subversive presence in the novel.

"All" Gowan's remarks are "equally hollow, and jesting, and full of mockery," as Wade says, because he presumes to be a man "of the world" who "understood mankind" and has dispensed with all faiths as mere vacant forms (2.21.650–51). His word for vanity is "smoke" in the *non credo* he vows to Clennam: "To keep up the pretence as to labor, and study, and patience, and being devoted to my art, . . . and all the rest of it—in short to pass the bottle of smoke, according to rule" (1.34.392–93). For this artist manqué, painting is his form of vain labor, for which quite literally "there was no profit under the sun" (Ecc. 2:11) since his paintings do not sell. When Clennam objects that the artist's is a serious calling, Gowan laughingly answers: "Clennam, I don't like to dispel your generous visions, and I would give any money (if I had any) to live in such a rose-coloured mist. But what I do in my trade, I do to sell. . . . All the rest is hocus-pocus. Now here's one of the advantages, or disadvantages, of knowing a disappointed man. You hear the truth" (393). This imaginative "truth," too, is smoke: the vanity of a disappointed man who "sees" that "most men are disappointed in life" (392) and who "sees" society as nothing but a long vista of replications of himself: "They all do it. . . . Painters, writers, patriots, all the rest who have stands in the market" (1.26.302). If Gowan accurately describes much of what we too see in *Little Dorrit*'s world, we also perceive the "defect in [his] mental vision" (2.7.493), a form of solipsistic hocus-pocus by which he can make realities outside himself—such as Clennam's earnestness— disappear.

Gowan's case, however, is not only the satiric object lesson Dickens at first intended in the "Languid artist career"[33] and the vanity of art without moral purpose. What makes this portrait less clear is the way it reflects Dickens' several different readings of Ecclesiastes in *Little Dorrit*. Dickens detects the biblical book's solipsism, is repelled by its thoroughgoing disillusion, and writes that rejection into his discredited artist-figure. But as the novelist follows out his later plan to "anatomise Gowan, and see what breeds about his heart,"[34] he uncovers a more disturbing possible truth when his character comes dangerously alive and Gowan's jaded wisdom finds echoes in Clennam's breast. Listening to Gowan lightheartedly advise him on the real emptiness at the heart of life, Clennam wonders whether there can be "a hopeful or a promising thing anywhere" (1.34.392). For the older, sadder Clennam, who has come to England to divest himself of all the vanities, there is just enough truth in what Gowan says to reinforce what Clennam knows from so much of his experience at middle life, that he who "increaseth knowledge increaseth sorrow" (Ecc. 1:18). With Gowan *Little Dorrit* entertains the possibility that the Preacher's doctrine really is the only operative Theorem of the Universe proved by experience. With Miss Wade—whose "History of a Self-Tormentor" is both a sermon on vanity (replete with variations on "I see" and deconstructions of received formula) and an inadvertent confession of vanity[35]—Dickens presents a bitter female version of Ecclesiastes in all those moments when no personal God or larger pattern of meaning is in view in his discourse. In the uninterpreted first-person narrative of this woman without a single transcendent idea, Dickens extends his imagination beyond satire to research the psychological implications of the irreligious theorem—without pointing its impiety through a single biblical allusion, indeed without disclosing any final attitude toward it. Although so thoroughly anatomized, to the end Wade remains what Meagles calls her, "a mystery" and a "dark spirit" (1.27.323).

With Mrs. Clennam, Gowan, and Wade, we move ever farther from satire strictly considered. But what literary code helps us to read Dickens' maddest sage, Mr. F's Aunt? There is no arraignment of vice here, no ordered system of values confirmed by our penetration of her illusions to the truth. Yet some "truth" seems to be concentrated in the Aunt, sharply and grossly told through caricature. In her "almost Solomonic" utterances (1.13.150) made with "burning indignation" (1.23.263), Dickens seems to create a wholly new genre: wisdom as apocalyptic (in its destructive phase). Both are encyclopedic modes, encompassing all of life and endeavoring to grasp its meaning[36]—an end to which the philosophizing Dickens of *Little Dorrit* seems to aspire. It is against such an effort that the Aunt concentrates her remarkable anarchic energies. Striking "into the conversation like a clock, without consulting anybody" (150), the Aunt arrives like an end-event in scenes where Clennam is present and, like other such events in this novel, perpetually returns. Following his primal apocalyptic moment when "the object of his old passion . . . shivered and broke to pieces" (when "the idea [of Flora does] not bear close comparison with the reality, and the contrast is a fatal shock to" the "mind," 142–43), the Aunt repeatedly appears like a series of aftershocks to remind Clennam of that shattering heuristic experience and all the disillusioning "wisdom" it sums up. Said to be "possessed of such a knowledge of life as no doubt with so many changes must have been acquired" (2.17.599), the Aunt comes on like the personification of experiential learning so disruptive that it does not increase sorrow merely, but evokes "peculiar terrors" to Clennam's mind (149). Depreciating Clennam's "temple of reason" as "a brass knob with nothing in it" (267) and calling him "a fool!" (150), Flora's companion radically destabilizes all intelligible language and rational patterns of thought.[37] Hers is not a form of wisdom that can be satirized as "false"—as sententious self-service, cynicism, or solipsism; it is wisdom as incomprehensibility, "with nothing in it" of use to humankind. Biblically considered, the Aunt's embodied conundrum gestures toward that ultimate absurdity to which Ecclesiastes returns after so much vain labor in his search for wisdom: "that which is afar off, and exceeding deep," which not even the wisest "can find . . . out" (7:24).

Confession and Dialogue

To ECCLESIASTES, Wisdom provides no privileged interpretation of experience; but then neither do his own skeptical investigations produce a definitive voice with which to speak. This inheritor of the Wisdom tradition has arrived at that stage of inquiry, as Carlyle described the nineteenth century, "when the mind having widened its sphere of vision, the existing Theorem of the Universe no longer answers the phenomena, no longer yields contentment; but must be torn in pieces, and certainty anew sought for in the endless realms of denial" (*CME* 28:26). Dean Stanley pointed out in one of his lectures on the Jewish church that "doubters and scoffers amongst our half-educated mechanics . . . make the Book of Ecclesiastes alternately the sanction of their own unbelief, and a ground of attack against the general faith of the Bible."[38] Yet that would be to oversimplify the real uncertainty at the heart of this book, which speaks with more than an unbelieving voice. In his popular Victorian commentary *Daily Bible Illustrations*, John Kitto observed that "from the apparently contradictory nature of its contents," Ecclesiastes has been variously interpreted as "the gloomy imaginings of a melancholy misanthrope," "the licentious suggestions of an Epicurean profligate," "the disputation of a wavering skeptic," and "a justification of God's providence in ruling the world."[39] Stanley heard in it an internal drama: "an interchange of parts, higher and lower, mournful and joyful, within a single human soul. . . . It is like the question and answer to the 'Two Voices' of our modern poet"; and in this Ecclesiastes represents, within the scope of one book, contradictions found elsewhere in Scripture.[40] Further, not only is the "dialogue" of Ecclesiastes many-sided; in contrast to the Book of Job, where the author questions the Wisdom tradition by dramatizing disputants in debate, Ecclesiastes' opponents are shadowy, present only as texts, reduced to unmarked quotations set side by side in illogical and discontinuous sequences. Modern biblical scholars dispute which passages were inserted by pious glossators to modify the Preacher's more heretical observations. But to Dickens, without the benefit of this scholarship, the book must have seemed a bewildering labyrinth of thought, in which one labors in vain to read one's "mere Whereabout" and to interpret its various philosophical positions "contending in boundless hubbub" (*CME* 28:32–33).

It is not just that the Preacher habitually points out contradictions between the providential theorem and his experience, but that he makes such observations within contradictory lines of argument which he appears to have constructed and from which he cannot extricate himself. One of his most common gambits is the antiphony of assertion and retraction: "a poor wise man . . . by his wisdom delivered the city; yet no man remembered that same poor man. Then said I, Wisdom is better than strength: nevertheless the poor man's wisdom is despised, and his words are not heard. The words of wise men are heard in quiet more than the cry of him that ruleth among fools. Wisdom is better than weapons of war: but one sinner destroyeth much good" (9:15–18).

As the ambivalent voices continue, Ecclesiastes begins to sound like Carlyle's modern doubting type who speaks not with the "certainty of Yes or No" but with the casuistry of "Yes *and* No; or . . . Yes *though* No." With such an "Ignatian method," Carlyle asks, "what will become of your religion?" (*LDP* 313). But making a leap of faith into the rhetoric of effortless assurance Carlyle called for is precisely what Ecclesiastes cannot do. His sharp criticism of Wisdom and his observations on the discrepancies of life are complicated by a many-sided dialogue of the mind with itself that self-consciously begins in the first chapter: "I communed with mine own heart, saying, Lo, I am come to great estate, and have gotten more wisdom than all they that have been before me in Jerusalem: yea, my heart had great experience of wisdom and knowledge" (1:16). Piling up compliments to himself, this "Solomon" persona immediately collapses the whole castle in the air: "And I gave my heart to know wisdom, and to know madness and folly: I perceived that this also is vexation of spirit" (v. 17). Chapter 2 recapitulates the same movement on a grander scale ("I made me great works; I builded me houses"); again, the skeptical strategy is to break down what he has built up, yet he returns not to God but to his own "vexation" with his own loss: "and there was no profit under the sun" (2:11).

Matthew Henry's teaching that the book is King Solomon's "recantation-sermon, in which the preacher sadly laments his own folly and mistake,"[41] points to the confessional quality of Ecclesiastes. Yet the circular structure of the book suggests something other than Henry's unidirectional salvific logic. To a skeptical reader the obsessive self-reference reveals the speaker's most troubling "vanity," of which he may not be aware: his pleasurable cultivation of self-consciousness, as he circles elegantly round his own central insight that "all" is self-concern and futility, repeatedly doubling back to his own empty center. One might then read Ecclesiastes not as pious sermon or faithful confession, but as a classic text of narcissism. It was just such a reading of existence that Carlyle had long repudiated. As early as his essay "Biography" (1832), he had attacked that "army of British authors" who do not "*see* anything whatever": "Nothing but a pitiful Image of their own pitiful Self, with its vanities, . . . hangs forever painted in the retina of these unfortunate persons; so that the starry ALL . . . does but appear as some expanded magic-lantern shadow of that same Image,— and naturally looks pitiful enough" (*CME* 28:58). This modern "Self-contemplation," as Carlyle had declared the year before in "Characteristics," "is infallibly the symptom of disease, be it or be it not the sign of cure" (*CME* 28:7). Yet try as Carlyle might to affirm a cure *through* a stage of doubt, this typical early essay convincingly portrays the skeptic's effort "to educe Conviction out of Negation" as a vain self-reflexive labor, circulating "in endless vortices; creat-

ing, swallowing—itself" (27). Carlyle's conclusion—"Hopeless struggle, for
the wisest, as for the foolishest!"—might be a paraphrase of Ecclesiastes' repeated confessions that his search for wisdom is futile. His deepest vortices
come cyclically throughout the book as a questioning of his own authority as
sage: "All this have I proved by wisdom: I said, I will be wise; but it was far from
me" (7:23; cf. 8:16–17). He confesses the pride of the seer's eyes—"All things
have I seen in the days of my vanity" (7:15)—even as he exposes the nothingness of what he sees. His obsession with his own skepticism presses him to
close his discourse with this ironic word of advice: "And further, by these, my
son, be admonished: of making many books there is no end" (12:12). Even
while asserting still his authority as teacher, he disconfirms it by concluding (yet
not concluding) as self-reflexively as he had begun. As Ecclesiastes says of
fools' words, his own nonsensical discourse creates and nearly "swallow[s] up
himself" (10:12)

No more than the Book of Ecclesiastes is *Little Dorrit* only a confident sermonic attack on Vanity Fair. Both are texts destabilized by their project of denying the received wisdom while seeking to establish certain truth by which to
live; both contradict themselves and are preoccupied with their own inconsistencies; both "circulate in endless vortices" around questions of the sage's—or
the artist's—authority; and the result for both is a specifically confessional form
of dialogism. Beyond its topical and satiric concerns, *Little Dorrit* is a profoundly autobiographical novel, written at a time of vocational and religious
crisis; and these find dynamic expression in the novel's subtly staged debates on
issues fundamental for Dickens that Carlyle had been addressing throughout his
career, issues that the *Latter-Day Pamphlets* (1850) had not closed for this disciple. While Dickens had long been Carlyle's admirer and by 1863 was still
insisting to his friend and mentor, "I am always reading you faithfully, and
trying to go your way" (13 April; D 3:348), *Little Dorrit* yields evidence of a
more uneasy literary discipleship in the mid-1850s; it illustrates that the "trying" was, at least during this period, ridden by ambivalence toward the Carlylean doctrine Dickens had sought to make his own. The result for biblical
allusion in *Little Dorrit* is a complex cycle of borrowings and revisions of formula: in writing this novel, Dickens seems to have been not only testing the
received wisdom of his Victorian sage against experience but also rereading
Carlyle through the lenses of Ecclesiastes—a book to which the allusions in
Carlyle's own earlier writings may have first drawn Dickens' reflective attention.
Ecclesiastes then becomes a tool of interpretation probably borrowed from Carlyle that Dickens turns back upon Carlyle himself. The evidence for this critical
rereading is that the chief themes treated ambivalently in the Preacher's book

are precisely those Carlylean themes on which *Little Dorrit* is most deeply conflicted: the value of work; the profit of learning through experience, especially
sorrow and renunciation; the certainty of providential order; and through all
these, the authority of the artist-sage. Because these themes, which shall be
taken up in sequence here, reach deep into beliefs Dickens shared with Carlyle,
the Preacher's book considered as dialogue is not only a subtext for Victorian
matters of public dispute; it becomes an expressive biblical precedent for
Dickens' troubled communings with his own heart.

Before the discussion turns to *Little Dorrit*'s fundamentally conflictive
themes, a further question must be considered: how is "Dialogue and Confession" related to "Sermon and Satire"? In its pursuit of both the satiric and the
novelistic modes I have discussed, *Little Dorrit* alternates between what
William Meyers has called "secure fixtures, clear judgements, confident assertions" and "unfixed dangers and ambiguities."[42] This fundamental indeterminacy reflects the indecisive beginnings of Dickens' novel for 1855–57: as is
well known, he shifted from a parable on irresponsibility satirically titled "Nobody's Fault" until the eve of publication, to a complex novel more hopefully if
also more ambiguously titled *Little Dorrit* (with its reminder of even the heroine's assumed identity and other fictions). In this work, Dickens attends to the
indeterminate qualities of human life with his most subtle novelistic means of
dissection and expression, making that finer delineation of experience most
notably lacking in the *Pamphlets*. Nonetheless, evidences of the original design
and of Carlylean rhetoric remain in *Little Dorrit* to plague critics who would try
to account for the novel's conflicting styles. I would suggest that the relationship
between the largely Carlylean satire and Dickens' more personal confession is
not simply contradictory but causal: the dangerous ambiguities into which the
novel travels issue, in part, from the extremity of its own satiric questioning, to
which Carlyle had led his disciple in the damning exposés of the *Pamphlets*.

This proposition requires a redefinition of the potentialities of satire. To this
point I have been arguing that, at least traditionally, satire is an art of closure: it
seeks at the least to clarify, by indirection, what is wrong and who is at fault.
The satirist, however, is under no obligation to provide positive alternatives to
what he attacks; he can work solely as a "demolition expert," as Kenneth Tynan
has said of G. B. Shaw, and it is irrelevant "if we ask a demolition expert when
his work is done: 'But what have you created?' "[43] Cumulatively, the effect of
Dickens' extensive satire in *Little Dorrit* is not closure at all but a radical reopening of issues. As Shaw himself perceived, *Little Dorrit* lays "dynamite"
under Victorian civilization;[44] but its blowing up of accepted formulas creates a
farther-reaching crisis of existential indeterminacy, in which (as Carlyle said of

the modern state of mind) "the worth and authenticity of all things seems dubitable or deniable" (*CME* 28:28). While Carlyle attacks this state of mind as Jesuitical unbelief in the *Pamphlets*, he had led Dickens like other disciples, in Clough's words, into this desert and left him there. Dickens' novel goes on from his satire to record what it means for the inner lives of his characters that Carlyle's "thrice-baleful Universe of Cant, prophesied for these Latter Days," has arrived (*LDP* 297). But Dickens does not define their malaise entirely in Carlyle's terms. Behind the characters' vanities lies the possibility that a universe of illusion is the one reality—a "still deeper Infinite of woe" not "chargeable on every one of us" (as Carlyle claimed, *LDP* 295) but nobody's fault. In this novelistic context, religious ideals and allusions to the biblical tradition become as problematic as they are for the subversive Old Testament writer—and as Ecclesiastes is in himself.

Work

AMONG ECCLESIASTES' voices are aphoristic directives to "labour under the sun," a phrase that is peculiar to this book and that occurs twenty-eight times in it. Like other Wisdom literature, Ecclesiastes provided support for nineteenth-century propagandists of the Goddess of Getting-on: "A feast is made for laughter, and wine maketh merry: but money answereth all things" (10:19). But his book also answers for those urging the higher value of work. If Samuel Smiles could ground the worldly advice of *Self-Help* in the proverbs of Solomon,[45] Victorian preachers opened to Ecclesiastes 9:10 for the all-sufficing text: "Whatsoever thy hand findeth to do, do it with thy might; for there is no work, nor device, nor knowledge, nor wisdom, in the grave, whither thou goest." This passage is often coupled with John 9:4: "I must work the works of him that sent me, while it is day: the night cometh, when no man can work."

Taken together, these two passages were not only a frequent resort of the chief Victorian apostle of work but the center around which Carlyle built his quasi-apocalyptic perorations, such as the climax of the "Everlasting Yea" chapter in *Sartor Resartus:* "Be no longer a Chaos, but a World, or even Worldkin. Produce! Produce! . . . Whatsoever thy hand findeth to do, do it with thy whole might. Work while it is called Today; for the Night cometh, wherein no man can work" (157; cf. "Characteristics," 43, and *LDP* 335). This repeated religioliterary strategy points to the importance of the Preacher's text on work—privileged as a means of closure to essays on doubt. It was in such a context that other nineteenth-century thinkers of all persuasions used the Preacher's proverb on work. Fitzjames Stephen's credo, as rendered by his brother, is typical: "Set to work upon the job that lies next to your hand, and so long as you are working well and vigorously, you will not be troubled with the vapours."[46]

Dickens' public recommendations of earnest labor, with himself as exemplar, were a constant theme. Yet as early as 1845, the private anxieties that provided the context for such earnestness suggest why work (especially good works) was so important. Responding to some bad news from Forster, Dickens wrote: "No philosophy will bear these dreadful things, or make a moment's head against them, but the practical one of doing all the good we can, in thought and deed. While we can, God help us! ourselves stray from ourselves so easily; and there are all around us such frightful calamities besetting the world in which we live; nothing else will carry us through it" (?2 March, P 4:275). Ten years later at a time when Dickens was taking great pains over *Little Dorrit* (*Life* 2:182), to Forster he wrote of how his sense of futility in his own work—even at the height of his career—led with a kind of psychic inevitability to ever more strenuous commitments to the work doctrine, even if it meant that he "must, please God, die in harness" (April 1856, D 2:765). Dickens admitted the desperation without understanding its causes—it is nobody's fault. Forster more perceptively relates this intensified restlessness and fatalism to the spiritual and intellectual wants of Dickens' temperament: his friend had "no 'city of the mind' against outward ills, for inner consolation and shelter" (*Life* 2:200). No wonder, then, that in 1856 Dickens (along with Carlyle) should find a place in Ruskin's roster of "nearly all our powerful men in this age of the world," artists who are "unbelievers; the best of them in doubt and misery; the worst in reckless defiance; the plurality, in plodding hesitation, doing, as well as they can, what practical work lies ready to their hands." Ruskin's rather dispiriting allusion here to Ecclesiastes 9:10 doctrine, which he had urged more heartily elsewhere, belies its inadequacy for unbelievers; consequently his type of the nineteenth-century artist in "Of Modern Landscape," a type for which the Dickens of the *Little Dorrit* period was a prime candidate, is troubled with "the vapours" like Ecclesiastes in a different phase of his thought: "speak[ing] ingeniously concerning smoke," the artist of the "cloudy" modern landscape paints things of "darkness" and "mutability," whatever "it is impossible to arrest, and difficult to comprehend."[47]

In its context Ecclesiastes 9:10 might be read as one of those moments when the confessor glimpses an exodus from his vortices of "smoke." But in his dialogical discourse, the "answer must needs prove, in great part, an echo of the question" (*CME* 28:4). If, in Bakhtin's terms, "every word is directed toward an *answer* and cannot escape the profound influence of the answering word that it anticipates,"[48] it is even more obvious that every answer includes its prompting question; and in Ecclesiastes the question predominates. The most frequent context in which the phrase "labour under the sun" occurs there is not in confirmations of the value of work, but in observations on the vanity of human toil. Indeed, on the theme of work Ecclesiastes' thought moves in bewildering cycles of contradiction. In chapter 2, for example, he announces that he "hated life; because the work . . . is grievous unto me: for all is vanity" (v. 17), but by verse 24, he is recommending man's enjoyment of "good in his labour," and in the next chapter he reasons, "there is nothing better, than that a man should rejoice in his own works; for that is his portion" (3:22).

Little Dorrit treats Carlylean work doctrine in terms of such contradictions. Officially the "clear design" of this novel (according to Forster) was simply to contrast "duty done and duty not done" (*Life* 2:185); and as I have suggested, the novel does expose varieties of millennial thinking and fatalism that deflect attention from the need for patient, exacting devotion to duty in this world. But Dickens' first full-fledged introduction of the theme of work dramatizes not Forster's clearly contrastive moral design but Ecclesiastes' conflicting attitudes. In chapter 2 of the first book Arthur Clennam presents himself as one of the "exhausted labourers" we saw on the "interminable plains" of chapter 1. His sympathetic complaint of having always been "grinding in a mill I always hated" until "Will, purpose, hope" have been "extinguished" is met by the aphoristic advice of "a sagacious man in business" (1.16.186) to set for London "with a will"; as for Clennam's darkened will, purpose, hope, he should "Light 'em up again!" (20). But for Arthur work has "bereave[d his] soul of good" (Ecc. 4:8), creating nothing but "the void in my cowed heart everywhere," as he tells Meagles. Arthur is Dickens' figure of the solitary man travailing in vain in Ecclesiastes 4:8. He has "neither child nor brother: yet there is no end of all his labour; neither is his eye satisfied with riches," for Arthur tells his mother, "I have seen so little happiness come of money. . . . It can buy me nothing" (1.5.47). When he does go to London as Meagles advises, ironically it is to give up work: "I have given up everything in life for the business, and the time came for me to give up that" (1.3.37).

Fortunately, Arthur does not have to choose between Meagles' Philistine practicality and Mrs. Clennam's Calvinist Mammon-worship. For he finds in Daniel Doyce a partner who offers the companionship in labor Arthur needs and who seems to justify the Victorian doctrine of work after all, when disinterested and devoted to a noble object. Doyce is vestured historically as one of the Captains of Industry to whom Carlyle commended the future in *Past and Present*[49] and as an exemplary nineteenth-century worker seems to satisfy the wisdom formulas of the age. Unlike Henry Gowan, he "believe[s] that in every service . . . a man must qualify himself, by striving early and late, and by working heart and soul, might and main" (1.17.202) since "time and tide wait for no one," as Doyce says (2.22.654). Victorian preachers such as Spurgeon (in his meditation on Ecc. 9:10) found this benign opportunism a timely theme for Victorian believers: "Let us not wait for large opportunities, or for a different kind of work, but do just the things we 'find to do' day by day. We have no other time in which to live. The past is gone; the future has not yet arrived; we never shall have any time but time *present*."[50] Doyce will "Take time by the forelock" and "Go in and win" (as Pancks advises elsewhere); he is one who knows how to redeem the time in the evil days, "not as fools, but as wise" (Eph. 5:15–16).

Doyce is further a wisdom figure in his understanding of Carlyle's counsel that no one works except under conditions: Daniel "faced his condition with its pains and penalties attached to it, and soberly worked on for the work's sake" (2.8.500), enjoying "his portion" regardless of ultimate profit. But, as in Ecclesiastes, the conditions, the contexts, pose difficulties. Despite the Victorian and specifically Carlylean formulas Dickens draws upon in this characterization, the surrounding "vapours" considerably cloud Doyce's worker-heroism. Like Ecclesiastes, he sagely speaks of injustice from "experience of these things" (1.10.115) and testifies later that trying to get his invention recognized has "aged," "tired," and "vexed" him (2.22.654), confirming Arthur's earliest observation of the man that the experience of vain labor has taken its toll (see 117). Moreover, as one who confesses to moments of self-doubt even if he does believe in his invention "as if the Divine artificer had made it" (2.8.501), Doyce contributes to *Little Dorrit*'s confessional dimension (see 114). A man who insists it is better to "put [the invention] by. Far better put it by. . . . It's all at an end" (2.8.502) echoes and reinforces Clennam's state of depressed resignation.

Carlyle's doctrine of work was ultimately part of his humanistic theodicy. "Evil," he wrote, ". . . is precisely the dark, disordered material out of which man's Freewill has to create an edifice of order and Good" through labor (*CME* 28:28). In *Past and Present* he had also argued that work yields knowledge (3.11.197–98), for labor provides the concrete testing by which men's powers are developed in the social organism. Arthur Clennam's experience in several ways does illustrate these ideas. If we look to the end of the novel, where Clennam is restored to the firm as a mark of his restoration of personal and social order in "a modest life of usefulness and happiness" (2.34.801), we sense Carlylean doctrine confirmed. From his earliest despairing speculations, as Barry V. Qualls observes, Clennam "must turn to the Carlylean prescription" that " 'Labour is Life' "; his "progress in self-discovery . . . is . . . to see 'what he was to do henceforth in life' "[51]—finding the vocation by which he is to earn his livelihood and doing good works as the novel's Good Samaritan (see 1.13.156–57, 2.20.635).

But Carlyle's promises of work's all-sufficing benefits are not realized for Arthur with complete certainty. There is no clear expression of any "self-discovery" Clennam gains from working with Doyce, nor does he notably exhibit self-understanding when he refuses to heed his partner's caution against speculating. His "highest and sole blessedness" (*CME* 28:15) is not work: it is marriage to Amy Dorrit. Moreover, while the narrator may seem to give uncritical assent to Arthur's Carlylean "code of morals" (1.27.311), one of the novel's darkest ironies is that his ideal imperils his spiritual well-being when "Duty on earth, restitution on earth" drives him in despair to enter voluntarily the Marshalsea Debtors' Prison—the novel's central symbol for the vanity of work, where he cannot do anything to pay off his debts. Imprisonment in the Marshalsea is an appropriate anticlimax to a life he judges "All in vain" (2.26.693), for although he has been ever so dutiful Clennam is Dickens' prime exhibit of the man who labors in vain to do his "Duty on earth." (The exhibition is extensive, involving nearly all the characters in some form of vain labor.) Like Carlyle's modern sufferers from doubt, Arthur's "best effort" is so often "unproductively spent not in working, but in ascertaining [his] mere Whereabout" (*CME* 28:28)—the labyrinthine mental confusions, mixed emotions, false leads, and practical no-thoroughfares of a plot that repeatedly dead-ends in little eddies of fruitless endeavor. Through most of the novel, Arthur's experience refutes Victorian worldly wisdom about work.

In his futile dialogues with Henry Gowan on the artist's calling, Arthur's defense of an Ecclesiastes 9:10 earnestness loses ground before the "smoke" Gowan calls "the truth": "'But it is well for a man to respect his own vocation, whatever it is; and to think himself bound to uphold it, and to claim for it the respect it deserves; is it not?' Arthur reasoned. 'And your vocation, Gowan, may really demand this suit and service. I confess I should have thought that all Art did'" (see 1.34.392–93). Arthur's "generous visions," as Gowan mocks them, are betrayed by the clichéd and apologetic way he confesses Carlylean-Dickensian doctrine. Arthur knows from his own marketplace experience money's fatal power to make a man's work vain—and more, the power of disillusion to empty labor of the meaning it could have. Since Gowan's jaded disappointment is anchored in the novel's larger questioning of "the fallacy of human projects" (1.18.213), the staged public debates on art between Gowan and Clennam have a deeper resonance, sounding Dickens' confession of his own anxieties in the mid-1850s about his vocation. Given his "despondency about public affairs" (to Forster, October 1855, D 2:700) and his personal "apprehension of some possible breakdown, of which the end might be at any moment beginning," in Forster's words (2:195), Dickens might well have been fearful for his work. As Carlyle had asked, "how can we *sing* and *paint* when we do not yet *believe* and *see*?"[52]

The Genesis theme of the "curse of perpetual and abiding physical toil" Ecclesiastes turns "into a toil in the mind which man cannot escape."[53] Dickens' descriptions of Clennam's fruitless practical endeavors soon yield to passages of speculation that are stylistic models of his mental vain labor to manage his contradictory inner voices. Were Dickens following Carlyle, he would have blamed this antihero's point of view: "If you have now no Heaven to look to," Carlyle wrote; "if you now sprawl, lamed and lost, sunk to the chin in the pathless sloughs of this lower world without guidance from above, know that the fault is not Heaven's at all; but your own!" (*LDP* 334). In *Little Dorrit* Dickens perceives, however, that while speculative skepticism can make "doing it" vain, the experience of labor's vanity can also drive a person into the painful vortices of speculation. Arthur Clennam is entrapped in this tautology, so that it is impossible to judge whether his attitude or his circumstances are at fault. And Dickens follows this character's "state of much perplexity" (1.26.298) so sympathetically that often the reader is hard-pressed to say where, in these "pathless sloughs," the "certain truth" Carlyle called for in the *Pamphlets* might be found. Indeed, whenever it becomes impossible to separate the narrator's voice from Clennam's rendered style, the Carlylean critic in Dickens becomes what he laments, and *Little Dorrit* sponsors the novelist's own divided state of mind.

Many of Clennam's most arduous speculative passages have to do with his relations with women, who serve as mediators for his relation with himself and the universe. In these communings, Arthur circles around the central subject, himself and the "void" in his "heart." In book 1, the chapter titled "Nobody's Weakness" is a model of such Ecclesiastian circumlocution, ending in suicidal longings for which the narrator has only sympathy: "And he thought—who has not thought for a moment, sometimes—that it might be better to flow away monotonously, like the river, and to compound for its insensibility to happiness with its insensibility to pain" (1.16.194–97; cf. Ecc. 9:5–6: "the dead know not any thing. . . . their love, and their hatred, and their envy, is now perished").[54] Even more convoluted are Clennam's conversations with Little Dorrit and his toil in the mind about her. In book 2, after he learns she loves him, Arthur wanders in a labyrinth of rationalizations until his thoughts come to a climax—or anticlimax—with a wonderfully ambivalent picture of her meaning for "his own poor story." It makes his love of her vain yet refuses definitively to cancel his hopes, thus making his labor of undoing the love equally futile: "Dear Little Dorrit! Looking back upon his own poor story, she was its vanishing-point. Everything in its perspective led to her innocent figure. He had travelled thousands of miles towards it; previous unquiet hopes and doubts had worked themselves out before it; it was the centre of the interest of his life; it was the termination of everything that was good and pleasant in it; beyond there was nothing but mere waste, and darkened sky" (2.27.714). Commenting on this pivotal passage, J. Hillis Miller stresses Arthur's perception that "only Little Dorrit gives form to his world and an orientation to his life," while Richard Barickman emphasizes that Amy is portrayed "as an end that is more like death than romantic consummation."[55] Equivocal like all Arthur's mental toils, this carefully constructed picture lends itself to both readings. In this optical illusion, another object lesson in point of view, now we see Amy, now we do not; now we believe, now we doubt. Ironically, this aporia is valorized by Arthur's code of "judge not" (1.13.158; cf. Matt. 7:1). At such moments, we see how Arthur's highest ideals rationalize temperamental needs—most obviously, the need not to reach for the object of his desire. Even the ideal issues in vanity.

The larger issue we see dramatized in these passages of romantic speculation is the plight of the man who cannot realize a worship for himself unaided in the modern world. At middle life in the mid-nineteenth century, the antiheroic (hence ironically named) Arthur finds himself in the position of Carlyle's "youth of these times" when "the Divinity has withdrawn from the Earth": "Time was, when if he asked himself, What is man, What are the duties of man? the answer stood ready written for him. But now the ancient 'groundplan of the All' belies itself when brought into contact with reality; Mother Church has, to the most, become a superannuated Step-mother, whose lessons go disregarded. . . . the Thinker must, in all senses, wander homeless, too often aimless, looking up to a Heaven which is dead for him, round to an Earth which is deaf." From his "sceptical, suicidal cavillings," Arthur's work with Doyce has not saved him. When "What are the duties of man?" has become unanswerable as Ecclesiastes 12:13 had answered it, the doctrine of work fails, for "there is nothing sacred under whose banner" Arthur Clennam "can act," either in Vanity Fair's secular faiths, or in the discredited creed of his superannuated stepmother (*CME* 28:29–30). Dickens then turns to the sacred female image: "Everything in its perspective led to her innocent figure," for there is nothing else—no operative Theorem of the Universe, no eye of Eternity—in what is otherwise a "dark air-canvas" (*CME* 28:28) of "waste, and darkened sky."

Amy Dorrit offers the only provisional closure possible for Arthur's speculative unease partly by embodying the antithesis of the sage's wisdom that human labor is vain. But on this as on other points, the novel shifts between "secure fixtures" and "unfixed dangers and ambiguities." The narrator early makes Amy a heroic exemplum of Carlyle's *"Work thou in Welldoing"* (*SR* 146): "Inspired?" he asks of his lowly heroine. "Yes. Shall we speak of the inspiration of a poet or a priest, and not of the heart impelled by love and self-devotion to the lowliest work in the lowliest way of life!" (1.7.70). But when Meagles points the lesson of Amy to his repentant ward—"Duty, Tattycoram. Begin it early, and do it well" (2.33.788)—his crude simplifications help us to see precisely the problem with "do the duty nearest to hand": its denial of intellectual and moral fineness. For what is the point of it without some analysis of the ends an Amy or a Tattycoram serves by doing her duty? In Meagles' sermonette, it becomes mere words—another empty formula.

Dickens' narrator often leads us to "think" of how Amy has worked (2.5.464); yet the cumulative effect of the novelistic presentation is to lead us to reflect on the futility of her work. Indeed, to borrow Clennam's words of praise, Amy's "patience, self-denial, self-subdual, charitable construction, the noblest generosity of the affections" (2.27.700)—all her spiritual, intuitive, and emotional giftedness—are rendered nearly impotent by her patient acceptance of a degraded condition in which she is "indispensable"—a condition the narrator declares "false even with a reference to the falsest condition outside the walls" (1.7.70). Far from being simply an inspiring example of noble work, even Amy sees herself in her confessional fairytale as the "tiny woman" forever spinning in vain at her wheel of fate and hiding love: an image that implies Ecclesiastes' most dismaying theorem of existence.[56] Although like Clennam's picture of "waste, and darkened sky" this is partly Amy's subjective distortion, it is significant that Dickens has Amy too tell the Ecclesiastian "narrative; the established narrative, which has become tiresome; the matter of course narrative which we all know by heart" (1.10.114).

In Riches, she comes to an excruciating awareness of the futility even of her love. With "no one to think for, nothing to plan and contrive . . . all she saw appeared unreal" (2.3.451). In Riches, the Whole Duty of Man no longer lies "ready written" for her. Even her mild presence reminding them all of the old days—and with no work to do, she can be nothing but a presence—does not improve their spiritual condition; she only drives them into ever more grotesque expressions of denial and ingratitude. In her relations with these people, there is "nothing to support life . . . nothing to do but die"—what, literally, she would have to do to cease being the bane of the family. Thus she too suffers from this novel's "enormous Life-in-Death" as she stares into the waters of the Grand Canal like Clennam gazing at the Twickenham river "flow[ing] away monotonously" (cf. Ecc. 1:7), or sinking into immobility in his prison room: this seems to be the climax—or anticlimax—of Amy's life of vain laboring in love. Even for the earnest characters of *Little Dorrit*, Ecclesiastian futilities modify the force of the Carlylean model from Ecclesiastes 9:10 amid the powerfully working fictions of Vanity Fair.

Learning from Experience

ECCLESIASTES' contradictory teachings on work derive from the indeterminacies of his larger project: his labor to "search out . . . all things that *are done* under heaven" in order to "see what was that good for the sons of men, which they *should do*" (1:13, 2:3; emphasis added). The Preacher's potentially antireligious procedure of learning through experience, not revelation, goes forward on the pious assumption that "wisdom" giving "life" will result (7:12; cf. 8:1, 5). The thrust of his researches, however, exposes the futility of evolving what men "should do" from what is actually "done." Learning ideal wisdom through experience is also vanity and vexation of spirit for the Dickens of *Little Dorrit*. Carlyle had long urged the artist to find the Ideal "here, in this poor, miserable, hampered, despicable Actual" and the supernatural in the natural (*SR* 156). But John Forster hinted that Dickens knew the futility of trying to deduce the ideal from actuality, when he wrote that his friend's "whole nature, was too exclusively made up of sympathy for, and with, the real in its most intense form, to be sufficiently provided against failure in the realities around him. There was for him no 'city of the mind' against outward ills, for inner consolation and shelter. It was in and from the actual he still stretched forward to find the freedom and satisfactions of an ideal. . . . But what he would have sought [in the world], it supplies to none; and to get the infinite out of anything so finite, has broken many a stout heart" (*Life* 2:200). Striving after experiential knowledge in the heuristic narrative structures I have noted, which seem to be "finding something out for us, something *real*," *Little Dorrit* seems driven by the urge to "[get] to the bottom of" the human problem and discover some answer for it, yet the novel repeatedly dead-ends in bafflement (see 2.25.688). The novel's often-noted air of weariness, like Ecclesiastes' "fatigue of the analysing faculties,"[57] seems to register the frustration Dickens encountered in the effort to get ideal wisdom out of the intractable yet elusive finite.

To Ecclesiastes, this effort is futile for particular reasons that Dickens explores in the fuller modern psychology and more sophisticated epistemology of *Little Dorrit*. In sum, what the Preacher learns through experience is that experiential learning yields contradictory, uncertain, impermanent (yet always the same), and intolerably painful results that do not "give life," indeed that exacerbate a longing for death. For this biblical writer whom Dean Stanley thought so "modern" and whose insights into the conditions of human learning were particularly compelling in the nineteenth century, there are both external and internal reasons for this kind of "vanity." These reasons merit review here, for they will suggest the grounds of Ecclesiastes' interest for Victorian writers and readers, especially the Dickens of *Little Dorrit*.

Observation turns up contradictory facts: evil men's days are prolonged, yet "He that diggeth a pit shall fall into it" (10:8). Moral categories conflict with social realities: "there be just men, unto whom it happeneth according to the work of the wicked" and vice versa (8:14). Such illogicalities and inequities in the external world cancel each other out, as do reversals of fortune; "time and chance happeneth to them all" (9:11) and "all go to one place" at death (6:6). Such reductive knowledge, of that which "hath been already of old time" (1:10), can only make the wisdom-seeker more jaded, for his experience produces no discoveries except that "there is no new thing under the sun." Thus Ecclesiastes is only too aware of how painfully the seemingly objective "facts" bear upon consciousness and shape moral and emotional response.

But he is also aware of how thoroughly the lessons of experience are mediated by human subjectivity—within the limits of memory, speculation, and imaginative discourse—and this experiential lesson most tellingly subverts the wisdom-seeker's project. Ecclesiastes has observed that men neither remember the past (2:16) nor can know the future (9:12); consequently they are doomed to repeat the past and to live in present uncertainty, spending their lives as a shadow (6:12; cf. Frederick, 1.8.78). Even if the future befalls by providential design, the uncertainty of men's knowledge still makes them wretched, as Ecclesiastes remarks with some irony, overturning the reassuring reading of Ecclesiastes 3: "Because to every purpose there is time and judgment, therefore the misery of man is great upon him. For he knoweth not that which shall be" (8:6–7). Preaching on this text, Queen Victoria's chaplain found comfort in the condition Ecclesiastes deplores: while conceding that human ignorance "contribute[s] much to the troubles and perplexities of life," he reasoned that "it is to the full as true, that the main of what shall befall us is matter of irrevocable appointment, to be averted by no prudence, and dispersed by no bravery. . . . In real truth, it is our ignorance of what shall happen which stimulates exertion: we are so constituted that to deprive us of hope would be to make us inactive and wretched." Thus Henry Melvill comes round to the duty nearest to hand: to know the future would unfit us "for those duties with which the present hour is charged."[58] But this Victorian lesson from the "real truth" of human actuality yields no sublime wisdom and encourages the suppression of the inquiring mind. The uncertainty of human projects persuades Ecclesiastes to the no higher counsel of opportunism: "In the morning sow thy seed, and in the evening withhold not thine hand: for thou knowest not whether shall prosper, either this or that, or whether they both shall be alike good" (11:6). The problem for both moralists is that without knowledge of consequences it is impossible to know for certain what is the *summum bonum*; hence, it is only too likely that reconcilers of the human condition will aim at some lower good to secure the certainty lacking in the important affairs of life.

Experiential wisdom can further turn to folly given the "many inventions" of the human imagination (7:29). Ecclesiastes sees that this fiction-making power both generates and arises from the production of language: "The beginning of the words of [a fool's] mouth is foolishness: and the end of his talk is mischievous madness" (Ecc. 10:13). Carlyle often glossed this favorite passage with his understanding of the reciprocal relation between words and mind: idle talk, he taught, is "precisely the beginning of all Hollowness, Halfness, *Infidelity*" (*CME* 28:84) because "False speech . . . falsifies all things; the very thoughts, or fountains of speech and action become false" (*LDP* 321). Carlyle condemned the ubiquity of "invention" as a peculiarly nineteenth-century disease, but Wisdom writers testify to the universality of his observation that "out of [speech] are the issues of life!" (*LDP* 312).[59] Such an insight could mean liberation from the tyranny of philosophical absolutes seen as mere products of the constituting and figuring powers of language. But in Ecclesiastes (while there will be more to say of his style), the emphasis on language as *theme* exacerbates his sense of entrapment in words: for not only does he declare fools' words vain, but repeatedly he seems to bracket his own acts of verbalization with the conclusive, yet so inconclusive and ambiguous dismissal, "this also is vanity."[60]

Under these external and internal conditions, whatever knowledge might be gained from experience brings "much grief" (1:18) and "despair" (2:20), prompting Ecclesiastes to praise the dead and the unborn because both "hath not seen the evil work that is done under the sun" (4:2–3). At length this chief of biblical soul-searchers abandons his high seriousness to counsel against the over-scrupulous conscience: "Be not righteous over much; neither make thyself over wise: why shouldest thou destroy thyself? Be not over much wicked, neither be thou foolish: why shouldest thou die before thy time?" (7:16–17). Ultimately, Ecclesiastes' awareness of the uncertainty of his knowledge leads to his admission of cosmic mystery—his privileged, nonexplaining answer to unbidden suffering, arbitrary chance, and human limit (see 8:16–17). His attitude, however, is not Carlyle's awe before the Universal Secret. The Preacher's raving reiterations drive home his vexation with the fact that "thou knowest not . . . thou knowest not the works of God" (11:5). While Ecclesiastes has often been read as a cautionary book warning against the forbidden questioning it pursues,[61] more immediately felt is its sharp sense of injustice that this mystery should be at all, given man's yearning to know—a "gift" of the Creator that "destroyeth the heart" (7:7).

As the theorizing of several characters makes pointed, *Little Dorrit* is preoccupied with the idea that learning from experience fosters the moral development of the individual, reminding us of Carlyle's "Eternal growth" in the "seedfield" of time. But this Victorian doctrine is even more problematic in *Little Dorrit* than in *Bleak House*, where Esther Summerson's progressive pilgrimage is to illustrate the moral usefulness of suffering and renunciation. Through many subtle gradations all the way to the denial of Carlyle's hopeful doctrine, Dickens shows in the later novel that experience yields uncertain insight, may cause regression rather than growth, and can deform the individual—such as the dented and incoherent Aunt. In the course of its researches into the finite, *Little Dorrit* makes precisely those qualifications of a formulaic Victorian ideal that Ecclesiastes makes of its received wisdom. Everywhere Dickens dramatizes epistemological uncertainty; explicitly he proposes the doctrine of experiential learning through the voices of untrustworthy spokesmen (such as Meagles and Wade) and stresses the conditions of perception under which lessons are learned (for Arthur, "the light of [Amy's] domestic story made all else dark to him"; 1.32.374). "There is no remembrance" for characters who dismiss the past without trying to understand it, or remember so selectively that their memories are organs of forgetting ("What's-his-name. He was there," says Clennam of Gowan, 1.26.299). As common as forgetfulness in this novel are mistaken prediction and the human misery it causes. Fearful about the uncertain future, the characters make up stories (like the princess tale in "Fortune-Telling") to protect themselves from the pain of hope; or they rationalize their lack of attention to consequences by doing some supposed duty nearest to hand and submitting to the irrevocable, as Melvill urged his hearers to do. Everywhere *Little Dorrit's* characters have "sought out many inventions," as does the narrator when he observes that "we all know how we all deceive ourselves—that is to say, how people in general, our profounder selves excepted, deceive themselves—as to motives of action" (1.13.137, a sentence also dramatizing the motions of the artist's language in shaping illusion, in the coy shift away from "we" to "people in general" here). Finally, experiential knowledge is intolerable. Carlyle confessed it in the *Pamphlets:* "no rapt Ezekiel in a prophetic vision imaged to himself things sadder, more horrible and terrible, than the eyes of

men . . . may now deliberately see" in "this false modern world" (313).
Dickens' opening vision of a terrifying sunscape without shadows, where the self
is intensely aware and pitilessly exposed,[62] projects this Ecclesiastian lesson
into setting; and the fact that modern experience leads to things "terrible to us,
to see" (1.27.323) Dickens repeatedly emphasizes in the abrupt discoveries that
bring dismay throughout *Little Dorrit* (for example, "I see it in your face," says
Bar to Physician on Merdle's suicide, 2.25.688; "Ah! We see enough!" cries
Arthur, observing Pet and Gowan, 1.27.204). Even after all his penetrative
seeing into human affairs, Dickens' narrator yields final judgment to "the
wisdom that holds the clue to all hearts and all mysteries" (1.29.224), although
not always so placidly as this conventional passage suggests. In short, experience can be a potent teacher in *Little Dorrit*, but the knowledge it brings is
relative to a whole panoply of human conditions and for some can destroy the
heart.

Dickens' novel of 1855–57 registers not only the author's personal ambivalence toward the doctrine of experiential learning but also the larger
cultural movement of a commonplace idea in transition. The empirical spirit of
the nineteenth century reinforced this doctrine preached by such moralists as
Samuel Smiles but ultimately undermined it by cultivating an ever finer sense of
"experience." As the inductive sciences were making moderns aware, Walter
Pater wrote in 1889, of "a world of fine gradations and subtly linked conditions,
shifting intricately as we ourselves change,"[63] "Lessons" learned from experience were becoming as discredited as the "Hard and abstract moralities" of
inherited ethical systems. Carlyle had early announced the death of superannuated "Mythuses," but partly in response to this new relativism he had fostered
his own abstract moralities in the 1850 *Pamphlets*. There, for example, he drew
a sharp distinction between two different battles of life: a noble one in which our
"sore toils . . . will themselves be blessed to us" if our guiding notion of the
universe be true; or "an ignoble devil-like and brutal" struggle if guided by
false notions and producing only the modern world's ills (*LDP* 297). Empowered
by a far more ambiguous sense of "false" and "true," and aware of the subtle
shifts of perception and language that change a fact into a fiction, the novelist of
Little Dorrit takes a position on experiential learning closer to Pater's than to
Carlyle's. In this mature fiction we find an extraordinary novelistic sympathy
with what Pater called "a more exact estimate of the subtlety and complexity of
our life," in which the noble and the ignoble are poignantly blended. The moments when Dickens abandons this kind of careful estimation to draw a lesson
from experience (such as at Merdle's death) stand out the more from the novel's
quietly realistic surface because the relativist method predominates, with its
refusal to extract lessons. The reader, learning from *his* experience of *Little*

Dorrit, is induced to eschew abstract moralizing and to develop the novelist's habit of forming proximate, revisable truths—"ideals" inextricably embedded in finite conditions of knowing which Ecclesiastes could not have followed out so intricately but had witnessed in the ancient world.

Miss Wade announces the doctrine of experiential learning in the second chapter of book 1: "My experience has been correcting my belief in many respects, for some years. It is our natural progress, I have heard" (22). For this embittered woman, "progress" is surely an ironic word: as she shows in her "History," the correction of belief can lead only to disillusionment, with the spiritual debility that brings to some natures. In chapter 13, we see the emptiness that Arthur's first presented adult learning experience yields. The narrator precedes the discovery with analysis that creates much sympathy for this "case": "Most men will be found sufficiently true to themselves to be true to an old idea. It is no proof of an inconstant mind, but exactly the opposite, when the idea will not bear close comparison with the reality, and the contrast is a fatal shock to it" (142–43). When the "fatal blow" comes in the form of a substantial and silly Flora, the experience is a "misfortune" to Clennam: "For, while all that was hard and stern in his recollection, remained Reality on being proved . . . the one tender recollection of his experience would not bear the same test, and melted away" (157–58). What "profit" can Clennam take from this discovery of vanity? The sympathy Dickens creates for Clennam makes Victorian doctrine on "the battle of life" absurdly inappropriate. Smiles' *Self-Help*, which popularized reductive versions of Carlyle's ideas, would counsel manly struggle in the "up-hill" fight: "All experience of life indeed serves to prove that the impediments thrown in the way of human advancement may for the most part be overcome by steady good conduct."[64] But in a battle wherein few "knew for what they fought, or why" (as Dickens' philosopher says in *The Battle of Life*, *CB* 302), no "steady good conduct" of any sort can make up for the loss of an ideal. Clennam has come to Teufelsdröckh's crisis of belief in himself and the order of things after the cruel betrayal of Blumine (Carlyle's "Flora"). For Clennam such a crisis is not Smiles' "wholesome stimulus" to wrest progress out of regress or to fight uphill, but a temptation to discover that there is no new thing in a monotonous life, "So long, so bare, so blank" (157), and to slide downhill:

> Therefore, he sat before his dying fire, sorrowful to think upon the way by which he had come to that night. . . . That he should have missed so much, and at his time of life should look so far about him for any staff to bear him company upon his downward journey and cheer it, was a just regret. He looked at the fire from which the blaze departed, from which the after-glow subsided, in which the ashes turned grey, from which they dropped to dust, and thought, "How soon I too shall pass through such changes, and be gone!"

To review his life, was like descending a green tree in fruit and flower, and seeing all the branches wither and drop off one by one, as he came down towards them.

"From the unhappy suppression of my youngest days, through the rigid and unloving home that followed them, through my departure, my long exile, my return, my mother's welcome, my intercourse with her since, down to the afternoon of this day with poor Flora," said Arthur Clennam, "what have I found!" (158)

Arthur's rhetorical question is his diffident way of avoiding Ecclesiastes' conclusion. But it turns into a real question, for Dickens builds into Clennam's "case" here an instance of skeptical apocalyptic: an ideational configuration (all the woman stood for to the idealistic youth) is disconfirmed by the facts, to be realistically revised in what Arthur *has* found, the figure who appears at this juncture announcing "Little Dorrit." Against any more hopeful knowledge, however, Arthur would defend himself. His overwhelming sense of the vanity of human projects and his personal vacuity would merely leave the ideal disconfirmed—subsiding, turning grey, dropping to "dust." Arthur's echo of Ecclesiastes 12:7 ("Then shall the dust return to the earth") suggests the Preacher's allegory on old age as the subtext for the configuration forming in Arthur's mind to replace his lost ideal: he makes his own little allegory (poetically depleted) out of the "dying fire" and the dropping tree, then explicates it in terms of his experience. Dickens' subtle rendering of Clennam's fiction in formation—so that we see and hear it temporally unfolding, stopping, beginning again—shows us the role of language in shaping illusion. We are also to see with considerable sympathy one man's vain, if conscientious, attempt to learn from failure. But Arthur learns "nothing," the end to which all things come.

The Merdle speculation into which Arthur is drawn is the novel's metaphor for the problem of his temperament: his speculative nature is compounded of his conscientiousness and his transcendental yearnings as well as the spiritual danger of endless introspection that depletes self-knowledge of usefulness for life. When Arthur becomes "The Pupil of the Marshalsea" (2.27.699), Daniel Doyce's sermon on learning through failure conveys Dickens' lesson on financial "speculation" but literalistically ignores the metaphoric implications of this word for Arthur's larger complexities. Indeed, especially with his suggestion that Arthur's mind and motives are a "machine" which can simply be readjusted, Doyce is blind to his own metaphors, to the way that language creates the illusion of philosophic certainty: " 'There are only three branches of my subject, my dear Clennam,' said Doyce, proceeding to mould them severally, with his plastic thumb on the palm of his hand, 'and they're soon disposed of. First, not a word more from you about the past. There was an error in your calculations. I know what that is. It affects the whole machine, and failure is the consequence. You will profit by the failure, and will avoid it another time. I have done a similar thing myself, in construction, often. Every failure teaches a man something, if he will learn; and you are too sensible a man not to learn from this failure' " (2.34.797). Like other of Doyce's pronouncements on the "struggle" of life (1.16.185), this echo of Victorian commonplaces is true in its way; as Smiles puts the idea, "probably he who never made a mistake, never made a discovery."[65] But the fictional context for Arthur's "mistake" considerably qualifies the truth of Doyce's ideally formulated sermon. For one thing, it is surely a perverse lesson to be teaching a man who has done nothing but force himself to learn from failure since the beginning of his story. In book 1 Clennam follows the dying fire meditation by telling Amy that he had "fancied I loved some one" but "found out my mistake, and I thought about it a little—in short, a good deal—and got wiser." Then, blind to *his* figuration, Clennam reinvokes his allegory of the downward journey (see 1.32.373–74), compelled to believe in his lesson even more by what Carlyle had called the prodigious influence of metaphors. To revise Smiles' formula for Clennam's case, he who has made a "mistake" has "never made [the] discovery" he might have made—that he and Amy are in love—had he not so insisted on the mistake and what he has "found" from it. As Flora puts this dilemma of self-deception, with its selective forgetting and blind prediction, "if seeing is believing not seeing is believing too" (2.9.517).

The only positive thing this pupil's Marshalsea experience has taught him seems to come too late: the awareness of "how much the dear little creature had influenced his better resolutions" (2.27.700). The narrator stresses the value of the lesson in conventional terms: "None of us clearly know to whom or to what we are indebted in this wise, until some marked stop in the whirling wheel of life brings the right perception with it. It comes with sickness, it comes with sorrow, it comes with the loss of the dearly loved, it is one of the most frequent uses of adversity. It came to Clennam in his adversity, strongly and tenderly" (700). But at this point Clennam's use of adversity is anything but sweet. With knowledge his sorrow increases. What he goes on to make of his discovery is to build up the dear creature's virtues so high that he depresses his own merits, "Until it seemed to him as if he met with the reward of having wandered away from her." To the narrator's praise of Arthur's "right perception" is added the ironic qualification that his oddly euphemistic use of "reward" implies here. Once again, his insight about himself and Amy can be expressed only as a distortion, and his language disguises his own foolishness from himself (just as the narrator's idealizing language would disguise the vanity of Arthur's knowledge from us). What we come to know from Clennam's experience is that the lessons of experience are learned in peril of utter ignorance amid the "twilight judgments of this lower world" (2.19.632).

We also see that given Arthur's spiritual plight, the realistic behavior Doyce recommends is not all the wisdom his partner needs. The workmanlike certainty of Doyce's creed is also out of date, like his "Divine artificer"; the distant clockmaker God of Paley's natural theology is appropriate to Doyce's generation, perhaps, but is no longer of service to nineteenth-century searchers who need a more immanent God, an Ideal *within* their Actual. Doyce may also be one of those Carlyle hailed near the end of "Jesuitism" who know "through all their being, the difference between Good and Evil" (*LDP* 334); but he never questions their coexistence in his orderly world, while Clennam's speculations imply just such a questioning. With his reiterated "I want to know" (2.28.725), this nineteenth-century Ecclesiastes quests after a deeper knowledge to which Doyce has no clue.

Nor does Dickens disclose that knowledge for him. The central secret of Arthur's origins, kept from him to the end by human contrivance, gathers metaphoric weight in the novel for larger unknowns. Unlike the ends of other Dickens novels that drive toward revelations, the resolution of *Little Dorrit* leaves many living issues "fraught with solemn mystery" (1.28.326). This privileged religious term, around which orthodox interpretations of Ecclesiastes typically close, had peculiar urgency in the era of the "March of Mind," which was unfolding an ever-thickening complexity of causes—be they mystery or muddle—that eluded formulation and obscured biblical schemes. Committed so extensively to rendering this "world of fine gradations and subtly linked conditions" in *Little Dorrit*, Dickens is nonetheless forced to admit that he holds no "clue to all hearts and all mysteries." Although such statements have a religious ambiance, in this novel they lack that note of earnest faith in the "Universal Secret" which Carlyle had long confessed. The scene of old Dorrit's death leaves the reader in bafflement rather than awe. Given the unavailability of the Seer's vision, the search for knowledge by "the sight of the eyes" (Ecc. 6:9) yields wisdom made vain by the conditions of human knowing.

The Teaching of Sorrow and Renunciation

THE BIBLE'S weariest sage finds "in much wisdom . . . much grief," yet from his book it is not clear whether "knowledge increaseth sorrow" (a pessimistic thought) or whether sorrow produces knowledge (a hopeful one). In chapter 7, he follows out the latter train of thought, sketching the framework for a doctrine of renunciation: "It is better to go to the house of mourning, than to go to the house of feasting: for that is the end of all men; and the living will lay it to his heart. Sorrow is better than laughter: for by the sadness of the countenance the heart is made better. The heart of the wise is in the house of mourning; but the heart of fools is in the house of mirth" (7:2–4). This clear teaching becomes clouded in the context of other statements Ecclesiastes makes on the meaning of sorrow. Its visitation on all obliterates moral discriminations between wise man and sinner (2:26). In the face of the fact that "all [man's] days are sorrows" (2:23), the Preacher repeatedly "commend[s] mirth, because a man hath no better thing under the sun, than to eat, and to drink, and to be merry" (8:15). Yet his assumption that mirth is within the range of human choice ("remove sorrow from thy heart," 11:10) is belied by the fact of unbidden suffering. Exactly what might be learned from sorrow, and whether renunciation is to be chosen, suffered resignedly, or repudiated by seizing the day of enjoyment: on these questions, the Preacher speaks in dialogical cycles of contradiction.

The ideal of renunciation was very attractive to Dickens, from his creation of Little Nell and the mutually self-sacrificing sisters of *The Battle of Life* to Sydney Carton and even Eugene Wrayburn. But self-denial was alien to Dickens' temperament, and not only because of his high spirits, as Forster was wont to point out. In a passage that makes critical distinctions between various experiential learnings in Dickens' life, Forster remarks that his friend's "early sufferings brought with them the healing powers of energy, will, and persistence, and taught him the inexpressible value of a determined resolve to live down difficulties; but the habit, in small as in great things, of renunciation and self-sacrifice, they did not teach; and, by his sudden leap into a world-wide popularity and influence, he became master of everything that might seem to be attainable in life, before he had mastered what a man must undergo to be equal to its hardest trials" (*Life* 2:194). In Ecclesiastes' self-contradictory utterances on sorrow, Dickens could find good biblical precedent for his own ambivalence toward an ideal he admired but could not reach, except on stage as the heroic Wardour in *The Frozen Deep*.[66] Whatever his personal limitations, Dickens could also find support in Ecclesiastes' teachings for the Calvinist gloom he believed psychically destructive and religiously false, "a most dismal and oppressive Charade" (*UT* 97). While the passage through a Valley of the Shadow is a recurrent conventional pattern in his books (as in Esther's Joban trials), Dickens was among those Victorians who did not consent unthinkingly to the notion that suffering was morally beneficial. In *Little Dorrit* not only Miss Wade and Mrs. Clennam but the central couple and others ranged across the moral scale of the novel's sufferings embody a variety of reservations about the teaching of sorrow and the renunciation ideal.[67] In these reservations, Dickens like Ecclesiastes queries his received wisdom—again, in Carlyle—yet without entirely abandoning it.

To Teufelsdröckh, it is vanity that makes us fancy we have not got the happiness we deserve, whereas to begin life one must discover "in man a HIGHER than Love of Happiness: he can do without Happiness, and instead thereof find Blessedness!" To love not pleasure but God is "the EVERLASTING YEA, wherein all contradiction is solved" (*SR* 153–54). Carlyle's worship of Sorrow, then, by which "the heart is made better," is not just resignation but, as *The Christian Year* would put it, the blessing of the rod in the yielding of the will to God.[68] Such worship was Carlyle's way of preserving the essence of Christianity without the intellectual difficulties of doctrines such as Incarnation and Atonement by which orthodoxy had rationalized suffering and comforted afflicted believers. In *Sartor Resartus*, reversing a pattern sketched earlier in this chapter, the casting out of Ecclesiastian vanity by self-denial leads to a natural-supernatural apocalypse and the discovery of the Godlike in man. Through "The Sorrows of Teufelsdröckh," "Experience is the grand spiritual Doctor," as the editor says (145); as he lies in the Centre of Indifference, Teufelsdröckh performs "the first preliminary moral Act, Annihilation of Self (*Selbst-tödtung*)" and illusion vanishes as he awakens to "a new Heaven and a new Earth" (149). Blessed with that end of alienation Revelation promises, he now names man "Brother" while "standing in the porch of that '*Sanctuary of Sorrow*'" to which he has been guided by divine forces (151). Teufelsdröckh has come to a Christian version[69] of the house of mourning, where the Preacher discovers the rudiments of brotherhood in the place of "the end of all men" (7:2).

In "Jesuitism" when Carlyle again invokes his ideal of *Selbsttödtung*, he looks specifically to the lessons of experience in Jesus' life (*LDP* 332). But if we probe further, Carlyle reveals in one of the more perverse moments in these "offensive and alarming" *Pamphlets* (295) a consequence of self-denial that Dickens will explore skeptically in *Little Dorrit*. This moment comes when Carlyle urges that Ignatius Loyola, his villain, should have consented (in his imputed words) "'To die forever, as I have deserved; let Eternal Justice triumph *so*, by means of me and my foul scandals, since otherwise it may not!' *Selbsttödtung*, Annihilation of Self, justly reckoned the beginning of all virtue: here is the highest form of it, still possible to the lowest man" (303). Carlyle's serious nonsense about Loyola does no actual harm to the doctrine of self-denial. But Dickens' portrait of Arthur Clennam as a "repentant outcast sinner" trying to find "healing solace to his conscience" by damning himself in a series of increasingly devastating self-denials casts a bleak light indeed on what this "transcendent act of virtue" (*LDP* 303) can come to. Dickens has even more to say in *Little Dorrit* than in *Bleak House* about the self-deceptive psychological uses of religion and morality. In this novel he also replaces the notion of blessing the rod with his own emphasis on healing the sick; and if Dickens' hero-worship of the Divine Teacher takes a cue from Carlyle, it is not the "man of sorrows" Dickens reveres—it is Amy Dorrit's "friend of all who were afflicted and forlorn" (2.31.770). Beyond these reconsiderations of received doctrine, there is a further dimension of the problem, obscurely represented in *Little Dorrit*, that reflects the persisting skepticism of its Ecclesiastes subtext. Here we also discover the psychic wilderness into which the loss of a creedal religion and a suffering God Incarnate throws Arthur Clennam, who renounces nearly everything but for nothing and with no divine aid. Even Amy Dorrit pointlessly suffers from the renunciation ideal and, somewhat surprisingly, can invoke no Divine Friend in the suffering of her days of vanity. Hence, even as the dangers of Calvinism and radical skepticism are emphasized in this novel, the limits of Dickens' liberalized Christianity bereft of some traditional comforts are also surreptitiously confessed. This is Dickens' darkest novel in its search for some center round which to crystallize belief, some lofty reason for self-denial, and some consoling explanation of suffering.

Turning to several key passages in *Little Dorrit*, we see the novelist registering his ambivalence toward Renunciation idealism by grounding it in the "confused human Actualities" of his characters' conditions and temperaments. Dickens' major statement of Arthur Clennam's "code of morals" is a paradigm of such skeptical modification. At first this creed appears to be simply noble and good: "As the fierce dark teaching of his childhood had never sunk into his heart, so the first article in his code of morals was, that he must begin, in practical humility, with looking well to his feet on Earth, and that he could never mount on wings of words to Heaven. Duty on earth, restitution on earth, action on earth: these first, as the first steep steps upward. Strait was the gate and narrow was the way; far straiter and narrower than the broad high road paved with vain professions and vain repetitions, motes from other men's eyes and liberal delivery of others to the judgment—all cheap materials, costing absolutely nothing" (1.27.311). This passage seems to call for a stable reading: it opens by denying that noble Arthur has been damaged by his experience, states his creed as the antithesis of otherworldly irresponsibility, and modulates into the absolute certainties of Dickens' satire on religious cant. Dennis Walder has usefully pointed out how in this passage Dickens reworked Matthew 7:13–14, usually taken to support the doctrine of election, to eliminate its "unwanted meanings."[70] But even if these clever reversals of Scripture's terms do make for an effective attack on "strait gate" theology that is really a "broad high road" of self-righteousness, this passage is surely equivocal as a statement of the hero's moral code. It may appear to be only what Walder calls it, "an expression of the broadly optimistic and practical view Dickens drew from the New Testament"; but in fact its language is carefully adjusted to create the ethos of the man who adopts this creed and to disclose the limitations of his point of view. Stylistic alliteration and repetition ("steep steps upward," "Strait," "narrow," "far straiter and narrower") recall the fact that Clennam has learned much (or little) from the rigid reiterations of a woman "brought up strictly, and straitly" on a Bible bound in the "straitest boards" (2.30.753, 1.3.30). With the final emphasis on "cost," Dickens reminds us too of her spiritual accounting methods. Arthur's intellect may have rejected his mother's otherworldly doctrine, but emotionally much of "the fierce dark teaching of his childhood" *has* "sunk into his heart." As we realize from his first announcement that he has "no will" (1.2.20) and his later confession that he has "habitually submitted" to his mother (1.5.45), the son raised on "2 Ep. Thess. c. iii v. 6 & 7" (where St. Paul warns against "walk[ing] disorderly")[71] suffers from the "repressed emotions" that such a creed has required (1.3.30, 1.26.310). And this creed now makes self-denial second nature to a man who calls himself "Nobody." If this code of "duty" and "restitution" contains telltale remnants of his childhood's legalistic themes, it is also notably deficient in Gospel; it omits, for example, the "Be ye therefore merciful" with which Luke introduces the motes and beams parable also recalled here (see 6:36–42). The child who has had "no more real knowledge of the beneficent history of the New Testament, than if he had been bred among idolaters" (30) is hardly likely in adulthood to draw the inspiring "optimistic and practical view Dickens drew from the New Testament." Given Dickens' novelistic qualifications, Arthur's self-denial is rather less than ideal—inextricable from circumstance and need.

The moral value of Arthur's particular acts of renunciation is further put in question by the ways irrevocable circumstance impinges upon acts of will. In Ecclesiastes' terms, what credit is it to the sage to renounce the house of mirth, if all men's days are sorrows? Carlyle had in fact argued pragmatically for *Selbsttödtung* by counseling accommodation to actuality: since no "Act of Legislature" has decreed any guarantee of happiness, "Make thy claim of wages a zero, then; thou hast the world under thy feet" (*SR* 153). Clennam half-heartedly takes Carlyle's advice, ever anticipating his disappointments by lowering expectation. In his farewell to romance, he turns an objective loss—Pet's rejection of him—into a noble act of self-denial, a mere vanity if the truth be known: "At that time, *it seemed to him*, he first finally resigned the dying hope that had flickered in Nobody's heart, so much to its pain and trouble; and from that time he became in his own eyes, as to any similar hope or prospect, a very much older man who had done with that part of life" (1.28.327, emphasis added). The vanity of hope for happiness cast out by *this* kind of self-deluding renunciation results in no apocalypse but the internal death emblematized by his floating of the roses upon the river. Over this funeral barge, nonetheless, the narrator lingers ("and thus do greater things that once were in our breasts, and near our hearts, flow from us to the eternal seas," 330), as though to memorialize the vanity of human wishes not renounced but simply lost. If this is merely that resignation to the inevitable we find in Ecclesiastes, its sentimentalization confesses that for the narrator as for Arthur, self-indulgence has replaced self-denial.

As I will argue more fully later, Amy's ideal is also embedded in her confused human actualities. Her acts of self-sacrifice for "the Family," her instinctive shrinking, and her unconsciousness of her needs derive from a background that encourages this behavior; the family in which she declines to assert a unique personal identity has all but denied her existence while demanding her complete self-devotion to *their* wants. To act as she does may be "heroic," but it is also a way to maintain the mechanisms of her involvement in the domestic life she needs. In book 2, the moral ideal that has defined her life reveals itself as a spiritual and psychological danger more clearly than before in the world of Riches, where self-denial has no purpose and now effects Amy's exile from family affairs. If she has scarcely ever had a self to indulge or deny, in Riches there is almost "no dear little thing left in the transformation" (2.17.602).

Arthur Clennam's renunciation code is even more clearly an ever-poised moral and psychological peril. As the sorrows of Arthur deepen, we see that his over-scrupulous conscience drives him (as the Preacher warns) nearly to "die before [his] time." In the Marshalsea prison, his house of mourning, Arthur seems to assume that his misfortune proves him a sinner (the view of Ecc. 2:26) and allows his Calvinist sense of deserved punishment nearly to crush him. As Carlyle puts this religious legacy, Nature "keeps silently a most exact Savingsbank . . . Debtor and Creditor, in respect to one and all of us; silently marks down . . . Debtor, Debtor, Debtor, day after day, rigorously as Fate . . . and at the end of the account you will have it all to pay, my friend. . . . neatly, completely, as sure as you are alive" (*LDP* 205). Dickens brings Clennam to debtors' prison partly to defeat this bookkeeping Theorem of the Universe, the Victorian formula by which Mrs. Clennam places acts of renunciation "to her credit . . . in her Eternal Day-book" (1.5.52). But the danger for Clennam is more than Calvinism perverted: as I have suggested, it is renunciation coupled with the loss of any transcendent faith. "Bred among idolators" and returning to a

London where "church bells of all degrees of dissonance" summon no one to church (1.3.26, 30), Arthur now pursues a self-denial motivated by no religious idea at all. When he repudiates openly his mother's business and beliefs, Arthur has "dared to say No, and yet cannot say Yea," but "dwell[s] as in a Golgotha, where life enters not, where peace is not appointed" to him (*CME* 28:31). In Arthur's case, a life of Calvinist self-denial has led on to the renunciation of belief and brings him to the edge of a void.

In other of Dickens' novels, such as *Bleak House* and *Great Expectations*, passing through the Valley of the Shadow implies a spiritual progress that makes suffering comprehensible. In *Little Dorrit*, that spiritual framework seems unavailable or inoperative for Amy and Arthur in their crises of near-death to the self; the God of their world, if present at all, works at an "untraversable distance" from their vain toils. If these two characters do have illusions that need to be purged, the sufferings they undergo are surely out of proportion to their sins. For Arthur, this disproportionate trial serves the generalization of the modern type he comes to embody. We sense this especially when he is descending into madness in the prison, where his "fever-paroxysms" are not "benignant," as they were part of Teufelsdröckh's larger scheme of cure (see 2.29.734). At this low point, Clennam's *Selbsttödtung* becomes indistinguishable from the modern malaise Arnold had called "depression," Pater "languor" and "endless regret," Ruskin "ennui, and jaded intellect," Carlyle "enchantment" and "paralysis." In "Of Modern Landscape," Ruskin painted the type brown and concluded: "The profoundest reason of this darkness of heart is, I believe, our want of faith." [72]

Dickens' "grave brown gentleman" of forty also suffers so disproportionately for his sins in order to become an expressive vehicle for the artist of the *Little Dorrit* period. In his skeptical cavilings about the doctrines of work, learning through sorrow, and renunciation, Dickens writes as the disciple who has found the sage's wisdom formulas empty because they do not speak to his own needs or capacities or to the realities he sees around him; and, with that self-pitying indulgence I have noted, through Clennam he laments being a "waif and stray everywhere" (1.2.19) without the authority that the Bible might have provided or that, in its stead, Carlyle had promised but belied in the desperate *Pamphlet* rhetoric. With a fierceness that defied all contrary evidence but brought no comfort, in the closing lines of "Jesuitism" Carlyle had insisted that this "restless gnawing ennui" *teaches:* it is a "prophetic Sermon from the Deeps [which] will continue with you, till you wisely interpret it and do it, or else till the Crack of Doom swallow it and you" (*LDP* 335, 337). But ennui teaches Dickens' Pupil of the Marshalsea nothing;[73] "going astray" in the night, he merely hears imaginary voices and answers them in the last trailing echoes of his dialogue of the mind with itself (735). There is no cosmic "Sermon" to interpret wisely or foolishly. There is finally nothing at all in his perspective except a woman wooing back to life the complex self Arthur's renunciations have nearly annihilated: "Little Dorrit, a living presence, called him by his name" (736).

In the novel's resolution, Dickens most fully puts the all-sufficiency of the renunciation ideal in question by showing that people need happiness as well as blessedness: and he does want it both ways, like Ecclesiastes. Through all his relations with Amy, Clennam has exhibited just this mixture of human needs. When in book 2 he refuses the offer of her fortune with "GOD bless you, GOD reward you! It is past," and when she responds, "weeping bitterly," "You will surely not desert me so!" (2.29.739–40), Dickens means his reader to feel the perversion of self-denial when enforced in such ignorance of the heart's affections. Arthur offers blessings that are torture to his beloved; and if his words "It is past" do recall Christ's from the cross,[74] the echo only draws attention to how difficult it is to execute a Christian ideal in the "poor, miserable, hampered, despicable Actual" of this world (SR 156).

Amy, too, has struggled against her own hopes for a life beyond self-denial. We see this most poignantly in the tale of the princess: with its Doppelgänger motif, this fiction enables Amy to flirt with despair and hope, entertaining alternate versions of her destiny with the self-renouncing tiny woman's death and the princess' continued life to tell the tale, which allows Amy to peep at her "Shadow" of love. Shy as she is to the end, however, the wonderfully convincing reality about this Dickens heroine is that she does, at last, ask for the happiness she needs: first, in terms of blessedness ("Pray, pray, pray . . . my friend!—my dear!—take all I have, and make it a Blessing to me!" 2.29.738), and then more directly: "Never to part, my dearest Arthur. . . . I am rich in being taken by you, I am proud in having been resigned by you, I am happy in being with you. . . . I love you dearly! . . . how blest at last my heart is!" (2.34.792). When we last see this pair they are "inseparable and blessed" (802). This is not "the EVERLASTING YEA, wherein all contradiction is solved," for they still walk "in sunshine and in shade." But in the midst of Vanity Fair, they have found that earthly beatitude which even the weary Ecclesiastes finds heart to preach: "Go thy way, eat thy bread with joy, and drink thy wine with a merry heart; for God now accepteth thy works. . . . Live joyfully with the wife whom thou lovest all the days of the life of thy vanity, which he hath given thee under the sun, all the days of thy vanity" (9:7–9).

Theorems of the Universe and the Artist

FOR CARLYLE the most telling spiritual fact is "the notion we have formed for ourselves of this Universe, and of our duties and destinies there" (*LDP* 296). The most revealing confessional fact about *Little Dorrit* is that it is not "formed" of one leading idea. Behind and through Dickens' embedded dialogues on work, learning through experience, and renunciation, he entertains contending "notions . . . of this Universe" with different conclusions about human duties and destiny, most pressingly those of the artist. Vocational and spiritual crisis come together in this confessional dimension of *Little Dorrit*. To Carlyle, the artist's work must announce a *"Fiat Lux"* to the century's doubts, reveal "God Almighty's Facts," and set readers working. Writing his "biography" of Amy Dorrit, a "record of the Divine Appearances among us" (*LDP* 324), the disciple of Carlyle strives to be faithful to his religious Theorem of the Universe, its apocalyptic faith, and its program for the artist. But in the same novel Dickens also explores the relative truth of a competing theorem given prominence in Ecclesiastes, as well as a possible third, subsumed under the second one here. All three propose some form of necessity, some stabilizing fiction of belief, benign or malign, to be read out of events; Ruskin summarized the fundamental aporia in *Little Dorrit* to which they point when he observed of the "inconsistency" in modern art that "the elements of progress and decline [are] strangely mingled in the modern mind."[75] These "notions," which drew Dickens' imaginative sympathy in the *Little Dorrit* period, are not each pursued with philosophical consistency, of course; and they are enmeshed in incident, narrative structure, characterization, dialogue, imagery, symbolism—in all those resources available to the rhetoric of fiction. But unlike Wayne Booth's rhetorician, Dickens creates out of these elements a shifting rhetoric that keeps his competing hypotheses in dialogic play. These rival theorems disrupt the univocity of the text by introducing thematic dissonances of the sort I have been discussing; they also contribute to the novel's heterogeneity by rationalizing the divergent, even irreconcilable artistic strategies pursued in the same work.

At the end of the first chapter and periodically throughout the text, Dickens reaches for a secure notion of order that he and Carlyle found indispensable: a conception of the world that encapsulates evil days in a design of good from all eternity, that sees human ambiguity and futility under the aspect of a higher clarity and purpose (intermittently revealed among men), and that drives toward the unveiling of truth by time. Periodically Ecclesiastes seems to glimpse such an order: "God shall judge the righteous and the wicked: for there is a time there for every purpose and for every work" (3:17; cf. 6:4, 12:14). Such passages,

modern biblical scholars argue, were added by later pious glossators introducing Hebrew notions of justice into a text notoriously bent on questioning those
ideas. If Dickens could find competing notions of the universe in Ecclesiastes,
he secures *Little Dorrit*'s apocalyptic paradigms in their most authoritative biblical source. The Hebrew conviction, as Carlyle puts it, "that wrong differs from
right as deep Hell from high Heaven" (*LDP* 302) is found throughout the Bible,
of course, but it reaches mature dramatic form in the Book of Revelation.

An apocalyptic reading of *Little Dorrit* is invited by its monthly cover design,
with Little Dorrit gliding through the prison door haloed by light as the central
emblem (see Rev. 3:20, 4:1), surrounded by visual signs of Britain/Babylon's
latter days. Equally prominent is the novel's basic structural device of the ironic
reversal from Poverty to Riches, Dickens' skeptical modification of the apocalyptic paradigm through which he exposes the transvaluation of values in the
Eye of the Great World (a specific Revelation theme; see 3:17–18). While the
mystic writer's symbols are in secret cipher, to be apprehended only by the
initiated, Dickens draws upon some of the more commonplace biblical archetypes recognizable to his Victorian audience: the "woman clothed with the sun"
(12:1) who bears the new age in pain, is persecuted by demonic forces but
protected by God in the wilderness, and embodies "the law of suffering and
renunciation";[76] a modern antichrist, surrounded by false prophets and wor-
shippers; in the fullness of time, the collapse of Babylon amid much general
lamentation and the judgment of all by their works. To some extent, these apocalyptic emblems are meant to accomplish in Dickens' novel what they do in the
Seer's discourse: they help us read contemporary actuality under the aspect of
eternity, not only to unmask Satan and Antichrist in the villains of the day, but
also to find, as Jacques Ellul writes, "in this present history, the Kingdom of
God hidden in this world."[77]

Inevitably Dickens attenuates the power of the apocalyptic symbols he re-
fashions as an almost wholly secular scripture; and his revisions suggest several
sorts of skeptical modification. Some of the symbols he domesticates, shifting
redemptive work to human hands and scenes. In Amy Dorrit's characterization,
as Alexander Welsh has shown, Dickens draws upon the Victorian cultural
mythology of the earthly bride who is to save from the City of Destruction and
from death. For Arthur Clennam, the Seer's vision is even more attenuated. As
Arthur recovers in the opening of the final chapter, a signal instance of secular
apocalyptic, Dickens gestures toward the "universal newbirth" Carlyle had
called for by describing an apocalypse of nature familiar from English Romantic
poetry which is made *present* to Arthur through a "voice" (as in Revelation): he
listens on "a healthy autumn day; when the golden fields had been reaped and

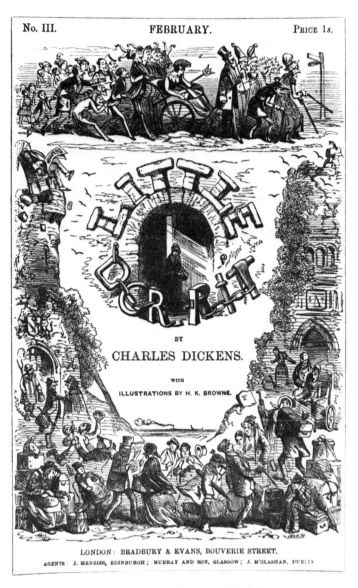

Cover design for monthly parts of *Little Dorrit*
(Hablot K. Browne)

Babylon the great is fallen, is fallen, and is become the habitation of
devils . . . and a cage of every unclean and hateful bird. . . . In one
hour so great riches is come to nought. (Rev. 18:2, 17)

And there appeared a great wonder in heaven; a woman clothed with the
sun. (Rev. 12:1)

ploughed again, when the summer fruits had ripened and waned, . . . when the apples clustering in the orchards were russet. . . . from the sea-shore the ocean was no longer to be seen lying asleep in the heat, but its thousand sparkling eyes were open, and its whole breadth was in joyful animation" (2.34.790). Insofar as this vision of a "new heaven and a new earth" is Dickens', he does providential work by recreating here the deadly sea images opening his first book and the deceptive eschatological harvest opening the second. But this natural-supernatural revelation ends in a "light" that is too "strong" for the jaded Arthur's eyes. Whatever religious impulses are present modulate into domestic desires for those "harvests of tenderness and humility that lie hidden in the early-fostered seeds of the imagination . . . in nursery acorns." This passage faintly echoes Carlyle on growth in time in *The French Revolution*, which Dickens knew intimately: "The Beginning holds in it the End . . . as the acorn does the oak"; there Carlyle depicts, too, "the summer's blossoming" and "the autumnal withering" (*FR* 3:103). But Carlyle's context is great historical "transactions," whereas Dickens' is one man's new birth in love. This domestication of apocalyptic marks the limits not only of Clennam's desire but also, evidently, of Dickens' own hopes for any larger transformation. And it is as distant from St. John's promised total integration as is the Day of Judgment from the end of *Little Dorrit*'s first chapter, where the sea "scarcely whispered of the time when it shall give up its dead."[78]

Other apocalyptic symbols, such as the messianic banquet and the river of life, Dickens parodies and ironizes in *Little Dorrit*. This kind of manipulation of the paradigms is authorized by St. John's book, where the dualistic vision requires ironic pairings (such as the verbal parody of honors paid to the Lamb in the worship of the Antichrist) that establish the meaning of the demonic as the inversion of the divine. These stable revisions, however, become genuinely skeptical in that Dickens' sense of irony far exceeds St. John's in the proportionate weight assigned to the blasphemous. As I have suggested, so extensive are *Little Dorrit*'s parodies of scriptural paradigms that the cumulative effect is to call the efficacy of Bible threats and promises into question. This depletion of the biblical symbols comes as a result of Dickens' commitment to contemporary observation, the project he shares with Ecclesiastes. Dickens insists he writes "history" (1.14.159); and in his imaginative reportage, we see not only how widely religious values have been abandoned and divine intervention interminably delayed, but also how the rise of historicism—with its sense that what is done cannot be undone—had challenged the formulas of renewal and forgiveness[79] and thus had helped to erase the apocalyptic horizon in the nineteenth century.

This sense of an unredeemable historical actuality also bears upon Dickens' narrative structure. In the course of St. John's book written for fellow Christians in prison, the whole world is delivered from captivity in the absolutely definitive confrontation between good and evil. Apocalypse thus completes a concordant vision that makes sense of history; from the absolute end with which Revelation starts—"end" as goal and as completion—we are able, Ellul writes, "to say what history is."[80] Despite Dickens' search for such ends and his exposure in words of an oppressive political order, no such final determinations as the Seer's are assured in *Little Dorrit*'s imprisoned world. Ironically what is so insistently called a "history" fails to make satisfactory sense of contemporary history, and the demonstrated need for a wider salvation than England's political redemption is mocked in Dickens' final picture of the resurgent City of Destruction. As Northrop Frye reminds us, the total cyclical mythos of apocalypse must include the epic of return as "disaster is followed by restoration, humiliation by prosperity."[81] In this novel Dickens' apocalyptic cycles are incomplete and his restorations sharply circumscribed. The "Golden Age revived" is indeed only a "most wonderful deception" (2.13.557, 556).

Despite these radical modifications of the apocalyptic paradigm, there is "Something Right Somewhere" in *Little Dorrit*'s world (title, 2.6)—presences as elusive as Dickens' indefinite pronouns suggest. Revelation's tableaux of beatitude and canticles of joy are structural interludes in the forward thrust of the action that represent the believer's advance participation "in the total presence toward which the action moves."[82] Even *Little Dorrit*'s labyrinthine narrative is penetrated periodically by visionary and prophetic glimpses. Carlyle would call them evidences of the "Transcendentalism, no less superlative," than the "Descendentalism" also found in humankind, manifestations of "GOD'S-PRESENCE" (*SR* 51–52). Dickens probably had something like this in mind ideally, although his reservations become inscribed in the novelistic language with which these evidences are presented. Even his affirmative statements dwindle away into qualification or become undone by their own telling metaphors, as when the narrator observes that "the stars came out in the heavens, and the fireflies mimicked them in the lower air, as men may feebly imitate the goodness of a better order of beings" (1.1.14). From John Baptist Cavaletto onward—forerunner of later "appearances"—nearly all the characters have such good imitative moments; but that "better order" would seem little more than the projection of the novelist's desire—so feeble are these imitations—were this not also the story of Little Dorrit, Dickens' godlike "Appearance in the Marshalsea" (title, 2.28) who brings light into the "troublous dim Time-Element" (*SR* 104) because she consciously imitates the Divine Teacher. As I will discuss further in the last section of this chapter, Amy stands timidly in the center of Dickens' religious design as well as in the heart of the prison, the present-and-absent "Something Right Somewhere" at the crux of the novel's belief and unbelief.

The apocalyptic paradigm—skeptically modified, domesticated, ironized though it may be—has specific further implications for Dickens' notion of the artist in this work. The first rests on an idea he saw as necessary to modern reading of Scripture, progressive revelation. Confirming the completeness of his vision, St. John concludes by warning against anyone adding to the prophecy (22:18), implying that God's revelation in general is "finished and done with." But this notion, Dickens wrote in a letter of 1863 on the *Essays and Reviews* controversy, he could not "in the least understand. Nothing is discovered without God's intention and assistance, and I suppose every new knowledge of His works that is conceded to man to be distinctly a revelation by which men are to guide themselves" (to W. F. de Cerjat, 21 May, D 3:352). From this theological idea Dickens drew one of his favorite analogies for the artist, proved by practice. As he wrote to Wilkie Collins: "I think the business of art is to lay [the] ground carefully, not with the care that conceals itself—to know, by a backward light, what everything has been working to—but only to *suggest*, until the fulfillment comes. These are the ways of Providence, of which ways all art is but a little imitation" (6 October 1859, D 3:125). Sometimes in *Little Dorrit* Dickens comes forward as just this sort of withholder and unfolder of the novel-world's secrets (see 1.9.95) and promises that Truth shall be revealed by Time (1.21.248, 1.15.173). In prominent portentous passages, he hints at a "vast" historical network of causes and effects in which the "multitude of travellers" are all caught up in one design, "the pilgrimage of life" (1.2.26, 1.15.173). The teleological suggestion here, as well as other references to "Destiny" and "Time," is not specifically religious, but it indicates a view of history as linear and governed by a progressive unfolding. Again a nineteenth-century historicism enters in to modify, but not disconfirm, the Revelation paradigm (which projects the radical disruption of history, not "progress" to a glorious goal). The many references to time and clocks ticking in *Little Dorrit* signal Dickens' preoccupation with one of Carlyle's leading themes: the "Time-Spirit" which has "environed and imprisoned us" (*SR* 103). One way to read the artist's activity in *Little Dorrit* is to accept his self-casting as patient Conductor of characters and reader through a minutely articulated time present, teaching us, as Michael Hollington writes, that the "true millennium is a . . . distant phenomenon, to be reached only through patient effort in time."[83]

Carlyle's teaching that all space and time is an organic web of causes and effects also entered into Dickens' conception of himself as a patient orchestrator of events. Presenting himself in the 1857 preface as one who has held the novel's "various threads with . . . continuous attention," the providential novelist announces that now "the weaving may be looked at in its completed state, and with the pattern finished" (p. lix). Carlyle's metaphor of the universe as the "loud-roaring Loom of Time" weaving "the vesture thou seest Him by" (*LDP* 326) led to his conviction that the man of letters is to illuminate this divine artistry by weaving (if he *must* write fiction) "an expository illustrative garment of Fact."[84] With the completion of the biographical *Little Dorrit*, Dickens had woven Carlyle's "fair tapestry of human Life"; and if he seemed, to one reviewer, "a weaver of odds and ends into a pattern resembling nothing in heaven or earth,"[85] such doubters see only "the wrong side of the pattern of the universe" (2.20.227), where all the "rough seams, tatters, and manifold thrums of that unsightly wrong-side" will necessarily appear (*SR* 51). That is how the universe appears for a time to Teufelsdröckh—and to Amy and Arthur—until he discovers, in his apocalyptic awakening, life's true artistry. Although the aesthetic metaphors, the organic filaments, and the dynamic conception of time here are Carlyle's and the nineteenth century's, the Bible read as a "wholly concordant structure," in Kermode's terms, implies this ultimate artistry; and the richly patterned artifice of Revelation implicitly confirms its own promises of a providential pattern working behind and through the obscure motions of historical events.

In the progressive revelation of his moral design, the artist of *Little Dorrit* drives toward Time's unveiling of God Almighty's "Facts" of good and evil. Yet as I have suggested, Dickens' fictional context, established with such minute and patient exactness, also provides support for our disbelief in his own executions of the moral pattern. This artist's voice, too, becomes problematic. In a novel of "studied ambiguity"[86] there seems something bogus about the narrative persona whose language is fit only for idol-breaking in the prophetic manner— who claims to know "as certainly as the sun belongs to this system" that Blandois is absolutely evil (2.6.473). Moreover, many readers have felt that the narrator's portentous predictions about fated encounters and the melodramatic mysteries of books 1 and 2 are anticlimactic. Dickens' strenuous attempts at closure in the five last chapters ("Closing In," "Closed," "Going," "Going!," "Gone") parody the conventions he is using. The unveiling of Truth by Time reveals itself to be a vain fiction of desire, driving the unenclosable narrative toward closure on evils that remain a mystery, substances never realized, and links never made in Dickens' promised "one idea and design" (letter to Forster, April 1856, D 2:766).

In the artist's refusal to produce a complete apocalyptic cycle or Everlasting

Yea to resolve all contradiction, there may yet be discerned a moral intention. Apocalyptic makes totalizing claims; Dickens, however, engaging his readers in what Richard Barickman (making a different argument) calls "morally instructive deception,"[87] writes a cautionary tale partly about the futility, even danger, of all-encompassing formulas for life—whether of the received traditions he entertains seriously (biblical or Carlylean) or of the new secular gospels he satirizes. Amy Dorrit tells such a cautionary tale in her story of the princess and the tiny woman. Pertinent here is this unstable narrative's skeptical revision of the "omniscient narrator" convention, with its implicit confirmation of life seen *sub specie aeternitatis* as in the Seer's book. In the course of the tale's unfolding, the rich and wonderful princess, faithfully following the tiny woman's lonely life to its predicted end, discovers that her vaunted "power of knowing secrets" comes to much less than expected: the role this observer learns is a rather more modest capacity for hearing pain confessed that she can neither alleviate nor wholly comprehend. The story's conclusion has only the sense of an ending with Amy's "That's all, Maggy," and leaves this listener "staring and ruminating" (1.24.286): the mystery of suffering remains—what it was. In the course of writing and rewriting his novel, Dickens the providential author, weaver of the pattern, orchestrator of causes and effects, repository of secrets, denouncer of villains, discovers himself after all to be just such a witness to the inconsolable griefs and enigmas of his characters' lives. As we shall see, this discovery has far-reaching implications for the dominant mode of *Little Dorrit*'s artistry.

The pressures for these revisions of the artist's role and of the Carlylean theorem on which it rests have their biblical locus in Dickens' Ecclesiastes subtext. Far more pervasive in the novel than apocalyptic teleology is the Preacher's cyclical conception of nature and history. His disposer of "a time for every purpose under the heaven" bears the name of "God" but does not resemble the Hebrew Jehovah: in its most pessimistic aspect, it is, as Carlyle wrote of the modern version of this theorem, "an iron, ignoble circle of Necessity [that] embraces all things" (*CME* 28:30). With an outlook that resembles contemporary determinism, the Preacher sees everything, even human feelings, as products of necessity in the depersonalized operations of nature's forces:[88] "To every thing there is a season . . . A time to be born, and a time to die; . . . A time to love, and a time to hate; a time of war, and a time of peace" (see 3:1–8). Such a vision of nature and history need not invite a wholly pessimistic reading. The calm beauty of Ecclesiastes' cadences doubtless has inspired the exalted resignation to the changing facts of life that we find in Christian interpretations of this passage. Matthew Henry was not dismayed by this picture of "the *wheel of nature* (Jam. iii.6)," in which "sometimes one spoke is uppermost and by and by the

THE STORY OF THE PRINCESS
(Hablot K. Browne)

Who is as the wise man? and who knoweth the interpretation of a thing? a
man's wisdom maketh his face to shine. . . . Yea farther; though a wise
man think to know [the work that is done under the sun], yet shall he not
be able to find it. (Ecc. 8:1, 17)

The Princess was such a wonderful Princess that she had the power of
knowing secrets. . . . [When the tiny woman died] she went in at once to
search for the treasured shadow. But there was no sign of it to be found
anywhere. (*LD* 1.24.286)

contrary; there is a constant ebbing and flowing, waxing and waning; from one extreme to the other does the fashion of this world change, ever did, and ever will."[89] Nor is Tennyson disturbed in his reconciling Prologue to *In Memoriam:*

> Our little systems have their day;
> They have their day and cease to be:
> They are but broken lights of thee,
> And thou, O Lord, art more than they.
>
> (lines 17–20)

In the Christian vision, the expectation that good will triumph places the Preacher's antithesis within a higher unity: as Spurgeon meditated on Ecclesiastes 10:7, "When the wheel turns, those who are lowest rise and the highest sink. Patience then, believer! eternity will right the wrongs of time."[90]

Even Ecclesiastes tells himself that there will be such a time of judgment. But on the whole, without any belief in an afterlife, and without knowledge of the times, Ecclesiastes inclines to a pessimistic interpretation of the cyclical universe. Indeed, his book conveys a horror akin to the feelings evoked by modern historicism's view of time marching on without stop: for there is no human transcendence of the Wheel of Nature, and no redemptive transhistorical purpose. If the Preacher envisions perpetual change, that change is "always the same, always the same" (as William Dorrit would say) in a kind of universal Marshalsea round from which there is no escape except in death. This is not the circular time of sacred myth, as Mircea Eliade interprets it—"a sort of eternal mythical present that is periodically reintegrated by means of rites" empowering religious man to transcend historical time. For nonreligious persons this troublous Time-Element is the "deepest existential dimension"; and in secular societies, where the "religious meaning of the repetition of paradigmatic gestures is forgotten," repetition, inherent in human life, leads to a pessimistic vision of existence.[91] Although the Preacher posits a directing force, his underlying horror undermines the religious terminology he uses, bringing us closer to the secular view of human beings as victims of contingency in an absurd world where "time and chance happeneth to them all" (Ecc. 9:11). The Preacher's world wears all the aspect of disorder of a totally desacralized universe.

From its opening circular paragraphs to the novel's reopening at its close in the Babel-builders' "uproar," Dickens presents a world whose forward thrust is repeatedly delayed by the *perpetuum mobile*, and whose God seems malevolent, faceless, or indifferent—at best a *deus absconditus*. R. Rupert Roopnaraine has found evidence of this novel's "metaphor of circularity" everywhere: announced in such repetitions as Pancks' "Fag and grind, fag and grind, turn the wheel, turn the wheel!" (2.32.779); embedded in the alternation of such contrasts as sun and shadow or poverty and wealth; and worked out narratively in such recursive movements as Amy's return to her Marshalsea lover as daughter. In Dickens' vision of the "whirling wheel of life" (2.27.700), Roopnaraine concludes, "there is nothing which we can call truly redemptive."[92] Roopnaraine's exegesis ignores a number of refinements in Dickens' more complex conception of time in *Little Dorrit:* for example, he slights the satirist's exposure of wrong attitudes toward time, such as Mrs. Clennam's willful denial of change; cyclical time is also satirized in the temporal framework of Vanity Fair—Society has not got to the substance of the millennium but perpetuates its vacuities "for ever and a day," parodying sacred mythological time, in its pagan rituals of idol worship. Roopnaraine sees a circle where I have suggested dialectic in the first chapter; and some of his circles are actually spirals, such as Amy's return to St. George's Church to be married, following a Carlylean notion of an upwardly progressive cyclic history.

The case for circular time in *Little Dorrit* can be overargued: yet the powerful forces of circularity are assuredly felt. If there can be such a thing as a "marked stop in the whirling wheel of life" that "brings the right perception with it," for Clennam it is an insight into Amy's goodness carrying him further downward in his cycle; and in Amy's tale of the princess, the spinning-wheel stops only at the tiny woman's death. According to Ecclesiastes' theorem, there can be no valorizing of historical time as there is in the Christian vision, with its belief in the intersection of eternal and temporal in the earthly existence of the Son of God.[93] For Dickens, who was attracted to an apocalyptic notion of history but had no belief in the Incarnation to sustain its hope, the redemption of time becomes an insoluble problem, and *Little Dorrit*'s Ecclesiastian repetitions reflect perhaps his bleakest view of it.

In Plornish and Clennam, Dickens entertains two radically different interpretations of these cycles of time. The sanguine reading of Ecclesiastes 3 that we find in Henry and Spurgeon turns up when the plasterer comes to offer consolation to Arthur in prison: "Mr. Plornish amiably growled, in his philosophical but not lucid manner, that there was ups, you see, and there was downs. It was in wain to ask why ups, why downs; there they was, you know. He had heerd it given for a truth that accordin' as the world went round, which round it did rewolve undoubted, even the best of gentlemen must take his turn of standing with his ed upside down and all his air a flying the wrong way into what you might call Space. Wery well then. What Mr. Plornish said was, wery well then. That gentleman's ed would come up'ards when his turn come, that gentleman's air would be a pleasure to look upon being all smooth again, and wery well then!" (2.27.712). Even when Dickens rescues Clennam from his upside-down position, all is not "wery well then"; Clennam is the sadder for his adventures on the wrong side of the pattern of the universe. Moreover, in its immediate context, Plornish's "It was in wain to ask why ups, why downs; there they was, you know" exposes his optimism as sheer faith, a rescuing fiction as necessary in an "ignorant life" as the opposing, fatalistic fiction that "Fortune . . . preserved an immoveable countenance" toward the Plornishes (1.31.357). Elsewhere the plasterer has no "crumb of comfort" (see 1.12.136–37; cf. Ecc. 4:1). If Plornish's madly inspired metaphors of the "rewolving world" seem a subjective distortion, so are the repeated cyclical metaphors of Clennam's allegorizing imagination through most of the novel. His poetical perpetual motion is still going in book 2 when, echoing Ecclesiastes' thought, he insists to Amy that they are destined to remain apart because he is "a ruined man . . . whose course is run, while yours is but beginning" (739).

Clennam's pervading theme of decay brings home in a personal case the novel's widespread imagery of a whole civilization's spiritual decrepitude. This imagery suggests a third possible Theorem of the Universe, which is included in the turning of the Great Wheel although its implications in the mid-nineteenth century were quite distinctively modern (and not cyclical). This is the idea of decadence, being given scientific attention in the new astrophysics as early as 1852 in Lord Kelvin's second law of thermodynamics, which proposed the necessity of cosmic entropy.[94] Already in *Bleak House* Dickens was developing a theory of moral entropy in English social life; in *Little Dorrit*, Ecclesiastes' allegory of the aging body as a decaying house is projected large onto a landscape of life in which time's ravages are everywhere and traditional structures are "mouldering to dust" (2.3.452). In book 1, Mrs. Clennam's house on crutches is surrounded by the archaeological ruins of churches; in book 2, European churches are "under suppositious repair," their scaffolding "fallen into decay" while neighboring houses have "grotesquely" deteriorated (6.474). In the course of the plot, it is as though a fatal spiritual disorder spreads from the heart of London to the birthplace of Western culture, where monuments of classical beauty are wasting away—as though the whole tradition of the West had become a "ruined spher[e] of action" (2.15.591). Everywhere, too, the degeneracy of the insupportable old traditions and the vacuity of their replacements account for the decline of art. From the apocalyptic perspective, *Little Dorrit* depicts the latter days, when men "shall . . . seek death, and shall not find it" (Rev. 9:6); from the Ecclesiastian, nearly all is sliding down the cycle of "a time to die." Again and again, the narrator returns to Ecclesiastes' riddle of "Death," "constant . . . to man" (2.33.782), "the great final secret of all life" (2.10.526).

The further question might fairly be asked: How are these radically different

Theorems of the Universe related in one fictional world? With their implicitly competing systems of valuation, they contribute to what Bakhtin would call the "Tower-of-Babel mixing of languages"[95] in a novel more specifically preoccupied with this biblical metaphor than any other of Dickens' fictions; and more than the others, *Little Dorrit* reflects that religious and irreligious "hubbub" on the Victorian scene which Carlyle had denounced nowhere more stridently than in the *Latter-Day Pamphlets*.

One way to view the relation between these antithetical world views would simply be through Ecclesiastes' notion that perpetual alternation is in the nature of things: Revelation and Ecclesiastes are *Little Dorrit*'s universal prison round of "Sun and Shadow," its religious-irreligious chiaroscuro. But more can be said than this if we think in terms of the two opposing tendencies of allusion to be found in Dickens' books. With its drive toward an all-encompassing design, Revelation represents the power of stable allusion and more than suggests the attraction of it. Ecclesiastes, with its uncertain and conflicting judgments, illustrates in the particular case of *Little Dorrit* the subversive influence of Dickens' unstable allusions. Further, like these two kinds of allusion, as my opening chapter has suggested, Dickens' two important subtexts for *Little Dorrit* "know about each other" and are structured in relation to each other, "dialogized" in Bakhtin's term. Again, Amy's tale of the princess offers an instructive parallel to what Dickens is doing in the larger work. In this story, which Amy tells as much to herself as to her listener, the fiction of a "reg'lar" princess with "wonderful" powers of discernment, like the Seer's, is an indispensable convention that the story be begun at all and the invitation then be issued, as Dickens issues it in *Little Dorrit*, "Come and see what I see!" That Ecclesiastian invitation brings into the story "things terrible to us, to see"; but significantly, it is through the princess fiction that they are seen. In the course of Amy's tale, this fiction is revised, but it is not completely discarded, for the princess outlives the radical diminution of her powers to tell the story of what she has observed and the dialogue in which she has engaged. In *Little Dorrit*, all the fictional embodiments of the apocalyptic theorem constitute a religious rhetoric that seems the necessary precondition for the author's subversive explorations. But as the Seer's yields to Ecclesiastian "seeing," the Christian vision is not abandoned; the subversions of certainty in Dickens' text make some kind of religious assurance all that much more necessary for the writer and his readers. Its claims, however, are sharply modified, for this twilight world at least. The evidence of Dickens' ending—surely among the most satisfying of closures in Victorian fiction—promises no larger redemption of evil days; it does modestly affirm a providential design yet operating in individual lives. And it does this without the fairytale-making conclusion of *Bleak House*. London's streets are still in hubbub, and the reader is left "staring and ruminating" like Maggy at the close of Amy's tale.

Dickens' humanistic revision of the religious theorem has important stylistic implications which can now be considered more fully. It is in his language that Dickens most successfully accommodates and surpasses Ecclesiastian confessionalism by encompassing its dead-ended skepticism with a more capacious, and more difficult, mode of stylistic consciousness. While the narrator responding to apocalyptic arrests some shams without mercy like Carlyle, most of the characters who make fictions in an "ignorant life" draw a more discriminating sympathy from another narrative persona who can "consider and adjust with great nicety" (1.10.116) to the case at hand—the morally alert, but modulated, qualifying, remarkably restrained voice with "large experience of humanity" in it (2.25.683). Physician, who in effect says, "Come and see," is the novel's model of how this narrative voice might "do it": no jaded wisdom-seeker, he is rather like the Jesus who "knew what was in man" (John 2:25).

In default of churchmen, Physician acts as confessor for people with their "wigs and paint off," listening to their "tendernesses and affections" as well as "much irreconcileable moral contradiction" in "the wanderings of [their] minds" (683–84). Although this medical man does Merdle no good and does not know his complaint, Physician does offer healing of a different sort: a confessor is one who forgives what he hears, even though this one "was oftener in [life's] darkest places than even Bishop." Embedded in a passage that playfully mimics Society's voices and jarring ironies,[96] a biblical voice emerges to make this potentially complex character an embodiment of the Sermon on the Mount—in Society: "Physician was a composed man, who performed neither on his own trumpet, nor on the trumpets of other people. Many wonderful things did he see and hear, and much irreconcileable moral contradiction did he pass his life among; yet his equality of compassion was no more disturbed than the Divine Master's of all healing was. He went, like the rain, among the just and unjust, doing all the good he could, and neither proclaiming it in the synagogues nor at the corners of streets" (683). If Dickens' echo here of Matthew 6:2 ("when thou doest thine alms, do not sound a trumpet before thee, as the hypocrites do . . . in the streets") immunizes Physician from the prevailing disease of vanity, the recall of Matthew 5:44–45 defines Dickens' antidote to the Ecclesiastian consciousness of evil: "I say unto you, Love your enemies . . . That ye may be as the children of your Father which is in heaven: for he maketh his sun to rise on the evil and on the good, and sendeth rain on the just and on the unjust." These biblical echoes draw attention to the distinctively Christian ethos missing from the Preacher's book (where even the oppressors need but have no "comforter," 4:1) and alien to the Carlyle of the *Pamphlets*. To Dickens, it is not only Physician's "large experience of humanity" but the man's equality of compassion that gives him the charisma of the "real"—at least "something real" (684)—even in Vanity Fair.

Dickens' nuanced novelistic language, as I have suggested, often dissolves ordinary moral categories in giving "a more exact estimate of the subtlety and complexity of our life." But he also wants a humanized version of the Christian model without abandoning the relativist realism that can be deduced from Ecclesiastes. In Physician's character he embodies a sermon on how the work of fiction writing done in chiaroscuro can become a moral act. It is the virtue of compassion inscribed into the dominant narrative persona's carefully modulated language that makes it possible not *only* to hear Mrs. Clennam as a false Old Testament prophet, or see her as an iconographic spectacle of the mourning fool, but also to respond to her as a human being whose sickness requires these verbal and physical arrangements. Listening to and recording such vanities, entering into them imaginatively, Dickens' work as a confessor—of his own affections, antipathies, and contradictions as well as others'—becomes a mode of compassionate attending upon the sick, while patiently doing justice to their "vacillations, inconsistencies, the little peevish perplexities of this ignorant life, mists which the morning without a night only can clear away" (2.29.618). And the way such religious affirmations in *Little Dorrit* so often remind us of the "immeasurable distance" between the Divine Disposer and earthly chaos makes it clear why such compassionate and just human writing is necessary, if the "troublous dim Time-Element" is to be redeemed in any degree at all this side of death. Further, such carefully adjusted and compassionate truth-telling, provisional and "Ignatian" though it be, lacking the final "clue to all hearts and all mysteries," is the one critical criterion of the artist's authenticity in *Little Dorrit*.

If Dickens also risks circling in endless vortexes of ambivalent speculation on the infirmity of the facts, there are important compensations even beyond the redemptive work of the narrative persona I have described. To see what these are, we need only return to Ecclesiastes and ask why, if everything is vain, he fashions his book at all. Certainly the Preacher speaks from experience when he writes, "there is nothing better, than that a man should rejoice in his own works" (3:22): for given the vast uncertainty of human projects, Ecclesiastes rejoices in the verbal performances that cast these indeterminacies into his own works of art. Out of weariness he makes the sonorous cadence; out of circularity he fashions a musical refrain; out of irreconcilable antitheses he sings an antiphonal litany of the "times." If "the stuff of which psychoses are made is in his book,"[97] Ecclesiastes asserts over this disturbance the control of a consummate artist who knows that language is the supreme fiction by which we imagine we order our experience. He casts about for maxims, parables, and figures with the skill of a man who has "sought out many inventions." He announces his conclusion that "There is no remembrance" yet fashions his lines for posterity: "To every thing there is a season. . . ." He takes pleasure in forming an enigma: "Cast thy bread upon the waters: for thou shalt find it after many days" (11:1). If his work is all in pieces, he polishes these brief units of literary discourse with his "might," unaware of some larger pattern in which all is artistically unified; and his riddles, gaps, and discrepancies give play to the reader's imagination in the construction of the text. He warns against "multitude of words" and writes with the terseness of classic gnomic literature, yet he produces the most redundant text in the Bible, with its elegantly circuitous variations on a single theme. In the vanity of his deft performances with Wisdom texts, he outwits the sages. But he reserves his *tour de force* for the concluding allegory on old age: and its enigmatic tropes and cumulative, rhythmic phrases disprove by their poetic beauty and vigor the possibility that this ancient sage has succumbed to the forces of disintegration he casts into symbols. Ecclesiastes' imaginative verbal constructions prove his potency; and that enjoyment of life he preaches issues most immediately, for the consumption of his audience, in the sober pleasures of his text.[98]

If Ecclesiastes the stylist is not paralyzed by the riddle of the universe, neither is Dickens by what he sees. For this popular writer, no doubt there were the pleasures of closure in his single-minded denunciations, which his audience expected and applauded. But one also imagines that the voice to which Dickens gives so much more of himself in *Little Dorrit* provided deeper pleasures, those of candor and discrimination, as he taught respect for nuance to his Victorian public by example. With both kinds of performance in this highly self-conscious novel—whether he is modernizing an apocalyptic emblem or outwitting the received wisdom in virtuoso displays of ambiguous prose—Dickens flaunts as always his enjoyment of fictional language. In *Little Dorrit*, it is the very means by which Dickens survives creatively "in the middest" and does the work that is his portion in the days of his vanity.

In this he takes Carlyle's lesson to heart that no man works save under conditions, but accepts the Ecclesiastian conditions of "fiction" which Carlyle had scorned in the *Pamphlets*. The novel's chief exemplar of specifically verbal work under a lively sense of the conditional is, ironically, one of the most practically lazy fools in the book and the "babbler" of whom Ecclesiastes 10:11 warns. Dickens' evident enjoyment in creating Flora Finching seems to be something more than the pleasure of putting an acute personal disappointment into comic perspective. Flora's methods of working with words are a wildly exaggerated mimicry of her creator's stylistic virtuosity; she too is a spokesperson for the Preacher as well as a parodist of his themes, bound in no "sluggish thrall" by her awareness of vanity.

In reopening the love story concluded so long ago, Flora immeasurably increases Arthur's sense of futility with the spectacle of her own vain labor, "going through all the old performances" (1.13.147). Yet as the theatrical metaphor suggests, she goes on "enjoying herself in the most wonderful manner" under these conditions, as one who rejoices in her own works. Whatever she does with words, she does it with her might, for they keep her afloat through all her delicious crises of existential indeterminacy. Her rapid changes of tone and topic, her different voices "contending in boundless hubbub," are an accelerated version of Ecclesiastes' changes of seasons "running on with astonishing speed" (144): now mourning (raising her handkerchief "as a tribute to the ghost of the departed Mr. F," 145), now dancing ("it was the morning of life it was bliss it was frenzy it was everything else of that sort in the highest degree," 1.24.277); now building up to a climax, then breaking down into anticlimax and "running into nonsense again"; now waging war on the lover who had deserted her, then making peace with a simper; getting and losing her train of thought ("I run away with an idea and having none to spare I keep it," 2.9.519–21); advancing to embrace "dear Arthur," refraining from embracing "Doyce and Clennam": only rarely observing "a time to keep silence," although Flora can do that, too.

Among the minor displays of her self-pleasuring performances are Preacherly proverbs about work and money: "business is equally business call it what you will" (264); "has she her health . . . for what is wealth without it" (518); "the laborer is worthy of his hire" (2.17.599; cf. Luke 10:7)—to which she adds on the vanity of labor, "I only wish he got it oftener and more animal food and less rheumatism in the back and legs poor soul." In the course of remarks on art, she tumbles into an economic analysis of "the extremes of rich and poor" (see 518); and she identifies Amy Dorrit as an exemplar of Ecclesiastes 9:10 (602). Flora's discourse is a patchwork of such commonplaces, but never does she take up any bit of received wisdom—even the romantic cliché—without presenting it skeptically or playfully, outwitting or out-nonsensing the Pauls and Virginias of this world.

The major themes she shares with the Preacher are time, mutability, old age, and death. Her repeated "there *was* a time" echoes Ecclesiastes 2, and she parodies his determinism with her "the decrees of Fate were beyond recall." If she pays "the tribute of a sigh to the instability of human existence" (2.23.665) like a comic sage, her adolescent manner at forty exacerbates Arthur's unstable sense of himself by suggesting that his "childhood and youth are vanity" too (Ecc. 11:10). The one obvious allusion to Ecclesiastes she tumbles into reveals her preoccupation, for it is taken from his allegory on old age: "When your mama and my papa worried us to death and severed the golden bowl—I mean bond but I dare say you know what I mean . . . —when they severed the golden bond that bound us and threw us into fits of crying on the sofa nearly choked at least myself everything was changed and in giving my hand to Mr. F I know I did so with my eyes open but he was so very unsettled and in such low spirits that he had distractedly alluded to the river if not oil of something from the chemist's and I did it for the best" (264). Ecclesiastes' verse, "Or ever the silver cord be loosed, or the golden bowl be broken, or the pitcher be broken at the fountain, or the wheel broken at the cistern" (12:6), arranges images in a still life of Death; the bowl is the lamp-oil holder suspended by a cord and, broken, suggests the light gone out.[99] Flora's accidental misnaming of the "golden chain" as "golden bowl—I mean bond" confounds cord and bowl to betray the several kinds of death on her mind, from the sudden breaking of a relationship down to Mr. F's suicidal threats and Flora's inadvertent confession that she did him in "for the best." When she says she carries these grimly humorous Ecclesiastian themes "stamped in burning what's his names upon my brow" (277), we realize that Flora's Cainlike exile to a prosy existence she manages to forget in the wonderful "many inventions" of her poetic speech. Perpetually they bring something new alive under her sun.

It is a critical commonplace that Flora is one of those who are entrapped in "what hath been already of old time" (Ecc. 1:10). But her critics take her "dear old days" too seriously. Like her deft management of proverbial lore, Flora exercises magisterial power over time despite her apparent victimization by it. From the transhistorical perspective of her free-floating imagination, she liberally reorders past, present, and future; she calls each moment into being on her own terms, achieving momentary concords—with all the pleasures of closure—and fostering revisability ("one more remark") with all the deliciousness of withholding closure and keeping the game alive. The effect of her talk about the past is not at all like Mrs. Clennam's "retrospective gloomy" voice (2.31.769), which determines the gloomy future she imagines; Flora celebrates the giddy sense of a present-tense indeterminacy in "her present disjointed volubility" (144), seizing her opportunities for enjoyment in "the present interview" (146) as they fly by her rapidly associating mind. She grasps Time by the forelock, knowing better than some of her critics that "The past is gone; the future has not arrived; we

never shall have any time but time *present*," as Spurgeon meditated on Ecclesiastes' opportunism theme.

Of course, these intimate tête-à-têtes are almost wholly solipsistic. Flora's
"business" with words is also quite deliberately a vain labor in that her ad-
vance-and-retreat style of "Ignatian" flirting ("or . . . but . . . when I come to
think of it") perpetually thwarts the very consummation she seems so devoutly to
wish. But then, under the conditions she "know[s] . . . very well" (146) of
being fat and forty, Flora realizes that entertaining fictive moments of romance is
so much better than the real thing. Her language is an art of what is possible
under these conditions, "not ecstacy," she admits, "but . . . comfort" (278)
amid the deprivations of her real world. Thus her house of feasting only pretends to be a house of mourning for past rose leaves and lavender. She knows "it
is good and comely for one to eat and drink" and does it with gusto, but more
than this she "enjoy[s] the good of all [her] labour" with words, her portion in
the days of her vanity.

Flora's paradise is not mythic like Mrs. Clennam's hell, a projection of naive
apocalyptic, but fictive in Kermode's skeptical sense—self-consciously called
forth from its remembered fragments, easily dashed and reconstructed to bring
provisional consolation, and giddy with genuine revisions that sometimes land
her in a plain truth. Flora's mode of thwarting herself and closing off dialogue we
judge or pity in the speech of many other characters; her life, as Dickens described his around this time, is a "so happy and yet so unhappy existence which
seeks its realities in unrealities, and finds its dangerous comfort in a perpetual
escape from the disappointment of heart around it" (*Life* 2:196). Nonetheless,
the hopeful comedy of Flora is that she discovers in every moment her buoyant
means of recovery through self-conscious fictional language. Her flexible style,
with which she accommodates herself to her losses and meets life's contrary
stresses, embodies her kindly advice to Amy Dorrit: "such is life you see my
dear and yet we do not break but bend" (276). Although Flora may be a "moral
mermaid" (147), a damnable "Moral Hybrid" from the Carlylean point of view,
in her words "and yet" lies the absurd hope of the human condition that carries
her—and carries *Little Dorrit*—forward, through all the trailing consequence of
unredeemed time.

Proverbial Wisdom and Living Gospel

SERMON AND confession together in *Little Dorrit* as in Ecclesiastes intensify the
pressures to locate affirmative values in the domain of experienced life. The
Preacher's intermittent "gleams of light"[100] are not neo-Platonic intimations of

another world but insights into the more pragmatic Possible in this one: "Go thy way, eat thy bread with joy, and drink thy wine with a merry heart"; "Live joyfully with the wife whom thou lovest"; "Whatsoever thy hand findeth to do, do it with thy might"; "the patient in spirit is better than the proud in spirit" (7:8). With reservations, Dickens dramatizes the good these proverbs counsel more extensively than my discussion has suggested. While the narrator advises and exemplifies "Patience" (1.21.248), for example, and Cavalletto raises it to the superlative degree in which the Griselda heroine embodies it ("patientissa-mentally," 2.28.725), patience is an equivocal virtue in *Little Dorrit*—needed in the *longueurs* of "the middest," but also fatal, valorizing domestic martyr-doms, or merely futile, sustaining ultimately useless activities like Pancks' "moleing," which unearths a legacy that does no good for the Dorrits. These typical qualifications of proverbial wisdom in *Little Dorrit* suggest that Dickens, neither quietist nor merely pragmatic like the Preacher, wants some more active and imaginative form of goodness, if he is to locate an Ideal within the Actual that answers Victorian needs.

Through the centuries, Christian commentators on Ecclesiastes have stressed the need for interpretive completion of a potentially heretical book. To Matthew Henry, the Preacher's vanity theme necessitates a salvation scheme: "If Solomon find all to be vanity, then the kingdom of the Messiah must come, in which we shall inherit substance." Revelation must complete Ecclesiastes' "There is no new thing": "If we would be entertained with new things, we must acquaint ourselves with the things of God, get a new nature; then *old things pass away, and all things become new.*"[101] In *Little Dorrit* Dickens reaches more earnestly than he had yet for the affirmation of a living gospel in Revelation and New Testament wisdom, mediating his vision through familiar religious codes that converge on his heroine. The saving texts are undeniably present, more explicitly than ever in this novel. Yet they fail to sustain Amy's immunity to criticism, and the fuller story eludes, even subverts, their religious logic. Not to be confused with Nell or Agnes, Amy is Dickens' best approximation of an Ideal in the Actual—and that means inevitable contamination. Dickens characterizes his "little Dorrit" born in the prison with the same novelistic attentiveness to her limitations and conditions as in his treatment of other ideals; and at some points these reservations prompt a critique of the Bible itself, of even the Gospel gone dead, become empty formula. Nonetheless, to the extent that Amy fails to be the stained-glass icon Dickens might have made of her, she succeeds as a novelistic heroine and lives as "good news" for Arthur in another sense of the word, the more credible and accessible for her subjection to the "vapours" and her refusal to be a transcendent object of worship.[102]

While many extravagant claims have been made for Amy Dorrit as a Christian figure, no one has more precisely set this "Paraclete in female form"[103] within the context of Victorian needs and conventions than Alexander Welsh. Welsh interprets Amy as a type of Christian wisdom embodying the promise of John 14:15–17: "If ye love me, keep my commandments. And I will pray the Father, and he shall give you another Comforter, that he may abide with you for ever; Even the Spirit of truth; whom the world cannot receive, because it seeth him not . . . but ye know him; for he dwelleth with you, and shall be in you." St. John's "Spirit of truth" is masculine, but in the older literature related to this passage, where the home is the proper setting for Wisdom teaching, Wisdom is personified as a woman of multiple roles, like Amy Dorrit—"sister" (Prov. 7:4), true wife to be loved rather than the "strange woman" (Prov. 5:20), and nurturing mother who is "from the beginning" (see Prov. 8:22; cf. Wisd. 7, 9:9).[104] Welsh's argument is that Victorian fiction transforms these biblical formulas to serve the domestic settings where struggles for the soul's salvation take place and heroes need a female "face of love and truth" (2.26.699). In this phrase, repeatedly associated with Amy Dorrit (see 1.35.406; 2.29.736), "truth" is not the correspondence of word to fact Carlyle insisted upon, the "plain truth" Amy imagines the family can "always go back to" (2.6.482), even less Ecclesiastes' corrosive honesty: her "love and truth" is her compassionate fidelity toward other human beings—the defining quality also of the narrative persona I have discussed.

St. John surpasses Ecclesiastes' "Fear God, and keep his commandments" by following the command in his own text with the promise of the Paraclete, a figure so obviously missing from the Preacher's world where there is "no comforter" (4:1). Likewise, as a type of Christian wisdom, Amy Dorrit transcends the limits of the Old Testament Wisdom tradition she continues; she thereby becomes a fit answer to Clennam's Ecclesiastian afflictions, instrumental in his redefinition of self as more than the skeptical "Philosopher" (2.28.725). Inspiring him "with an inward fortitude" that matches her own (2.29.737), Amy cures Arthur of his debilitating uncertainty; her Christian belief makes up for his lack of it; her faithful preservation of the saving truth of the past is the "remembrance" Ecclesiastes denies and Arthur needs. Most of all her love—an answer the Preacher barely glimpses—fills the "void" in Arthur's heart, his deepest vanity. Amy (aimée) is the antidote to all the deathly forces driving him downward, just as in the other Wisdom book traditionally ascribed to Solomon, "love is strong as death" (Song of Sol. 8:6).[105]

Such a typological background is essential to understanding Dickens' overt strategies of establishing his heroine's superiority, but it does not fully describe his practice in the text. Indeed, as soon as we begin to interpret the phrase "love and truth" in any of its contexts, its meanings begin to proliferate and it no longer serves to contain a readable Amy Dorrit. In Dickens' practice, to be "love and truth" for another—father, lover, reader—is far more difficult than Welsh acknowledges for both Amy and the narrator; it is not simply a grace with which one is endowed but a moral challenge, a practical virtue to be won daily through subtle acts of moral discrimination, and often scarcely distinguishable from folly. One pair of examples can suggest the range of relative success with which "love and truth" is realized in *Little Dorrit:* when the narrator exclaims, "how true the light that shed false brightness around him!" (1.9.93), he seems seduced by his own paradox to ignore the evil Amy perpetuates by worshipping her father; on the other hand, Amy's "pretending a little" at the end of the story, as she vows she will always be "comforting and serving you with all my love and truth" (2.34.792), offers real comfort that may be far better for Arthur—at least from one point of view—than the "plain truth" she conceals by having him burn the codicil.

Whenever it appears in this novel, the "face of love and truth" seems to arrive like a miracle; in psychological terms, it is the realization of the infant's desire for complete security as it gazes on its mother's face. But in the skeptical adult contexts of *Little Dorrit,* the face breaks into facets, that is, its solidity is fractured as various points of view develop on it in the course of interpretation. The most doubtful of these materializes when Dickens lets us see that Amy's significance as "a face of love and truth" is even a stumbling block to Arthur's salvation which he must overcome. Welsh does not inquire into the questionable '.ses heroes make of such formulas, but the iconographic tradition on which he draws illustrates the problem: in English Romantic poetry, the iconic female face is a mirror of the poet's self in which he seeks to confirm his own vocation. Dolores Rosenblum has observed that although the poet may long "for a living face, what he projects is a dead mask. Its power resides not in its capacity to originate meaning, but in its ability to appear and disappear—or to be sum-moned and dismissed—in the poet's serious game of mastering himself and 'reality.'"[106] Such a "reified" face, however, prevents that intersubjective seeing "face to face" of healthier human interaction between living beings who change and grow. It thus becomes a narcissistic delusion that arrests self-devel-opment. Because Dickens had long associated his own "love and deep truth" with the ideal woman of his young manhood, Maria Beadnell (see letters to Mrs. Winter, 10 and 15 February 1855; D 2:627, 628–29), and had often linked the iconic female to his heroes' integrity of selfhood, it is the more impressive that in *Little Dorrit* he is able to dramatize the solipsistic uses of the "face of love and truth" convention in portraying Clennam's illusion of his ideal beloved. In so doing, Dickens' novel manages to break out of some of the "sacred and salutary" formulas it uses for religious heroines—if only, as we shall see, to invoke another set of conventions.

Even though Clennam has warned himself not to "make a kind of domesticated fairy of her" (1.22.252), he becomes Little Dorrit's iconographer because he needs a form for his ideal (see *CME* 28:31)—a need she also shows in her idealizations of him. It is also part of his Nobody strategy to distance the object of his desire. Musing in the Marshalsea, he imagines her into what begins as narrative but quickly translates its temporal distances into the static spatial ones of a perspective painting so provocative it calls for a second reading here: "Looking back upon his own poor story, she was its vanishing-point. Everything in its perspective led to her innocent figure. He had travelled thousands of miles towards it; previous unquiet hopes and doubts had worked themselves out before it; it was the centre of the interest of his life; it was the termination of everything that was good and pleasant in it; beyond there was nothing but mere waste, and darkened sky" (2.27.714). In Dickens' extraordinary elaboration of this dream moment, which recalls his dream of Mary Hogarth in Italy,[107] the female figure becomes an iconic optical illusion able to be "summoned and dismissed" like the Romantic visionary's muse. But Clennam is a dreamer manqué; and, given his Ignatian state of mind, this unstable iconographic arrangement does not help him "believe . . . more steadily" (in Dickens' words) any more than the dream figure of Mary Hogarth, draped in blue like a Raphael Madonna, helped Dickens to settle the urgent question he had asked his ideal, "What is the True religion?" (to Forster, ?30 September 1844, P 4:196). Arthur's picture coquettes with time and space, presence and absence, shifting from the personal "she" to the impersonal "it," undecided in its direction of movement (back from or "towards" her?), and ambivalent in its attitude toward a "vanishing-point" that is at once a "centre" and "the termination of everything." It is not just that Clennam needs to stabilize his image; he needs to relinquish his tendency toward what Carlyle would call idolatry, even though Carlylean motives underlie Clennam's worship of the Godlike in this human being. So long as Amy is an iconic "face of love and truth" or a religious "figure" rather than a person, Clennam will not be released from narcissistic self-contemplation.[108] In the Carlylean dynamic of redemption that, in part, moves this novel toward its conclusion, Amy—if she is a true representative of Reality—must possess the "living force and truth" to break the false conventional formulas put artificially around her. Reversing the common self-reflexive pattern by which people in *Little Dorrit* project their own images as idols for worship, Dickens' heroine must become her own iconoclast.

Amy's late "appearance" in the Marshalsea is at first as elusive as Clennam's sense of providential order. Just when he has fallen into a nightmarish reverie, she appears to him as a hallucinated "figure" in a dreamy *tableau vivant:*

> One of the night-tunes was playing in the wind, when the door of his room seemed to open to a light touch, and, after a moment's pause, a quiet figure seemed to stand there, with a black mantle on it. It seemed to draw the mantle off and drop it on the ground, and then it seemed to be his Little Dorrit in her old, worn dress. It seemed to tremble, and to clasp its hands, and to smile, and to burst into tears.
>
> He roused himself, and cried out. And then he saw, in the loving, pitying, sorrowing, dear face, as in a mirror, how changed he was; and she came towards him; and with her hands laid on his breast to keep him in his chair, and with her knees upon the floor at his feet, and with her lips raised up to kiss him, and with her tears dropping on him as the rain from Heaven had dropped upon the flowers, Little Dorrit, a living presence, called him by his name. (2.29.735–36)

Although it may also be read as a sentimental dramatization of fantasy fulfilled, this scene is staged to show the disintegration of a dream image by the presence of an actuality, following a dynamic we have seen elsewhere in the novel. As Amy steps out of a frame (as often, a doorway) to become "as large as life" (1.14.171), the perspective painting in whose vast distances Clennam's hopes had seemed to terminate now reverses its directions and "she" (not "it") comes toward him. Not an icon or romantic ideal, Amy has become a "living presence" and can thus begin to be "gospel" for Arthur. Her particularized face (no general "figure" projected into the void) becomes the "mirror" by which he sees not an ideal hero-image but the prisoner's degradation. As Arthur's consciousness is awakened to them both in their historical actuality (he has "changed"), he becomes a man with a "name" related to another living being in time and space.[109] When Arthur and Amy are "married, with the sun shining on them through the painted figure of Our Saviour on the window" (2.34.801), it is Jesus who has become the "figure"; these two human beings—who have always been "interested" in each other "out of [their] own individuality" (1.22.252)—though momentarily haloed do not become fixed in ritual postures. Turning from the church, they descend into the London turmoil to practice not the new religion but the arts of living. In their "modest" way, they are exempla in a Carlylean lesson that each human soul, no icon or fictive projection, is a living work of art.

Throughout the novel other characters too try to enclose Amy in "Jesuitical" formulas they only half-believe, making her over into a creature of fairytale (1.18.206), a painting, even a Raphael Madonna (2.24.676, 2.9.518), an emblem and a holy relic (1.14.171). The proliferation of such conventions suggests that Amy both provokes and eludes any easy formulation, and that Amy as ideal is very much the creation of human minds, just as Paul Dombey's Jesus is first (and perhaps last) an *objet d'art* and the waves symbolism in *Dombey* subjective projection. This novelistic backdrop in *Little Dorrit* is the creation of Dickens' own understanding, which we have seen maturing through *Bleak House*, of what John Stuart Mill in an essay of this period called "The Utility of Religion."[110] Despite Dickens' capacity for producing such a context, in which the conditions of knowing and believing modify claims to absolute truth, the novelist nonetheless succumbs on occasion to Clennam's temptation to hypostatize Amy as a religious "figure." Many critics of the novel have taken Dickens' lead: A. E. Dyson, for example, calls Amy "truly Christlike . . . in an unanswerable sense."[111] What are we to make of such claims? If Dickens can humanize and particularize the ideal "face of love and truth," how firmly is he committed to the other Christian conventions he employs in presenting his heroine, in J. Hillis Miller's words, as "the mystery of divine goodness incarnate in a human person"?[112]

Alistair M. Duckworth has raised this question in his quasi-Derridean critique of *Little Dorrit*: "Of all the god-terms in the novel, 'Little Dorrit' seems most in need of 'deconstruction.' As she is Clennam's 'center,' his alpha and omega, so she is the novel's fundamental ground, its 'primary signified.' As many critics have argued, she is the 'real' or 'natural' base beneath the fictions, surfaces, and 'genteel mystifications' of life in society. She corresponds, it would seem, to Derrida's definition of the 'transcendental position.' . . . As all of Clennam's perspectives lead to her 'innocent' figure, so the novel seems to rest on the metaphysical concept of truth itself."[113] Although Duckworth is unnecessarily collapsing Clennam's view of Amy with the novelist's here (and stabilizing a most unstable picture), there are certainly moments in the novel that seem to give Amy a "transcendental position" through allusive connections with Christ. In the passage staging Amy's return to the prison, the iconic formulas are broken and the doorway frame left behind only to place Amy in another conventional framework that claims to precede all convention: the Christian doctrine of Real Presence. As a channel of that ultimate reality, Amy is then allusively connected in this passage with "the painted figure of Our Saviour" who stands at the door and knocks (like Holman Hunt's contemporaneous *The Light of the World*, 1851–56; cf. 1.13.159; see illustration on book title page) and, in calling Clennam by his name, with the true Shepherd who "entereth in by the door" and "calleth his own sheep by name" (John 10:2–3). As Amy Dorrit becomes through these associations the door of salvation (v. 9),[114] whatever qualifications of the salvific "face of love and truth" convention that Dickens has inscribed into his text would seem to be unwritten. Indeed, those epiphanic moments when Amy becomes, insistently, a "living presence" seem to bid for that leap of faith Ecclesiastes cannot take—to discover that religion is not merely a "tale that is told" or a pleasing design, but bears witness to an Actuality redeeming all others, the substance wanted in Vanity Fair.

Thus does the novel itself lead F. R. Leavis to call Amy "indefectibly real"[115] and others to claim for her an "unanswerable" Christian status based on her privileged access to Reality, which she achieves through the indefectible mimesis of her imitation of Christ. But as Duckworth and Janice M. Carlisle have argued, Amy cannot be a "god-term" because she involves herself in deception, assumes roles, and makes fictions[116]—unlike Christ as "the Way, the Truth, and the Life" (although not unlike the Jesus of the tricky parables). Amy's particular acts of fictionalization may not be so problematic, if "love and truth" does not require strict veracity; but they are important items in a wider array of novelistic strategies, to be discussed here, through which Dickens dismantles his god-term in Little Dorrit. Further, Amy's acts of fiction making possibly help us to see as parallel the novelist's own efforts to endow her— through biblical allusion and iconography—with the very godlike qualities he also qualifies. These qualifications are needed not because built-in deconstructive readings are necessarily the best ones for all literary works, but because in this novel of "studied ambiguity" and questioning of formula, a credible heroine must be enmeshed in its thematized problems of knowledge and interpretation. In order to maintain Amy's poise as the Ideal in the Actual (as he does through most of the story), Dickens must neither spiritualize her out of this world nor merely expose her as a "prevaricating little piece of goods!" (as Fanny charges): he must make Amy's lowly heroism convincing by grounding it in her compassionate participation in others' miseries, confusion, and guilt. As these complexities unfold in the story, the New Testament texts associating her with Christ also serve as measures of her defective virtue, the limits of her "imitation," just as we immediately grasp the difference if we juxtapose the crowned and regal figure in The Light of the World with the image of Dickens' diminutive heroine coming through the prison door in Browne's illustration. The allusions meant to exalt her then have an ironic effect; they also prove insufficient both as guides to conduct and as guarantors of redemption from the evils of Dickens' "lower world." These insufficiencies do not wholly discredit the religious tradition he is using, but they betray a suppressed dissatisfaction with biblical ideals in Little Dorrit that finally draws it away from transcendental solutions to accept the literary and humanistic ones with which the novel provisionally closes.

How then does Dickens qualify Amy's transcendental status? First, if Amy Dorrit is "Christlike," it is a Christ with a very human face that she imitates—

not the "only-begotten Son of God" of the Nicene Creed but the Jesus of *The Life of Our Lord*, the human child who "will grow up to be so good that God will love him as his own son" (14). In *Little Dorrit*, where the piety of this *Life* is almost wholly muted, it is this "little child" who "shall lead them," this supremely human healer and friend whom Amy emulates and of whom, on one occasion, she preaches. If the impulse which eliminated the Incarnation from *The Life of Our Lord* also modifies any "transcendental position" that might be claimed for Amy Dorrit, that is not to deny the moral superiority of both figures in their respective "histories." In *The Nemesis of Faith*, Markham Sutherland argues that Christ's goodness was the more impressive for his being only "very Man," proceeding in darkness like the rest of us. Seeing "Indistinctly,"[117] Amy Dorrit is good despite uncertainty, her own littleness, and her painful sense of difference from the others, a uniqueness that does not protect her from the pain.

Amy's transcendental position is further modified, paradoxically, by her association with the Sermon on the Mount. Because this is the sapiential discourse of one whom Scripture calls "the wisdom of God" (1 Cor. 1:24), Amy is thus linked with another specifically Christian form of wisdom to counter Clennam's vain Ecclesiastian kind as well as his Old Testament legalism. The choice of this "handbook of Christian conduct" as one subtext for her story, however, underlines Dickens' faith in good human deeds rather than in God's mighty saving acts in *Little Dorrit*.[118] Moreover, when critically examined, this New Testament text turns out to be less stable than supposed; its "rules of living" are not, as Forster wrote in his review of Dean Stanley's biography of Dr. Arnold, "equitable, plain, explicit, compendious and complete: raising no doubt or dogma."[119]

Forster's remark about dogma *was* correct and suggests one reason for the Sermon's attractiveness to Victorian Broad Church liberals.[120] As Martin Dibelius points out, the Sermon "has nothing to do with [the] larger message of the Incarnation, Salvation and Redemption"; this is what makes it closer to Jewish Wisdom literature[121] in its ethical formulations. Its Golden Rule and the Beatitudes in Matthew's longer version (5:1–7:29) present models of Christian behavior, while the abominations and the "woes" in Luke's comparable Sermon on the Plain (6:20–49) define in uncompromising terms the ungodly life (and in ways particularly relevant to *Little Dorrit*). The Sermon on the Mount also sets forth "the righteousness of the Gospel as contrasted with the righteousness of the Law"[122] in Jesus' antitheses ("Ye have heard that it was said. . . . But I say unto you . . .": Matt. 5:21–48). Without understanding that Jesus did not aim to overthrow the Old Testament or Jewish customs, Dickens nonetheless grasped the central proclamation of these antitheses especially for his time of empty religious formula: Jesus demands a change in attitude of men whose institutional religion had become a mere formality. The preacher of the Sermon emerges as a champion of the anticonventional; but unlike the questioning Preacher of Ecclesiastes, Jesus urges a change of heart that the "spirit" and not merely the "letter" of the Law prevail (a distinction Dickens often invoked in defining his religious position).

All this would seem to make the Sermon a firm ground of belief to guide "Duty on earth . . . action on earth" in *Little Dorrit* (1.27.311) and serve as the basis for Dickens' liberal Christian creed. Yet its relation to earthly action is precisely the beginning of this text's instability. The Beatitudes and the expansions of the Law that follow in Matthew preach a kind of sublime nonsense: so radical are the Sermon's demands ("if thy right eye offend thee, pluck it out;" Matt. 5:29) and so decisively yet vaguely futuristic are the Beatitudes (*when* "shall" the pure in heart "see God"?) that the Sermon finally makes no "terms at all with this world," as James R. Kincaid writes of *Little Dorrit* (and see Matt. 6:20).[123] If this biblical text is to be useful in defining where duty lies, it must be *made* so by human interpretation; and since applications of the Sermon vary, Jesus' discourse turns out to be no stable and self-sufficient foundation for ethics but an enigma to plague generations of Bible readers. It strands us uncomfortably on the same dilemma that Dickens strives to resolve in *Little Dorrit:* how to find and live the Ideal *in* the Actual. While neither the Sermon nor the characters whose ideals are inspired by it give the novel a stable center of belief, however, Dickens still makes as much of this subtext as he can in his provisional affirmations of what people might "do" to find riches (beatitude) amid the poverty of the earthly kingdom.

One thing he does with it is to work into *Little Dorrit* his version of the Sermon's antitheses between the Old Dispensation and the New: "Set the darkness and vengeance against the New Testament," he reminded himself in the Number Plan for book 2, chapter 31.[124] Amy Dorrit "does it" for him when she preaches a sermon to Mrs. Clennam that echoes all the chief emphases of *The Life of Our Lord*, if it also eliminates the more radical demands of Matthew's Gospel:

> "O, Mrs. Clennam, Mrs. Clennam, angry feelings and unforgiving deeds are no comfort and no guide to you and me. My life has been passed in this poor prison, and my teaching has been very defective; but, let me implore you to remember later and better days. Be guided, only by the healer of the sick, the raiser of the dead, the friend of all who were afflicted and forlorn, the patient Master who shed tears of compassion for our infirmities. We cannot but be right if we put all the rest away, and do everything in remembrance of Him. There is no vengeance and no infliction

of suffering in His life, I am sure. There can be no confusion in following Him, and
seeking for no other footsteps, I am certain!"

In the softened light of the window, looking from the scene of her early trials to
the shining sky, she was not in stronger opposition to the black figure in the shade,
than the life and doctrine on which she rested were to that figure's history. It bent its
head low again, and said not a word. (2.31.770–71)

In this tableau of "Sun and Shadow," the woman so "poor in spirit," who had
"seemed the least, the quietest, and weakest of Heaven's creatures" (1.9.92),
shows forth the teaching of 1 Corinthians 1: "God hath chosen the foolish things
of the world to confound the wise" and "things which are not, to bring to nought
things that are" (vv. 27–28). Moreover, this Nobody figure, who dismisses her
"defective" teaching, does not merely adopt a conventional religious language
that suppresses the personal (as do others for whom formula usurps individual
life) and belies its own hollowness: Amy's heartfelt eloquence stylistically
enacts the new order of which she speaks. And as she does this, she brings
about one of the novel's more stable moments of dialogical resolution, when one
voice has cast out another. In this confrontation the providential novelist has
arranged between Law and Gospel, Amy Dorrit reverses the perverted speech
habits that have sustained Mrs. Clennam's perverse judgments through many
secret years,[125] even as the whole sermon embodies Amy's will to "bless them
that curse" her. Thus does this character as living gospel overturn the Law's
formulaic "love thy neighbour, and hate thine enemy" (Matt. 5:43–45).

However persuasive in its form and content, Amy's sermon does not convert
Mrs. Clennam to "later and better days"; even her watered-down scriptural
ideal is far too radical for this confirmed old sinner's actualities. Amy's "in-
spired and soul-inspiring Eloquence, whereby Religion itself were brought
home to our living bosoms" (*CME* 28:22), is a performance for the Victorian
reader, rather, who may yet be able to "remember the life and lessons of Our
Lord Jesus Christ," as Dickens wrote his children, "and try to act up to them"
(*LOL* 127). Moreover, Amy's offer of forgiveness cannot be realized because
Dickens' antithesis of the Old and New Dispensations serves the staging of an
End-event that exacts its penalty: that moment in *Sartor Resartus* when "the
dead Letter of Religion own[s] itself dead, and drop[s] piecemeal into dust," so
that "the living Spirit of Religion . . . [may] arise on us, newborn of Heaven,
and with new healing under its wings" (92). Sealing this moment, Dickens'
sunset breaks out in the iconographic splendor of a Sunday School leaflet Easter
illustration: "From a radiant centre, over the whole length and breadth of the
tranquil firmament, great shoots of light streamed among the early stars, like

signs of the blessed later covenant of peace and hope that changed the crown of thorns into a glory" (771). As a burst of light into a dark narrative, this moment has apocalyptic force, seeming to offer one of *Little Dorrit*'s most striking anticipatory glimpses of beatitude, like Carlyle's "symbols of eternal covenants" that span the "weltering seas of trouble" in the *Pamphlets* (324). Read skeptically, however, it only places Little Dorrit's acts into the framework of the past of *The Life of Our Lord*, and while it fairly shouts "Do Not Forget" the "later covenant," it makes no larger resurrection promises for the novel's future days. Spatially the rays of light point outward and toward the viewer, but temporally the "signs" in the sky point backward to "glories" that Dickens may have confessed in his account of Our Lord's resurrection, but that may "expire" (as they do in another, skeptically apocalyptic sunset passage, 2.3.454)[126] in these latter days, when Bible promises may no longer hold. Amy Dorrit *is* an imperfect agent of "peace and hope," of course, but Carlyle's faith in "eternal" covenants is missing. Meantime we are left with a religious vision that commands attention to its own constructedness in the conventionality of its images emblazoned on the sky. By the novel's close the transformation of suffering seemingly promised here but actually only recalled is realized imperfectly for very few, and in this world amid "uproar," not the next. The elusiveness of Dickens' religious vision is felt most fully, however, in his treatment of Arthur Clennam's relation to his Ideal in the Actual.

It would be wholly inappropriate for Amy to preach a Christian sermon to Arthur—and Amy is always respectful of her hearers; but she seems to be herself such a "delivering angel" (as Kitto calls a text in Ecclesiastes) in her embodiment of saving texts from the Sermon on the Mount for him. As Carlyle had urged biography should do, hers "wraps in it a message out of Heaven" (*LDP* 326), what it means to *do* the Word (see Matt. 7:21). Amy's living gospel, set in "the lowliest way of life" (1.7.70), is bodied forth in a concrete narrative to benefit the reader, like "the beneficent history of the New Testament":

> For Wisdom dealt with mortal powers,
>   Where truth in closest words shall fail,
>   When truth embodied in a tale
> Shall enter in at lowly doors.
>   (*In Memoriam*, stanza 36, lines 5–8)

But no more than the synoptic Gospels in the nineteenth century does Amy's "tale" provoke no difficulties of interpretation. Indeed, a Higher Critic reading the various versions of her "history" found in *Little Dorrit* might object that, far from being a "transcendental ground" for the novel, the "truth" of her story is always shaped by the belief-needs of the audience and the storyteller, including Dickens and Amy herself (who tells her "short story" in several variants). The importance of point of view is nowhere more evident than in Clennam's interpretation of Amy's "living gospel," a piece of experience "shifting intricately as we ourselves change." Moreover, for his story, this lesson is neither specifically Christian nor resistant to the variable interpretations Dickens' reader is permitted to make, even as he or she is observing Clennam misinterpreting. Arthur misreads Amy's embodied Sermon; and she does not perfectly conform to the biblical model.

Clennam does not think he appreciates her incarnate gospel until a "marked stop in the whirling wheel of life" brings his "right perception" of "how much the dear little creature had influenced his better resolutions" (2.27.700). This "remembrance of her virtues" comes too late for Clennam to "do" anything in remembrance of her, but it serves to persuade him that Amy actually realizes the very ideals he has had such difficulty realizing himself: "to judge not, and in humility to be merciful, and have hope and charity" (1.13.158). These articles in Clennam's humanistic code echo both Sermon versions (Matt. 7:1 and Luke 6:37), as well as St. Paul's little sermon on love in 1 Corinthians 13. In piling up Amy's moral, if not necessarily religious, characteristics in the sermon he preaches to himself in book 2, chapter 27, Clennam implicitly recognizes the qualities celebrated in the Beatitudes. Unlike that "mound of meekness" Casby (2.32.778), Amy really is poor in spirit and meek, "One weak girl!"; she is merciful and a peacemaker in her "charitable construction" and "noblest generosity of the affections"; she is persecuted for righteousness' sake, "toiling on, for a good object's sake . . . against ignoble obstacles"; and she bears this persecution bravely and compassionately like Dickens' Jesus, turning the other cheek and asking forgiveness for her enemies (Matt. 5:39, 44–45). In her evident "patience, self-denial, self-subdual," and devotion to duties at hand, Amy would seem to be not exactly "Perfection. Best of Amys!" in Fanny's terms (2.24.677), but "perfect" in the sense of Matthew 5:48 ("Be ye therefore perfect"): single-minded, completely devoted.[127] Pure in heart, this "pure girl" hungers and thirsts after righteousness in this world. If some do not "see [her] good works, and glorify [her] Father which is in heaven," Clennam sees her light shine and glorifies *her*, just as he sees the light "shine on others and hail[s] it" (1.13.158; cf. Matt. 5:16). (Reciprocally, she makes *him* into the Good Samaritan, stabilizing their always ambiguously uneasy relationship into a moral parable rather than a love story; see 2.4.457.)

Like other Divine Appearances in Carlyle's gospel, Amy is likely to be overlooked—even when she is overestimated. In Clennam's interpretation of Amy's

Sermon, we see more of his need for an ideal than we do of Amy's character, which his "remembrance of her virtues" has distorted. His epithet "one weak girl!" ignores the flaw in her meekness—an almost fatal timidity in the face of life, born of her prison seclusion—as well as the strength of her self-assertions and her evidences of womanly need. Clennam may need to stress her "charitable construction," but, like Christ, at times she brings not peace but a sword (see "Taking Advice," 2.14). She is not merely a silent sufferer; quietly she raises objections to others' misreading of her (for example, "Don't say that, dear Fanny. I do what I can for them," 1.20.238). Her affections are more than "generous," as Clennam will discover when he rereads her letters from Italy. She may be single-mindedly devoted to duty, but the scene where Amy is piteously torn between her "O thank you, thank you!" and "But, O no, O no, O no!" (1.32.376) shows that she does have inner conflict. Not simply a "pure girl," she "can't look . . . out of a child's eyes" (1.14.170) but must see with the eyes of experience. These qualifications of Amy's religious ideal, however, are what help to make her a living gospel for Arthur, who needs more than her goodness. We see this need when, at the end of this passage, the effect of the Sermon's idealizations is only to shame the humiliated man the more. Such a remote ideal has no transforming power over Arthur's actualities now, in prison and disgrace. Dickens is not interested in discrediting values in which he confessed his faith; as a novelist, however, he observes the lives of characters who suffer from ideals—from their inaccessibility and from their tyranny over the imagination, a tyranny exacerbated by the general condition of entrapment intensifying the need for transcendence.

The Sermon's ideals are both blessing and bane in Amy Dorrit's life, and that ambiguity also calls quiet attention to the subtext's inadequacies. Like Dickens' Jesus, a good man who "didn't mind himself when he was doing . . . good" (LOL 22), Amy does her good works unobtrusively: she fasts not openly like hypocrites such as Mrs. Clennam, but "in secret" (Matt. 6:16–18), saving her broken victuals for her father's repast. In contrast to her vain father's anxieties, like the lilies of the field she is not anxious about what she shall eat, drink, or put on; but she is very anxious for her family's physical needs in a life of poverty that requires the most careful economies, not the Sermon's attitude of "the Lord will provide" (see 2.15.590: "I—hum—can, with the—ha—blessing of Providence, be taken care of"). She also knows that life is "more than food, and the body more than clothing" (see Matt. 6:25–34). But this higher knowledge separates her from the family for whom her sacrifices are made—and whom she needs precisely because she finds no compensation in gratifying her own physical wants, nor even in the kingdom Jesus bids his hearers seek first, for she expresses no otherworldly hopes. In Amy's story we find even the reverse of wisdom. She can be morally discriminating (while Jesus urges us not to turn the borrower away in Matthew 5:42, Amy asks Clennam not to lend to her father); but on the whole she casts her pearls before swine, who trample them "and turn again and rend" her (Matt. 7:6). Like the Beatitudes to some interpreters, Amy's life preaches sublime nonsense for a "righteousness' sake" that is abstract in having almost no beneficial spiritual effect on those who turn on her the more for their recognition of her virtues. Indeed, her goodness strands her in a spiritual no-man's-land from which Clennam cannot rescue her because she lives only too much "in secret" and refuses to acknowledge her womanly need of him. For all her quiet virtue, Amy is not rewarded "openly," as Jesus promises (Matt. 6:18), until the end so long delayed. Further, the novel calls for goodness larger in range than Amy's unobtrusive domestic offerings. Here the Sermon subtext, by so stressing personal virtue, provides no help for determining where public duty lies with the causes of wider ills—such as the capitalist ideology that requires debtors' prisons and generates a cultural neurosis about the "Getting On" of Matthew 6:25. If Dickens had lost all social and political faith by the time he wrote *Little Dorrit*, the Bible did nothing to redirect or revive it.

Equally troubling are prayer and blessing in *Little Dorrit*, two important themes of the Sermon. If Jesus warns against obtrusive public praying (Matt. 6:5), Amy prays in quiet corners of the novel for "pity on all prisoners and captives" (1.19.219) and for the earthly salvation of her father: "O spare his life! O save him to me! O look down upon my dear, long-suffering, unfortunate, much changed, dear dear father!" (1.19.224). But these prayers do not achieve the desired effect, as even the desperation of Amy's language anticipates. Her prayers are not answered except in one respect very important to Dickens: in the "pity" this human daughter can offer Dorrit, as she already has done in saying the prayer at all. In this revision of the Sermon's teaching on prayer, the expression of concern is its own reward—consolation that is decidedly limited. Likewise, Jesus' promises in Matthew 7:7 ("Ask, and it shall be given you; seek, and ye shall find; knock, and it shall be opened unto you") are realized only insofar as Amy herself gives, helps others find, opens—as when she opens up the mystery of print to Maggy and helps the girl find a livelihood.

Amy is also one of those characters (like her father) who are always saying "God bless you!" when God's blessings are so notably absent. Such exchanges can be efficacious for binding together small human communities of concern, and Dickens hints—just barely—that they echo some larger good ("perhaps she may have been as audible above—who knows!—as a whole cathedral choir," 1.14.165). But these beatitudes are often ironic and can even be cruel, such as Clennam's "God bless his wife and him!" when Pet and Gowan have made a disastrous marriage (1.28.327). Humanly administered blessings in *Little Dorrit* are shadowed like all human action, in a world of systemic evils that wants some bolder mode of remediation from "above" or on earth than these fragile gestures of goodwill.

Dickens' Jesus, a wronged hero, does not die for the sins of the world but is merely victimized by evil men. Amy belongs to a long line of suffering Dickensian innocents whose strength of renunciation is hard to judge morally, to distinguish from the weakness of submission to powerful circumstances or the stronger wills of others. To the limited extent that Amy is identified with *this* Jesus, she elicits the reader's pity, perhaps, but not admiration. More damaging, between the gaps of his imperfectly realized religious design, Dickens lets his reader see something masochistic about her martyrdom and infantile[128] about her need to dismiss an adult life with Arthur to go "home" to the prison of her childhood. Her preference for "not my Christian name" but "Little Dorrit" signals her reluctance to put away certain childish things (2.11.536: is "Little Dorrit," then, an unchristian name?). If Amy is Jesus' "Child of the Parable" who enters the kingdom,[129] the childlike Christianity by which she is to "lead" others is morally ambiguous and, as I have suggested, at least partially fictive. Only when Amy becomes "something more womanly" at the end of book 2 (29.737), and has broken out of these ideal formulas enough to reach for the object of her desire, can her preservation of childlike qualities into adulthood recall Clennam's sense of his intrinsic goodness and empower his potential recovery of the kingdom within.

Amy's most important "Christlike" role is that of intercessor, praying mercy for a number of sinning fellow humans who need her mediation with God and with the novelist as well. In the Sermon on the Mount, Jesus sets forth a divine model of forgiveness that incorporates both Gospel and Law: "And forgive us our debts, as we forgive our debtors. . . . But if ye forgive not men their trespasses, neither will your Father forgive your trespasses" (Matt. 6:12–15). Despite Dickens' explicit echoes of the Sermon's teachings on forgiveness, however (see 1.5.45), in *Little Dorrit* the economy of debt and repayment operates rather differently, where it operates at all, from the divinely instituted model. Alexander Welsh points out that as faith in a personal God weakens, the doctrine of forgiveness loses its premise as well as its efficacy to remediate evil, while "the morality of strict consequences, . . . obligation and duty" become "sanctions much more weighty . . . than forgiveness," especially given the growth of determinism in the nineteenth century.[130] A third result of this attenuated faith is the appearance of the intercessory female in the Victorian novel. It was one of

Dickens' favorite fictions, which he indulged most fully in *The Old Curiosity Shop*'s "picture" of "the Good Angel of the race—abiding by [the family] in all reverses—redeeming all their sins" (69.637). Rewriting the Little Nell figure in Little Dorrit, Dickens operates this stereotype in some newly complex patterns reflecting his later understanding of the problem of forgiveness. Amy Dorrit is at once more and less than "the Good Angel of the race"; her "forgiveness" must also be supplemented by formulas of debt and repayment, and guilt must be released through melodramatic events quite outside the circle of her powers.

If Amy fails to intercede for the stricken Mrs. Clennam, Amy is only a little more successful in interceding for her father with the novelist, who grants this unrepentant old sinner at least the return of his youthful face in death. Of course, this form of clemency is not what Amy had asked for; but death must come—a direct result, presumably, of late hours in castle-building on the Roman campagna. For all Amy's angelic life-giving powers, deeds have consequences that even Little Dorrits cannot contravene.

In fact, Amy's final intercession for her father culminates a pattern of "Christian" behavior that the novel invites the reader to question. Toward others Amy does scruple to make critical judgments tempered by mercy (for example, on the Pet and Gowan, Fanny and Sparkler marriages). But up to Dorrit's death, Amy has been doing nothing but "redeeming all [his] sins" in ways that make us doubt her moral scrupulousness, for her forgiving perpetuates the very wickedness she would absolve. And Amy's case is compromising because she sees so much in her "watchful love" (2.29.621). As a child she is said to be "Innocent, in the mist through which she saw her father" (1.7.76), but as she gains experience Amy's forgiveness is no longer based on ignorance nor so innocent. Two kinds of "mist" cloud her judgment still. One is her daughterly love, in all its ambiguity. The other is that she "see[s] everything with that ineffaceable brand" of the cruel prison spikes (1.24.283). This awareness of mitigating circumstances easily shades into the rationalization and special pleading that erode moral categories, as Clennam notices when Amy objects that her freed father should have to pay all his debts when he has suffered so long (see 1.35.409). In this passage, Clennam absolves the "confusion" in Amy's system of absolution that ignores the law of consequences and the narrator absolves Clennam for criticizing her, but the memorable point in this awkward moment of rationalization on all hands is that Amy needs to *be* absolved. There *is* something dishonest about the fact that, while Amy secretly sheds "tears of compassion for [her father's] infirmities," like the Master, what she publicly acknowledges is that she pities his misfortune; and the fiction, like others in the novel, is self-serving, for it helps support an idealization Amy very much needs amid her actualities, "but too content to see him with a lustre round his head" (1.19.224). What makes her fiction a "Jesuitical" form of half-belief is that she knows both the theory of mitigating circumstances and the idealization which it supports are fictive. (In "Little Dorrit's Party," she admits the "degradation" she knows Clennam has seen, but then expressly seeks to enlist him in pious pretense about old Dorrit that will help them both "think better of him!" [see 1.14.164–65].)

In short, Amy's Christlike acts foster her systematic evasion, which is only too well-designed to sustain Dorrit's own more elaborate evasions. She thus helps to deaden his conscience, so that he commits new acts of ingratitude against her, which she must then "forgive" in an endless prison round of unredeemed sins. Dickens lets his reader see this in the dynamics of family relations, while giving his narrator license to absolve Amy of *her* sins: she too is a victim of circumstances, a "Child of the Marshalsea," and a little Dorrit. The narrator also places Amy's limited seeing within his own wider vision, which considers and adjusts judgment and mercy with great nicety to suit Dorrit's peculiar case. On the same page as Amy's simple absolving prayer, he says, "Only the wisdom that holds the clue to all hearts and all mysteries, can surely know to what extent a man, especially a man brought down as this man had been, can impose upon himself. Enough, for the present place, that he lay down with wet eyelashes, serene, in a manner majestic, after bestowing his life of degradation as a sort of portion on the devoted child upon whom its miseries had fallen so heavily, and whose love alone had saved him to be even what he was" (1.19.224). This narrator pleads a more profound ignorance than her fictive one in this twilight world—and he no more offers to say on what grounds her love *is* justified than he names exactly "what he was." In the reminder that Dorrit has been "brought down," the slight comic distance in the middle ("wet eyelashes, serene . . ."), and the final clause, this narrative voice is ultimately compassionate toward old Dorrit; but we also sense here how the efficacy of merely human forgiveness tends to dissolve into mist in *Little Dorrit*, and evil remains—what it is.

Amy's forgiving is unavailing in another sense: it does not release her from internal contradiction. In the system of forgiveness as a divine-human exchange, the payoff in forgiving *to be* forgiven is peace of mind. But the many acts of forgiveness that texture Amy's daily life do not dissolve her internal tension between her knowledge of good and evil, although they may keep some awareness of evil at bay. Amy's pain continues because there are still debts to be paid—paid again and again in her overwhelming sense of duty and her attempts to shoulder the burden of others' sins.

Amy's intercession for Arthur Clennam is as cloudy as that for her father and only partially availing in the resolution of Arthur's story, even though her loving affection, come of age, is what seems in the most obvious way to save him from self-mistrust. Alexander Welsh asks why Clennam needs an intercessor at all: another wronged hero, Arthur seems "more sinned against than sinning" and is as innocent of charges hurled against him as he is of complicity in his parents' crimes.[131] But why, then, does he feel, "anchor[ed] by the haunting topic" of the family guilt, like "a criminal . . . chained in a stationary boat on a deep clear river, condemned . . . always to see the body of the fellow creature he had drowned lying at the bottom" (2.23.658)? The strange power of this image suggests that Clennam's sense of guilt is anchored in something real: not his illegitimate birth, a bogus issue in itself, but in his anger at his parents' injustice toward him in childhood (to name only the most obvious psychological cause). As Arthur's first outburst against his parents reveals, he has nursed this "sullen sense of injury in his heart" (1.3.30) over the years; but he has turned the anger inward and against himself. Its outward face in middle life is his self-repressed manner, with which he defends himself against his unacceptable aggressive feelings, and the crisis of "will" he voices, which involves the self-enforced passivity of a man fearful to act on what he feels. Imagining himself vaguely complicit in his parents' crimes, the "haunting topic," is a natural expression of Arthur's neurotic confusion of fault.

In psychological terms, Clennam needs to be released from this repressed anger and guilty feelings about it; in traditional moral terms, he can be saved only if he replaces "Do Not Forget" (as a motto of grievance) with the quasi-Christian formula of "Forgive and forget." To Dickens, memory is essential in the psychologically healthy and moral life, for what is forgiven must first be remembered; one cannot "forget and forgive." Amy Dorrit's forgetful kind of forgiveness, which covers up a multitide of sins with charitable fictions, cannot help Clennam work through either the therapeutic process of remembrance and release, or the moral one of forgiving that he might be forgiven.

Amy acts as intercessor by forgiving *for* him. That part of the family secret which involves hurt to her she dismisses "freely" ("all forgiven, all forgotten," 2.33.788) and in so doing abridges the law of consequences not for Mrs. Clennam but for her son. As Arthur "forgives"—through her mediation—so he gains peace of mind and can go forward into a happy future with Amy. The flaw in this scheme, of course, is that the wrong Amy forgives is not precisely the wrong Arthur needs to forgive—a much larger debt, which has depleted his whole life. Amy never has to sound the depths of his anger, and she so arranges things that Arthur never has to confront it either. Like Doyce urging him to forget the past without ever really analyzing it, Amy gets "things perfectly arranged without [Arthur's] knowledge" so that "a new and prosperous career [can be] opened before" them all as partners, business and marital (2.34.797). The "sullen sense of injury in his heart," the problematic speculations, the crisis of will, the quests for reparations, and most importantly the quest for origins merely dissolve, like the lines in old Dorrit's face, as "all the affairs [become] smooth" (797). Arthur never exposes his anger, analyzes his sense of guilt, or even forgives his parents for what he does know of them. Conveniently, his mother's paralysis and death help to keep the secrets of Arthur's anger and guilt "safe," as Amy puts it (788). This conspiracy of persons and events helps to preserve the fiction of the hero's innocence, but it short-circuits any realistic process of healing we might have expected in this reflective man's story.

While Dickens lets his redeeming female work secretly to dissolve sin, the plot's melodramatic machinations confess the inadequacy of this human substitute for the Redeemer. Justice is not abridged; debtors must pay. Clennam pays for his release not through his imprisonment and illness alone but through displaced punishments: the decisive collapse of the Clennam house, bringing Mrs. Clennam to her knees, and the crushing of the scapegoat Blandois (Arthur's double) under its ruins.[132] Economically, letting Clennam have it both ways, these acts also wreak vengeance on his two enemies. While he relinquishes no secrets, they burst forth from Affery and Mrs. Clennam. Other explosive revelations help to generate the sense of relief that attends Arthur's last scenes.[133]

Dickens' resolution of Clennam's spiritual crisis, in short, is neither realistic nor religious but literary, requiring the writer to manipulate many fictional counters into patterns of mirroring, reversal, and displacement in order to create a sense of closure. This resolution testifies to the inadequacy of the divine model Dickens has used as well as to the profound ambiguity of human solutions, just as his mid-Victorian heroine, more than Nell, reflects the exacerbated problem of evil in Dickens' time. When divine grace can no longer be invoked, unaided humans must somehow live with the knowledge that stooping to forgive (when they do try to do it) may be morally ambiguous at best, and hoping to banish their demons yet another vanity.

If forgiveness in *Little Dorrit* can be but a "chasing of the wind"—if as in Ecclesiastes there seems still to be in the world "a crookedness not to be straightened, a void not to be filled"[134]—how does Dickens manage to leave his reader with the sense that a rebirth has occurred even in the corrupt heart of the Marshalsea prison?

The subject of regeneration, C. H. Spurgeon proclaimed, "is the hinge of the gospel; it is the point upon which most Christians are agreed,"[135] including Dickens: the metaphors of rebirth arise again and again in his work. Certainly

they belong to the conventional repertoire of Victorian fiction; they also hold a
primary place in the apocalyptic prose of Carlyle, to whose rebirth imagery
Dickens was powerfully drawn the more he became aware of the difficulties of
actual social and personal reform.[136] Again, as Dickens' realistic hopes for
change waned, literary solutions became more attractive—and even more obviously "literary" than the artifice of narrative structuring I have noted are these
archetypes of rebirth, a privileged part of that poetry of religion which Matthew
Arnold believed would be "our ever surer and surer stay." Where God seems
absent, Victorian eloquence is yet at midcentury a powerful invention for evoking at least linguistic traces of the divine.

Little Dorrit feels like a hopeful novel because it moves from a parched sunscape to rituals that bring water, flowers, and abundance into the Marshalsea
prison, and finally to that morning when "Little Dorrit . . . came into the prison
with the sunshine" (2.34.798). It is not that "morning without a night" bringing
no more pain, but it does signal the hopeful beginning of one man's regeneration
in a world of the dead and dying. Arthur's madness is arrested when an angelic
voice—at a "door . . . opened" not in heaven but on earth—speaks of "things
which must be hereafter" (Rev. 4:1) to a man oppressed by history who so needs
a sense of the future Amy helps him to imagine. She comes "as a bride adorned
for her husband" (Rev. 21:2) in the old dress she will wear on their wedding day;
but more than this, she is the "woman clothed with the sun" who undergoes the
trials of the wilderness and points the way of salvation in St. John's vision (Rev.
12). In Dickens' humanistic re-envisioning, Amy is that salvation, awakening
the imprisoned Clennam and showing him that "wherein thou even now stand-
est, here or nowhere is thy Ideal" (*SR* 156) with her in the earthly city. Other
emblems of hope in *Little Dorrit*'s final chapter recall the principal religious
images Carlyle had invoked amid the wild desperation of his last *Pamphlet*—the
imagery of regenerative nature, the clear and widening prospects, the growing
light, human pilgrimage through the actual.

While Carlyle had long demonstrated "the wondrous agency of *Symbols*" (*SR*
175), Dickens' are the more convincing for being embedded in a "Very quiet
conclusion."[137] Apocalyptic's yearning for total Presence is considerably modified by the inductions into experience *Little Dorrit* fosters. Heaven does not
descend to earth and the words of consolation are not those of St. John's angel
but the declarations of human love by a woman who insists, quite rightly, "You
praise me far too much" (2.34.791). Yet even while her transcendent stature is
disconfirmed, this heroine is not discredited. A "trace" of divinity, though it
remind us of what is absent, gives the imagination work to do and is still a

present consolation, if not Presence itself. Sustaining others by her loving fidelity, some provisional truths, and saving fictions, Amy Dorrit is Dickens' living gospel in the "living grave" of the prison world. Here much is buried, but it is only within this Actual that the conventional skeptic in Arthur Clennam may yet be revised, if not the man reborn.

6

Dying unto Death: Biblical Ends and Endings in *Our Mutual Friend*

THE GARDEN ON THE ROOF
(Marcus Stone)

> . . . until there shall be written against my life, the two words with
> which I have this day closed this book:—THE END.

> "Postscript in Lieu of a Preface,"
> *Our Mutual Friend* (1865)

> ". . . and the story is done, and God bless you my Beauty,
> and God bless us all!" . . .
> "But *is* the story done?" said Bella, pondering.
> "Is there no more of it?"

MORE THAN ANY OTHER of Dickens' late novels, *Our Mutual Friend* is "about ends: whatever sense of direction or purpose can be salvaged from experience."[1] Alexander Welsh's words about Victorian fiction are peculiarly appropriate for a novel that dramatizes salvage as a human purpose, for good or ill, and strives itself to resuscitate traditional "ends"—reasons for living, solutions to riddles, terminations of doubt—"In these times of ours" (the book's opening phrase). *Our Mutual Friend* is about ends in the face of the end, but not the blowing up of society as in *Bleak House* or personal death alone: this novel takes on all those deathly forces "of the world, worldly" and "of the earth, earthy" (2.2.294; cf. 1 Cor. 15:47) that encroach upon human artifacts, that threaten people's capacities for making meaning. *Our Mutual Friend* thus plunges its readers into a fictional world of "texts" and of "dust"—the verbal and scribal debris of a decadent moneyed civilization, and the material chaos "without and before book" (2.1.263) that threatens the immaterial cosmos of humanly ascribed values. From the opening scene, where a mysterious man is "On the Lookout" for "Tokens. . . . Marks . . . Signs . . . Appearances" (1.11.179) of "something" in the foul river that will sustain his living, and where Dickens' reader is engaged in looking out for signs of the scene's meaning, *Our Mutual Friend* presents life ("this day") as a text ("this book") to be interpreted, easily or with difficulty, for vicious or benign ends. The alternative to such acts of reading—"Reading of the sea" (3.10.605), the river, the sky, the fire, faces, corpses, one's place in the social hierarchy, one's "weaknesses," one's soul—is sinking back into the "Dismal Swamp" of materiality, where the mere remains of "human warious" decompose the "general panoramic view" (1.7.126).

Calling attention to this central metaphor of reading, *Our Mutual Friend* is constructed as "a vast anthology of texts and fictions," in Robert S. Baker's words:[2] printed money ("L.S.D."), "Alfred Davids" and other legal documents, "Found Drowned" notices, the "printed bill 'Veneering for ever,'" Sloppy's newspaper, the Inspector's missals, Lady Tippins' Cupidon, Jenny's "bright little books" of fairy tales, *The Decline and Fall of the Roman Empire*, classical myth and medieval legend, the *Annual* (or "Animal") *Register*, *The Newgate Calendar*, *The Complete British Housewife*, *The Compleat Angler*, John Harmon's "English, French, and Italian" books, Veneering's library of "bran-new books," Merryweather's *Lives and Anecdotes of Misers*, Irish ballads, hunting songs, James Thomson's *Seasons*, *The Beggar's Opera*, plays of Shakespeare, *The Mysteries of Udolpho*, *Gulliver's Travels*, S. J. Arnold's *The Death of Nelson*, "Auld Lang Syne," *Marmion*, *In Memoriam*, the Gospel According to Podsnap, the Books of the Insolvent Fates, riddles, proverbs sacred and profane, and a golden treasury of conventional phrases (on display especially in the titles of chapters, of books, and of the novel itself). Amid this peculiarly literary (and musical) kind of heteroglossia—bringing into the novel an extraordinarily wide range of allusion—sacred texts, rubrics from the Book of Common Prayer, and religious archetypes precariously, often only momentarily, emerge to speak a religious word. Compared to the status of religious allusions in Dickens' middle period, their position in *Our Mutual Friend*, even where privileged, is considerably diminished—imaginatively depleted, of the dust, dusty, or emptied of religious content; nor can their words give interpretive stability[3] to the novel's welter of human voices raised against the silence and the dark.

The "embodied conundrum" of this novel is the riddle of mortality; and to this amoral "Riddle Without an Answer" (2.6.339) Dickens opposes two kinds of reading, with their corresponding texts. The first is represented by the way Mr. Venus, an artist in the "human warious," deftly articulates bones with his perfect knowledge of anatomy; as he tells Wegg: "if you was brought here loose in a bag to be articulated, I'd name your smallest bones blindfold equally with your largest, as fast as I could pick 'em out, and I'd sort 'em all, and sort your wertebrae, in a manner that would equally surprise and charm you" (1.7.128). Unlike the editor of *Sartor Resartus* with his bag of biographical fragments from which to construct the "mysterious ME" of his hero, to Venus the human skeleton is a stable, perfectly readable text (so long as all the parts are there and fit). When Wegg is first hired to read for Mr. Boffin, he imagines his job will be this easy and takes on the air of "an official expounder of mysteries" (1.5.97). But as their voyage into the open seas of Print goes on, the "labouring bark" of this minimally literate reader becomes "beset by polysyllables, and embarrassed among a perfect archipelago of hard words," and he has "to take soundings every minute, and to feel the way with the greatest caution" (3.14.639). Until he gets to the book on misers (that congenial subject), Wegg's texts are highly unstable, awash with unknowns. From the tensions between these two kinds of reading, of the intelligible (or only deceptively complicated) and of the genuinely problematic, Dickens' novel is generated in the reader's experience. But while in *Bleak House* and *Little Dorrit* biblical texts were involved in both kinds of interpretation, in *Our Mutual Friend* Dickens has returned to an earlier manner in his use of scriptural allusion, as in other things. Sometimes a fairytale teller, sometimes the Famous Author articulating the Laws of his world,[4] the voice that guides easy reading is also the biblical voice drawing upon Scripture and Prayer Book as sources of stable moral values, recognizable figures, and familiar language as Dickens conducts the religious satire, several moral plots, and the stories of rebirth. The intelligence in this novel that complicates reading, on the other hand, creating gaps in the text or forcing the reader to revise his judgments and expectations, is not biblical: it assumes other voices to which the moral designs are deaf; it sounds human depths amid a surrounding high comedy of surfaces; it fractures the perspectives from which Dickens' several stories are told; it nervously switches from past to present tense; and it "complete[ly] transform[s] . . . tone and milieu from chapter to chapter" and "juxtapos[es] . . . incompatible fragments in a pattern of disharmony or mutual contradiction" like "a cubist collage."[5] It sometimes deliberately withholds the facts in order to test the reader's capacity for correcting errors of interpretation,[6] but it also attends upon the secrecy of the text like Kafka's doorkeeper in "Before the Law." While some of the novel's deliberate ambiguities are clarified (such as the Boffin deception), the accumulation of these other, indeterminate meanings prevents interpretive closure and thus affects the way we read even the clear moral parables Dickens tells in *Our Mutual Friend*.

For all Dickens' stratagems, therefore, to educate the reader to find "something to trust in, and care for, and think well of" (2.11.405), to find ends, he is left pinioned on Boffin's "chief literary difficulty" when hearing Plutarch's *Lives*, the problem of "What to believe": "for some time he was divided in his mind between half, all, or none; at length, when he decided, as a moderate man, to compound with half, the question still remained, which half? And that stumbling-block he never got over" (3.6.538). Although Dickens' novel embodies the possibility of provisional solutions in such difficulties,[7] it works mightily toward what John Harmon declares *such* "a quantity of believing!" (4.5.755) that we cannot endorse the happy resolutions with the credulity they require, given the darker parables we have read. The conclusion's belief in traditional (if not finally biblical) ends is salvaged at the cost of too much complexity, as though Dickens would finally arrange his fiction like Miss Peecher's "little work-box of thoughts, fitted with no gloomy and dark recesses" (3.11.609), or had taken up the Podsnap flourish—"Nothing else To Be—anywhere!" (1.11.175). Dickens never achieves this "high simplicity" (1.15.234), but the impulse drives the book to its end. After the main plots have been worked out, with the exorcising of villains and the baptismal "rebirths" of several characters, sealed by Boffin's hearty "God bless us all!" Bella asks, "But *is* the story done?" (4.13.845). That there is "more of it" Dickens' last chapter reminds us by resurrecting the secular voices of Society, which dismiss the voices of modest moral awareness in this final scene and babble on into the reader's present world.

1

"Now it's too late for me to begin shovelling and sifting at alphabeds," Mr. Boffin tells Wegg (1.5.94). The old histories come alive for him, but the remark of this "scholar in Dust" signals a general condition in *Our Mutual Friend:* texts—language of all kinds, but especially biblical—are in danger of becoming, if they have not already become, waste-heaps of dead quotations to be shoveled and sifted but not reclaimed. Dickens' satire on a money-scavenging society exposes this near-universal devaluation of religious currency; unfortunately, his own creative practice in *Our Mutual Friend* also suffers from the condition he would expose, as though he had lost interest in or heart for the literary reclamation of the Bible for his time.

In the Scrip Age Carlyle had damned in "Hudson's Statue" (*LDP* 257), where the "Fathers of the Scrip-Church"—contractors and chairmen of boards—"piously" interpret the Bible of Mammon to neophytes like Veneering (3.19.690), the deadest of traditional words are "Christian" and "God" (or better, for its suggestion of provender, "Providence"). The name of "Christian" is taken in vain by the scavenging charities (1.17.259), but it is most often on the lips of speculators in human flesh like Fledgeby, who denotes his victims by this name. Riah's addressing him as "Generous Christian master" brings out that reversal of expected meanings this good Christian society has effected through love of money. As one of the idols of a Mammon-worshipping age, Podsnap not only takes the name of Providence in vain but, like Dombey, appropriates God's creative and destructive powers, in determining with a wave of his arm what will be and not "Be—anywhere!" Reading from a red-letter edition of "the Gospel according to Podsnappery" (3.8.566), he makes a mockery of Carlyle's "Divine appearances" in asking a foreign dinner guest if he has "Observed in our Streets . . . any Tokens. . . . Marks . . . Signs, you know, Appearances— Traces" of "our Constitution, Sir. It was Bestowed Upon Us By Providence" (1.11.179). On another occasion he appropriates Jesus' words with "you shall have the poor always with you" (188; cf. Matt. 26:11) to put down "the meek man" (surely one of the kingdom of heaven), who has hinted that something is wrong with the economic system. What "Providence has declared" (an "absurd and irreverent conventional phrase," says the narrator) is, of course, only what Podsnap means and wants (188, 175).

Dickens brings out the callousness of this appropriation in rendering the Catechism and Collect of the Scrip Church, which has reduced social responsibility to the word "Shares," a system of buying and selling human flesh. It is the one thing needful (Luke 10:42): "As is well known to the wise in their generation, traffic in Shares is the one thing to have to do with in this world. . . . Where does he come from? Shares. Where is he going to? Shares. What are his tastes? Shares. Has he any principles? Shares. . . . Sufficient answer to all. . . . O mighty Shares!" (1.10.159–60). Financial lingo also gets into Podsnap's version of the marriage service; what "his standard Young Person" has to do "with such matters" is "to take as directed, and with worldly goods as per settlement to be endowed" (2.5.327). The one wedding we witness under the auspices of the Scrip Church—conducted (according to Twemlow's script) by "the Reverend Blank Blank, assisted by the Reverend Dash Dash"—is entirely devoid of the Prayer Book words for the Solemnization of Matrimony, substituting in their place Lady Tippins' calculations ("Bride; five-and-forty if a day, . . . veil fifteen pound") and concluding in a disjointed list suggesting by its syntax that Bride and Bridegroom have not been "joined together" before God ("Ceremony preferred, register signed, Lady Tippins escorted out of sacred edifice by Veneering . . ."; see 1.10.163–65).[8] The real marriage vows come afterward as a business deal; reaffirming it later, Sophronia inadvertently echoes Galatians 6:2 ("Bear ye one another's burdens, and so fulfill the law of Christ"): "My husband and I deceived one another when we married; we must bear the consequences of the deception—that is to say, bear one another, and bear the burden of scheming together for to-day's dinner and to-morrow's breakfast—till death divorces us" (3.17.689). As in the narrator's punning on "Shares," in which the financial meaning of the word reverses its social denotation, Galatians' vision of communal sharing is radically overturned by the pressure of money values—as is *what* should be "borne." Given the fatal power of money to deplete social meaning, this marriage of scavenging schemers need not await the Great Divorce; like the mercenary Dombey wedding, which turns into a funeral, the Lammles' union is already deathly—for Sophronia, a state of fitful dying unto death.

Just as "you never g[e]t a sign out of bodies," as the Inspector says sagely (1.3.69), so the corpses in the Social Chorus never mean anything by the few once-religious words they do use. Eugene Wrayburn carelessly explains the significance of the dead sign:

> "But then I mean so much that I—that I don't mean."
> "Don't mean?"
> "So much that I only mean and shall always only mean and nothing more, my dear Mortimer. It's the same thing." (2.6.336)

It is a case of what Carlyle called "mere words." Eugene—whom Headstone sees as solely made up of words (see 3.11.615) and whose "name" is the "text" of Bradley's sermon to Lizzie (2.15.457)—reduces the several biblical expressions he uses to the level of all his other mock-texts, such as "A fair day's wages for a fair day's work" (1.13.213). Typically, he says that Mortimer has had "a light thrown" on the pots and pans Eugene has purchased, "which, when you only saw them as in a glass darkly, you were hastily—I must say hastily— inclined to depreciate" (2.6.348–49; cf. 1 Cor. 13:12). Jenny Wren satirically scolds Eugene as "a precious godfather" (3.10.595), for he is a giver of reductive and abusive names that deplete the meaning of signs: besides the rechristening of "Mr. Dolls" and "Schoolmaster," Eugene further reduces the shrunken Riah in calling him sarcastically a "Patriarch"; and he declares to Mortimer, "it comes into my mind that—no doubt with an instinctive desire to receive him into the bosom of our Church—*I* gave him the name of Aaron!" (3.10.598). A dead sign to Eugene—a stereotypical name for a Jew toward whom Eugene's feelings are dead—it may not be to Dickens, if he had in mind Garrett Stewart's version of its genealogy: as Moses' brother and his people's first high priest, Aaron is a fitting namesake for Jenny's priestly confidant, for she has prophetic visions.[9] Such associations, however, like Riah himself, are mere "ghost[s] of a departed Time" (2.15.465) in "these times of ours" from which Eugene's language suffers.

If Carlyle's "long *Scavenger Age*" has arrived (*LDP* 329), religious words have become lifeless objects to be manipulated in low society as well as high. Rogue Riderhood's key phrase of self-description, "a honest man as gets my living by the sweat of my brow" (3.8.572), is oblivious to the curse he reinvokes each time he so *defends* himself and to the Fall of which his every appearance reminds us. (And his Old Adam is not drowned in his ineffectual river baptism.) Like Carlyle's Mammon-worshippers who kiss the outside of their closed Bibles, this "honest" rogue says "I kisses the book" (3.11.612); and he has the vague notion that swearing by the names of two famous kings ("Alfred David") or, by "this here world-without-end-everlasting chair" (1.12.198), will warrant his lies. Such is life in the Scavenger Age that for his daughter, Pleasant, the rituals of the Church have all become sanctions of violence, ineffectual rites to prevent it, or pretentious "masquerade" (see 2.12.407). No wonder Pleasant's visions of "Eden"—a more pleasant setting in which to gull sailors (407)—are corrupted by the money-violence of Scrip-scavenging: its one "true business precept," as for that other poisoned Eden in *Martin Chuzzlewit*, is to "Do other men, for they would do you" (*MC* 11.241).

This is dust indeed; but even at the school, which is to raise street urchins out of the world "without and before book," and which displays "peaceful texts from Scripture on the wall" (3.11.618), the "latest Gospel according to Monotony" (2.1.268) prevails to empty the New Testament of meaning. Providing no anti-dote to the ridiculous "Adventures of Little Margery" and the darkly commercial "experiences of Thomas Twopence" (263) are the reading lessons out of the New Testament: "by dint of stumbling over the syllables and keeping their be-wildered eyes on the particular syllables coming round to their turn, [the pupils] were as absolutely ignorant of the sublime history, as if they had never seen or heard of it"—which, of course, they have not, for these texts are "jumbled" into bits of sound, like the shattered crockery and bone in the Mounds. Every Sun-day night, the children are addressed "for a mortal hour" by a "chief execu-tioner": "drawling on to My Dearerr Childerrenerr, let us say, for example, about the beautiful coming to the Sepulchre; and repeating the word Sepulchre (commonly used among infants) five hundred times, and never once hinting what it meant," while an assisting "acolyte" darts at the sleeping infants and wakes them up, "as an infallible commentary" (264–65). The Baptist *Freeman*'s complaint that Dickens' attack on "feeding . . . children with ill-digested scraps of biblical lore" was "a wretched attempt to caricature a Sunday School"[10] missed Dickens' satiric points about the fractured Code in a Scav-enger Age: in an age without God, where (as Carlyle said) soul is synonymous with stomach, the Bible is nothing but "scraps" among other scraps and cannot bring meaning or people to life. Like this preacher's ineffectual Easter Story, Charley's first two scriptural allusions suggest as much.[11] When Mortimer asks this errand boy whether efforts were made to determine if the drowned Harmon could be restored to life, Charley answers in devalued biblical code: "You wouldn't ask, sir, if you knew his state. Pharaoh's multitude that were drowned in the Red Sea, ain't more beyond restoring to life. If Lazarus was only half as far gone, that was the greatest of all the miracles" (1.3.61). To the reader who knows the plot outcome, the allusion to Lazarus is stably ironic, for Harmon will come back from the dead (though by no miracle); but to Charley, its jocular use in the context of Mortimer's serious, hopeful question suggests the child's materialist disbelief in miraculous restorations in "these times of ours," whatever may have happened in Bible times—the dead are dead for good. Ironically, although Charley through reading has become biblically knowledgeable—"at home in the Red Sea," as Mortimer says—his views on life and death (and later, scavenging in Society) are not far from his father's river notions at home: "What world does a dead man belong to? T'other world. What world does money belong to? This world. How can money be a corpse's? Can a corpse own it, want it, spend it, claim it, miss it?" (1.1.47). Although even Gaffer Hexam, articulating the catechism of his trade here, seems to believe in an afterlife (unlike the younger generation), an eternal perspective has no restorative bearing on his views of this life, where corpses are fair game for birds of prey moving over the face of the waters. Indeed, his language of otherworldly belief helps to sanction this-worldly crimes. And for Charley, "becoming civilized" means learning only to "ea[t] one another" (4.17.888) in more genteel acts of cannibalism, such as consuming his sister and then the teacher with whom he had read the spiritually defunct tale of Lazarus at school.

The biblical words displayed in the speech of these characters are "like inscriptions over the graves of dead businesses" on the Thames (1.14.219), for in this novel Christianity has gone out of business for Mammon's sake. The new problem in *Our Mutual Friend* is that so many of Dickens' own religious allusions have also become but dead quotations, bits of authoritative discourse that have no dialogic relation to other voices in the novel; nor does the new Mammonism explain why the Word has become to Dickens "an object, a *relic*, a *thing*"[12] merely to be displayed.

Certainly this problem is symptomatic of the larger one that Henry James identified, if exaggerated, in his infamous 1865 *Nation* review of *Our Mutual Friend*: "the conduct of the story," he said, meaning "no compliment," "betrays a long-practised hand."[13] What we find in many of the examples I have given are not fresh borrowings from Scripture indicating Dickens' own dialogic engagement with its meaning, but mere imitations of his own earlier manner. While more extensive in this story of mistaken identity and baptismal self-renewal than I have indicated,[14] Dickens' many plays on the catechism questions "What is your Name?" and "Who gave you this Name?" (*BCP* 321) are really replays from *Bleak House*'s more imaginative uses of the motif. (Its utter vacuity in the later novel is dully summed up by King George the Third's reported words, "What, what, what? Who, who, who? Why, why, why?"; 1.10.164.) The

Mammon-worship inversions of Scripture texts had abounded with more point and humor in *Little Dorrit*'s satire. The perversions of Prayer Book ritual had found more extensive, and more damning, treatment in *Dombey and Son;* Dickens had similarly made sharp satiric points with the liturgy in *Bleak House.* The Gospel according to Monotony we recognize from *Hard Times* and garbled preaching to children from Chadband's orations to Jo. In *Our Mutual Friend,* other familiar biblical phrases come from Dickens' pen—again—as though he was dipping into his inkwell of cultural clichés rather than reaching for parallels with point. There *was* point to be told that Florence Dombey heaped coals of fire on her father's head—the phrase summed up much of that painful relationship; but when the narrator informs us that Fledgeby "proceeded to heap coals of fire on [Twemlow's] sensitive head" (3.13.632), no serious moral or psychological issue is at stake, Twemlow is merely gulled by Fledgeby's speech into feeling guilty, and the tension of St. Paul's counsel to be kind to one's enemies is lost. Equally blunted rather than pointed is the pledge that a reformed Venus will "betake himself to the paths of science, and . . . walk in the same all the days of his life" (3.14.649): the catechism phrase arose naturally in the speech of Captain Cuttle, but it is ill-adapted to the nonreligious idiom of Venus and suddenly makes him dull.

The "long-practised hand" also betrays itself in Dickens' unimaginative uses of biblical types, and here the Famous Author who "knows their tricks and their manners" gets in the way of Dickens the later, subtler psychologist. His Mrs. Lammle is a curious half-realized portrait—she sees through and perpetuates sham, yet has maternal and moral instincts she expresses to her own social harm and finally quells. Dickens lets us glimpse this brief coming-alive of a Society corpse, yet he deadens her unnecessarily by having her bestow on Bella a "Judas order of kiss" (3.5.533), a reference that tells us less than we already know of Sophronia. Jenny's "Oh, you prodigal old son!" (2.2.293—not as amusing as Charles' rechristening John Dickens his "prodigal father") does not tell us anything about the Cleavers' relationship beyond their reversal of roles and the father's waste of three pennyworths on rum; and the Bible model does not even apply, for he is not repentant, and she does not forgive him. It is part of Dickens' subversion of his Christian readers' expectations to make Riah a Good Samaritan ("I cannot pass upon my way and leave you weeping here alone," he says to a "stranger" in the street, 2.15.462).[15] But Dickens carries this idealization too far when he has Riah offer to tend the pummeled Fledgeby because "it is the custom of our people to help." We secretly applaud when Jenny scolds him—"Godmother, godmother, godmother! I really lose all patience with you. One would think you believed in the Good Samaritan"—even though we may

THE PERSON OF THE HOUSE AND THE BAD CHILD
(Marcus Stone)

"Oh, you prodigal old son!" (Jenny Wren, *OMF* 2.2.293)

well be disturbed by her touch of anti-Semitism: "If your people don't know better than to go and help Little Eyes, it's a pity they ever got out of Egypt" (4.9.797). If Dickens was redressing his earlier error of exploiting a Jewish stereotype in *Oliver Twist*, turning Fagin the deceptive Bad Samaritan into Riah the perfectly Good one makes no *literary* advance. Dickens' satiric parable on that "remarkable Christian improvement" of his society, the state's making "a pursuing Fury of the Good Samaritan," asserts a by now mechanical point about "a type of many, many, many" (3.8.569). Quoting from Scripture directly becomes a way of driving his point into the ground, as when he insists it is "worth thinking of, perhaps, my fellow-Christians" that if "the Samaritan had in the lonely night, 'passed by on the other side,' [Betty Higden] would have most devoutly thanked High Heaven for her escape from him" (573). Replete with Samaritanisms, *Our Mutual Friend* (the very title, perhaps, evoking another) masks the further mere repetition of this design as invention in the elaborate case of Noddy Boffin. He poses as the helper of Rokesmith, (twice called "a needy chap that I pick up in the street," 3.15.655), appears to become no generous friend at all in the miser interlude, and turns out genuinely helpful— but at the cost of any of the real imaginative complexity or moral challenge that Dickens had sometimes found in Jesus' parable.

Inevitably in this series of types Bradley Headstone, "under a spell," "chained heavily" to his crime of murder, becomes Cain. But need we be told in a chapter title—and in the overemphasis in Marcus Stone's illustration of Bradley Headstone *in extremis*, with the captioned painting of "Cain and Abel" hung above the self-tormented figure—that it is "Better To Be Abel Than Cain" (4.7)? And in what way is Eugene an Abel except as the victim of a homocidal jealousy? If the point needs to be made that these two characters are "brothers"—like other twins in this novel of split and doubled identities—the stalking of each by the other and the explosion of the murderous deed at the point of Eugene's crisis as he confronts his wicked thoughts far more masterfully establish Headstone as Wrayburn's darker self. (Indeed, to insist on the Abel-Cain *contrast* in a title is to deflect attention from the men's more provocative similarities.) By the time of *Our Mutual Friend*, the association of villains with Cain has become a Dickens tic; the writer is no longer making any imaginative capital of it, as he had in *Great Expectations*. The more one meditates on the parallel in the later novel, the more irrelevant differences appear. The Cain association does become more meaningful in terms of Carlyle's writings: as Barry V. Qualls reminds us, in *Sartor Resartus* Carlyle had called attention to "a whole world of internal Madness" inside each person, which breaks out in Teufelsdröckh when he walks "in the temper of ancient Cain," finding the universe "one huge, dead,

BETTER TO BE ABEL THAN CAIN
(Marcus Stone)

And I shall be a fugitive and a vagabond in the earth; and it shall come to pass, that
every one that findeth me shall slay me. (Gen. 4:14)

immeasurable Steam-engine" (*SR* 127, 133), like the dead world Headstone's mechanical education has made. When Dickens' schoolmaster breaks loose from this routine "like an ill-tamed wild animal" (3.2.609), he becomes Carlyle's Cain, not the Bible's; and when he strikes Eugene, the dilettante metaphorically confronts "his own Cain-like selfishness."[16] If Qualls' literary detective work tells us much about Dickens' literary source of inspiration (Byron, too, should be considered even if Dickens, like Carlyle, disparaged him), it also illustrates how little the details of this biblical paradigm apparently meant to Dickens at this point in his career. It also suggests how sometimes he resorts to a conventional type as though to harness morally the criminal sympathies unleashed through these disturbing characterizations of social violence; their origins can be safely anchored in the legend of Cain and Abel.

Within the complex, multiperspectival world of *Our Mutual Friend*, these conventional formulas, like others in the satire, serve as the proverbial "fingerpost" (4.13.846) telling us which way our judgment of characters should go. The problem is that they reduce Mrs. Lammle, Mr. Dolls, Eugene Wrayburn, and Bradley Headstone to biblical caricature. In such cases we see that the Word reduced to "the mere word is not to the purpose" (1.10.172) of interesting us in these figures, although Dickens' earlier, more imaginative engagements with biblical models could do so (for example, Esther Summerson as Queen Esther and Job). Thus we cannot know or care much about Dolls as an ironic Prodigal Son; he *does* shock us into belief in him with his own muddled "I am NOT mere child, sir. Man. Man talent" (3.10.603). It is just such revealing speech and the intricately woven lengths of prose Dickens gives us around his biblical signs that interest us in these lives. As we become more concerned with knowing than with judging them, the moral points become muted; indeed, we wonder at times in this novel where the moral grounding has gone. Because Dickens as psychologist does want us to know these creatures as they are, his reversion to familiar biblical types in this late, multivocal fiction makes them sound against the backdrop of more nuanced voices like dead or dying quotations, words that do not resonate. Like Riah's quaint speech, they are "ghosts of a departed Time"— that fictive age when moral values were simpler, perhaps—before the collecting of the dust heaps had commenced.

2

OUR MUTUAL FRIEND is about ends and new beginnings. Near the close of chapter 2 of book 1, when Mortimer believes he has finished his desultory story of

"The Man from Somewhere" or Nowhere, who is expected to complete the fairy-tale by inheriting a fortune, a paper "arrives in an extraordinarily opportune manner" bearing news of the real conclusion. "The story is completer and rather more exciting than I supposed," Mortimer declares. "Man's drowned!" (59). To the Society chorus and their storyteller, this ending comes as a relief amid dull after-dinner talk; life has seemed to offer a more complete sense of closure than the weary Mortimer had been able to bring off in his fiction. Dickens' irony, of course, is that this Lazarus found drowned will come back from the grave to defeat, at least symbolically, the illusions of a money world so dead that it craves a sensational story. And Harmon's symbolic "rebirth," along with Bella's dying to worldly ambitions and Eugene's reformation, are meant to signal, as Andrew Sanders writes, Dickens' belief in "the individual's potential for re-generation and . . . his ability to overcome the social ills to which he is heir."[17] But this is not the only story Dickens tells in *Our Mutual Friend*. Mortimer's "real-life" ending, which happily turns out a fiction, could have been simply true; after all, the real power of Harmon's later version of the story is the sense of mortal danger it conveys in his struggle with mercenary assassins and the muddy Thames—with the worldly and earthy powers that would have obliter-ated the text of his life. Harmon nearly did drown; others really do. From the novel's first narrated death scene to its last, its single resonating Bible subtext for the darker parable Dickens tells—"for dust thou art, and unto dust shalt thou return" (Gen. 3:19)—threatens to "usur[p] the places of the peaceful texts from Scripture" (3.11.618) that he so prominently displays as moral pointers and that underlie his plots of human regeneration.

We sense this threat, for example, in the way Dickens destabilizes his own moral parable of Gaffer Hexam's merited end. As Qualls points out, "The novel opens 'emblematically' with the modern age's version of a fisher of men . . . hunting for dead bodies with coin on them."[18] Such stable ironies are a familiar form of demonic inversion in Dickens; they do not necessarily disprove a pro-vidential universe, in which the providential novelist will "Kill Gaffer re-tributively" (Dickens' plan for Number 4).[19] When this grisly fisherman en-tangles himself in his own lines and his corpse becomes his last prey, we are to see as "tremendous" a "punishment" as that reserved for John Harmon's mur-derer: "but it was not of my bringing about," Harmon says. " 'Of whose then?' asked Pleasant. The man pointed upwards with his forefinger, and, slowly re-covering that hand, settled his chin in it again as he looked at the fire" (2.12.411). But this stable reading of Hexam's death Dickens then works to destabilize in an extraordinary passage immediately following the discovery of the body:

Soon, the form of the bird of prey, dead some hours, lay stretched upon the shore, with a new blast storming at it and clotting the wet hair with hailstones.

Father, was that you calling me? Father! I thought I heard you call me twice before! Words never to be answered, those, upon the earth-side of the grave. The wind sweeps jeeringly over Father, whips him with the frayed ends of his dress and his jagged hair, tries to turn him where he lies stark on his back, and force his face towards the rising sun, that he may be shamed the more. A lull, and the wind is secret and prying with him; lifts and lets fall a rag; hides palpitating under another rag; runs nimbly through his hair and beard. Then, in a rush, it cruelly taunts him. Father, was that you calling me? Was it you, the voiceless and the dead? Was it you, thus buffeted as you lie here in a heap? Was it you, thus baptized unto Death, with these flying impurities now flung upon your face? Why not speak, Father? Soaking into this filthy ground as you lie here, is your own shape. Did you never see such a shape soaked into your boat? Speak, Father. Speak to us, the winds, the only listeners left you! (1.14.221–22)

In this passage, all the Burial Service Hexam will have, Dickens shifts between a reportorial, curiously detached, and even playful voice (with which he also describes corpses in "Travelling Abroad"), the solemn overtones of the moral parabler, and Lizzie's elegy of inconsolable loss—the wail of all "anxious worried women," as in Eliot's *The Dry Salvages*, whose men are lost at sea: "And the ground swell, that is and was from the beginning, / Clangs / The bell." To Lizzie thinking earlier of her father's suspected guilt, "the great black river with its dreary shores" had stretched "away to the great ocean, Death" (1.6.115). Now, in the unfatherly care of the elements, Hexam pays the due of the curse in his name, but it is not only his text: distress, as he had said, "is for ever a going about, like sut in the air," and its cause remains a question that Lizzie's elegiac cry reopens even as Dickens' moral design would close it. As Gaffer asks, "Have we got a pest in the house? Is there summ'at deadly sticking to my clothes? What's let loose upon us? Who loosed it?" (119, 121). The Fall text from Genesis 3:19 that Rogue Riderhood is always recalling, as well as the Cain story the narrator insists upon, would contain the curse by explaining it;[20] but *Our Mutual Friend*'s preoccupation with "dust" in the biblical sense—its repeated reminders that all "are living and must die" (3.3.503), that there is "one sure termination" of manifold human ends (4.11.822)—suggests that Dickens remains unconsoled by such traditional resignations. Gaffer Hexam's baptism "unto Death, with these flying impurities now flung upon [his] face," reverses the hopeful promises of Romans 6:4 with which Dickens underwrites his rebirth parable. Death is and was from the beginning everyone's mutual "friend," and no morally certain ending of justice served when fathers die can stay the encroachments of that close, sedimentary, silent community.

At the other end of the novel and the moral scale is Betty Higden's pious deathbed "at the foot of the Cross" (3.8.575). Dickens counterposes to "the laws of the physical world" that bring on "the shadow of advancing Death" the grace of "all the Light that shone on Betty Higden," which "lay beyond Death" (566). Yet here again Dickens' shifting style of presentation fosters a curiously unstable reading, which offers several interpretations of her end, never really works out the religious one, and brings Betty's story under the advancing shadow of the darker parable. Although Lizzie as the Victorian Angel of Death will lift the old woman "as high as Heaven" (577), Betty is on a "pilgrimage" (574) not to the promised land but to "Death" (repeatedly capitalized), as though the "end" she seeks to gain (574) is only the shrine erected to this dark god; the aim to "die independent"—a meaningful phrase for the old woman fleeing the indignities of state charity, yet surely a heavily ironic juxtaposition of words—preoccupies her thought more than union with God in heaven. Even though she reaches her goal, the substance we are to assign her expressions of faith in the "Lord" who "will see [her] through it!" (574) begins to evaporate with Dickens the psychologist's emphasis on Betty's diseased imagination and his account of the "visionary hands" and voices that lead her on her journey (574)—are they heaven-sent or hallucination? The scene where she finds her "journey's end," the "great building, full of lighted windows" near "a plantation of trees" (574), presents through her eyes the iconography of the Celestial City[21] as merely a place to die. While the narrator sees the upper Thames "dimpled like a young child, playfully gliding . . . unpolluted by the defilements that lie in wait for it on its course," Betty's vision of the river is defiled by her morbidity: she hears "the tender river whispering to many like herself, 'Come to me, come to me! . . . I am the Relieving Officer appointed by eternal ordinance to do my work. . . . My breast is softer than the pauper-nurse's; death in my arms is peacefuller than among the pauper-wards. Come to me!'" (567). The grisly echo of Matthew 11:28 here calls attention to the discrepancy between this voice, which Betty hears, and another, which is silent in her world: "Come unto me, all ye that labour and are heavy laden, and I will give you rest." Like old Harmon taking "precautions against his coming to life" (1.2.58), like his son unwilling to surface and burying himself under "heaped mounds upon mounds of earth" (2.13.435), like Jenny Wren inviting others to "Come up and be dead," like Headstone forcing Riderhood to "Come down!" to a watery grave (4.15.874), Betty in her simpler way longs only to die—"like us all, every day of our lives when we wake . . . instinctively unwilling to be restored to the consciousness of this existence, and [desiring] to be left dormant" if we could (3.5.505).

Even Betty's "gentler fancies" are polluted by the "bitterness" the narrator claims she never feels and Dickens cannot let her express because, as a Christian foil to public charity's perversion of Christianity, Betty must be charitable. But it is hard to articulate a Christian ideal in her circumstances. The narrative voice falters as Dickens' anger at the injustice of her death creeps into her rendered thoughts; the juxtaposition of this voice with her charitable constructions suggests inadvertently that beneath them anger *is* there in Betty: "Those gentlefolks and their children inside those fine houses, could they think, as they looked out at her, what it was to be really hungry, really cold? . . . Bless the dear laughing children! . . . If they could have seen dead Johnny on that little bed, would they have understood it? . . . 'Ah me! The dead and I seem to have it pretty much to ourselves in the dark and in this weather! But so much the better for all who are warmly housed at home!'" (567–68). Dickens' finally enclosing her thoughts in quotation marks, in a passage where they were earlier rendered without such typographical signals, does not solve the problem; the anger seeps through, making the charitable constructions less credible. But even as the entrée of the social reformer's voice exposes something about the Betty Higdens of this world he would rather not see, his language contains, even covers up, something else: the "horror" of Betty's suicidal longing, which is called a "horror of falling into the hands of Charity" (569) rather than into the postlapsarian human condition—"the vast blank misery of a life suspected" (1.6.115) that her plight suggests (and her "innocence" protests) in a fictional world so palpably fallen.

At such recurrent cruxes, Dickens' narrator typically retreats from metaphysical (and theological) problems. Cryptically Milvey does this for him at Johnny's funeral: "Some of the Reverend Frank Milvey's brethren had found themselves exceedingly uncomfortable in their minds, because they were required to bury the dead too hopefully. But, the Reverend Frank, inclining to the belief that they were required to do one or two other things (say out of nine-and-thirty) calculated to trouble their consciences rather more if they would think as much about them, held his peace" (2.10.386). Now, at Betty's funeral, Dickens would remind us of the "other things" we are to think of in this world rather than the Four Last Things: "'WE GIVE THEE HEARTY THANKS FOR THAT IT HATH PLEASED THEE TO DELIVER THIS OUR SISTER OUT OF THE MISERIES OF THIS SINFUL WORLD.' So read the Reverend Frank Milvey in a not untroubled voice, for his heart misgave him that all was not quite right between us and our . . .

sister in Law—Poor Law" (3.9.577). But even as he is making his social points
about the Poor Law, Dickens destabilizes the Burial Service as a rite of consolation and reads even the hopes raised by Betty's faith in "the Power and the
Glory" in a "not untroubled voice." For if the rite's words are set in small
capitals literally to enlarge their ironic inappropriateness to her end (despite *her*
"HEARTY THANKS" for the grace to "die independent"), the irony is at the Prayer
Book's (and Betty's) expense, not only at society's; the otherworldly words of the
Church, directed to a God "PLEASED" with her death, deflect attention from
remediable injustice in "THIS SINFUL WORLD," another religious phrase that
seems to valorize the status quo. Christian hope in the afterlife is further put in
question by the narrator's interpretation of the simple, heartfelt response of
Sloppy, who cannot "in his conscience as yet find the hearty thanks required of
it" by faith (577). If Betty's example is to tell us that "God is good" (1.16.246),
the story of her end is so constructed as to remind us of the social, material, and
perhaps cosmic forces that are not good, that also baptize her "unto Death."
Shifting between the mediating perspectives of the psychologist, the social reformer, and the believer, Dickens presents this "Respected Friend in More Aspects Than One" (title, 3.3), as he presents nearly everything in this novel;
within its play of meanings, the religious is only one among several possible
interpretations. It is one associated, moreover, with the "illogical . . . and
light-hearted" thinking (574) of an old woman who does not belong to, is destroyed by, "these times of ours," and whose faith like Riah's may be but the
"ghost of a departed Time."

"Though they do not express orthodox Christian doctrine," J. Hillis Miller
has written, "Dickens' novels are religious in that they demand the regeneration
of man and society through contact with something transcending the merely
human."[22] Amid the worldly and the earthy, Dickens engages his readers in
scanning the general panoramic view for "tokens" and "appearances" of such a
transforming power. Several critics have suggested Romans 6:3–4 as Dickens'
text for the parable of regeneration in *Our Mutual Friend*, a text at the heart of
the baptismal rite: "Know ye not, that so many of us as were baptized into Jesus
Christ were baptized into his death? Therefore we are buried with him by baptism into death: that like as Christ was raised up from the dead by the glory of
the Father, even so we also should walk in newness of life."[23] But in this novel,
Dickens' baptismal pattern serves no biblical end: just as *Our Mutual Friend*
asks the catechism questions but does not give the catechism answers, so the
need of its mired world for the transcendent is met by a wholly human perception about processes of change brought about by wholly human means, not by
the mutual "friend of all who were afflicted and forlorn," as Amy Dorrit calls

Jesus (*LD* 2.31.770).[24] The novel's problem, according to Miller, is "how to assume death into life—without simply and literally dying,"[25] especially since dying unto death can bring no certainty of eternal life, only relief from pain (see 2.9.384). Behind that is the problem of interpretation continually posed in this fictional world of tricky surfaces and ambiguous depths: what is genuine life, as opposed to the many forms of life in death?—another way of asking after ends. Undoubtedly, Dickens' baptismal motif is far more extensive here than in *Dombey and Son*. But in *Our Mutual Friend* even Dickens' secular reading of the Order of Baptism, which means different things for characters so variously reanimated, does not provide the stable text wanted in the face of "dust"; and while the rebirth pattern in Dickens' main plots borrows some of the poetry of religion, his over-insistence on the baptismal symbolism only calls attention to the ways fact is failing the traditional Christian paradigm.

From the opening chapter's introduction to the vocation of making one's "living" from the quirky corpses in the river, Dickens invites his readers into continual acts of discriminating who and what is dead or alive. The Veneerings might be alive if they were not so emphatically "bran-new people" (1.2.48) and did not have an Analytical retainer whose mournful sighing "such is life!" (49) suggests, instead, "such is death!" With Lady Tippins' "grisly little fiction" (54) of her eternal youth and Podsnap's "fatal freshness" (50), with Sophronia Lammle's false "it imparts new life to me, to see my Alfred in confidential communication with Mr. Boffin" (4.2.707), even with Twemlow's astonished "and I AM!" (2.3.296), we are in the realm of Dickens' stable ironies, by which he instructs us in the ways Society's dead take on the mere appearances of life. Like Pleasant Riderhood's "Sweet delusion" that "the old evil is drowned out of" her father when he falls into the river (3.3.506, 505), these characters only imagine their forms of revival and immortality; and the Social Chorus exists to keep up such fictions among mutual friends.

With other characters, however, we experience some of the genuine suspense and mystery of Riderhood's rescuers as he wavers between the realms of the living and the dead:

> Stay! Did that eyelid tremble? . . .
> No.
> Did that nostril twitch? . . .
> Over and over again No. No. But try over and over again, nevertheless.
> See! A token of life! An indubitable token of life! . . .
> He is struggling to come back. Now, he is almost here, now he is far away again.
> Now he is struggling harder to get back. (504–5)

In scene after scene, we watch Boffin, Harmon, Bella, and Eugene for signs of their coming to life; through these uncertainties of interpretation Dickens would have us learn to discard the fatal illusions of the money world for the "true golden gold" of the living "heart" (4.13.843). But just as Riderhood in this scene does come back, and with the new superstition upon him that he "can't be drowned" (4.1.702), so these four central characters achieve through their varying brushes with "death" not only new knowledge but a kind of fairytale invulnerability to further drowning, to the social and material forces "with a thirst for sucking them under" (1.14.219). All instabilities are stabilized in their mutual happy endings. If Dickens has decomposed the world, in U. C. Knoepflmacher's terms, he has recomposed it in an ideal design, "the 'nowhere' of symbol, myth, and fairy tale."[26] But as "once upon a time" casts out "These times of ours,"[27] Dickens thwarts his own serious intentions by locating his ideal outside the actualities of a novel he has himself problematized—despite the advance he had made in finding his Ideal in the Actual in *Little Dorrit* and incorporating this paradox into its ending.

In *Our Mutual Friend*'s comic extended version of the deathbed watch, we observe Noddy Boffin come alive, go dead, and come alive again. From our first view of him, with his "overlapping rhinocerous build" giving the appearance of sheer materiality (1.5.90), we see a character who longs for transcendence and renewal: "Print" is what "open[s]" up his world, for "This night, a literary man—*with* a wooden leg" (material, yet textual) "will begin to lead me a new life!" (97). Boffin's association with the biblical Nicodemus, to whom Jesus gave his famous explanation of spiritual rebirth in answer to the question, "How can a man be born when he is old?" (see John 3:1–8),[28] becomes only spuriously ironic as his story unfolds: the Golden Dustman, dying the death of the rich and taking up the new self of fortune (3.5.525), seems to "Fal[l] into Bad Company" and "Worse Company" (titles, 3.5 and 6), reaches "His Worst" (title, 15), "Rises a Little" and "Sinks Again" (titles, 4.2 and 3), and finally "Help[s] to Scatter Dust" (title, 13) after all. His is a wholly readable story, achieving only apparent complexity (and a spurious "rebirth" of what has never died). When he turns miserly, "A kind of illegibility . . . stole over Mr. Boffin's face" (3.5.534), but when he returns to the "high simplicity" of his real self, "all those crooked lines of suspicion, avarice, and distrust" dissolve into "the shining countenance of Mr. Boffin" (4.13.839) blessing all.

John Harmon's case parallels Boffin's because he, too, only pretends to be "dead" and "reborn." Harmon comes back from his fourteen-year exile as though from the dead, "timid, divided in my mind, afraid of myself and everybody here" (2.13.423). In this state he has come close to death, as he will again literally in his fall into the Thames. These are not, however, the deaths from which he is said to be "reborn." The pattern upon which so many interpretations of this novel are founded requires Harmon to descend also into his own depths—"an impersonal and anonymous realm" like the water, in Miller's words, where he loses "all sense" of "distinct identit[y]"—and, through this "drowning" of the Old Adam, to emerge the better man.[29] H. M. Daleski argues that Harmon baptized in the Thames "lets go, as it were, of a divided self whose will to live has been sapped"; this "profound spiritual experience" is then "confirmed" by his decision to renounce the fortune, which indicates "the consolidation of his newly accepted values."[30] Perhaps this is the moral design Dickens had in mind; but it is not quite the story he tells. Harmon's fall into the Thames is a merely physical struggle for survival in which he regains, rather than loses, consciousness of self, and then at one remove: he is still alienated from himself in crying, "This is John Harmon drowning! John Harmon . . . call on Heaven and save yourself!" (2.13.426). His recognition of his double is merely a plot detail; it signals no self-recognition, as Eugene's parallel case does, for Harmon has no shadow. The decision to go underground is undertaken because of new reinforcement of "the moral timidity that dates from my childhood," as he says (427), not out of a new sense of purpose; and the resolve to stay as dead as everyone thinks he is seems more the response of a weak man to social pressure than the determination of a newly strong one to take on the moneyed world. Emerging from near-death only to "die" to others' knowledge for ill-considered reasons, Harmon finds he has "now to begin life" as "Rokesmith," but assuming a false identity is not in itself walking "in newness of life."

In the plot, the rebirth pattern for Harmon means even less than it does in Boffin's sham case, because with this noncomic character we sense that Dickens might have done so much more, especially given his new subtleties of psychological analysis elsewhere in this novel. This "living-dead man" (2.13.430) has wonderfully paradoxical lines ("I have no clue to the scene of my death," 422), and bizarre moments of disorientation disturb his double life: "looking into a churchyard on a wild windy night," he feels that he "no more hold[s] a place among the living than these dead do," and knows that he lies "buried somewhere else, as they lie buried here. Nothing uses me to it. A spirit that was once a man could hardly feel stranger or lonelier, going unrecognized among mankind, than I feel" (422). Dickens tempts the reader's speculation when he endows Harmon with such a consciousness; but although he writes "something" into Harmon's face that tells of his "terrible strait" (1.16.242), somehow Dickens cannot get past this legible surface. The whole Harmon story reads like an extended Memoranda Book note (an idea for a character rather than the "real thing"). Dickens has outlined an interesting psychological condition, but he never explores it here as he had in an earlier Nobody figure, Arthur Clennam, whom Harmon superficially resembles. We never see the man "divided in . . . mind" that Harmon merely tells us of, as we see Clennam wrestling with self-division; we never understand why Harmon urges himself so portentously not to "evade" reconstructing his story (423), or why the apparently noble decision that "John Harmon shall come back no more" (430) is not evasion of another kind—of a sort more than hinted by the vehement self-alienation of his rhetoric, "Cover him, crush him, keep him down!" after Bella's refusal of her hand (435; Clennam's self-repression crosses with Bradley Headstone's passion here). Dickens never explores the reasons for Harmon's reluctance to come to life because the author must preserve the purity of his hero's motives toward the Boffins and the much-tried Bella; Harmon must not have, like Eugene, "wicked thoughts."

Dickens' reluctance to explore his own conception voids the whole baptismal paradigm of its meaning, for Harmon's experience of such "horror" (428) should have fostered some deeper self-understanding but does not. Nancy Aycock Metz argues that in telling his own story, he saves himself through "articulation," pieces his words "together coherently and so regain[s] a sense of who he is": his efforts, she writes, "stand as a model at the novel's heart and center of the peace that can be gained through dispassionate self-questioning, patience, and discipline willingly entered into."[31] The narrator seems to support this therapy when he tells us that what Harmon seeks is "the power of knowledge; the power derivable from a perfect comprehension of his business" (1.16.241). But in a novel that fragments perspectives on the truth and insists upon mysteries of life and death, there can be no "perfect comprehension of his business"; and in Harmon's articulating what is chiefly an interpolated story of adventure and detection, there seems little enough anyway—save questions of times and places confused then—to *understand* in "th[inking it] out, from the beginning to the end" (430), in encircling all in a stable pattern. At the end of this entirely silent soliloquy, Harmon—who has never questioned himself as Bella has, and who suppresses more than disciplines himself—buries his text under mountains of dust. The Inspector may exclaim upon hearing Harmon's secret, "what a game was this to try the sort of stuff a man's opinion of himself was made of!" (4.12.832), yet the hero is never really on trial, except in the later scene staged for Bella's more convincing renewal. In spite of his emergence from underground at the close of the story, Harmon remains "nobody, . . . and not likely to be known" (1.8.140), least of all by himself.

If in Harmon's story we sense a factitious rebirth pattern that yields no new understanding of human depths, only substitutes for their exploration, in Eugene's regeneration we have a more suspenseful and convincing account. This character, who begins "buried alive in the back of his chair" (1.2.53)—a sign of his dormancy if also his potential for dying to the Society world—displays slight tokens of better life that we watch with interest as his story develops. Dickens' lethargic gentleman-sinner will not "Turn or Burn," but he begins to make his "Turning" (title, book 4) when he tells Lizzie, "You don't know how the cursed carelessness that is over-officious in helping me at every other turning of my life, WON'T help me here. You have struck it dead, I think, and I sometimes almost wish you had struck me dead along with it" (4.6.760). But he needs more than her disturbing presence in his world: he too must be ritually baptized unto death to find life—"In an instant with a dreadful crash, the reflected night turned crooked, flames shot jaggedly across the air, and the moon and stars came bursting from the sky. Was he struck by lightning?" (767). Qualls points out the probable Carlylean background for this event, Teufelsdröckh's "Baphometic Fire-baptism": "The Everlasting No had said: 'Behold, thou art fatherless, outcast, and the Universe is mine (the Devil's)'; to which my whole Me now made answer: '*I* am not thine, but Free, and forever hate thee!' It is from this hour that I incline to date my Spiritual Newbirth . . . ; perhaps I directly thereupon began to be a Man" (*SR* 135). Teufelsdröckh awakens "to a new Heaven and a new Earth"; Wrayburn, to Jenny's fancies of flower scents and songbirds. But as Qualls observes, this is hardly Carlyle's godlike universe, merely a fanciful projection of belief[32] in the domestic setting where Dickens typically realizes apocalyptic hope. Like Dombey with Florence, Wrayburn merely believes in Lizzie, who has the power of all such women in Dickens, as Eugene says, to "recall me!" (824) to some tentative belief. "I shall find out that my husband has a mine of purpose and energy, and will turn it to the best account?" Lizzie asks. "'I hope so, dearest Lizzie,' said Eugene, wistfully, and yet somewhat whimsically. 'I hope so. But I can't summon the vanity to think so. How can I think so, looking back on such a trifling wasted youth as mine! I humbly hope it; but I daren't believe it. There is a sharp misgiving in my conscience that if I were to live, I should disappoint your good opinion and my own—and that I ought to die, my dear!' " (825). If this passage modulates from the wistful and whimsical to the morbid, it conveys at least that uncertainty of tone we know in Eugene; he is confessedly, now, a member of the human race as Reverend Frank Milvey sees the lot—"all a halting, failing, feeble, and inconstant crew" (3.9.578). Dickens largely abandons this more realistic vision of an imperfect character's redemption only when Eugene mends to become a "resurrection man" who can press upon Mortimer fervent cliché: "In turning to at last, we turn to in earnest" (4.16.885).

To claim as Robert S. Baker does that Eugene "embodies the pattern of spir-

EUGENE'S BEDSIDE
(Marcus Stone)

"Stay and help to nurse me," said Eugene [to Jenny Wren], quietly. "I should like you to have the fancy here, before I die." (*OMF* 4.10.807)

itual development that underlies the novel's complex and episodic surface and that helps to shape the crowded events of Dickens' masterpiece into a unified whole"[33] is surely to exaggerate both the happy results of Eugene's cure and the literary power of his story within the novel, while unnecessarily assuming that there need be such a single privileged pattern for this work to be a "masterpiece." On the other side, it seems not quite fair to find, with Robert Garis, that Eugene's rebirth is only "a tastefully managed diagram of symbolic intention,"[34] although the Marcus Stone illustration Dickens approved is precisely such a diagram of the edifying deathbed, the enthroned dying one surrounded by prayerful, attentive figures (notably, female Alpha and Omega figures at head and foot). Although we may wish for more demonstration, Eugene's change is the most convincing in the novel;[35] it is even more so than Bella's, whose independent wit finally lapses into "mysterious disappearances" (in Harmon's embrace, her "last resting-place"; 3.16.674, 671) and who gets back in the end all she has renounced, stamped with the guarantee that wealth can no longer corrupt her.[36] On his sickbed, Eugene may seem "less sexual partner than dependent patient for his working-class bride," as Deirdre David believes,[37] but he is not a stuffed Husband for Wife, like Venus' canary—"There's animation! On a twig, making up his mind to hop! Take care of him; he's a lovely specimen" (1.7.125). In Eugene's last scene with Mortimer, he regains some of his old animation in his chaffing talk about "M.R.F." and "our Tippins" (4.16.884–85). His earnestness is strained, like that of a man in a fever, but even Lizzie can twit him about looking "flushed" and talking Society talk, while Eugene finds a way of keeping up his "old airy manner" even with her (886). If our belief in his reformation through her influence is weakened, it is chiefly because Dickens idealizes the working-class woman (who can recite Prayer Book English while rowing at top speed to rescue her lover) rather than because Dickens has failed to make Eugene "a Man."

If Bella must confront the lustful self that does not "improve upon acquaintance" (3.9.583), in order to recover her true depths of feeling, and if Eugene must see his "thoughts" of "wickedness" starting up "unbidden" from the deep (4.6.766), the encounter with the depths does not always have such beneficent effect in *Our Mutual Friend*. Bradley Headstone intimates this darker parable when he says to Lizzie, " 'No man knows till the time comes what depths are within him. To some men it never comes; let them rest and be thankful! To me, you brought it; on me, you forced it; and the bottom of this raging sea,' striking himself upon the breast, 'has been heaved up ever since' " (2.15.454). With Headstone, Dickens explores the dark side of the rebirth paradigm, for (to borrow words for Eugene) the "frequent rising of [this] drowning man from the deep, to sink again" is "dreadful" to behold throughout his part of the story (4.10.810). By letting go of his schoolteacher identity, false to begin with, Headstone unleashes the animal. For him there is no Christian renewal, no re-articulation in the unified self of Jungian belief; there can be only a suicidal baptism unto a death that ends his torment.

Meanwhile, as these voided or variously efficacious rites of immersion go forward, underwritten by a New Testament text that Dickens has wholly secularized, "sheer matter shows through," in Miller's words[38]—through the novel's fictions of living and of believing that can effect only provisional forms of transcendence. "Whence can [the dust] come," the narrator asks in the old Ecclesiastian manner, "whither can it go?" (1.12.191; cf. Ecc. 1:6). The human world is encompassed by the nonhuman, for the dust moves from nowhere to nowhere; all one has is the time between. If "The wind sawed, and the sawdust whirled" about in the "hopeless city . . . invested by the great Marsh Forces of Essex and Kent," the reader of the sky in *Our Mutual Friend* who follows this pointing finger upward does not find any hopeful tokens there: "wild disorder" of clouds blown by wind reigns (1.12.204); "the sun itself" seen "through circling eddies of fog, showed as if it had gone out and were collapsing flat and cold" (3.1.479); above the necropolis of London, there can be seen "no rent in the leaden canopy of its sky" (191), or if "a ragged tear of light" should rip "the dark clouds," all they show is "a great grey hole of day" (1.14.219). In the unfatherly care of these elements, those not granted the poetry of religion or a visionary belief find church towers only as "dark and dingy as the sky that seems descending on them, . . . no relief to the general gloom" (2.15.450), while amid a "foggy sea, . . . the great dome of Saint Paul's seem[s] to die hard" (3.1.479).

3

WHEN MR. WEGG, "in a hospitable glow" that is all delusion, greets Venus, "you come, brother . . . shedding a halo all around you," he is asked to explain what kind of halo he means: " 'Ope, sir. That's *your* halo." But Mr. Venus appears "doubtful on the point, and looked rather discontentedly at the fire" (3.6.538–39). In *Our Mutual Friend* Dickens tells the dark parable of Genesis 3:19 and writes over it a fictional pattern of renewal in which readers like the doubtful Venus cannot wholly believe. Yet, against the general panoramic view of dust and descending gloom, churches that are dead or monstrous, the blank sky, "the voiceless and the dead," Dickens sets "a child—a dwarf—a girl—a

MORE DEAD THAN ALIVE
(Marcus Stone)

For dust thou art, and to dust shalt thou return. (Gen. 3:19)

something" (2.1.271) who can see more and witness to what she sees. To Garrett Stewart, Jenny Wren personifies the Romantic idea: she is one who has been baptized by the imagination to transcend, even if in glimpses, her own condition "of the world, worldly" and "of the earth, earthy" (2.2.294).[39] What do we make of this claim, as well as others for Jenny as a religious figure? Jenny's most radiant text is her version of the "Come unto me" passage—her beatific vision of "the children that I used to see early in the morning," unlike herself or the poor and the cruel children she knows: "All in white dresses, and with something shining on the borders, and on their heads. . . . They used to come down *in long bright slanting rows*, and say all together, 'Who is this in pain! Who is this in pain!' When I told them who it was, they answered, 'Come and play with us!' When I said 'I never play! I can't play!' they swept about me and took me up, and made me light. Then it was all delicious ease and rest till they laid me down, and said, all together, 'Have patience, and we will come again.' . . . And I used to cry out, 'O my blessed children, it's poor me. Have pity on me. Take me up and make me light!' " (2.2.290, emphasis added). If Jenny's vision reminds of popular religious prints of Jacob's dream,[40] her own intense energy of imagination has transformed conventional iconography into a personal revelation that makes her face "light" in the retelling and sheds light even for Eugene Wrayburn. From within the "golden bower" of her beautiful hair, her halo of " 'ope," Jenny can call forth imaginative worlds that lift her "so high" above the sordid thoroughfares of getting and spending that she sees a transcendent plane of meaning: as she tells Fledgeby on the rooftop of Pubsey and Company, "And you see the clouds rushing on above the narrow streets, not minding them, and you see the golden arrows pointing at the mountains in the sky from which the wind comes, and you feel as if you were dead" (2.5.334; see illustration on chapter title page).

In striking contrast to Marcus Stone's realistic drawing of the city view from the rooftop, with its lines of dismal chimney smoke drifting skyward, the iconography of Jenny's strangely laconic vision sets the earthly below the heavenly city, with the golden arrows in the sky slanting upward (reversing the direction of the children coming "down in long bright slanting rows") to pave the golden streets. In this suggestively "Christian" context, we grasp one meaning of her "dead" in the contrast to Fledgeby in this scene: all he hears is "the City's roar"; all he sees is "the smoke" in the rooftop world and "nothing written on the face of the earth and sky but the three letters L. S. D." (324). Like the world-bound visitor to the city of Tamara in one of Italo Calvino's "Cities and Signs" parables, Fledgeby's gaze "scans the streets as if they were written pages: the city says everything [he] must think, makes [him] repeat her discourse."[41] When Jenny cries to those "down in the dark," "Come up and be dead! Come up and be dead!" (334–35), her incantation sets the terms of freedom from the Mammon world: to "be dead" is to be deaf to the "roar" of the city's signs. In Christian terms, it is dying to this world that Jenny urges on those who rise up to her rooftop, as though "out of [the] grave" (334). Thus, in her invitation to "death" and scorn for being "called back to life" (334), the rebirth paradigm is confirmed in an ironic reconstruction of it, as she overturns the meaning of worldly terms.

What both the "Christian" and the "Romantic" interpretations leave out, however, are the fictive strategies of Jenny Wren's visionary voice (and the ways they show she is not deaf to other voices). However personal, her visions are still too close to conventional iconography to resemble the nonreligious epiphanies in certain modernist fictions; even less are they the integrating moments of *claritas* in the older mystic tradition. More precisely, they are Victorian allusions pointing backward to this tradition, reluctant completely to abandon it but unable to recreate it without calling attention to their own allusiveness by self-conscious literary and pictorial device. Further, even more transparently than the radiant sunset passage in *Little Dorrit*, the vision from Jenny's rooftop is a paradigm of signification, indeed a diagram of it. In its depiction of "golden arrows pointing," it shows she knows their tricks and their manners, those transcendentalists, always gesturing in the direction of the sky (like John Harmon pointing upward and Jenny here "holding up her slight transparent hand," 334). In her diagram, the signified is notably absent, or blocked from view by metonymy ("the mountains" associated with the gods), while what we *see* are the signifiers pointing, observing the human process by which such visions as her earlier more naive one are made. And the arrows now point from earth to heaven instead of coming down to earth. In Dickens' highly self-conscious late novel, Jenny's visions are more like deliberately constructed rescuing texts than spontaneous eruptions of the power of Presence into her world; and to Eugene dying, her picture of the children is only "a pretty fancy" he "should like [her] to have . . . here, before I die" (4.10.807). In later life, that child's vision is also considerably revised by adult awareness. The angels' "Come and play with us!" becomes the ambiguous invitation, issued by Jenny herself, "Come up and be dead," and their unequivocal promise ("we will come again") becomes only uncertain supposition: as she tells Sloppy later, her bridegroom "is coming from somewhere or other, I suppose, and He is coming some day or other, I suppose. *I* don't know any more about him, at present" (4.16.883). Such expectation is finally reduced to an "extraordinarily good joke" shared with Sloppy, if not the grimly humorous mock-apocalyptic we find in *Little Dorrit* (where Uncle Freder-

ick in the theater pit cries, "I am coming, I am coming!" as he creeps "forth by
some underground way which emitted a cellarous smell," 1.20.231).

If the golden arrows do not point to any divine center, their strenuous pointing
is in itself significant, as is the self-consciousness of Jenny Wren's religious
language. What they chiefly signify is the human power of Jenny herself, a
"golden arrow," bringing the world of dead signs alive in her curious,
provocative uses of words. With her we hear that there may be life yet in what
Eugene has described as a fatal flaw—that one might "only mean and . . .
always only mean and nothing more"—for in such human acts of ascribing
value, dust is transcended by texts. Reading them is as important as making
them; later on, this imaginative producer of words will become the "interpreter"
on Eugene's deathbed "between this sentient world and the insensible man"
(4.10.809). It is precisely because Jenny *can* choose to be deaf to the insentient
world—the world of the dust heaps—and only because she is also aware of it
that she is attuned to the feeblest of human signals showing signs of life.

In Jenny Wren, Dickens brings together his secularized baptismal motif with
his Romantic perception that the language of imagination can bring alive new
selves even in this world.[42] This perception is central to his continued use of
rebirth symbolism, which has always seemed to me less a function of his belief
in heavenly rebirth (as Andrew Sanders argues in *Charles Dickens, Resurrectionist*), than the expression of a conviction he confirmed through his experience
as a maker of fiction. Perpetually proliferating new fictive voices, roles, and
worlds throughout his career, he was a "resurrectionist" of himself as well as a
"resurrection man" for Victorian readers through his transforming powers of
imagination. Nonetheless, however much she resembles her maker, however
redemptive her acts of articulation and interpretation, the fact that Jenny Wren
is not the novel's "original Word,"[43] nor any human words in this book the
unifying Logos, Dickens quietly shows us. In their immediate contexts, Jenny's
verbal creations, even more than Florence Dombey's fancies, are as much disturbing as consoling; by their note of complaint, self-pity, or eccentricity they
remind us of her need for them and of the dissonances to which she must momentarily pretend to be deaf to have them at all. Her means of escape reflect the
conditions she would transcend; her voice everywhere anticipates the "worldly"
discourse. Even her repeated "Come up and be dead . . . dead!"—a coy translation indeed, if not outright denial, of Jesus' "Come unto me" as the Resurrection and the Life—discloses its preoccupation. Death, too, invades Jenny
Wren's texts, reminding us that the resurrective powers of the merely human
word are constrained in the event by all that does, in fact, lie outside language.

In their larger contexts, the visions of this wise but crooked child—momentary enough, and contradicted by other things she says and does—are only one among many perspectives in the novel's play of many voices and modes of consciousness. That multivocity denies any ideal center or unifying word that might be "perceptible," in J. Hillis Miller's terms, "from the outside by Providence or by the omniscient eye of the narrator."[44] In *Our Mutual Friend's* dense matrix of contradictory and dissonant signs, each of Jenny Wren's "Appearances" is simply like all such human inventions in Dickens—the one thing needful for "all who see it." For these readers at least, her visionary texts are distinguishable from others—including Dickens' dead and dying biblical quotations—by their curious momentary power to show forth an ambient "radiance." Then the door of religious interpretation shuts, and we are left outside to read her life and *Our Mutual Friend*, as best we can, as wholly secular stories.

4

ARE WE BAPTIZED unto death or life? In the last chapter *Our Mutual Friend* leaves its readers with the problem of "which half" to believe, which ending to impose, by reinvoking the Social Chorus to rewrite the text of Eugene and Lizzie's story as a *mésalliance*, "a ridiculous affair" emptied of all moral content (4.17.888). Seeming to dismiss their point of view for good, at the conclusion of his Number Plans for "The Voice of Society" Dickens placed the apparently rhetorical question, "And is it worth much, after all?"[45] But if the grisly fictions of Society are resurrected once again only to be exposed, the remarkable capacity of these civilized cannibals to survive on scavenged gossip and false coin, and the power of all the cultural death forces they recall for the reader, tends to reopen the rhetorical query as a real question "after all": not about the moral "worth" of Podsnappery, but about the value and possibility of life and art in a declining and falling civilization. None in this world has ears to hear the parable of Eugene and Lizzie but Twemlow brought finally to life, who finds his own voice at last in defending "the feelings of a gentleman" about the marriage (891); and Mortimer, whose spirit "brightens" as he seems to distinguish, more consciously than he has as yet, false social voices from true (892). Yet what, one might ask, are these realizations worth—will they make for renewal in this world? Although Twemlow rejects narrow social definitions of "the gentleman" and applies a moral one to Eugene, this aging aristocrat never completely transcends the consciousness of his class, as John Lucas has observed;[46] and in interpreting the parable less as a story of rebirth than as a revised society romance of the gentleman raising the waterman's daughter to be "the greater lady"

(891), Twemlow retails a version of those same classist and sexist fictions that had fed Bradley Headstone's passion for Lizzie and thus helped nearly to bring about Eugene's death. And Mortimer seconds Twemlow's sentiments. For transcending the falsifications of such socially determined modes of thought, for being reborn to genuinely new consciousness in this decadent civilization, Dickens offers little hope in his final chapter.

Meanwhile, the "rosy path" he strikes out through the novel's waste land to the tune of "O 'tis love . . . that makes the world go round!" (4.4.738) leaves London's drugged populace, its babble of voices, and the dust mountains undisturbed—to be reclaimed for literary purposes nearly sixty years after in T. S. Eliot's poem of modern life most influenced by Dickens, with its fragments of texts shored against ruins and its even more tenuous biblical voice. Dickens may have settled for himself certain limited social questions in *Our Mutual Friend*, but amid the dying gestures of religious types and designs in his last completed novel he is still asking after ends—what life, art, is "worth much, after all?"; and the "overwhelming question" of life or death remains. As Eliot's Twemlow continues that internal dialogue elsewhere:

> And would it have been worth it, after all,
> After the cups, the marmalade, the tea,
> Among the porcelain, among some talk of you and me,
> Would it have been worth while,
> To have bitten off the matter with a smile,
> To have squeezed the universe into a ball
> To roll it toward some overwhelming question,
> To say: "I am Lazarus, come back from the dead,
> Come back to tell you all, I shall tell you all"—
> If one, settling a pillow by her head,
>> Should say: "That is not what I meant at all.
>> That is not it, at all."

Coda

ESPITE DICKENS' SATIRE on the depletion of religious language and Christian charity in the Scavenger Age, the biblical "fingerposts" guiding his moral plots, and the "Christian lessons" he said he had "studied . . . to inculcate" in his books (*UT* 415) and secularizes in his last completed parable of dying unto life: despite these and other efforts "to reconstruct a world out of a world deconstructing, like modernist texts, all around" him,[1] *Our Mutual Friend* remains a radically unstable text. As such, it has been a sourcebook for those very post-Victorian works to which George Levine has compared the disintegrating nineteenth-century world. The tensions within this novel have left vital and intact none of those conserving scriptural formulas Dickens had so long used, along with other things, to stabilize his fictions; and with the possible exception of a single image from the Burial Service, the novel engages imaginatively with none of that darker biblical material which had at least secured the profound unease of *Bleak House* and *Little Dorrit* within the conventions of the sacred text.

It has been the task of this book to show, however, that not a facile security but reconstruction was Dickens' more energetic intent, one he shared with other major imaginative thinkers of his time despite their different endowments of temperament and intellect. From the beginning, through scriptural allusion Dickens had practiced a form of writerly literary criticism—a sort of lower biblical criticism, if you will—in which he weighed, rejected, revised, and tried to recuperate the fractured Code for Victorian needs, within his larger project of producing expressive commercial fiction. Although his consistent testimonials over the years to personal belief in "the life and lessons of Our Saviour" suggest a simple acceptance of biblical material as unproblematic in itself, he knew, indeed often complained bitterly (and once in doggerel to Lady Blessington), that "they" had "Squabbled for words upon the altar-floor, / And rent The Book, in struggles for the binding." No matter how far Dickens removed himself from the squabbling or objectified the squabblers in his "Wrong Reverends" caricatures, what "they" had done (or undone) could not be ignored. Dickens inherited for his fictional purposes a "Book" thus unbound, its words (if not always "mere words" to Dickens) wrenched from familiar patterns of meaning and commanding new attention as human creations. Such a predicament—or liberation from old lendings—calls for not prayer and fasting so much as human intervention; indeed, the humanizing of the Bible invited it. In selecting certain prominent fragments (such as the Sermon on the Mount) and in attempting to bind them together and into his novels, Dickens was responding in his own way to the call Carlyle had issued to his contemporaries—Thomas and Matthew Arnold, Tennyson, Froude, George Eliot, Dean Stanley, Ruskin, and so many others answered it—to conceive the new Mythus. Without the formal religious training some of these eminent Victorians had, tied to no sect, and suffering from no family tyranny of expected piety and devotion, Dickens lacked the personal urgency to reexamine Scripture that many of his fellow Victorians felt; but that he should revise, not merely receive, his Bible at a time of needful revision and even radical rewriting—such as the century's many efforts (including *The Life of Our Lord*) "to reconceive the Christ"—is quite to be expected of a writer so much attuned to his time.

It should hardly be further surprising to find this popular novelist reworking the Bible's conventions in conventionally Victorian ways. His "essentializing" of Christian gospel, his use of scriptural stories as myths, his responses to Job and Ecclesiastes, his skeptical reproduction of Genesis archetypes, his domestication of Apocalypse, his borrowings of tone and content from Old Testament prophecy: all reflect common nineteenth-century attitudes toward these texts, as well as nineteenth-century textual preferences. At the same time, these new conventions, new ways of reading the Bible, were inherently more unstable than the old conventions by virtue of their being in formation, widely debated, and under threat from without. When these hermeneutic instabilities then disturb Dickens' reconstructive project and conspire with other things to prevent its completion, the familiar dialogue of the mind with itself ensues—another Victorian convention. Dickens nonetheless seized upon this fluid situation for biblical language with the originating energy of a writer who could turn an imitation into an inimitability; and so we find in him newly thoughtful, provocative, and sometimes wonderfully absurd applications of Bible texts—from Sairy Gamp's "Rich folks may ride on camels but it ain't so easy for 'em to see out of a needle's eye" (*MC* 25.474), and the "Meethosalems" and "Methoozellers" who mangle Hebrew syllables, to Society's "polite new reading[s]" of Scripture that are merely forgetful (like Mrs. Merdle's Job—"as poor as Thingummy," *LD* 1.33.384) or positively blasphemous, through all those darkly ironized religious formulas Dickens flung in the face of "a Christian people."

This last recalls us to the context wider than biblical controversy for Dickens' revisions of Scripture. In his encounter with places like Tom-all-Alone's, where "few people are known . . . by any Christian sign" (22.278), the implications of a larger world of defaced or erased Christian signs were likely pressed most indelibly on Dickens' consciousness; and as the young boy had discovered in his own experience of Tom's, it was also a world where one might wake up one day and discover that "no one," least of all a divine rescuer, "made any sign" (*Life* 1:21). In his fiction Dickens' efforts to signify by reviving biblical texts and types are, in part, his answer to such erasures and silences. It is not always, as we have seen in *Our Mutual Friend*'s dead quotations, an answer that incorporates its prompting question. But in the most richly biblical and complex of Dickens' novels, the voices of Scripture and Prayer Book are dialogically engaged with other, "worldly" voices. That dialogue is just beginning in *Oliver Twist* and fading out in *Our Mutual Friend*; in *Dombey, Bleak House*, and *Little Dorrit* it is central and formative, helping to generate the structural and stylistic tensions by which these novels exist as expressive and enigmatic works of art.

Not merely intertextual play for its own sake, these dialogues reproduce in Dickens' texts the multivocal languages, "contending in boundless hubbub," that this remarkable mimic and parodist heard on the nineteenth-century scene and overheard in his own heart. They thus bring into his work that not so heavenly host of Victorian readers, who are invited to take part in the unresolved play of voices for their entertainment and edification. In an age when "Hard and abstract moralities" are dissolving, however, edification is not the comparatively straightforward business it was for Bunyan, when he urged his reader to "lay my Book, thy Head and Heart together" (B 37). Through the multiplied hermeneutic possibilities of Dickens' mature fiction, he is still inviting his audiences to reread the Bible, their times, and themselves as they make their way through the book, participating imaginatively in the making and revising of interpretations. In accepting those invitations, his readers might join in the reconstructive project so much wanted; but they also are liable to discover its impossibility—swallowed up by "dust," evaporated as "fiction," or baffled by the secrecies of both the Bible and Dickens' text.

Notes

1. The Fractured Code in Dickens' Fiction

1. Northrop Frye, *The Great Code: The Bible and Literature* (New York: Harcourt Brace Jovanovich, 1982), pp. xvi and xi.

2. Arthur Penrhyn Stanley, *Sermon Preached by Arthur Penrhyn Stanley, D. D., Dean of Westminster, in Westminster Abbey June 19, 1870 (The First Sunday after Trinity), Being the Sunday Following the Funeral of Charles Dickens* (London: Macmillan, 1870), pp. 4, 5–6.

3. Ibid., pp. 10, 12.

4. George H. Ford, *Dickens and His Readers: Aspects of Novel-Criticism Since 1836* (New York: W. W. Norton, 1965), p. 109.

5. J. M., "How Dickens Sells," *The Book Monthly* (August 1906), p. 773. B. W. Matz in "The Cult of Dickens," *The Book Monthly* (October 1904), p. 26, reports a reader who wrote, "no other works—except the Bible—have so stirred the soul"; *The Dickensian* (22 [July–September 1926]: 150) notes with approval "an aged grandfather . . . who thinks he can prepare himself for the next world by reading Dickens in this world." See also *Life* 1:126, 300, and 2:314–16.

6. Dr. Thomas Arnold, Sermon 37, *Christian Life, Its Course, Its Hindrances, and Its Helps* (London: B. Fellowes, 1841), pp. 408, 400.

7. Stanley, *Sermon*, p. 12.

8. Frank Kermode, *The Genesis of Secrecy: On the Interpretation of Narrative* (Cambridge: Harvard University Press, 1979), pp. 25, 23, 28.

9. Ibid., p. 15.

10. Ibid., p. 45.

11. Ibid., pp. 27–28.

12. G. B. Shaw, Introduction to *Hard Times* (London, 1912), reprinted in *The Dickens Critics*, ed. George H. Ford and Lauriat Lane, Jr. (Ithaca: Cornell University Press, 1961), p. 128.

13. [E. B. Hamley], "Remonstrance with Dickens," *Blackwood's Magazine* 81 (April 1857): 495, complained of both kinds of parables: when some "luminary tells him that it is the duty of a great popular writer to be a great moral teacher, . . . straightway a piece of staring morality is embroidered into the motley pattern"; Dickens also "addresses himself to the melancholy task, setting to work to illustrate some enigma which Thomas

Carlyle perhaps, or some such congenial dreary spirit, . . . has left rather darker than before."

14. Thomas Carlyle to John Forster, 16 February 1874, quoted in W. Forbes Gray, "Carlyle and John Forster: An Unpublished Correspondence," *Quarterly Review* 268 (January–April 1937): 282.

15. Kermode, *The Genesis of Secrecy*, p. 47.

16. G. B. Shaw, Introductory Epistolary to Arthur Bingham Walkley, in *Man and Superman, Plays of George Bernard Shaw* (New York: New American Library, 1960), p. 255.

17. Unsigned review, "Charles Dickens," *Blackwood's Magazine* 109 (June 1871): 694.

18. Alexander Welsh, *The City of Dickens* (Oxford: Clarendon Press, 1971), p. 180.

19. In reply to a remonstrance, Dickens called this "a much-abused social figure of speech impressed into all sorts of services"; see William Kent, *Dickens and Religion* (London: Watts and Company, 1930), p. 52.

20. Unsigned review of *Dombey and Son, North British Review* 7 (May 1847): 110.

21. Humphry House, *The Dickens World*, 2d ed. (London: Oxford University Press, 1942), p. 110.

22. See Julian Moynahan, "The Hero's Guilt: The Case of *Great Expectations*," *Essays in Criticism* 10 (January 1960): 61. For a dissent to Moynahan's reading, see Dennis Walder, *Dickens and Religion* (Boston: George Allen and Unwin, 1981), p. 203.

23. Dennis Walder treats "The Social Gospel" in *Bleak House* on pages 140–69 of *Dickens and Religion*. I am indebted to Walder's work on Dickens and religion.

24. See Bert G. Hornback, *"Noah's Arkitecture": A Study of Dickens's Mythology* (Athens: Ohio University Press, 1972); Jane Vogel, *Allegory in Dickens* (University: University of Alabama Press, 1977); Theresa R. Love, *Dickens and the Seven Deadly Sins* (Danville, Ill.: Interstate Printers and Publishers, 1979); Michael Wheeler, *The Art of Allusion in Victorian Fiction* (New York: Barnes and Noble, 1979), pp. 61–77; Welsh, *The City of Dickens*; Andrew Sanders, *Charles Dickens, Resurrectionist* (New York: St. Martin's Press, 1982); and Barry V. Qualls, *The Secular Pilgrims of Victorian Fiction: The Novel as Book of Life* (New York: Cambridge University Press, 1982), pp. 85–138.

25. Wolfgang Iser, *The Implied Reader: Patterns of Communication in Prose Fiction from Bunyan to Beckett* (Baltimore: Johns Hopkins University Press, 1974), p. 288.

26. Welsh, *The City of Dickens*, pp. 141, 228.

27. Dickens, "A Sleep to Startle Us," *Household Words* (13 March 1852), reprinted in *Miscellaneous Papers, Plays, and Poems*, 1:316. In this essay on his tour of a Ragged School, Dickens urges his "Dearly beloved brethren" to "come out of the controversies for a little while, and be simply Apostolic thus low down!" Compare Dr. Arnold's argument in his Introduction to *Christian Life*, pp. lxv–lxvi, that social, moral, and intellectual evils go neglected while churchmen debate the necessity of Apostolic Succession.

28. On Tractarianism, see Dickens to Mrs. Sydney Smith, 11 November 1847, P 5:194; on Unitarianism, see Walder, *Dickens and Religion*, pp. 12–14; on "the Colenso

and Jowett matter," see Dickens to W. F. de Cerjat, 21 May 1863, D 3:352; on Old Testament controversy, see Dickens to de Cerjat, 25 October 1864, D 3:402; on Dickens' Broad Church sympathies, see his response to Forster's *Examiner* review (12 October 1844) of Dean Stanley's *The Life and Correspondence of Thomas Arnold,* "I respect and reverence his memory, beyond all expression. I must have that book. Every sentence that you quote from it is the text-book of my faith" (?13–14 October 1844, P 4:201); on scientific thought, see, e.g., Ann Y. Wilkinson, *"Bleak House:* From Faraday to Judgment Day," *English Literary History* 34 (June 1967): 225–47, and William F. Axton, "Religious and Scientific Imagery in *Bleak House," Nineteenth-Century Fiction* 22 (March 1968): 349–59.

29. Lady Dickens writes in her Foreword to *The Life of Our Lord:* "This life of Our Lord was written without thought of publication, in order that his family might have a permanent record of their father's thoughts. After his death, this manuscript remained in the possession of his sister-in-law, Miss Georgina Hogarth. On her death in 1917 it came into the possession of Sir Henry Fielding Dickens. Charles Dickens had made it clear that he had written *The Life of Our Lord* in a form which he thought best suited to his children, and not for publication. His son, Sir Henry, was averse to publishing the work in his own lifetime, but saw no reason why publication should be withheld after his death. Sir Henry's will provided that, if the majority of his family were in favour of publication, *The Life of Our Lord* should be given to the world. It was first published, in serial form, in March 1934" (*LOL* 7–8).

30. In "Two Views of a Cheap Theatre," Dickens speculates that many find "the verse-form" of the New Testament hard to read, "imagin[ing] that those breaks imply gaps and want of continuity. Help them over that first stumbling-block, by setting forth the history in narrative" (*UT* 44).

31. Dickens to Forster and to S. R. Starey, 24 September 1843, *The Letters of Charles Dickens,* Pilgrim ed., 3:572, 574. The example Dickens gives in the second letter has to do with the concept of "the Lamb of God," the subject of some "injudicious catechizing" of children at a Ragged School.

32. Compare Dickens, "Two Views of a Cheap Theatre": people can "work out their own salvation if they would, by simply, lovingly, and dutifully following Our Saviour, and . . . needed the mediation of no erring man" (*UT* 43); the narrator's apostrophe to Jo (*BH* 25.323); and Dickens' will, in which he exhorts his children "to try to guide themselves by the teaching of the New Testament in its broad spirit, and to put no faith in any man's narrow construction of its letter here or there" (*Life* 2:422).

33. Rev. Chauncy Hare Townshend, *The Religious Opinions of the late Rev. Chauncy Hare Townshend,* published as directed in his will, by his literary executor [Charles Dickens] (London: Chapman and Hall, 1869), p. 18. Compare Dickens' directive that the women of Urania Cottage were to hear "the *New* Testament" but were not to be subjected to "injudicious use of the Old" (3 November 1847), in *Letters of Charles Dickens to the Baroness Angela Burdett-Coutts,* ed. Charles C. Osborne (New York: E. P. Dutton, 1932), p. 93.

34. Dickens is, however, very explicit about the physical aspects of crucifixion (*LOL*

105–6) and includes two particularly violent narrative climaxes, the deaths of Judas (99) and of Ananias and Sapphira (121).

35. Matthew Arnold, Preface to *God and the Bible* (1875), reprinted in *Matthew Arnold Prose and Poetry*, ed. Archibald L. Bouton (New York: Charles Scribner's Sons, 1927), p. 409.

36. One such rationalist, William Kent, comments on Dickens' "selective process" for accepting miracles: he "pick[s] out as credible everything that is clearly beneficent. Those which a lover of his race might wish to have happened are accepted without any apparent strain of credulity" (Kent's *Dickens and Religion*, pp. 18–19).

37. It follows that a Jesus who is not true God must be radically idealized; the hero of *The Life of Our Lord* never becomes angry, ironical, or witty, is not tempted by the Devil, does not wrestle with God's will in Gethsemane, is not poor (only "very simply dressed; almost like the poor people," p. 60). His chief human attribute is his capacity for suffering and compassion. The need for idealization (as well as Dickens' ignorance of typology and his conventional taste in painting) seems also to lie behind his execration of John Millais' painting, *Christ in the House of His Parents*, in "Old Lamps for New Ones," *Household Words* (15 June 1850), reprinted in *Miscellaneous Papers, Plays, and Poems*, 1:193–99. See also Herbert L. Sussman, *Fact into Figure: Typology in Carlyle, Ruskin, and the Pre-Raphaelite Brotherhood* (Columbus: Ohio State University Press, 1979), pp. 47–56.

38. Dickens' "A Christmas Tree" climaxes a series of impressionistic images from Christ's life with the Crucifixion's "one voice . . . 'Forgive them, for they know not what they do'" (reprinted in *Selected Short Fiction*, ed. Deborah A. Thomas [Harmondsworth: Penguin, 1976], p. 134).

39. Dr. Arnold's Sermon 17, in *Sermons* (London: B. Fellowes, 1844), 1:198–99, sums up for me Dickens' attitude, indicates how common it was, and places him critically in relation to orthodox Christianity: "Now first, I believe that there are many, who, in a very strict sense, may be said, not to know who the Son of God is. They call him their Saviour, but if they are asked what he has done for them, they would say that he has taught them their duty, and told them that if they did well, they should go to heaven hereafter. Thus they consider him in fact as a great prophet, but are never led to regard him with that faith, and love, and adoration, which his character, as revealed in the Scriptures, demands. I am not speaking of those who avow their disbelief in his divinity; but of those . . . who . . . habitually lose sight of [Jesus Christ's] office of Saviour and Mediator, and regard him only as a teacher. . . . their opinions and practice are more those of the disciples of John the Baptist, who preached repentance, than of the Apostles of Christ, who taught together with repentance towards God, faith towards Jesus Christ our Lord."

40. Angus Wilson, Introduction to *Edwin Drood*, quoted in Harland S. Nelson, *Charles Dickens* (Boston: Twayne Publishers, 1981), p. 179. Steven Marcus in *Dickens from Pickwick to Dombey* (New York: Simon and Schuster, 1965), p. 68, offers a more qualified estimate: "Dickens was of course a Christian—Dostoevsky called him 'that great Christian' [in *A Writer's Diary*]—which is to say that, living when he did, his

involvement with Christian culture was by nature profound, passionate, contradictory and, as frequently as not, adverse."

41. House, *The Dickens World*, p. 111.

42. Ibid., p. 112. The contemporary controversy on future punishment is parodically replayed in the catechizing of Jo at the Coroner's Inquest, when his "Can't exactly say what'll be done to him arter he's dead if he tells a lie to the gentlemen here" is put aside with "This won't do, gentlemen!" and Jo is dismissed, like F. D. Maurice from King's College, London, in 1853 as a professor of truth (*BH* 11.134).

43. George P. Landow, *Victorian Types, Victorian Shadows: Biblical Typology in Victorian Literature, Art, and Thought* (Boston: Routledge and Kegan Paul, 1980), p. 175, discusses Carlyle's manipulations of typology "for effect" as decadent, heralding his tradition's demise. With Dickens we are in "the hazy, ill-defined borders between religious and secular discourse in an age when these territories continually shifted" (p. 225); Dickens takes the Broad Church position Landow describes, that types were "not divinely instituted signs of specific events," all pointing to Christ as the center of history, but general symbols of religious ideas to be employed figuratively (p. 31). For a general discussion of Victorian novel types, see also John R. Reed, *Victorian Conventions* (Athens: Ohio University Press, 1975), pp. 20–24.

44. George Eliot, *Middlemarch*, ed. Bert G. Hornback, Norton Critical Edition (New York: W. W. Norton, 1977), 1.1.1.

45. Walder, *Dickens and Religion*, p. 119, discusses a *Martin Chuzzlewit* revision of Psalm 37:25 that casts David as a jejune bard in the light of modern problems.

46. See Hans W. Frei, *The Eclipse of Biblical Narrative: A Study in Eighteenth- and Nineteenth-Century Hermeneutics* (New Haven: Yale University Press, 1974), p. 7; and Robert Alter, *The Art of Biblical Narrative* (New York: Basic Books, 1981), p. 16.

47. Erich Auerbach, *Mimesis: The Representation of Reality in Western Literature*, trans. Willard R. Trask (Princeton: Princeton University Press, 1953), p. 16.

48. George Levine, *The Realistic Imagination: English Fiction from Frankenstein to Lady Chatterley* (Chicago: University of Chicago Press, 1981), p. 4.

49. See Earl Miner, "Allusion," *Princeton Encyclopedia of Poetry and Poetics*, ed. Alex Preminger et al., enl. ed. (Princeton: Princeton University Press, 1974), p. 18, and M. H. Abrams, "Allusion," *A Glossary of Literary Terms*, 3d ed. (New York: Holt, Rinehart and Winston, 1971), p. 8.

50. See Wheeler, *The Art of Allusion in Victorian Fiction*, pp. 2–4, for a fuller discussion of these definitions; I use his terms *marked* and *unmarked quotation* and *adopted text*.

51. Stephen C. Gill, in "Allusion in *Bleak House*: A Narrative Device," *Nineteenth-Century Fiction* 22 (September 1967): 148, finds in these allusions "simultaneously menace and compassion," but he does not read the passage quite the way I do.

52. See Wheeler, *The Art of Allusion in Victorian Fiction*, p. 161.

53. Ziva Ben-Porat, "The Poetics of Literary Allusion," *PTL: A Journal for Descriptive Poetics and Theory of Literature* 1 (1976): 126–27.

54. Wayne Booth, *A Rhetoric of Irony* (Chicago: University of Chicago Press, 1974), p. 233. See his whole discussion in part 3, pp. 230–77.

55. Wheeler, *The Art of Allusion in Victorian Fiction*, p. 25.

56. Wayne C. Booth, *The Rhetoric of Fiction*, 2d ed. (Chicago: University of Chicago Press, 1983), pp. xiii and 112.

57. Henry Melvill, "Songs in the Night," Sermon 12 (February 1837, Cambridge), in *Sermons*, ed. the Right Reverend C. P. M'Ilvaine (New York: Stanford and Swords, 1950), 1:228. Compare C. H. Spurgeon, "Songs in the Night," Sermon 11, in *Sermons of Rev. C. H. Spurgeon*, 2d ser. (New York: Robert Carter and Brothers, n.d.), pp. 167–87.

58. Frank Kermode, *The Sense of an Ending: Studies in the Theory of Fiction* (New York: Oxford University Press, 1966), p. 6.

59. Qualls discusses "the novel as book of life," tracing the Victorians' understanding of fictional narrative as an assurance of "some knowable order" back to Quarles, Bunyan, and revaluations of the Puritan and the Romantic traditions through the lenses of Carlyle (see Introduction to *The Secular Pilgrims of Victorian Fiction*, pp. 1–16).

60. See *The Late John Wilkes's Catechism of a Ministerial Member; Taken from an Original Manuscript in Mr. Wilkes's Handwriting, Never Before Printed, and Adapted to the Present Occasion* (London: William Hone, 1817); *The Sinecurist's Creed, or Belief, as Used Throughout the Kingdom*, in Hone's *Weekly Commentary*, no. 11 (London, 1817); and *The Political Litany, Diligently Revised; To Be Said or Sung, Until the Appointed Change Come, Throughout the Dominion of England and Wales, and the Town of Berwick upon Tweed* (London: William Hone, 1817). I am grateful to the Houghton Library for permission to view these materials and three pamphlets containing the trial testimony showing that Hone used for his defense religious satire by Church divines (beginning with Martin Luther). He was acquitted.

61. The Book of Common Prayer is also used to judge the government (40.502 and n. 5), Guppy (38.480–81), Smallweed, Richard (45.545 and n. 2), and Lady Dedlock (56.667; cf. *BCP* definition of "Sacrament"), but not the Bagnets, who playfully revise their catechism with impunity (49.587 and n. 1).

62. See R. C. D. Jasper, "The Prayer Book in the Victorian Era," in *The Victorian Crisis of Faith*, ed. Anthony Symondson (London: Society for the Promotion of Christian Knowledge, 1970), pp. 107–21.

63. See Walder, *Dickens and Religion*, pp. 159–60.

64. Gill, "Allusion in *Bleak House*," p. 149.

65. Wolfgang Iser, *The Act of Reading: A Theory of Aesthetic Response* (Baltimore: Johns Hopkins University Press, 1978), p. 6.

66. [Wilkie Collins], "To Think, or Be Thought For?" *Household Words* 14 (13 September 1856): 193–98.

67. The grid in which I have placed literary allusion is a simplified version of Paul Hernadi's scheme in "Literary Theory," *Introduction to Scholarship in Modern Languages and Literatures*, ed. Joseph Gibaldi (New York: Modern Language Association, 1981), pp. 98–115.

68. Herman Meyer, *The Poetics of Quotation in the European Novel*, trans. Theodore and Yetta Ziolkowski (Princeton: Princeton University Press, 1968), p. 4.

69. M. M. Bakhtin, "Discourse in the Novel," in *The Dialogic Imagination: Four Essays by M. M. Bakhtin*, ed. Michael Holquist, and trans. Caryl Emerson and M. Holquist (Austin: University of Texas Press, 1981), pp. 275, 273.

70. Ibid., p. 324.

71. Ibid., p. 292. Hornback reads the Babel phase of Genesis mythology primarily as a story of noncommunication (*"Noah's Arkitecture,"* pp. 104–5), but Dickens' use of the story is wider than this.

72. See Bakhtin, "Discourse in the Novel," pp. 342–44. I think the very artistic failure of Dickens' "dead quotations," however, indicates the presence of heteroglossia and its power to reduce the authoritative word (which rejects dialogue) to "an object, a *relic*, a thing" (p. 344). In a sense even these relic-words—"sharply demarcated" and "inert," "resistant to stylistic play"—are structured in relation to the surrounding dynamic vocal contexts, respond rigidly to them, reveal their own failure in relation to them—not likely the effect Dickens intended, of course.

73. Ibid., p. 262.

74. Peter K. Garrett, in *The Victorian Multiplot Novel: Studies in the Dialogical Form* (New Haven: Yale University Press, 1980), discusses a parallel strategy in plotting, applying Bakhtin's ideas in ways that complement my argument about Dickensian allusion.

75. See Sanders' chapter on *The Old Curiosity Shop* in *Charles Dickens, Resurrectionist*, pp. 64–93, for a discussion of these multiple attitudes that does not, however, interpret their multiplicity as I do.

76. For an illuminating discussion of Bakhtin's problems with authoritative discourse, see Caryl Emerson, "The Tolstoy Connection in Bakhtin," *PMLA* 100 (January 1985): 68–80.

77. See Qualls, *The Secular Pilgrims of Victorian Fiction*, pp. ix, xi, and "The WORD Made Novel," pp. 1–16.

78. Terry Eagleton, *Literary Theory: An Introduction* (Minneapolis: University of Minnesota Press, 1983), p. 69.

79. Bakhtin, "Avtor i geroi v esteticheskoi deiatel'nosti" (Author and Protagonist in Aesthetic Activity), in *Estetika slovesnogo tvorchestva* (The Aesthetics of Verbal Art) (Moskva: Iskusstvo, 1979), p. 34; quoted in Caryl Emerson, p. 70.

80. No attempt will be made here to represent the full range of responses to the novels considered; George H. Ford and Philip Collins have made the most important contributions to our knowledge of Dickens' readers, and I am indebted to both scholars. The one contemporary study we have on Dickens' biblical allusions, "Charles Dickens' Use of the Bible," *Temple Bar* (1869): 225–34, is a pious compilation to illustrate Dickens' veneration for the Holy Book. The chief dissenting voice comes from William Kent, who finds Dickens' uses of Scripture perfunctory.

81. Booth, *The Rhetoric of Fiction*, p. 112. The theoretical overlappings and diver-

gences of Booth and Iser form a larger topic that cannot be taken up here adequately; I focus on only their divergent tendencies. Booth's reader does "creative" work and must "collaborate" with the author by making inferences (especially where the narrator is unreliable), deciphering puns and allusions, or "providing mature moral judgment" (pp. 307–8), but this reader's basic role toward the text is that of a recipient of its meanings, a "subordinate" of the author, who "makes his reader, as he makes his second self"; the goal is their "complete agreement" (p. 138). While Iser too can sometimes treat the reader as subordinate to the author's intentions, on the whole he does not use this kind of language and would not agree to Booth's goal here. Partly under the influence of Bakhtin, as Booth generously acknowledges, he qualifies his earlier argument in his "Afterword to the Second Edition" (p. 415) and produces an elaborate schema of various authors and audiences (pp. 427–31). Booth clarifies his changing position further and fully acknowledges Bakhtin's impact on it in his Introduction to Mikhail Bakhtin, *Problems of Dostoevsky's Poetics*, ed. and trans. by Caryl Emerson, Theory and History of Literature, vol. 8 (Minneapolis: University of Minnesota Press, 1984), pp. xiii–xxvii.

82. Iser, *The Implied Reader*, p. 288. Iser discusses repertoires and strategies at greater length in *The Act of Reading*, pp. 53–103.

83. Harry Levin, *The Gates of Horn: A Study of Five French Realists* (New York: Oxford University Press, 1963), p. 31.

84. Iser, *The Implied Reader*, p. 28.

85. Dickens, "Rather a Strong Dose," review of *The History of the Supernatural in All Ages and Nations, and in All Churches, Christian and Pagan, Demonstrating a Universal Faith*, by William Hewitt (1863), in *All the Year Round* 9 (21 March 1863), reprinted in *Miscellaneous Papers, Plays, and Poems*, 2:254.

86. Dickens would not "disparage . . . the intelligence" of his readers (see "Two Views of a Cheap Theatre," *UT* 44) and "contest[ed]" Wilkie Collins' "disposition to give an audience credit for nothing" (7 January 1860, D 3:145). Compare letters from Dickens to G. H. Lewes, ?9 June 1838, P 1:404; to Collins, 14 October 1862, D 3:309; to G. H. Wills, 20 December 1863, D 3:374; to Bulwer Lytton, 18 December 1861, D 3:268. Monroe Engel argues that Dickens "had a tenderness of concern for his audience perhaps related to that tenderness he looked for between a writer and the character of whom he writes"; see "Dickens on Art," *Modern Philology* 53 (August 1955): 36. "Tenderness" is only one possible descriptive term; one also thinks of "discretion" or simply "respect." Dickens insisted that the emanations of his own mind took on independent life; characters are creations to be nurtured and coaxed, listened to, even suffered, but not to be "conducted" in the high-handed editorial manner.

87. See John Holloway, *The Victorian Sage: Studies in Argument* (New York: W. W. Norton, 1953), pp. 4–17.

88. Iser, *The Implied Reader*, p. 284.

89. [John Eagles], "A Few Words about Novels—a Dialogue," *Blackwood's Magazine* 64 (October 1848), reprinted in *Dickens: The Critical Heritage*, ed. Philip Collins (London: Routledge and Kegan Paul, 1971), p. 231.

90. Iser, *The Implied Reader*, p. xiv.

91. For an example of the refusal to be baldly didactic in a Victorian novel that problematizes its message, see Charlotte Brontë's final address to "the judicious reader putting on his spectacles to look for the moral" in *Shirley* (1849), ed. Andrew and Judith Hook (Harmondsworth: Penguin, 1974), 3.14.599.

92. Christopher Norris, *Deconstruction: Theory and Practice* (New York: Methuen, 1982), p. 122.

93. T. S. Eliot, "Tradition and the Individual Talent" (1919), in *Selected Essays*, new ed. (New York: Harcourt, Brace and Company, 1950), p. 5.

94. Iser, *The Act of Reading*, p. 10.

95. "The Spirit of Fiction," *All the Year Round* 18 (27 July 1867): 118. The internal evidence of style suggests that Dickens did not write this article.

2. Early Biblical Boz: The Case of *Oliver Twist*

1. Steven Marcus, *Dickens from Pickwick to Dombey* (New York: Simon and Schuster, 1965), p. 76.

2. "There is a sort of Radicalish tone about *Oliver Twist* which I don't altogether like"; Rev. Richard Harris Barham, contributor to *Bentley's Miscellany*, in a letter to Mrs. Hughes (April 1837) in *The Life and Letters of the Rev. Richard Harris Barham*, by his son (1870), 2:24; quoted in Kathleen Tillotson, *"Oliver Twist," Essays and Studies* 12 n.s. (1959): 102.

3. Alexander Welsh, *The City of Dickens* (Oxford: Clarendon Press, 1971), p. 141.

4. Marcus, *Dickens from Pickwick to Dombey*, pp. 67–68. I am indebted to Marcus' fine discussion of the Bunyan parallel.

5. *Oliver Twist*, ed. Kathleen Tillotson (Oxford: Clarendon Press, 1966), p. 385.

6. Herman Meyer, *The Poetics of Quotation in the European Novel*, trans. Theodore and Yetta Ziolkowski (Princeton: Princeton University Press, 1968), p. 6.

7. Peter Brooks, *The Melodramatic Imagination: Balzac, Henry James, Melodrama, and the Mode of Excess* (New Haven: Yale University Press, 1976), discusses the nineteenth century's need for the definitive closures of melodrama in these terms. In Kathleen Tillotson's Introduction to the Clarendon *Oliver Twist*, she discusses the revisions Dickens made in 1846 to tone down emotional exaggeration (pp. xxxvi–xxxvii), but of course much melodrama remains.

8. Lauriat Lane, Jr., sees a "spiritual progression" from the "partial redemption" suggested by "Mr. Brownlow's conditional generosity" to the "total redemption" offered in "the Maylies' all-embracing kindness and forgiveness," but these shifts are merely external to a hero who does not change himself; see "The Devil in *Oliver Twist*," *The Dickensian* 52 (Summer 1956): 135.

9. The persistence of good through trial is also the pattern of Esther Summerson's

narrative (see my chapter 4), where Dickens transforms the Bunyan paradigm with an enormous gain in psychological complexity; she reaches her heavenly city on earth only after much wrestling with her credible internal demons. In the light of the evil that has entered her life and that lurks around it in the complex set of doubles for her character (Lady Dedlock and Hortense), as well as in the other narrative, it is impressive that Dickens can create a specifically Christian heroine—again unlike Oliver—even while showing us the evasions fostered by her religious rhetoric.

10. Roger Sharrock, Introduction to *The Pilgrim's Progress*, p. 15.

11. Bert G. Hornback, *"Noah's Arkitecture": A Study of Dickens's Mythology* (Athens: Ohio University Press, 1972), pp. 18–21, discusses the otherworldly rhetoric in *Oliver Twist* and also finds the resolution finally morbid.

12. Marcus, *Dickens from Pickwick to Dombey*, p. 79.

13. J. Hillis Miller, *Charles Dickens: The World of His Novels* (Bloomington: Indiana University Press, 1958), pp. 38–39.

14. Dayton Haskin, "The Burden of Interpretation in *The Pilgrim's Progress*," *Studies in Philology* 79 (Summer 1982): 278.

15. Ibid., p. 275.

16. Humphry House, *The Dickens World*, 2d ed. (London: Oxford University Press, 1942), p. 42.

17. Sallie McFague TeSelle, *Speaking in Parables: A Study in Metaphor and Theology* (Philadelphia: Fortress Press, 1975), p. 33, describes this movement of parable.

18. John Dominic Crossan, *The Dark Interval: Towards a Theology of Story* (Niles, Ill.: Argus Communications, 1975), p. 56. I am indebted to Crossan's rather specialized theology of parable, based on some of the work of Claude Levi-Strauss, for my definitions here.

19. John Dominic Crossan, *In Parables: The Challenge of the Historical Jesus* (New York: Harper and Row, 1973), p. 64.

20. Matthew Arnold, "The Study of Poetry" (1880), in *Essays in Criticism*, 2d ser., ed. S. R. Littlewood (New York: St. Martin's Press, 1958), p. 10.

21. Notably, Dickens interpreted the parable of the Good Samaritan simply and literally; not for him are the elaborate interpretations of patristic allegory, for which he would have had neither taste nor training, discussed by Frank Kermode in *The Genesis of Secrecy: On the Interpretation of Narrative* (Cambridge: Harvard University Press, 1979), pp. 35–37.

22. Dennis Walder, *Dickens and Religion* (Boston: George Allen and Unwin, 1981), p. 53.

23. Dr. Thomas Arnold, *Sermons* (London: B. Fellowes, 1844), 2:65.

24. See John R. Reed, *Victorian Conventions* (Athens: Ohio University Press, 1975), pp. 89–93, especially his discussion of Thackeray's use of the type in *The Adventures of Philip on His Way Through the World, Showing Who Robbed Him, Who Helped Him, and Who Passed Him By* (1861–62).

25. Henry Morley, "The Predatory Art," in *Charles Dickens' Uncollected Writings from*

"*Household Words,*" *1850–1859*, ed. Harry Stone (Bloomington: Indiana University Press, 1968), 2:570. Two months later Dickens published a note exonerating the secretary (16 May 1857).

26. See Reed, *Victorian Conventions*, p. 89.

27. The simplest form of demonic inversion is the curse. The thieves apply the epithet "Christian" to each other and to Sikes' dog (18.112). The thieves also invert biblical values when they transpose the Devil and Providence (see 51.336 and 19.119). Demonic inversion—precedented in the Book of Revelation, where the Antichrist rules over a world that is a demonic parody of the divine world—becomes a full-scale systematic technique in *Bleak House*, where such ironic allusions encompass the "respectable" folk protected from such contamination in *Oliver Twist*.

28. J. Hillis Miller, "The Fiction of Realism: *Sketches by Boz, Oliver Twist*, and Cruikshank's Illustrations," in *Dickens Centennial Essays*, ed. Ada Nisbet and Blake Nevius (Berkeley and Los Angeles: University of California Press, 1971), p. 113.

29. Clarendon *Oliver Twist*, p. 385.

30. H. M. Daleski, *Dickens and the Art of Analogy* (London: Faber and Faber, 1970), p. 49. I am indebted to Daleski's discussion of the conflicts in *Oliver Twist*.

31. Tillotson, Introduction to the Clarendon *Oliver Twist*, pp. xi–xvi.

32. See Arnold Kettle, "Dickens: *Oliver Twist*," *An Introduction to the English Novel* (New York: Harper and Row, 1968), 1:124.

33. James Anthony Froude, *The Nemesis of Faith*, 2d ed. (London: John Chapman, 1849), pp. 17–18.

34. Kettle, "Dickens: *Oliver Twist*," 1:122.

35. Compare Miller, *Charles Dickens: The World of His Novels*, p. 61.

36. Kermode, *The Genesis of Secrecy*, p. 126.

37. I find only two apocalyptic allusions in *Oliver Twist:* the narrator's warning that "dark evidences of human error . . . are rising . . . to Heaven, to pour their after-vengeance on our heads" (30.186; I discuss this passage in chapter 3); and Monks' words as he drowns the locket, "If the sea ever gives up its dead, as books say it will, it will keep its gold and silver to itself, and that trash among it" (38.242; cf. Rev. 20:13).

38. *The Unitarian Lectures at Liverpool* (Liverpool, 1839), pp. xii, 5–6; quoted in Geoffrey Rowell, *Hell and the Victorians: A Study of the Nineteenth Century Theological Controversies Concerning Eternal Punishment and the Future Life* (Oxford: Clarendon Press, 1974), p. 49.

39. House points out that while debates raged in theological circles, Dickens refers to the Devil and hell "ambiguously; they might be either literal or metaphorical, so that details of belief are left open" (*The Dickens World*, p. 112). Michael Wheeler discusses Dickens' more imaginative use of "hell" in *Hard Times* in *The Art of Allusion in Victorian Fiction* (New York: Barnes and Noble, 1979), pp. 61–77. By the time of *Little Dorrit*, hell has become "an old dark closet . . . with nothing in it" to Arthur Clennam (1.3.33).

40. Quoted in Sir Walter Moberly, *The Ethics of Punishment* (1968), p. 329; cited in Rowell, *Hell and the Victorians*, p. 14.

41. Marie Hamilton Law discusses "The Indebtedness of *Oliver Twist* to Defoe's *History of the Devil*" in *PMLA* 40 (December 1925): 892–97. Lauriat Lane, Jr., corrects some of her emphases and comments: "Probably Dickens found little in Defoe's *History of the Devil* that he was not already aware of. On the other hand, the tone of Dickens' remarks to Forster does suggest that Defoe's treatment of the devil was fresh enough to make an impression. . . . this organized treatment may have further stimulated his interest" ("The Devil in *Oliver Twist*," pp. 132–33).

42. Rev. C. H. Spurgeon, *Sermons of Rev. C. H. Spurgeon*, 2d ser. (New York: Robert Carter and Brothers, n.d.), p. 438.

43. Rowell, *Hell and the Victorians*, pp. 13–14.

44. Unsigned review, *Spectator* 11 (24 November 1838): 1114–16, reprinted in *Dickens: The Critical Heritage*, ed. Philip Collins (London: Routledge and Kegan Paul, 1971), p. 43.

45. R. H. Horne early pointed out the "immoral tendency" of Dickens' cross purposes; see *A New Spirit of the Age* (1844; reprinted, World's Classics Edition, 1907), pp. 26–27, quoted in Philip Collins, *Dickens and Crime*, 2d ed. (New York: St. Martin's Press, 1965), pp. 263–64.

46. A. J. Duffield to F. W. Farrar, 9 January 1789, quoted in Rowell, *Hell and the Victorians*, p. 149.

47. Collins discusses Dickens' paradoxical and changing position in *Dickens and Crime* as an attitude of increasing "severity towards criminal offenders" accompanied by "an ever-increasing intimacy with the criminal mind" (p. 22).

48. Spurgeon, *Sermons*, p. 426.

49. Miller, *Charles Dickens: The World of His Novels*, p. 67.

50. Froude, *The Nemesis of Faith*, p. 15.

51. Daleski, *Dickens and the Art of Analogy*, p. 75.

52. Italo Calvino, *Invisible Cities*, trans. William Weaver (New York: Harcourt Brace Jovanovich, 1972), p. 97.

53. Howard Schwartz, "Afterword: Kafka and the Modern Parable," in *Imperial Messages: One Hundred Modern Parables*, ed. Schwartz (New York: Avon, 1976), pp. 326–27.

3. Transitional Dickens: Biblical Schemes and New Worlds in *Dombey and Son*

1. Steven Marcus, *Dickens from Pickwick to Dombey* (New York: Simon and Schuster, 1965), p. 355.

2. William J. Roffey, "Essex Street Chapel: A Note on Dickens's Attendance There," *The Dickensian* 22 (July–September 1926): 186–87, quoting from J. Panton Ham, "Para-

bles of Fiction: A Memorial Discourse on Charles Dickens" (London: Trübner and Company, 1870).

3. See Michael Steig, *Dickens and Phiz* (Bloomington: Indiana University Press, 1978), pp. 104–5, and "Iconography of Sexual Conflict in *Dombey and Son*," *Dickens Studies Annual*, vol. 1, ed. Robert B. Partlow, Jr. (Carbondale: Southern Illinois University Press, 1970), pp. 161–67. See also Q. D. Leavis, "The Dickens Illustrations: Their Function," in F. R. and Q. D. Leavis, *Dickens the Novelist* (New York: Pantheon, 1970), p. 356; and John R. Reed, "Emblems in Victorian Literature," *Hartford Studies in Literature* 2, no. 1 (1970): 28–30.

4. See, e.g., A. E. Dyson, "The Case for Dombey Senior," *Novel* 2 (Winter 1969): 133–34; and Andrew Sanders, *Charles Dickens, Resurrectionist* (New York: St. Martin's Press, 1982), pp. 94–130.

5. Unsigned review of *Dombey and Son* in *North American Review* 69 (October 1849): 405; and [John Eagles], "A Few Words About Novels—a Dialogue," *Blackwood's Magazine* 64 (October 1848), reprinted in *Dickens: The Critical Heritage*, ed. Philip Collins (London: Routledge and Kegan Paul, 1971), p. 231. Even Dickens admits in chapter 60, "It was not in the nature of things" that Dombey "should be softened" (p. 469).

6. Unsigned review of *Dombey and Son* in *Rambler* 1 (1 January 1848): 64; and Julian Moynahan, "Dealings with the Firm of Dombey and Son: Firmness *versus* Wetness," in *Dickens and the Twentieth Century*, ed. John Gross and Gabriel Pearson (Toronto: University of Toronto Press, 1962), p. 127.

7. John Forster, *The Examiner* (28 October 1848), p. 692; and Arthur Dudley, "Charles Dickens," *Revue des Deux Mondes* 21 (1848): 901–22, trans. in *The People's Journal* 5 (1848): 229–31.

8. Leavis and Leavis, *Dickens the Novelist*, p. 2.

9. See Number Plans for 10, "Appendix B: The Number Plans," *Dombey and Son*, ed. Alan Horsman (Oxford: Clarendon Press, 1974), p. 844.

10. Kathleen Tillotson, *Novels of the Eighteen-Forties* (Oxford: Oxford University Press, 1954), p. 201, quoting from a letter of 1848 in *Letters of Matthew Arnold to Arthur Hugh Clough*, ed. H. F. Lowry (1932), p. 97.

11. See an unsigned review of Samuel Smiles' *Lives of the Engineers* (1861) in *The British Quarterly Review* 35 (1 April 1862): 263: "it is a thought of deep truth, that the Deity should have permitted man . . . to adjust and control the masses and forces of the material creation, so that they shall subdue one another to his service, and enable him to assert in his history so largely the sublime dominion of mind over matter."

12. Plans for Number 1, in Clarendon *Dombey and Son*, p. 835.

13. Rob's schooling at the Charitable Grinders turns his "social existence" into something "more like that of an early Christian, than an innocent child of the nineteenth century," for he is "stoned in the streets" for his charity attire (6.57). He becomes a Prodigal Son (22.258–59) and a Cain (255) in this Dombey world of false Christianity.

14. The family baptisms also incorporated a host of "literary" allusions into the names

of Dickens' children: Macready, Walter Landor, Francis Jeffrey, Alfred Tennyson, Count D'Orsay, Sydney Smith, Henry Fielding, and Bulwer Lytton.

15. "Holy Baptism," in *The Christian Year*, Canterbury Poets, ed. William Sharp (Newcastle-on-Tyne: Walter Scott Press, 1827), p. 263.

16. Sanders' *Charles Dickens, Resurrectionist* is devoted to exploring Dickens' wide-ranging use of the motif of rebirth, a most fluid conception that extends from St. Paul's historical and theological ideas of resurrection to Dickens' revision of Jesus' words to Nicodemus, "every man who seeks heaven must be born again, in good thoughts of his Maker" (letter to David Dickson, 10 May 1843, P 3:485); it includes the notions of good deeds springing from the exemplary deathbed, the eternal rebirth of hope, the change of heart, the gain time brings out of loss, nature's self-renewal, and (surely the bottom line in resurrection philosophy) the fact that "life must go on." In my view, as Dickens works out the fictional possibilities in this spectrum, the natural and psychological meanings of rebirth tend to replace the religious ones associated with Sydney Carton's favorite text, "I am the Resurrection and the Life"; but this Sanders wants to deny in his effort to convince that the earthly renewals in the fiction are anchored in Dickens' Christian belief in heaven.

17. Cousin Feenix, despite his name, will never find rebirth in the waters of Baden-Baden, nor does the accident of putting "his noble name into a wrong place, and enrol-[ling] himself as having been born, that morning" of the wedding avail (31.373); cf. Sol Gills, 4.29.

18. Unsigned review of *Dombey and Son*, *Parker's London Magazine* (May 1848), p. 201.

19. William Kent, *Dickens and Religion* (London: Watts and Company, 1930), p. 120, quotes this clergyman in 1861 objecting to a penny reading of this sketch in Stowmarket. In "The Bloomsbury Christening," the godfathers and godmother "promised to renounce the devil and all his works—'and all that sort of thing'—. . . 'in less than no time'; and . . . the whole affair went off in the usual business-like and matter-of-course manner" (*SB*, p. 555).

20. Robert C. Elliott, *The Power of Satire: Magic, Ritual, Art* (Princeton: Princeton University Press, 1960), p. 274.

21. The emotional vacuum is epitomized in religious clichés such as Mrs. Chick's counsel to Florence, "all grief is unavailing, and . . . it is our duty to submit" (18.204); cf. Cuttle's "what can't be cured must be endoored" (32.393, a proverb that appears in Rabelais and in Burton's *Anatomy of Melancholy*; see Alfred H. Holt, "Captain Cuttle's Quotations," *The Dickensian* 28 [Autumn 1932]: 305). In contrast, the "poor excommunicated Miss Tox watered her plants with her tears" (29.353; cf. Ps. 6:6 and *Paradise Lost* 10.1089–90).

22. [Charles Kent], *The Sun* (13 April 1848). For Dickens' response to this review see letter to the editor of *The Sun*, 14 April 1848, D 2:78–79.

23. Walter Bagehot, "Charles Dickens," *National Review* (October 1858), reprinted in *Literary Studies*, ed. Richard Holt Hutton (London: Longmans, Green, 1898), 2:156.

24. Forster, *The Examiner* (28 October 1848), p. 692, quoting Mrs. Anne Marsh.

25. For example, Henry Melvill (Queen Victoria's chaplain), whose sermon on Psalm 68:10 insisted that poverty is a divine appointment and saw it serving the purpose of "displaying the comparative worthlessness of earthly possessions"; God has also "thrown [spiritual] advantages round poverty which will be said to counterbalance its disadvantages." See Sermon 8, "The Provision Made by God for the Poor," and Spital Sermon on Matthew 26:11 in *Sermons*, ed. the Right Rev. C. P. M'Ilvaine (New York: Swords, Stanford and Company, 1838), pp. 162–63, 425.

26. Dennis Walder (*Dickens and Religion* [Boston: George Allen and Unwin, 1981], p. 138) notes this allusion to Carlyle as well as to *Paradise Lost*.

27. Quoted in Kent, *Dickens and Religion*, p. 77.

28. For a discussion of these strategies, see John Holloway, *The Victorian Sage: Studies in Argument* (New York: W. W. Norton, 1953), pp. 7–10.

29. [E. B. Hamley], "Remonstrance with Dickens," *Blackwood's Magazine* 81 (April 1857): 495.

30. Carlyle to Robert Browning, 23 June 1847, in *Letters of Thomas Carlyle to John Stuart Mill, John Sterling, and Robert Browning*, ed. Alexander Carlyle (London: T. Fisher Unwin, 1923), p. 284.

31. Entry for Sunday, 22 April 1832, in *Two Note Books of Thomas Carlyle*, ed. Charles Eliot Norton (1898), reprinted in *A Carlyle Reader: Selections from the Writings of Thomas Carlyle*, ed. G. B. Tennyson (New York: Modern Library, 1969), p. 25.

32. M. M. Bakhtin, "Discourse in the Novel," in *The Dialogic Imagination: Four Essays by M. M. Bakhtin*, ed. Michael Holquist, and trans. Caryl Emerson and Michael Holquist (Austin: University of Texas Press, 1981), p. 280.

33. John Forster, review of Arthur Penrhyn Stanley, *The Life and Correspondence of Thomas Arnold* . . . (1844), in *The Examiner* (12 October 1844), p. 644.

34. Marcus, *Dickens from Pickwick to Dombey*, p. 51.

35. Lord Jeffrey to Dickens, 31 January 1847, reprinted in *Critical Heritage*, p. 217.

36. Dr. Thomas Arnold, Sermon 16 on Matthew 6:10 in *Sermons* (London: B. Fellowes, 1844), 1:189.

37. Moynahan, "Dealings with the Firm of Dombey and Son," p. 129.

38. Only facetiously and from a child's point of view does Dickens express a sense of the difficulties of Scripture (see 8.85, 12.133, 39.456).

39. Forster, *The Examiner* (12 October 1844), p. 644.

40. The anonymous reviewer of *Dombey and Son* no. 16 in the *Rambler* 1 (1848) noted disapprovingly that religious feeling is not a cause of her virtue but "merely . . . one of the flowers that spring spontaneously out of her pure and gentle nature. We are not sure that there is any one distinct recognition of the claims of duty or principle throughout." Notably, there is no ethical struggle when Florence flees the Dombey home, no hint from Dickens "that in this there was any dereliction of duty, any thing to excuse, any thing to atone for" (65).

41. See J. W. T. Ley, "Sentimental Songs in Dickens," *The Dickensian* 28 (Autumn

1932): 313–21, for several such attributions in *Dombey and Son*. *The Beggar's Opera* allusion Cuttle also attributes to the Bible: " 'Tis woman as seduces all mankind. For which, you'll overhaul your Adam and Eve, brother" (56.667). When Cuttle and Bunsby read the Last Will and Testament of the missing Gills, they improvise the most absurdly unfeeling funeral service imaginable out of nautical quotations and poetical clichés (see 39.464).

42. When Dickens chose for the first public reading from his own works scenes he entitled *The Story of Little Dombey*, the only one of fifteen scripts during the 1850s and 1860s with a deathbed, Dickens' personal intention seems to have been to create a community of sorrow, rather than of reconciliation and hope, that might help him continue to mourn Mary Hogarth's death. The anguish he went through in this reading's rehearsals (as attested by Mamie Dickens, *My Father as I Recall Him* [New York: E. P. Dutton, 1897], p. 9) suggests he was not yet reconciled to that death. On the public impact of Paul Dombey's death, see Forster, *The Examiner* (28 October 1848), pp. 692–93; and Lord Jeffrey's letters to Dickens of 14 December 1846, 31 January 1847, 5 July 1847, and 12 September 1847, reprinted in *Critical Heritage*, pp. 216–18.

43. Bagehot, "Charles Dickens," 2:158.

44. Unsigned review of *Dombey and Son* no. 1, in *Economist* (10 October 1846), reprinted in *Critical Heritage*, p. 215.

45. Leavis and Leavis, *Dickens the Novelist*, p. 17.

46. See Walder, *Dickens and Religion*, pp. 133–34, for a discussion of popular traditions Dickens draws upon.

47. Tennyson, *Memoir* 2:367, quoted in *Victorian Poetry and Poetics*, ed. Walter E. Houghton and G. Robert Stange, 2d ed. (Boston: Houghton Mifflin, 1968), p. 162, n. 1. Dickens often expressed his belief in a divine guiding hand (see Walder, *Dickens and Religion*, p. 8, and Mamie Dickens, *My Father as I Recall Him*, pp. 144–45).

48. Kent, *Dickens and Religion*, pp. 44–45.

49. Unsigned review of *Dombey and Son* in *North British Review* 7 (May 1847): 116; R. H. Hutton, "The Genius of Dickens," reprinted in *Brief Literary Criticisms*, ed. E. M. Roscoe (London: Macmillan, 1906), pp. 56–57.

50. Lord Jeffrey to Dickens, 14 December 1846, reprinted in *Critical Heritage*, p. 216.

51. Marcus, *Dickens from Pickwick to Dombey*, p. 352.

52. See Alexander Welsh, *The City of Dickens* (Oxford: Clarendon, 1971), pp. 164–79.

53. Sanders, *Charles Dickens, Resurrectionist*, p. 103, interprets this story as "derived . . . from St. Paul's natural analogy for the resurrection of the body together with Polly's own admixture of love and hope and memory" and seems to give a fair account of Dickens' beliefs and intentions; yet he does not take into account the flaunted fictive character of this "Once upon a time" (*DS* 3.20) idealization of death, Mamas, and daughters' pure hearts, as well as its overt purpose as "a comfort" (21) to the sobbing child, akin to Polly's "there there there! There, poor dear!"

54. *North British Review,* p. 117. Compare the *Carlow College Magazine* (August 1870) on Nell, Kit, Paul, Florence, and Little Dorrit: "What are they, after all, but the types of mere natural goodness, with naught in them of the supernatural, nor aught of that eminent heroism which nerved an Aloysius, a Cecilia, an Agnes, or a Vincent of Paul. They are of the earth, earthy, and yet attempered to a something higher, partaking rather of the good fairy, than of the Saint" (p. 215).

55. Walder notes this allusion in *Dickens and Religion,* p. 131.

56. In minor arabesques gracing the novel's ending in reconciliation, Miss Tox brings Rob to admit that "it's never too late . . . to mend" (59.707–8), although this is just the sort of weaseling mimicry this "penitent cove" (46.531) has learned to cultivate; and Mrs. MacStinger tells Cuttle, "I bear no malice now. . . . I hope I go to the altar in another spirit" (60.714–15), although Phiz's illustration, "Another Wedding," shows MacStinger (Bunsby well in hand) triumphant and surrounded by all her Amazonian kind.

57. Moynahan, "Dealings with the Firm of Dombey and Son," p. 125. Barbara Hardy, *The Moral Art of Dickens* (New York: Oxford University Press, 1970), p. 58, interestingly contrasts the converted heroes ("analysed and dramatized in external action, like figures in a Morality Play") with "the converted heroines [who] are analysed and dramatized as realistic characters involved in a complex process" of long inner conflict. Hardy finds Edith Dombey "the finest and fullest analysis of the type" and offers her own fine analysis, pp. 6–69. She observes, "A. O. Cockshut remarks that Dickens's good characters make goodness seem very easy. Characters like Edith . . . make goodness seem very hard"; and in the *Dombey* context, where Edith "achieves a form of earned cynicism," "damnation seems the only honest course" (pp. 67–68). As I argue below, the falseness of Dombey's change is largely exposed by the contrasting difficulty of change of heart for Edith, who is given limited attention in this chapter because so little of the biblical attends her more realistic case (a significant omission).

58. Moynahan makes this argument; so does Nina Auerbach in "Dickens and Dombey: A Daughter After All," *Dickens Studies Annual,* vol. 5, ed. Robert B. Partlow, Jr. (Carbondale: Southern Illinois University Press, 1976), p. 113.

59. For example, "the rolling of [Dombey's] sea of pride" (40.471); the division of Edith and Dombey as "if seas had rolled between them" (27.327); "no chilled spring, lying uncheered by any ray of light in the depths of a deep cave, could be more sullen or more cold than" Dombey (47.541); in the depths of Edith's hatred for Carker, "too far down for her threatening eye to pierce, though she could see into them dimly, lay the dark retaliation [adultery?], whose faintest shadow seen once and shuddered at, and never seen again, would have been sufficient stain upon her soul" (46.538).

60. David D. Marcus, "Symbolism and Mental Process in *Dombey and Son,*" vol. 6, *Dickens Studies Annual,* ed. Robert B. Partlow, Jr. (Carbondale: Southern Illinois University Press, 1977), p. 58.

61. Ibid., p. 59.

62. Ibid., p. 60.

63. See Marcus, *Dickens from Pickwick to Dombey*, pp. 313–14. In *Dickens at Work* (London: Methuen, 1957), p. 94, John Butt and Kathleen Tillotson read the monthly cover design as an illustration of "Pride of Wealth must have a Fall" (a formula that unites the personal moral fable with the Carlylean parable on Mammonism); but one can also see in its little figures at the mercy of a precarious, collapsing design, a third and nonreligious story of human fate.

64. Moynahan, "Dealings with the Firm of Dombey and Son," p. 129.

4. Biblical Reading in the Later Dickens: The Book of Job According to *Bleak House*

1. In a speech to the Metropolitan Sanitary Association (10 May 1851), Dickens declared it "certain . . . that the air from Gin Lane will be carried, when the wind is Easterly, into May Fair" (*The Speeches of Charles Dickens*, ed. K. J. Fielding [Oxford: Clarendon Press, 1960], p. 128). In Job, the East Wind is the agent of God's wrath against rich "oppressors" (see Job 27:21); on this and other texts about the East Wind bringing trouble see Russell M. Goldfarb, "The East Wind as Biblical Allusion in *Bleak House*," *Dickens Studies Newsletter* 12 (March 1981): 14–15. Edwin M. Eigner discusses a pestilent East Wind in Exodus in *The Metaphysical Novel in England and America: Dickens, Bulwer, Melville, and Hawthorne* (Berkeley and Los Angeles: University of California Press, 1978), p. 196. On other associations see Frederic Schwarzbach, "A Note on *Bleak House:* John Jarndyce and the East Wind," *Dickens Studies Newsletter* 6 (September 1975): 82–84, and M. J. Crump, "Dickens's Use of the East Wind: A Further Note," *Dickens Studies Newsletter* 9 (June 1978): 46–47.

2. On the manuscript of Numbers 1 and 2 before publication began was "Bleak House and the East Wind" (see "A Note on the Text," Norton Critical *BH* 778–79), a title incorporating two Joban motifs. The ruined or desolate habitation (see Job 3:14, 8:15, 8:22, 15:28) is usually associated with wickedness and injustice; but some such desolations (e.g., the falling of Job's house upon his children) cannot be explained by prophetic logic. Hence "Bleak House," like "In Chancery" and other titles, points both to suffering that is legible (traceable to social and personal causes) and to that which seems "without cause" (Job 2:3).

3. See, e.g., Ann Y. Wilkinson, in *"Bleak House:* From Faraday to Judgment Day," *ELH* 34 (June 1967): 225–47, and William F. Axton, "Religious and Scientific Imagery in *Bleak House*," *Nineteenth-Century Fiction* 22 (March 1968): 349–59.

4. "Poetic and prophetic Genesis" is Northrop Frye's phrase to describe the place of the Book of Job at the head of the second half (poetry, prophecy, and Wisdom books) of the Old Testament canon (see *The Great Code: The Bible and Literature* [New York and London: Harcourt Brace Jovanovich, 1982], p. 193).

5. Peter K. Garrett, "Double Plots and Dialogical Form in Victorian Fiction," *Nineteenth-Century Fiction* 32 (June 1977): 15.

6. Quoted in Nahum N. Glatzer, *The Dimensions of Job: A Study and Selected Readings* (New York: Schocken Books, 1969), p. ix.

7. Charles Haddon Spurgeon, *Morning by Morning; or, Daily Readings for the Family or the Closet* (New York: Sheldon and Company, n.d.), p. 49. John R. Reed, *Victorian Conventions* (Athens: Ohio University Press, 1975), pp. 12–20, discusses the convention of sending a Job-like character through "the valley of the shadow of death" in nineteenth-century fiction.

8. James Anthony Froude, "The Book of Job," *Westminster Review* (1853), reprinted in *Short Studies on Great Subjects* (New York: Charles Scribner and Company, 1870), 1:253.

9. Ernest Renan, *The Book of Job*, trans. A. F. G. and W. M. T. (London, 1889), reprinted in Glatzer, *The Dimensions of Job*, p. 119.

10. Froude, "The Book of Job," 1:235, 252, 231, 267, 268.

11. Paul Scherer, "Job," *The Interpreter's Bible*, ed. George Arthur Buttrick et al. (New York: Abingdon Press, 1954), 3:907, 906.

12. Samuel Terrien, *The Interpreter's Bible*, 3:886.

13. Harry Levin, *The Gates of Horn: A Study of Five French Realists* (New York: Oxford University Press, 1963), p. 31.

14. Frye, *The Great Code*, p. 198.

15. John Ruskin, "Fiction, Fair and Foul—1," in vol. 34 of *The Works of John Ruskin*, Library Edition, ed. E. T. Cook and Alexander Wedderburn (London: George Allen, 1908), pp. 273, 272.

16. Matthew Henry, *Job to Song of Solomon*, vol. 3 of *Matthew Henry's Commentary on the Whole Bible* (McLean, Va.: MacDonald, n.d.), p. 2. Although it antedates the Victorian period, Henry's work was widely influential in the nineteenth century as "the poor man's commentary, the old Christian's companion, suitable to everybody, instructive to all," according to Spurgeon; Henry's name was "a household word" (see *Commenting and Commentaries* [New York: Sheldon and Company, 1876], p. 13). Popular commentators like Henry reconciled the story of the patient sufferer with the poetry of the rebel by emphasizing the epilogue. Christian typologists could also rescue this book for the life of faith by interpreting Job as a type of Christ, humbled only to be exalted, forsaken by God but interceding for his friends, and affirming the resurrection faith in 19:25 (see Henry, *Commentary on the Whole Bible*, 3:2).

17. See J. Hillis Miller, *Charles Dickens: The World of His Novels* (Bloomington: Indiana University Press, 1958), p. 168. In this earlier essay, Miller finds that there is a true if intermittent Providence in *Bleak House*, but in his later Introduction to *Bleak House*, ed. Norman Page (Harmondsworth, England: Penguin, 1971), he argues that the novel "remains poised" between "its commitment to a traditional interpretation [of events] and a tendency to put all interpretations in question" (p. 34).

18. In "Dickens at Work on *Bleak House:* A Critical Examination of His Memoranda

and Number Plans," *Renaissance and Modern Studies* 9 (1965): 47–65, H. P. Sucksmith has shown how carefully Dickens built into *Bleak House* an "ironic providence or fate." The instability of the novel lies in part, however, in the coexistence of stylistic and allusive indeterminacy with the plot's providential patterning, marked by such determinate allusions as George Rouncewell's "I have my reward" (55.658; cf. Matt. 6:16) and the prophetic narrator's "Tom has his revenge" (46.553; cf. Rom. 12:19). Stephen C. Gill discusses the latter in "Allusion in *Bleak House:* A Narrative Device," *Nineteenth-Century Fiction* 22 (September 1967): 152–53.

19. Froude, "The Book of Job," 1:265.

20. George P. Landow, *Victorian Types, Victorian Shadows: Biblical Typology in Victorian Literature, Art, and Thought* (Boston: Routledge and Kegan Paul, 1980), p. 109. On Job as a figure of Christ, see my note 16. Although the self-sacrificial Queen Esther could also be seen as a type of Christ, St. Jerome calls her "a type of the church," who "frees her people from danger and, after having slain Haman whose name means iniquity, hands down to posterity a memorable day and a great feast" (see letter 53, "To Paulinus," in *St. Jerome: Letters and Select Works*, vol. 6 of *A Select Library of Nicene and Post-Nicene Fathers of the Christian Church*, 2d ser., trans. and ed. Philip Schaff and Henry Wace [New York: Christian Literature Company, 1893], p. 101; cf. Jonathan Edwards, who sees Esther as the church presented "as a chaste virgin to Christ," in *Notes on the Bible*, vol. 9 of *The Works of President Edwards*, ed. Edward Williams and Edward Parsons [1847; reprint, New York: Burt Franklin, 1968], pp. 191–93). Catholic commentaries in the Reformation period treated Esther as a type of the Blessed Virgin (see Lewis Bayles Paton, *A Critical and Exegetical Commentary on the Book of Esther*, International Critical Commentary [New York: Scribner's, 1908], p. 108).

21. Matthew Arnold, "The Scholar-Gypsy," line 195. This Joban section of the poem offers a melancholy memorial to another dejected sufferer, but in recalling *In Memoriam* Arnold forgets to mention Tennyson's faithful conclusion—like a skeptical Bible reader unconvinced by the triumphant ending of Job.

22. The Joban theme of death in life is treated by Garrett Stewart in "The New Mortality of *Bleak House*," *English Literary History* 45 (Fall 1978): 443–85.

23. This allusion may also recall the sealing of the elect in Revelation (see 22:3, 4), just as Esther's being "set apart" by her false comforter, Miss Barbary, points to her elect status despite Barbary's effort to make her a Cain. In contrast, Chadband's forehead "smokes" as though he has come from the pit where God casts Satan and "set[s] a seal upon him" (Rev. 20:3).

24. Froude, "The Book of Job," 1:249.

25. Martin Buber, *The Prophetic Faith*, trans. Carlyle Witton-Davies (New York, 1949), reprinted in Glatzer, *The Dimensions of Job*, p. 59.

26. Renan, *The Book of Job*, p. 114.

27. R. A. F. MacKenzie, S.J., "Job," in *The Jerome Biblical Commentary*, ed. Raymond E. Brown, S.S., Joseph A. Fitzmyer, S.J., and Roland E. Murphy, O. Carm. (Englewood Cliffs, N.J.: Prentice-Hall, 1968), 1:515. The lament is "a prayer of petition

in which a sufferer appeals to God for a hearing, describes his affliction . . . , and beseeches God to put an end to it and save him." This is also the structure of Shakespeare's sonnet 111 (addressed to his patron), which Dickens quotes prominently in his preface; this generating nonbiblical allusion for *Bleak House* is appropriate to the satire, but also suggests the writer's anxieties about his nature being "subdued / To what it works in" (p. 3) as he writes the novel.

28. Renan, *The Book of Job*, p. 113.

29. E. Cobham Brewer, *The Dictionary of Phrase and Fable* (New York: Avenel Books, 1978), p. 499.

30. Terrien, *Interpreter's Bible*, 3:893: The writer of Job "ran the whole gamut of tones: he could be coarse (as in 15:2) or vehement (as in 16:18), gruesome (as in 17:14) or humorous (as in 17:16), tender (as in 14:13ff) or passionate (as in 19:13–19). He used all shades of irony, from earthly sarcasm (as in 12:2) to heavenly persiflage (as in 39:3ff)."

31. W. J. Harvey, *Character and the Novel* (Ithaca, New York: Cornell University Press, 1965), p. 92.

32. In contrast, Sandra K. Young, in "Uneasy Relations: Possibilities for Eloquence in *Bleak House*," *Dickens Studies Annual*, vol. 9, ed. Michael Timko, Fred Kaplan, and Edward Guiliano (New York: AMS Press, 1981), p. 70, infers that "verbal facility, playing with words, is a quality [Esther] denies in herself."

33. Wolfgang Iser, "Indeterminacy and the Reader's Response in Prose Fiction," in *Aspects of Narrative*, ed. J. Hillis Miller (New York: Columbia University Press, 1971), pp. 18–19.

34. Bert G. Hornback, *"Noah's Arkitecture": A Study of Dickens's Mythology* (Athens: Ohio University Press, 1972), p. 87. J. Hillis Miller places the opening "in a world near the beginning of time" (*Charles Dickens*, p. 160).

35. Nahum Glatzer observes that the author of Job probably "expected the reader to view the Job drama against the background of Genesis 3" and notes both allusions and parallels (*The Dimensions of Job*, pp. 8–9). To Frye, the Book of Job is "the epitome of the narrative of the Bible" (*The Great Code*, p. 193): "Job seems to have gone the entire circuit . . . , from creation and fall through the plagues of Egypt, the sayings of the fathers transmitting law and wisdom, the flash of prophetic insight that breaks the chain of wisdom, and on to the final vision of presence" (p. 197). Henry comments that the scriptural books preceding Job "have hitherto been, for the most part, very plain and easy, narratives of matter of fact, which he that runs may read and understand. . . . but here we are advanced to a higher form in God's school, and have books put into our hands wherein are *many things dark and hard to be understood*" (*Commentary on the Whole Bible*, 3.iii).

36. Wolfgang Iser, *The Implied Reader: Patterns of Communication in Prose Fiction from Bunyan to Beckett* (Baltimore: Johns Hopkins University Press, 1974), p. 34. Analogous to the skeptical revision of Genesis in chapter 1 is the narrator's ironic description of Chesney Wold (41.514) in terms that echo the Creation story; Gill discusses this passage in "Allusion in *Bleak House*," pp. 151–52.

37. On the relation of the name *nōah* to *nāham* (to console), see Eugene H. Maly, "Genesis," *Jerome Biblical Commentary*, 1:15. On the political implications of the novel's ironic Noah's ark motif (e.g., 40.495–96 and 504), see Richard D. Altick, "*Bleak House:* The Reach of Chapter One," *Dickens Studies Annual*, vol. 8, ed. Michael Timko, Fred Kaplan, and Edward Guiliano (New York: AMS Press, 1980), p. 76. On this motif as positive, see Thorell Tsomondo, "'A Habitable Doll's House': Beginning in *Bleak House*," *The Victorian Newsletter*, no. 62 (Fall 1982), pp. 7, 5. Waters rise and recede at Chesney Wold throughout the story, as in Job 12:15; and the sketch of Miss Flite letting her birds go free on the monthly number covers visually recalls Noah and the dove.

38. See Henry, *Commentary on the Whole Bible*, 3:3: "His name *Job*, or *Jjob*, some say, signifies *one hated* and counted as an enemy. Others make it to signify one that grieves or groans; thus the sorrow he carried in his name might be a check to his joy in his prosperity." *Iyov* (Job) is close to *Oyev* (enemy), as Glatzer suggests (*The Dimensions of Job*, p. 17). Terrien relates the name *'iyyôbh* ("Job") to the Hebrew verb *'āyabh* (to be hostile, to treat as enemy) and connects it with the Arabic stem *'wb* (to come back, to be penitent) (see *Interpreter's Bible*, 3:908).

39. Axton, "Religious and Scientific Imagery in *Bleak House*," p. 357.

40. In *Creation and Fall: A Theological Interpretation of Genesis 1–3*, translated from *Schöpfung und Fall* (Munich: Chr. Kaiser Verlag, 1937) by John C. Fletcher (New York: Macmillan, 1959), Dietrich Bonhoeffer suggests a related general reason for the anger in *Bleak House:* "Man . . . finds he is in the middle, knowing neither the end nor the beginning, and yet . . . coming from the beginning and going towards the end. He sees that his life is determined by these two facets, of which he knows only that he does not know them" (p. 14). God raises this problem in Job 38:4, "Where wast thou when I laid the foundations of the earth? declare, if thou hast understanding." Compare with Richard on being in the middle: "how *can* I be more settled? . . . I was born into this unfinished contention with all its chances and changes" (23.288).

41. For *Bleak House*'s serpent motif begun here, another biblical source (besides the snake of Genesis 3) is Mordecai's dream of dragons come "forth ready to fight" on "a day of darkness and obscurity" when "the whole righteous nation. . . . cried unto God" for aid; see the apochryphal additions to Esther 11:5–11. Dickens could have read the Apochrypha in the family Bible, now on loan to the Dickens House Museum, London.

42. Allusion identified by Susan Shatto, "A Commentary on Dickens's *Bleak House*" (Ph.D. diss., University of Birmingham, England, 1974).

43. Maly, "Genesis," 1:15.

44. That Dickens replays this scene on other occasions (e.g., in chapters 20 and 32) suggests the attractiveness of the pagan world view underlying this Old Testament story of God and Satan, drawn from the international folklore of the ancient East (see Terrien, *Interpreter's Bible*, 3:879); much of the impersonal narrator's commentary implies that capricious, cruel gods rule the world.

45. Ford and Monod identify this allusion (see Norton Critical *BH*, p. 10, n. 3).

46. J. Hillis Miller emphasizes the stylistic importance of the present tense for these apocalyptic disappearances: "things . . . happe[n] one after the other in an eternal present formed out of the instantaneous annihilation of what has just occurred" (see *Charles Dickens*, p. 176).

47. Dickens' preoccupation with mortality in *Bleak House* is tempered by his awareness that people also unnecessarily choose death in life. The allusion to 1 Peter 1:24 ("all flesh is as grass") in Vholes' "making hay of the grass which is flesh" (39.482) constitutes a cannibalizing of the Peter text for a natural man who does not live by the Word, which endures forever. The fuller verse ("all the glory of man as the flower of grass. . . . withereth," cf. Isa. 40:6) suggests the fate of Richard's blooming prospects under Vholes' deathly care. Esther's burning of Woodcourt's dried nosegay, "dust in an instant" (44.539), recalls the Burial Service and suggests her 1 Peter attitude toward her fleshly needs; as with Vholes, the allusion is ironic—neither *must* choose death.

48. See Jeremiah's curse against his day in 20:14 and 15:10. Froude points out the incompatibility of the Job poems with the discourse of the prophetic period, "an ill occasion for searching into the broad problems of human destiny; the present is all-important and all-absorbing" ("The Book of Job," 1:239).

49. For example, the "appointed night" for Esther's receipt of Jarndyce's proposal (44.536), a false climax, and the "appointed . . . time" for Esther's fairytale-like restoration (60.714, 64.749); compare with Esther 9:27, the "appointed time" for celebration of a divine rescue from death. Ford and Monod (p. 391, n. 1) identify the Job 7:1 allusion.

50. Peter Brooks, *The Melodramatic Imagination: Balzac, Henry James, Melodrama, and the Mode of Excess* (New Haven: Yale University Press, 1976), pp. 55, 20.

51. Paul Zweig, *The Adventurer* (New York: Basic Books, 1974), p. 173, also connects gothic romance "with incipient Jobs."

52. Froude, "The Book of Job," 1:258. See also Harold Dekker, Introduction to John Calvin's *Sermons from Job*, sel. and trans. Leroy Nixon (Grand Rapids: Eerdman's, 1952), p. xxxii.

53. Brooks, *The Melodramatic Imagination*, p. 2.

54. These texts occur several chapters after Daniel reads the writing on the wall at Belshazzar's feast; to this Dickens alludes obliquely in Krook's prefigurative wall-writing (cf. 41:507–8 and Dan. 5:5), as Michael Ragussis notes in "The Ghostly Signs of *Bleak House*," *Nineteenth-Century Fiction* 34 (December 1979): 264. But this is another ironic allusion: just as Krook is neither real melodramatic villain nor prophet, so the implications of his writing are illegible to those who try to read it.

55. Brooks, *The Melodramatic Imagination*, p. 33.

56. "Dickens' Working Plans," memorandum for Number 10, in Norton Critical *Bleak House*, p. 787.

57. Bruce Vawter, C. M., "Introduction to Prophetic Literature," *Jerome Biblical Commentary*, 1:224.

58. See ibid., 1:236. Dickens also uses the prophetic image of the stones crying out

against evil (see Luke 19:40 and Hab. 2:11) with Caddy (5.47) and Tulkinghorn (48.583) but his point is that the stones *do not* cry out—the prophetic signs are dumb.

59. Brooks, *The Melodramatic Imagination*, p. 11.

60. George J. Worth, *Dickensian Melodrama: A Reading of the Novels* (Lawrence: University of Kansas Press, 1978), p. 127.

61. Other things reinforce the preposterous Guppy's comic divinity: a running headline in the Charles Dickens Edition for chapter 13 reads "Under the eye of Guppy" (Norton Critical *BH*, p. 800); he imagines other "swells" want to "depose him," and "in the most ingenious manner takes infinite pains to counterplot, when there is no plot" (20.244).

62. Ford and Monod identify this allusion (p. 391, n. 2). The point of the Twenty-Third Psalm satire is that in legal and commercial London there are no guiding shepherds concerned for justice and the public welfare (see 32.392, 48.584, 37.460 and 468, 39.482, 42.514, and 57.682; Job 24:2, Ps. 44:22, and Rom 8:36).

63. Like Job, whose words and life are "wind" (6:26, 7:7), Krook has longed for death; he has been heard below "humming, like the wind" his own death song on his birthday (see 32.398). Job's pride ends "in dust and ashes" when he confesses he has presumed to know God's mysteries (42:6); Krook has pride in secrets he does not understand and ends in a "log of wood sprinkled with white ashes" (403). These and other ironic linkages to the Joban subtext make Krook less clearly a prophetic emblem for evil.

64. Brooks, *The Melodramatic Imagination*, p. 50.

65. Renan, *The Book of Job*, p. 112.

66. Froude, "The Book of Job," 1:230.

67. Dickens also parodies the resurrection theme in Bucket: "Like man in the abstract, he is here to-day and gone tomorrow—but, very unlike man indeed, he is here again the next day" (53.626). But Hortense points out his limitations as a resurrection man who cannot restore Tulkinghorn to life, Lady Dedlock to honor, or Sir Leicester to his former pride; then "It is but the death, it is all the same" (see 54.652–53)—the "same death eternally" yet again.

68. Froude, "The Book of Job," 1:266.

69. Renan, *The Book of Job*, p. 111.

70. See Lawrence Frank, " 'Through a Glass Darkly': Esther Summerson and *Bleak House*," *Dickens Studies Annual*, vol. 4, ed. Robert B. Partlow, Jr. (Carbondale: Southern Illinois University Press, 1975), p. 111.

71. Esther's central encounter with the incongruous—her discovery of the surprising kinship with Lady Dedlock—is in concentrated form akin to many other moments of confusion, disorientation, and "shock" in her narrative (e.g., Chancery discoveries in 5.52). The establishing and disruption of configurations, a process essential to learning and to reading, does go on in Esther's narrative for her and for Dickens' reader, although not in steady progression toward conclusive knowledge.

72. For other appreciations of Esther's psychological portraiture that have most influenced this essay, see William Axton, "The Trouble with Esther," *Modern Language Quarterly* 26 (December 1965): 545–57, and "Esther's Nicknames: A Study in Rele-

vance," *The Dickensian* 62 (Autumn 1966): 158–66; Q. D. Leavis, " 'Bleak House': A Chancery World," in F. R. Leavis and Q. D. Leavis, *Dickens the Novelist* (New York: Pantheon, 1970), pp. 118–79; Alex Zwerdling, "Esther Summerson Rehabilitated," *PMLA* 88 (May 1973): 429–39; Crawford Killian, "In Defence of Esther Summerson," *Dalhousie Review* 54 (Summer 1974): 318–28 (and see p. 326 on the "Watch ye therefore" allusion); Lawrence Frank, " 'Through a Glass Darkly': Esther Summerson and *Bleak House*," pp. 91–112; and Paul Eggert, "The Real Esther Summerson," *Dickens Studies Newsletter* 11 (September 1980): 74–81. Michael Slater, *Dickens and Women* (Stanford: Stanford University Press, 1983), pp. 255–57, has more recently contributed a succinct, telling analysis of Dickens' contradictory Esther.

73. "The Sensational Williams," *All the Year Round* 11 (13 February 1864): 14–15.

74. Ragussis' phrase (see "The Ghostly Signs of *Bleak House*," pp. 264–65): Summerson "finds herself in the wilderness of ink, in 'the immense desert of law-hand,' like her Old Testament counterpart, the orphan 'Queen' (lix, 704), who reverses Haman's law of the dead letters in a striking prefiguration of the New Testament." See also Eigner, *The Metaphysical Novel in England and America*, p. 198: "her fate, like that of the biblical heroine, is to rise from a despised birth to become the beautiful and redeeming queen of her oppressed, leaderless people." Harland S. Nelson, *Charles Dickens* (Boston: Twayne, 1981), p. 178, reads the Aunt's "you are set apart" (3.19) as a signal of the child's queenly election to save her people.

75. See Zwerdling on the advantage of first person, "Esther Summerson Rehabilitated," p. 433. Fredric V. Bogel, in "Fables of Knowing: Melodrama and Related Forms," *Genre* 11 (Spring 1978): 100, thinks Dickens withholds irony from Esther.

76. See Robert Alter, *The Art of Biblical Narrative* (New York: Basic Books, 1981), p. 34.

77. Henry, *Joshua to Esther*, vol. 2 of *Commentary on the Whole Bible*, p. 1121. Henry Melvill (chaplain to Queen Victoria) also emphasizes this theme in "The Sleepless Night" (on Est. 6:1) in *Sermons*, ed. the Right Reverend C. P. M'Ilvaine (New York: Stanford and Swords, 1850), 2:51–60.

78. Especially in the apocryphal additions, Esther also provides a relevant subtext for the *Bleak House* satire on "the pestilent behavior of them that are unworthily placed in authority" (Apoc. Est. 16:7; cf. "most pestilent of hoary sinners," 1.6, and "all authorities in all places . . . where false pretenses are made, and where injustice is done," 32.403).

79. Demetrius R. Dumm, O.S.B., "Tobit, Judith, Esther," in *The Jerome Biblical Commentary*, 1:629.

80. Henry, *Commentary on the Whole Bible*, 2:1127.

81. Ibid., 2:1127. Mordecai and Jarndyce both also refuse to bow down to the secular powers.

82. Dumm, "Tobit, Judith, Esther," 1:630–31.

83. John Kitto, "Woman," in *The Kings of Israel*, vol. 2 of *Daily Bible Illustrations* (New York: Robert Carter and Brothers, 1872), p. 10.

84. Frank, " 'Through a Glass Darkly': Esther Summerson and *Bleak House*," p. 94.

85. Carey A. Moore, trans., *The Anchor Bible: Esther* (Garden City, N.Y.: Doubleday, 1971), p. xxxiv. Although she disavows the compliment (17.207–9, 45.547), Esther is associated by Skimpole (43.527), by Jarndyce (8.89), and sarcastically by Richard (45.546) with the female biblical figure of Wisdom (see Prov. 8 and 2 Sam. 20:16) who is sister and friend, to be loved rather than the adulteress (Prov. 7:4–5). Susan Shatto notes the many proverbial phrases in Esther's speech; see "New Notes on *Bleak House*—Part I," *Dickens Studies Newsletter* 6 (September 1975): 78. The identification of Esther with Wisdom is, however, unstable because Esther *is*, as she says so often, "foolish" as well as wise.

86. Mordecai dreams that from the people's cry "as it were from a little fountain, was made a great flood, even much water. The light and the sun rose up, and the lowly were exalted" (Apoc. Est. 11:10–11); the river "is Esther" (10:6). *Bleak House*, after a failed Deluge, moves through Esther's two baptisms that enable her to become a renewing presence wherever "It rain[s] Esther" (wherever Esther reigns), even if she cannot redeem the world. As a Wisdom figure, Esther Summerson is also associated with the fountain of life (Prov. 10:11, 16:22), a biblical image that connotes length of days, riches, large family, goods, success, and prestige in this life—rewards Job and Esther Summerson finally gain.

87. Henry, *Commentary on the Whole Bible*, 3:iii.

88. MacKenzie, "Job," 1:515.

89. Esther's allusion to Proverbs 13:12 in 24.307 occurs in a passage of gnomic phrases as though she is practicing proverb-making. Her long list of anomalies, however, represents Job's view of Proverbs, for the whole point is that evil is not punished and good rewarded as in Wisdom literature. The other narrator likewise reveals the limits of biblical and worldly wisdom through calling Vholes "Diligent, persevering, steady, acute in business" (39.483; Ford and Monod note this allusion to Rom. 12:11 and Prov. 22:29). Vholes turns up again in Esther's Narrative with "honesty being my golden rule" (51.608) and "the labourer is worthy of his hire" (609; Luke 10:7). In 49.588 the other narrator explicitly asks whether "there be any truth in adages."

90. Both narratives are peopled with false patriarchs exposed by ironic biblical allusion; e.g., Turveydrop ("Strike deep, and spare not," see 23.293 and n. 4; cf. 1 Sam. 15:3); Sir Leicester ("as if he were nodding down . . . from a Mount," 29.358—presumably Sinai, since he is upholding the law here; see also Prov. 22:28, which confirms his conservative social views: "Remove not the ancient landmark, which thy fathers have set"); and playful allusions to "Methoozellers" (11.134) and Noah's drunkenness (30.376).

91. See George Ford, *Dickens and His Readers: Aspects of Novel-Criticism Since 1836* (New York: W. W. Norton, 1965), pp. 67–71.

92. See Barry V. Qualls, *The Secular Pilgrims of Victorian Fiction: The Novel as Book of Life* (Cambridge: Cambridge University Press, 1982), pp. 114–19, for a pertinent discussion of this pilgrimage, a Romantic revision of the Puritan progress to salvation.

93. Henry, *Commentary on the Whole Bible*, 3:iv.

94. "Dickens' Working Plans," Norton Critical *Bleak House*, p. 786.

95. Eigner, *The Metaphysical Novel in England and America*, p. 197.

96. Joseph I. Fradin, "Will and Society in *Bleak House*," *PMLA* 81 (March 1966): 95–96. It seems necessary to dualistic treatments of *Bleak House* to insist on Esther's consistency, lucidity, and exemplary religious orientation in order to distinguish her sharply from the other narrator; for critics bound to the form of this argument, see, e.g., J. Hillis Miller, *Charles Dickens*, pp. 210–11, 213; Leonard W. Deen, "Style and Unity in *Bleak House*," *Criticism* 3 (Summer 1961): 207–8, 214; Robert A. Donovan, "Structure and Idea in *Bleak House*," *English Literary History* 29 (June 1962): 200–201; and Harvey, *Character and the Novel*, pp. 89–99.

97. Esther echoes Song of Solomon 8:6 when she refers to Ada's "love that nothing but death can change," a not necessarily hopeful revision of the biblical idea (51.613). The novel's major opposition is love against death, as I argue below; but Esther's being "Dickens's emblem of hope in a dark world" because she loves, as Harland S. Nelson argues (*Charles Dickens*, pp. 177–82), is far more problematic than is often assumed.

98. Ford and Monod identify this allusion (p. 307, n. 3). Significantly, Esther omits the second half of this proverb: "but when the desire cometh, it is a tree of life."

99. More than the social satire allusion it appears to be, this phrase from the catechism is part of the child's answer to the question, "What did your Godfathers and Godmothers then [do] for you?" By recalling the baptismal vows, the allusion suggests the theme of parental irresponsibility in which Lady Dedlock is implicated. This scene in chapter 38 also marks the beginning of Esther's maturity in facing her inner demons, which she must then renounce for herself.

100. Lady Dedlock also serves as a Job figure, particularly at her crisis: in 55.666–67, she is denounced by an invisible accuser, throws herself on the floor and buries her face, believes there is no escape but in death, is hunted, is whirled away like a leaf before a mighty wind, protests her innocence (of the murder), is homeless, is sought but not found, is a lonely figure; in 59.710–12 she is pursued by would-be comforters and saviors, is unrecognizable (as is Job in suffering), is obsessed with writing (see Job 19:23–24) but does it "almost in the dark" (710), and loses her way. These parallels are not anchored by any formal allusions I could trace.

101. Eigner, however, reads this passage as "the beginning of Esther's queenly power, which had long lain dormant" (*The Metaphysical Novel in England and America*, p. 199); Qualls believes "the pattern of felt grace is on this meditation. Esther discovers in the random happenings of her life a divinely ordained pattern," like Bunyan, although the quest for innocence is Romantic (*The Secular Pilgrims of Victorian Fiction*, pp. 117–18). It is ironic that Esther declares her innocence of birth from Romans 8:28, a key proof text for the Calvinist doctrine of election; Spurgeon uses Romans 8 in Sermon 5, "Election," in *Sermons*, 2d ser. (New York: Robert Carter and Brothers, n.d.), p. 73.

102. Frank, "'Through a Glass Darkly': Esther Summerson and *Bleak House*," p. 101.

103. Froude, "The Book of Job," 1:269.

104. Ibid., 1:262.

105. In the spirit of mature love and pity, not cheerful-evasive charity, Esther revises Deuteronomy 32:32, a diatribe against Sodom and Gomorrah, in her elegiac reference to "all the ashey fruit [the Chancery suit] casts ashore" (27.472; Ford and Monod, n. 7, also suggest more immediate sources). Mature love also motivates Sir Leicester's Christian message, "Full forgiveness" (56.669). The complexity of the "love" theme is indicated, however, in Phiz's illustration, "Sunset in the long Drawing-room at Chesney Wold," which groups Good Samaritan with Venus and Cupid images; see Michael Steig, *Dickens and Phiz* (Bloomington: Indiana University Press, 1978), pp. 149–50. *Bleak House*'s Good Samaritan motif is extensive: George has rescued Phil Squod from a ditch and nursed Hawdon; Jo is aided by the brickmakers, Esther and Jarndyce, Snagsby (with the "balsam" of coin) and Woodcourt on Jo's deathbed; Jarndyce refers to the theme of selfless help in a truncated, humanized version of Matthew 25:40 ("forasmuch as she [Charley] did it unto the least of these——!") in 15.190, a chapter full of Joban sufferings contrasted with acts of charity.

106. Spurgeon, Sermon 6, "The Anxious Inquirer" (on Job 23:3) in *Sermons*, 3d ser., p. 98.

5. The Seer, the Preacher, and the Living Gospel: Vision and Revision in *Little Dorrit*

1. Barry V. Qualls, in *The Secular Pilgrims of Victorian Fiction: The Novel as Book of Life* (Cambridge: Cambridge University Press, 1982), pp. 100–102, discusses the religious prison-labyrinth emblem as Dickens used it.

2. Frank Kermode, *The Sense of an Ending: Studies in the Theory of Fiction* (London: Oxford University Press, 1966), p. 8. The novel is also replete with "end effects in the text" by which the conclusion "is supplemented in advance"; on this technique see Kermode, "Sensing Endings," *Nineteenth-Century Fiction* 33 (June 1978): 155.

3. Even before Rigaud has introduced the *vanitas, vanitatum* theme, skeptical revision of apocalyptic has invaded Dickens' mode of description in the opening paragraphs, where there is "no new thing" under the "stare and glare" for those gathered to trade, "descendants from all the builders of Babel" (1.1.1). Their vain building suggests another sense in which "vanity" reigns here: the monotony of the work done by "exhausted labourers in the fields" (1.1.2). Ecclesiastes too reads the natural world as a parable of human futility (1:3–9). At the close of chapters 1 and 2, Dickens reenacts Ecclesiastes 1:5 ("the sun also ariseth, and the sun goeth down"); the dominant note at the end of chapter 2 is resignation to circumlocutory motion "under the sun" (Ecc. 1:3). The incidents of chapter 2 also parody or otherwise correct apocalyptic models: the officials' "mighty production of papers" (1.1.21) parodies the opening of the Book of Life and

sealing of the blessed (Rev. 20:12–13); the bejeweled banquet in "Christian style" (pp. 21–23) is a mock paradisal banquet, a "disenchanted feast" (1.8.150); Miss Wade corrects Mr. Meagles' complacent Christian talk of reconciliation and also makes an ominous prediction that perverts the language of the Golden Rule or the Lord's Prayer (especially given Pet's response, "O, Father!"), while echoing Ecclesiastes 1:9, "that which is done is that which shall be done" (see p. 24).

4. Kermode, *The Sense of an Ending*, p. 124.

5. Ibid., p. 18.

6. K. J. Fielding, *Charles Dickens: A Critical Introduction* (London: Longmans, Green, 1958), p. 146; cf. John Holloway's Introduction to *Little Dorrit* (Harmondsworth: Penguin, 1967), p. 27.

7. A. P. Stanley, Lecture 28, *Lectures on the History of the Jewish Church* (1863), reprinted in *A Selection from the Writings of Dean Stanley*, ed. Anthony S. Algen (New York: Charles Scribner's Sons, 1894), p. 345.

8. Henry, *Job to Song of Solomon*, vol. 3 of *Matthew Henry's Commentary on the Whole Bible* (McLean, Va.: MacDonald, n.d.), p. 979.

9. See, e.g., Sylvia Bank Manning, *Dickens as Satirist* (New Haven: Yale University Press, 1971), p. 9.

10. Lionel Trilling, "*Little Dorrit*," *Kenyon Review* 15 (Autumn 1953): 590.

11. Northrop Frye, *Anatomy of Criticism* (New York: Atheneum, 1968), pp. 233, 230.

12. For a fuller treatment of this literary connection, see my article, "The Arts in These Latter Days: Carlylean Prophecy in *Little Dorrit*," *Dickens Studies Annual*, vol. 8, ed. Michael Timko, Fred Kaplan, and Edward Guiliano (New York: AMS Press, 1980), pp. 139–96. For earlier discussions of these two writers, see Michael Goldberg, *Carlyle and Dickens* (Athens: University of Georgia Press, 1972); William Oddie, *Dickens and Carlyle: The Question of Influence* (London: Centenary Press, 1972); Richard Stang, "*Little Dorrit*: A World in Reverse," in *Dickens the Craftsman: Strategies of Presentation*, ed. Robert B. Partlow, Jr. (Carbondale: Southern Illinois University Press, 1970), pp. 140–64; and John Holloway's Introduction to the Penguin *Little Dorrit*, pp. 16, 20–23.

13. Frye, *Anatomy of Criticism*, p. 234.

14. "The Spirit of Fiction," *All the Year Round* 18 (27 July 1867): 119.

15. Robert C. Elliott, "Satire," in *Princeton Encyclopedia of Poetry and Poetics*, enl. ed., ed. Alex Preminger (Princeton: Princeton University Press, 1974), p. 738.

16. Holloway notes *The Whole Duty of Man* as an anonymous devotional manual published in 1658, possibly by the eventual Provost of Eton, Richard Allestree (Penguin *LD*, p. 904, n. 8).

17. Alexander Welsh, *The City of Dickens* (Oxford: Clarendon Press, 1971), p. 66, n. 32, also notes the *Benedicite, omnia opera Domini* canticle in the Book of Common Prayer.

18. See R. C. Elliott, *The Power of Satire: Magic, Ritual, Art* (Princeton: Princeton University Press, 1960).

19. David Gervais, in "The Poetry of *Little Dorrit*," *Cambridge Quarterly* 4 (Winter

1968–69): 46–47, compares Dickens' speech at Merdle's death with Parliamentary Barnacle rhetoric and similarly argues that it dismisses his more complex effects achieved with this character elsewhere.

20. In Carlyle's "Fire-whirlwind," creation and destruction are simultaneous. Since Dickens draws upon *Sartor Resartus* for Clennam's story, he may well have a Carlylean whirlwind in mind here (see book 3, chapter 5, "The Phoenix"), although the apocalyptic cycle is incomplete and Carlyle is disproved.

21. See F. R. Leavis, "Dickens and Blake: *Little Dorrit*," in F. R. and Q. D. Leavis, *Dickens the Novelist* (New York: Pantheon, 1970), pp. 272–73, on this aspect of the prose.

22. Frye, *Anatomy of Criticism*, p. 224.

23. Appropriately the biblical allusions of book 1 yield in book 2 largely to classical literary and painterly ones as the Dorrits acquire culture; here, too, it is "the—hum—precepts of Mrs. General" to which Dorrit alludes (see 2.5.462–63) rather than biblical ones.

24. C. H. Spurgeon, "The House of Mourning, and the House of Feasting," Sermon 6 on Ecclesiastes 7:2, in *Sermons of Rev. C. H. Spurgeon*, 2d ser. (New York: Robert Carter and Brothers, n.d.), p. 89.

25. Mike Hollington, in "Time in *Little Dorrit*," in *The English Novel in the Nineteenth Century: Essays on the Literary Mediation of Human Values*, ed. George Goodin (Urbana: University of Illinois Press, 1972), makes this point (p. 109) and discusses the novel's deterministic fictions (pp. 115–16).

26. Bert G. Hornback, in *"Noah's Arkitecture": A Study of Dickens's Mythology* (Athens: Ohio University Press, 1972), p. 105, sees the office as a Tower of Babel; Dickens disperses the clan over the face of the earth (see 1.34.390–91; cf. Gen. 11:8). Hornback (pp. 105–7) also discusses a Noah's ark archetype in the "ship of state" motif and in drifting ships like Arthur and Gowan.

27. For example, see Dickens' letter to W. C. Macready (4 October 1855): "the English people are habitually consenting parties to the miserable imbecility into which we have fallen, *and never will help themselves out of it*" (D 2:694–95).

28. John Ruskin, "Of Turnerian Topography," vol. 4 of *Modern Painters*, vol. 6 of *The Works of John Ruskin*, ed. E. T. Cook and Alexander Wedderburn (London: George Allen, 1904), p. 29.

29. See Dennis Walder, in *Dickens and Religion* (Boston: George Allen and Unwin, 1981), p. 188. Walder also notes (p. 189) the appropriate painting of a scene in Joshua 10:13 hanging in her room, in Browne's illustration, "Mr. Flintwinch mediates as a friend of the family."

30. Unsigned review, "The Collected Works of Charles Dickens," *British Quarterly Review* 35 (1 January 1862): 150.

31. A. P. Stanley, Preface to *The Bible: Its Form and Its Substance*, Three Sermons Preached Before the University of Oxford (Oxford: John Henry and James Parker, 1863),

p. iv. Dickens' belief in progressive revelation is discussed below in the section titled "Confession and Dialogue."

32. This god's voice thunders in Mrs. Clennam's curses; her perversion of the "just dispensation of Jehovah" is a felt presence in her parallel constructions, her neat epigrammatic formulas; the "will of the disposer of all things" confused with her will exerts its force through her own frequent imperative mood and imperious active verbs (2.30.755). Her "it is appointed" construction mystifies the identity of her unseen god, but the emphasis her verbal rhythms often place on the first-person pronouns betrays the solipsism of her worship (e.g., "Not unto me the strength be ascribed; not unto me the wringing of the expiation!" (p. 754).

33. Plan for Number 5, chap. 17 (Clarendon *LD*, p. 811). For a general discussion see Paul D. Herring, "Dickens' Monthly Number Plans for *Little Dorrit*," *Modern Philology* 64 (August 1966): 22–63.

34. Plan for Number 12, chap. 6 (p. 818).

35. The whole procedure of her "History" self-consciously follows the skeptical experiential method of recounting incidents, trying illusions, and presenting the dismaying conclusions, always the same: vanity and vexation. To an extraordinary degree she returns to the Preacher's "I see" and "I know" (and their equivalents). The whole project is self-reflexive, like his, but she also sharply anatomizes the "vanity" of those around her (p. 644—a word Dickens chose over "pride" in the original manuscript, n. 4) and carefully disavows "Vanity" for herself (p. 648). Ecclesiastes caught her type: a woman "more bitter than death . . . whose heart is snares and nets, and her hands as bands" (7:26).

36. William A. Beardslee, "The Apocalypse," in *Literary Criticism of the New Testament* (Philadelphia: Fortress Press, 1970), p. 54.

37. See Alan Wilde, "Mr. F's Aunt and the Analogical Structure of *Little Dorrit*," *Nineteenth-Century Fiction* 19 (June 1964): 37; and James R. Kincaid, *Dickens and the Rhetoric of Laughter* (Oxford: Clarendon Press, 1971), p. 219.

38. Stanley, *Lectures*, p. 342.

39. John Kitto, *Daily Bible Illustrations . . . : Job and the Poetical Books*, evening ser. (New York: Robert Carter and Brothers, 1872), p. 353.

40. Stanley, *Lectures*, p. 343.

41. Henry, *Commentary on the Whole Bible*, 3:979.

42. William Meyers, "The Radicalism of *Little Dorrit*," *Literature and Politics in the Nineteenth Century*, ed. John Lucas (London: Methuen, 1971), p. 87.

43. Kenneth Tynan, *The Observer* (22 July 1956), quoted in James Sutherland, *English Satire* (Cambridge: Cambridge University Press, 1958), p. 1.

44. G. B. Shaw, Preface to *Great Expectations* (Edinburgh: R. and R. Clark, 1937), p. xi.

45. Samuel Smiles, *Self-Help*, rev. and enl. ed. (New York: Thomas Y. Crowell, n.d.), clusters many of these proverbs in chapter 9, "Industry and Thrift," pp. 296–97; he also often echoes Ecclesiastes 9:10 (see p. 75).

46. Leslie Stephen, *Life of Fitzjames Stephen* (London: 1895), pp. 453–54, quoted in Walter E. Houghton, *The Victorian Frame of Mind, 1830–1870* (New Haven: Yale University Press, 1957), p. 258. See also the Preface to J. A. Froude, *The Nemesis of Faith*, 2d ed. (London: John Chapman, 1849), p. vi.

47. John Ruskin, "Of Modern Landscape," vol. 3 of *Modern Painters*, vol. 5 of *The Works of John Ruskin*, pp. 322, 318, 317. Later Ruskin specifies: Dickens is one of "our popular authors" who "set themselves definitely against all religious form, pleading for simple truth and benevolence," while Carlyle (along with Tennyson) is "doubtful and indignant" (p. 323).

48. M. M. Bakhtin, "Discourse in the Novel," in *The Dialogic Imagination: Four Essays by M. M. Bakhtin*, ed. Michael Holmquist, trans. Caryl Emerson and Michael Holmquist (Austin: University of Texas Press, 1981), p. 280.

49. Daniel Doyce, "a man as knows his tools and as his tools knows" who inspires his men's cheering "like the rush of their whole history" (2.22.654–55), is just the hero to body forth Carlyle's theme that " 'Tools and the Man,' that were now our Epic" ("Corn-Law Rhymes," *CME* 28:162).

50. Rev. C. H. Spurgeon, *Morning by Morning; or, Daily Readings for the Family or the Closet* (New York: Sheldon and Company, n.d.), p. 331.

51. Qualls, *The Secular Pilgrims of Victorian Fiction*, p. 104.

52. Thomas Carlyle to John A. Carlyle, 1 October 1833, in *The Collected Letters of Thomas and Jane Welsh Carlyle*, ed. Charles Richard Sanders (Durham, N.C.: Duke University Press, 1977), 7:9.

53. Duncan Black MacDonald, *The Hebrew Literary Genius: An Interpretation, Being an Introduction to the Reading of the Old Testament* (Princeton: Princeton University Press, 1933), p. 201.

54. Jerome Beaty, "The 'Soothing Songs' of *Little Dorrit:* New Light on Dickens's Darkness," in *Nineteenth-Century Literary Perspectives*, ed. Clyde de L. Ryals (Durham, N.C.: Duke University Press, 1974), pp. 228–29, discusses the river in *Little Dorrit* 1.16 as an emblem of escape from time but notes nothing suicidal about Clennam's state of mind. Dennis Walder reads the "dream-like, visionary element" in Clennam's river-thoughts in 1.28.330 as a sign of his "saving apprehension of a truly religious view of life" (*Dickens and Religion*, p. 191).

55. J. Hillis Miller, *Charles Dickens: The World of His Novels* (Bloomington: Indiana University Press, 1958), p. 246; Richard Barickman, "The Spiritual Journey of Amy Dorrit and Arthur Clennam," *Dickens Studies Annual*, vol. 7, ed. Robert B. Partlow, Jr. (Carbondale: Southern Illinois University Press, 1978), p. 179. Stang sees Amy presented here as a multi-dimensional possibility in contrast to the two-dimensional people of surface in the novel ("*Little Dorrit:* A World in Reverse," p. 156).

56. See Barickman, "The Spiritual Journey of Amy Dorrit and Arthur Clennam," p. 177.

57. Richard G. Moulton, *A Short Introduction to the Literature of the Bible* (Boston: D. C. Heath, 1901), p. 154.

58. Henry Melvill, "The Advantages of a State of Expectation," Sermon 10, in *Sermons*, ed. the Right Reverend C. P. M'Ilvaine (New York: Stanford and Swords, 1850), 1:103–4.

59. Carlyle counseled, "Thy words, let them be few, and well-ordered" (*LDP* 213); Ecclesiastes, "let thy words be few" (5:2). Both sages ironically belie their own advice, Carlyle through the "multitude of words" in his many volumes, Ecclesiastes through his "sundry curious variations on the same tune" (*LD* 1.12.137) that all is vanity.

60. I am indebted to Anne Davison, a Rutgers University graduate student of Professor Barry V. Qualls, for this reading of "the ambiguity [Ecclesiastes] creates by not directly specifying the antecedent for 'this,'" which can refer both to the human circumstance he has just observed and to "his own vain acts of articulation" ("Ecclesiastes: A Performing Self Unmasked," unpublished seminar paper, 15 February 1983, p. 4).

61. See, e.g., Kitto, *Daily Bible Illustrations*, p. 353.

62. Elaine Showalter, "Guilt, Authority, and the Shadows of *Little Dorrit*," *Nineteenth-Century Fiction* 34 (June 1979): 26–27, discusses the sunscape without shadows in terms of Dickens' fear of exposure.

63. Walter Pater, "Coleridge," in *Appreciations, with an Essay on Style* (1889; reprint, London: Macmillan, 1908), pp. 66–67.

64. Smiles, *Self-Help*, p. 352.

65. Ibid., p. 349.

66. Dickens collaborated on *The Frozen Deep* with Wilkie Collins during the *Little Dorrit* period, when the renunciation plot of *A Tale of Two Cities* was also forming in his mind; see George H. Ford, *Dickens and His Readers: Aspects of Novel-Criticism Since 1836* (New York: W. W. Norton, 1965), p. 67; see also Dickens' letter to John Forster describing himself as "Wardour to the life!" in a Carrick Fell rescue adventure with Wilkie Collins (9 September 1857, D 2:880).

67. Barickman, to whose discussion of renunciation I am indebted, cites several false forms of it ("The Spiritual Journey of Amy Dorrit and Arthur Clennam, p. 177). Gowan mockingly praises the "beautiful sacrifice" of the Saint Bernard system (2.1.429); William Dorrit mocks unwittingly by stressing that he does not wish to "sacrifice" Amy, who must make an impressive match (2.15.590); Dickens also mocks Clennam's teaching of sorrow in Tinkler (see 2.5.461).

68. See, e.g., the verse in *The Christian Year*, Canterbury Poets, ed. William Sharp (London: Walter Scott, 1827), pp. 186–87, on Ephesians 3:13.

69. Charles Frederick Harrold identifies the "Sanctuary of Sorrow" as Wilhelm Meister's hall where murals of Christ's life are to be seen; see his edition of *Sartor Resartus* (Indianapolis: Odyssey Press, 1937), p. 189, n. 1.

70. Walder, *Dickens and Religion*, p. 181.

71. Walder, p. 190, identifies this allusion.

72. Ruskin, "Of Modern Landscape," *Modern Painters*, 3:322.

73. Showalter ("Guilt, Authority, and the Shadows of *Little Dorrit*," pp. 39–40) argues that Arthur does learn in meditating on his suppressed feelings for Little Dorrit, cultivat-

ing his memory, and confronting his demons. But there is much delusion mingled with his discoveries and imprisonment drives him near to insanity (cf. Ecc. 7:7: "Surely oppression maketh a wise man mad").

74. Barickman, "The Spiritual Journey of Amy Dorrit and Arthur Clennam," p. 186.

75. Ruskin, "Of Modern Landscape," *Modern Painters*, 3:327.

76. Jean-Louis D'Aragon, S.J., "The Apocalypse, " in *The Jerome Biblical Commentary*, ed. Raymond E. Brown, S.S., Joseph A. Fitzmyer, S.J., and Roland E. Murphy, O. Carm. (Englewood Cliffs, N.J.: Prentice-Hall, 1968), 2:482.

77. Jacques Ellul, *Apocalypse: The Book of Revelation*, trans. George W. Schreiner (New York: Seabury, 1977), pp. 24–25.

78. Although this passage in 2.34.790 "seems to assert unequivocally a doctrine of presence," Alistair Duckworth writes, that presence although not unavailable is "in fact an indefinitely deferred (differed) value, a 'trace,' not a presence." See "*Little Dorrit* and the Question of Closure," *Nineteenth-Century Fiction* 33 (June 1978): 126–28.

79. Welsh, *The City of Dickens*, pp. 116–17.

80. Ellul, *Apocalypse: The Book of Revelation*, p. 24.

81. Frye, *Anatomy of Criticism*, p. 316.

82. Beardslee, "Literary Criticism of the New Testament," p. 61.

83. Hollington, "Time in *Little Dorrit*," pp. 120, 123.

84. Carlyle, *History of Frederick the Great*, vol. 12 of *Works*, p. 431.

85. [E. B. Hamley], "Remonstrance with Dickens," *Blackwood's Magazine* 81 (April 1857): 503.

86. Robert Garis, *The Dickens Theatre: A Reassessment of the Novels* (Oxford: Clarendon, 1965), p. 165. Garis admits the subtlety, interrupted by "single-minded denunciations," but seems to find it bogus.

87. Barickman, "The Spiritual Journey of Amy Dorrit and Arthur Clennam," p. 167.

88. O. S. Rankin, "Introduction to the Book of Ecclesiastes," in vol. 5 of *The Interpreter's Bible* (New York: Abingdon, 1956), p. 17.

89. Henry, *Commentary on the Whole Bible*, 3:995.

90. Spurgeon, *Morning by Morning*, p. 140.

91. Mircea Eliade, *The Sacred and the Profane: The Nature of Religion*, trans. Willard R. Trask (New York: Harper and Row, 1959), pp. 70–71, 107.

92. R. Rupert Roopnaraine, "Time and the Circle in *Little Dorrit*, " *Dickens Studies Annual*, vol. 3, ed. Robert B. Partlow, Jr. (Carbondale: Southern Illinois University Press, 1978), pp. 54–58, 75.

93. Eliade, *The Sacred and the Profane*, pp. 72, 112.

94. See Jerome Hamilton Buckley, *The Triumph of Time: A Study of the Victorian Concepts of Time, History, Progress, and Decadence* (Cambridge: Harvard University Press, 1966), pp. 66–67.

95. Bakhtin, "Discourse in the Novel," p. 278.

96. Nancy Aycock Metz, "Physician as Cliché and as Character," *Dickens Studies Newsletter* 13 (June 1982): 40–41, discusses this prose.

97. Glenn Gaius Atkins, "Exposition of the Book of Ecclesiastes," vol. 5 of *The Interpreter's Bible*, p. 24.

98. For the idea of Ecclesiastes as a performer in language, I am indebted to Anne Davison, whose work draws upon Richard Poirier, *The Performing Self: Compositions and Decompositions in the Language of Contemporary Life* (New York: Oxford University Press, 1971).

99. Roland E. Murphy, O. Carm., "Ecclesiastes (Quoheleth)," *Jerome Biblical Commentary*, 1:540.

100. Atkins, "Exposition of the Book of Ecclesiastes," p. 25.

101. Henry, *Commentary on the Whole Bible*, 3:982, 984.

102. Michael Slater, *Dickens and Women* (Stanford: Stanford University Press, 1983), p. 258, also discusses Little Dorrit as a credible feminine ideal placed in an imperfect world. To Barbara Hardy, *The Moral Art of Dickens* (New York: Oxford University Press, 1970), p. 16, Amy though not complex is "a very effective character who manages to be both symbolic and sufficiently a creature of time and place" and "Dickens's most successfully heroic character since Oliver Twist." While Dennis Walder recognizes "moments when she lives," his Amy Dorrit "remains an etherealised figure" and "icon-like" (*Dickens and Religion*, pp. 194, 192). Walder's general view of the novel, however, comes close to and has influenced mine: if "there is a new urgency with which spiritual consolation is yearned after," there is also "a new realism with which it is grasped." In this "first, perhaps the only, novel of Dickens's in which plot, character and scene are all closely involved with religion," Dickens may fall "back upon a fundamentally, but not exclusively, humanist approach," but "it is not without the deepest struggle to reach a more 'ideal' and transcendent form of belief, a struggle which paradoxically links his inner life with his times even when he seems to be moving away from them" (p. 172).

103. Trilling, "Little Dorrit," p. 590.

104. See Welsh, *The City of Dickens*, pp. 165–66, 171–73, and 176–79. When Dickens employs the rich-poor antithesis in the closing love scenes, he is also following through with the Wisdom literature texts on "a virtuous woman . . . far above rubies" (Prov. 31:10) and Wisdom itself as "inexhaustible wealth" (see Prov. 3:15, 8:18–19, 20:15; cf. Clennam, 1.35.405, on Amy as "riches").

105. In my view, Amy is not the ominous "angel of death" Welsh makes of her (*The City of Dickens*, pp. 207–9). She can perform her gracious, life-giving offices precisely because she is "untroubled" by death (1.14.171); and if her wisdom is "the virtue that enables one to face death" (*The City of Dickens*, p. 211), it is also biblically associated with "life"—her "modest life of usefulness and happiness" with Arthur (2.34.801).

106. Dolores Rosenblum, "Face to Face: Elizabeth Barrett Browning's *Aurora Leigh* and Nineteenth-Century Poetry," *Victorian Studies* 26 (Spring 1983): 322–23.

107. In this vista of the iconic face, Clennam projects large upon the universe the grotto with the missing religious statue which he had seen in the bleak courtyard at Miss Wade's (see 2.20.635); compare with Dickens' dream of Mary Hogarth in Italy when he fell asleep one night wondering about the face of a missing religious picture over the altar

in his bedchamber (P 4:196–97). Both Dickens and Clennam fill in the religious gap with their dream-women.

108. As Garis writes, *contra* Trilling's idealizations, Amy has been for Arthur "rather too much a Beatrice, a Paraclete in female form" (*The Dickens Theatre*, p. 184).

109. Dianne F. Sadoff, "Storytelling and the Figure of the Father in *Little Dorrit*," *PMLA* 95 (March 1980): 234–45, discusses the father-daughter incest motif and finds the Clennam-Amy relationship a static narcissistic paradise of desire (p. 241).

110. John Stuart Mill remarks that the usefulness of religion "did not need to be asserted until the arguments for its truth had in a great measure ceased to convince" (see *Nature, The Utility of Religion, and Theism*, 3d ed. [London: Longmans, Green and Company, 1885], p. 70).

111. A. E. Dyson, *The Inimitable Dickens: A Reading of the Novels* (New York: St. Martin's Press, 1970), p. 211.

112. Miller, *Charles Dickens*, p. 243.

113. Duckworth, "*Little Dorrit* and the Question of Closure," p. 119, quoting from Jacques Derrida, "The Purveyor of Truth," *Yale French Studies* 55 (1976): 94.

114. Harland S. Nelson, *Charles Dickens* (Boston: Twayne, 1981), p. 184, sees in Amy's name a linking of "*do(o)r*" and love: "She is the little door, the way; and the way is love, because that is her given name." He also links these ideas with the Matthew 7:14 "strait gate" passage embedded in Clennam's moral code and reads Amy's image on the monthly cover design in terms of the needle's eye parable, appropriate for a seamstress. (Amy's last name also contains the novel's formula for duty, "do it.")

115. F. R. Leavis, "Dickens and Blake," p. 226.

116. Duckworth, "*Little Dorrit* and the Question of Closure," pp. 128–30; Janice M. Carlisle, "*Little Dorrit*: Necessary Fictions," *Studies in the Novel* 7 (Summer 1975): 195–214.

117. Dickens noted in his Number Plan for 6, chapter 20, that the theater should be "Indistinctly seen, as Little Dorrit saw it," a phrase Dickens underlined three times (Clarendon *LD*, p. 814).

118. John L. McKenzie, "The Gospel According to Matthew," *Jerome Biblical Commentary*, 2:62. Protestant theology (like Dickens and Forster here) has tended to see the Matthean Beatitudes (privileged because they occur in the Sermon on the Mount) primarily as articulating an ethic to live by, although Luke's offer something more which Dickens could not affirm, escatological comfort (God's kingdom come will overturn social actualities); and both Matthew and Luke offer a theodicy of suffering. See "The Beatitudes," in *The Dictionary of Biblical Tradition in English Literature*, gen. ed. David L. Jeffrey, forthcoming from W. B. Eerdmans, 1987.

119. John Forster, review of A. P. Stanley, *The Life and Correspondence of Thomas Arnold*, in *The Examiner* (12 October 1844), p. 645.

120. Dean Stanley, for example, linked the Beatitudes' teaching to Buddha's, in "The Beatitudes," Sermon 10 in *Sermons for Children*, Preached in Westminster Abbey (New York: Charles Scribner's Sons, 1887), pp. 98–100.

121. Martin Dibelius, *The Sermon on the Mount* (New York: Charles Scribner's Sons, 1940), pp. 9–10.

122. McKenzie, "The Gospel According to Matthew," 2:62.

123. Kincaid, *Dickens and the Rhetoric of Laughter*, p. 193. *The Dictionary of Biblical Tradition* notes that Shakespeare, sensing this incompatibility between human experience and the Sermon's teaching, makes only ironic allusions to the Beatitudes (see, e.g., Falstaff in *The Second Part of Henry the Fourth*, 5.3.143–45).

124. Plan for Numbers 19 and 20 (Clarendon *LD*, p. 827).

125. Mrs. Clennam's impersonal and passive language disguises ill-doing; Amy's personal and active speech urges well-doing. With her "let me implore you to remember," Amy's more persuasive imperatives counter the strong-willed woman's commands and especially the stern motto "Do Not Forget." While the old sinner uses euphemisms for herself ("an instrument"), Amy calls sins by their right names ("vengeance"), yet without saying directly, "You are vengeful," holding out hope to Mrs. Clennam in the spirit of Christ's "Judge not" (Matt. 7:1).

126. In this earlier scene, which perhaps the later sunset is to correct, Amy muses that the water "might run dry, and show her the prison again . . . all lasting realities that had never changed" (a skeptical revision of Rev. 20:13).

127. Donald Juel, with James S. Ackerman and Thayer S. Warshaw, *An Introduction to New Testament Literature* (Nashville: Abingdon, 1978), p. 101.

128. On Little Dorrit's infantilization see Showalter, "Guilt, Authority, and the Shadows of *Little Dorrit*," p. 38.

129. Trilling, "Little Dorrit," p. 590. Miller, *Charles Dickens*, p. 240, calls Amy "Dickens' dramatization of the idea expressed in Christ's words: 'Except ye . . . become as little children, ye shall not enter into the kingdom of heaven' " (Matt. 18:3).

130. See Welsh, *The City of Dickens*, pp. 109–11.

131. Ibid., pp. 107–9.

132. Sadoff, "Storytelling and the Figure of the Father in *Little Dorrit*," p. 237, discusses Rigaud as Clennam's double.

133. See Randolph Splitter, "Guilt and the Trappings of Melodrama in *Little Dorrit*," *Dickens Studies Annual*, vol. 6, ed. Robert B. Partlow, Jr. (Carbondale: Southern Illinois University Press, 1977): 130–32, on these mechanisms of melodrama.

134. The phrase "chasing of the wind" is a translation of "vanity" by R. B. Y. Scott, *The Way of Wisdom in the Old Testament* (New York: Macmillan, 1971), p. 178; the second phrase here, quoted by Scott (p. 179), is a translation of Ecclesiastes 1:15 by R. Gordis in *Koheleth: The Man and His World*, 3d ed. (1968), p. 148.

135. Spurgeon, "Regeneration," Sermon 14 on John 3:3, in *Sermons of Rev. C. H. Spurgeon*, 3d ser. (New York: Robert Carter and Brothers, n.d.), p. 210.

136. Goldberg, *Carlyle and Dickens*, p. 157.

137. Last words of the Number Plans (Clarendon *LD*, p. 828).

6. Dying unto Death:
Biblical Ends and Endings in *Our Mutual Friend*

1. Alexander Welsh, *The City of Dickens* (Oxford: Clarendon Press, 1971), p. 228.

2. Robert S. Baker, "Imagination and Literacy in Dickens' 'Our Mutual Friend,'" *Criticism* 18 (Winter 1976): 57.

3. See Barry V. Qualls, *The Secular Pilgrims of Victorian Fiction: The Novel as Book of Life* (Cambridge: Cambridge University Press, 1982), p. 135.

4. This rather overbearing laying-down of the law is everywhere evident in *Our Mutual Friend*, sometimes contradicting or oversimplifying the novel's experience; e.g., *apropos* of Old Harmon and the Boffins Dickens asserts: "And this is the eternal law. For, Evil often stops short at itself and dies with the doer of it; but Good, never" (1.9.146).

5. J. Hillis Miller, *Charles Dickens: The World of His Novels* (Bloomington: Indiana University Press, 1958), p. 284.

6. This is Rosemary Mundhenk's argument in "The Education of the Reader in *Our Mutual Friend*," *Nineteenth-Century Fiction* 34 (June 1979): 41–58.

7. See Nancy Aycock Metz, "The Artistic Reclamation of Waste in *Our Mutual Friend*," *Nineteenth-Century Fiction* 34 (June 1979): 59–72.

8. Bella's and John's marriage, however, is no less mechanical; see 4.4.732.

9. Garrett Stewart, *Dickens and the Trials of Imagination* (Cambridge: Harvard University Press, 1974), p. 212.

10. Quoted in William Kent, *Dickens and Religion* (London: Watts and Company, 1930), pp. 55–56.

11. So ill-digested are Charley's "scraps of biblical lore" that he mixes them with scientific facts, unaware of any contradiction, when he tells Lizzie proudly, "That's gas, that is, coming out of a bit of a forest that's been under the mud that was under the water in the days of Noah's Ark" (1.3.71).

12. M. M. Bakhtin, "Discourse in the Novel," *The Dialogic Imagination: Four Essays by M. M. Bakhtin*, ed. Michael Holquist, and trans. Caryl Emerson and Michael Holquist (Austin: University of Texas Press, 1981), p. 344.

13. Henry James, review of *Our Mutual Friend* in *The Nation* (21 December 1865): 786–87, reprinted in *Dickens: The Critical Heritage*, ed. Philip Collins (London: Routledge and Kegan Paul, 1971), p. 470. Dennis Walder, in *Dickens and Religion* (London: George Allen and Unwin, 1981), p. 198, finds that "at times Dickens manipulates the familiar themes with a self-conscious air which robs them of [their] force."

14. See "Lightwood's catechism" in 2.6.348 and 15.465; Wegg's and Boffin's versions, 1.5.91–92; Bella's, 4.5.754; Miss Peecher's, 2.11.394.

15. On this occasion Dickens also Christianizes Riah's speech by having him echo Mark 8:5 in advising Lizzie, "Shake the dust from thy feet and let him [Charley] go" (2.15.462).

16. See Qualls, *The Secular Pilgrims of Victorian Fiction*, pp. 130–31.

17. Andrew Sanders, *Charles Dickens, Resurrectionist* (New York: St. Martin's Press, 1982), p. 166.

18. Qualls, *The Secular Pilgrims of Victorian Fiction*, p. 123. Annabel M. Patterson, in "*Our Mutual Friend:* Dickens as the Compleat Angler," *Dickens Studies Annual*, vol. 1, ed. Robert B. Partlow, Jr. (Carbondale: Southern Illinois University Press, 1970): 256, discusses Dickens' inversions of the "fishers of men" verse in the "Anglers Song," Walton's *The Compleat Angler*.

19. Ernest Boll, "The Plotting of *Our Mutual Friend*," *Modern Philology* 42 (November 1944): 105.

20. The novel presses farther back for evolutionary causes: "All about this was quite familiar knowledge down in the depths of the slime, ages ago," grins the alligator at Venus' shop (3.14.647).

21. Miller, *Charles Dickens*, p. 291, makes this suggestion about Betty's Celestial City images.

22. Ibid., p. 315.

23. See Patterson, "*Our Mutual Friend:* Dickens as the Compleat Angler," p. 260; Sanders, *Charles Dickens, Resurrectionist*, pp. 176–77.

24. U. C. Knoepflmacher, in *Laughter and Despair: Readings in Ten Novels of the Victorian Era* (Berkeley and Los Angeles: University of California Press, 1971), p. 161, would argue otherwise: "Christ . . . hovers as an imponderable presence throughout this novel of transformations and resurrections. He is suggested by Riah," is "evoked by Jenny's puzzling words about her imaginary bridegroom: 'He is coming from somewhere or other, I suppose,'" and "may even be one of the figures suggested by the novel's elusive title."

25. Miller, *Charles Dickens*, p. 316.

26. Knoepflmacher, *Laughter and Despair*, p. 167; see the discussion of Dickens' "double process of decomposition and cohesion," pp. 137–43.

27. John M. Robson, "*Our Mutual Friend:* A Rhetorical Approach to the First Number," *Dickens Studies Annual*, vol. 3, ed. Robert B. Partlow, Jr. (Carbondale: Southern Illinois University Press, 1972): 201, makes this contrast.

28. Sanders, *Charles Dickens, Resurrectionist*, pp. 175–76, discusses the Nicodemus parallel and reminds us of Dickens' other character by this name, Nicodemus Dumps, in "A Bloomsbury Christening."

29. See Miller, *Charles Dickens*, pp. 322–25.

30. See H. M. Daleski, *Dickens and the Art of Analogy* (London: Faber and Faber, 1970), pp. 331–33.

31. Metz, "The Artistic Reclamation of Waste in *Our Mutual Friend*," p. 63; compare Baker, "Imagination and Literacy in Dickens' 'Our Mutual Friend,'" pp. 60–61: "Dickens repeatedly stresses the sheer difficulty that Harmon experiences in organizing his thoughts both at the time of his attempted murder . . . and during the creation of his text"; but Dickens would not have to so "stress" the point if he had dramatized it. My

reading of Harmon's text-within-the-text is that he constructs it with remarkable ease considering the experience he is describing.

32. See Qualls' discussion, *The Secular Pilgrims of Victorian Fiction*, pp. 131–32.

33. Baker, "Imagination and Literacy in Dickens' 'Our Mutual Friend,'" p. 72.

34. Robert Garis, *The Dickens Theatre: A Reassessment of the Novels* (Oxford: Clarendon Press, 1965), p. 229.

35. Ellen Moers, in *The Dandy: Brummell to Beerbohm* (Lincoln: University of Nebraska Press, 1960), pp. 246–50, treats the likely reason for this imaginative engagement with Eugene's fate, Dickens' sympathy for the later "grey" figures in his fiction.

36. Barbara Hardy, *The Moral Art of Dickens* (New York: Oxford University Press, 1970), pp. 49–51 and 75–77, discusses Bella's unsatisfying conversion.

37. Deirdre David, *Fictions of Resolution in Three Victorian Novels: North and South, Our Mutual Friend, Daniel Deronda* (New York: Columbia University Press, 1981), p. 77.

38. Miller, *Charles Dickens*, p. 310.

39. Stewart, *Dickens and the Trials of Imagination*, pp. 199, 205.

40. Walder, *Dickens and Religion*, p. 204.

41. Italo Calvino, "Cities and Signs 1," in *Invisible Cities*, trans. William Weaver (New York: Harcourt Brace Jovanovich, 1972), p. 14.

42. Compare Baker, "Imagination and Literacy in Dickens' 'Our Mutual Friend,'" p. 71: "*Our Mutual Friend* celebrates not a mystical vision of redemption through Christ but a secularized version of regeneration through the logos of language and imagination."

43. Stewart argues that Jenny is, in *Dickens and the Trials of Imagination*, p. 216.

44. Miller, *Charles Dickens*, p. 292.

45. Boll, "The Plotting of *Our Mutual Friend*," p. 122.

46. John Lucas, *The Melancholy Man: A Study of Dickens's Novels* (London: Methuen, 1970), p. 338.

Coda

1. George Levine, *The Realistic Imagination: English Fiction from Frankenstein to Lady Chatterly* (Chicago: University of Chicago Press, 1981), p. 4.

Index